NEGIMA!

5

Ken Akamatsu

TRANSLATED AND ADAPTED BY
Douglas Varenas

LETTERED BY
Steve Palmer

LONDON

Published in the United Kingdom by Tanoshimi in 2006

1 3 5 7 9 10 8 6 4 2

First published in serial form by Shonen Magazine Comics and subsequently published in book form by
Kodansha Ltd, Tokyo in 2004. Copyright © 2004 by Ken Akamatsu.

Published by arrangement with Kodansha Ltd., Tokyo and with Del Rey,
an imprint of Random House Inc., New York

Tanoshimi
The Random House Group Limited
20 Vauxhall Bridge Road, London, SW1V 2SA

Random House Australia (Pty) Limited
20 Alfred Street, Milsons Point, Sydney
New South Wales 2061, Australia

Random House New Zealand Limited
18 Poland Road, Glenfield
Auckland 10, New Zealand

Random House (Pty) Limited
Isle of Houghton, Corner of Boundary Road & Carse O'Gowrie
Houghton 2198, South Africa

Random House Publishers India Private Limited
301 World Trade Tower, Hotel Intercontinental Grand Complex,
Barakharnba Lane, New Delhi 110 001, India

Random House Group Limited Reg. No. 954009

www.tanoshimi.tv
www.randomhouse.co.uk

A CIP catalogue record for this book is available from the British Library

Papers used by Random House
are natural, recyclable products made from wood grown in sustainable forests.
The manufacturing processes conform to the environmental regulations of the country of origin

ISBN 9780099505020 (from Jan 2007)
ISBN 0 09 9505029
Printed and bound in Germany by GGP Media GmbH, Pößneck

Translator and Adaptor— Douglas Varenas
Lettering — Steve Palmer
Cover Design — David Stevenson

A Word from the Author

Finally, here's Volume 4 of *Negima!* Between trying to guide his tumultuous group of students through a wild field trip in Kyoto and Nara and dealing with a new menace, Negi-sensei has his hands full! (The field trip will continue into the next book.)

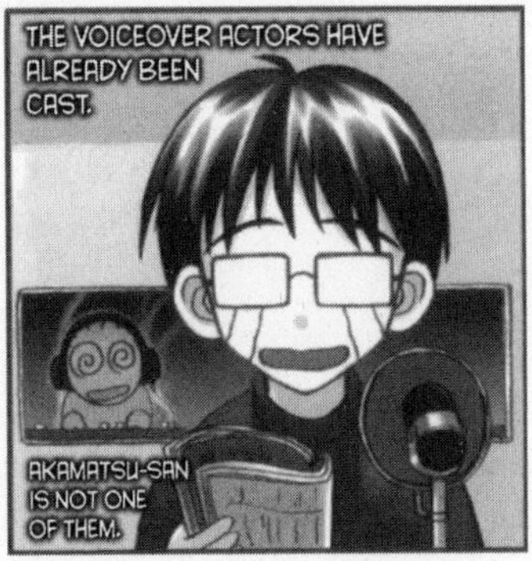
THE VOICEOVER ACTORS HAVE ALREADY BEEN CAST.
AKAMATSU-SAN IS NOT ONE OF THEM.

By the way, the "Character CD" of the digitized classmates of *Negima!* is now on sale. We've got thirty-one talented voice actors helping create a maxi CD single packed with imaging, mini-dramas, and more of each character. As a bonus, we included a Pactio Card (Probationary Contract). Don't miss it! For more information, check out my website.

Ken Akamatsu
http://www.ailove.net

Honorifics

Throughout the Tanoshimi Manga books, you will find Japanese honorifics left intact in the translations. For those not familiar with how the Japanese use honorifics, and more important, how they differ from English honorifics, we present this brief overview.

Politeness has always been a critical facet of Japanese culture. Ever since the feudal era, when Japan was a highly stratified society, use of honorifics — which can be defined as polite speech that indicates relationship or status — has played an essential role in the Japanese language. When addressing someone in Japanese, an honorific usually takes the form of a suffix attached to one's name (example: "Asuna-san"), or as a title at the end of one's name or in place of the name itself (example: "Negi-sensei," or simply "Sensei!").

Honorifics can be expressions of respect or endearment. In the context of manga and anime, honorifics give insight into the nature of the relationship between characters. Many translations into English leave out these important honorifics, and therefore distort the "feel" of the original Japanese. Because Japanese honorifics contain nuances that English honorifics lack, it is our policy at Tanoshimi not to translate them. Here, instead, is a guide to some of the honorifics you may encounter in Tanoshimi Manga.

-*san*:   This is the most common honorific, and is equivalent to Mr., Miss, Ms., Mrs., etc. It is the all-purpose honorific and can be used in any situation where politeness is required.

-*sama*: This is one level higher than -*san*. It is used to confer great respect.

-*dono*: This comes from the word *tono*, which means *lord*. It is an even higher level than -*sama*, and confers utmost respect.

-*kun:*   This suffix is used at the end of boys' names to express familiarity or endearment. It is also sometimes used by men among friends, or when addressing someone younger or of a lower station.

-*chan:*   This is used to express endearment, mostly toward girls. It is also used for little boys, pets, and even among lovers. It gives a sense of childish cuteness.

Bozu: This is an informal way to refer to a boy, similar to the English term "kid".

Sempai: This title suggests that the addressee is one's "senior" in a group or organization. It is most often used in a school setting, where underclassmen refer to their upperclassmen as *sempai.* It can also be used in the workplace, such as when a newer employee addresses an employee who has seniority in the company.

Kohai: This is the opposite of *sempai,* and is used toward underclassmen in school or newcomers in the workplace. It connotes that the addressee is of lower station.

Sensei: Literally meaning "one who has come before," this title is used for teachers, doctors, or masters of any profession or art.

-[blank]: Usually forgotten in these lists, but perhaps the most significant difference between Japanese and English. The lack of honorific means that the speaker has permission to address the person in a very intimate way. Usually, only family, spouses, or very close friends have this kind of permission. Known as *yobisute,* it can be gratifying when someone who has earned the intimacy starts to call one by one's name without an honorific. But when that intimacy hasn't been earned, it can also be very insulting.

魔法先生ネギま!

MAGISTER NEGI MAGI

5

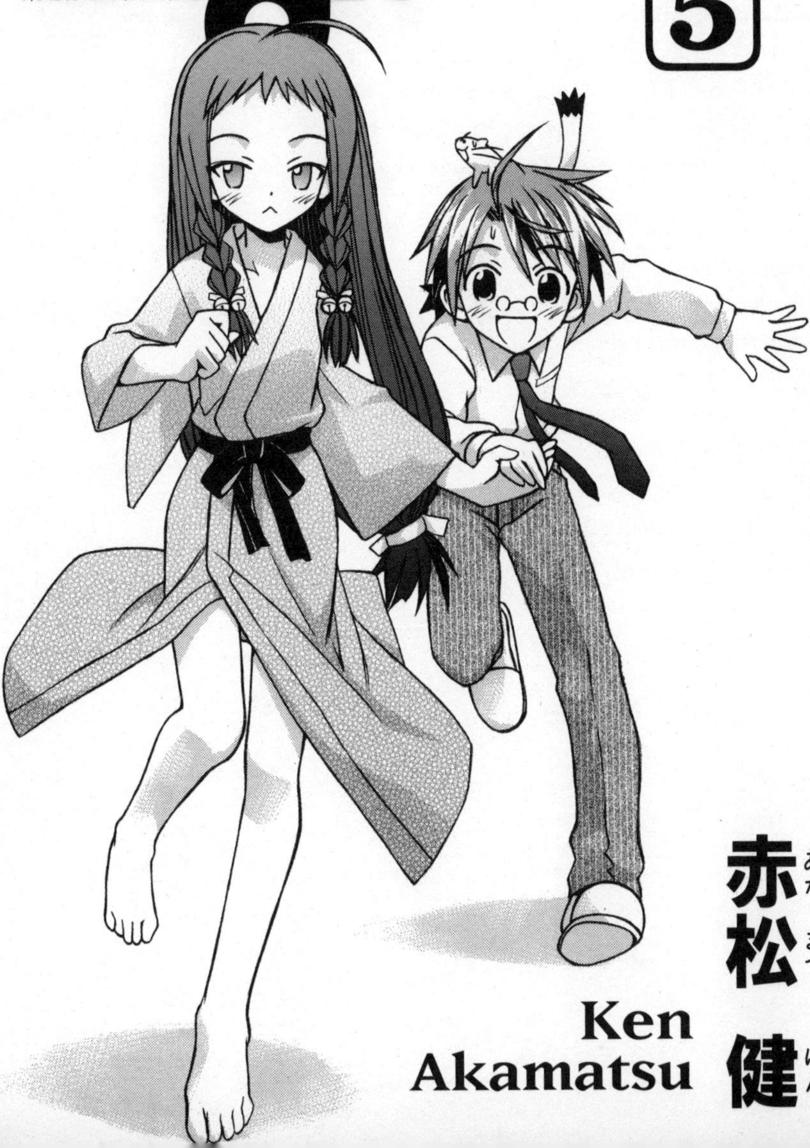

赤松健

Ken Akamatsu

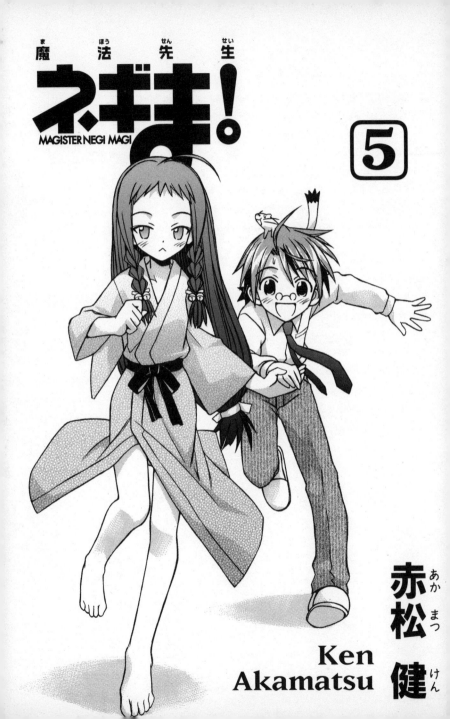

CONTENTS

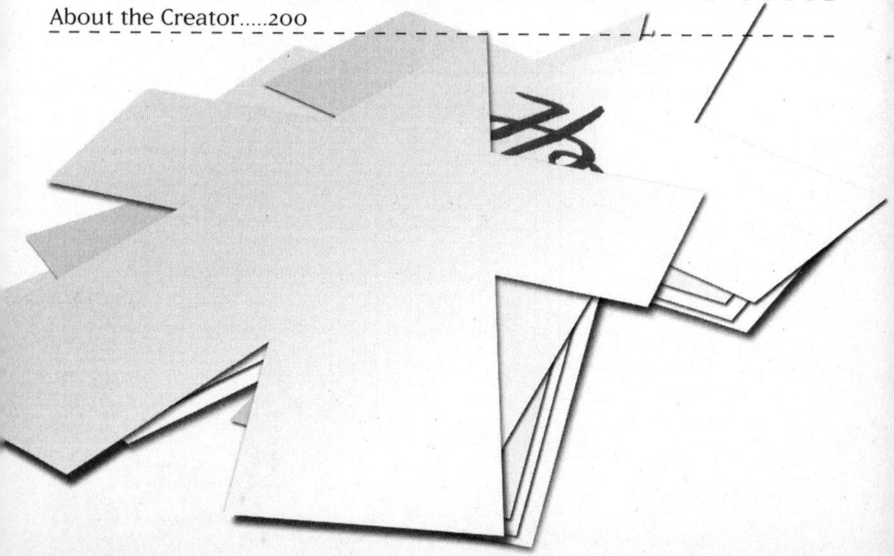

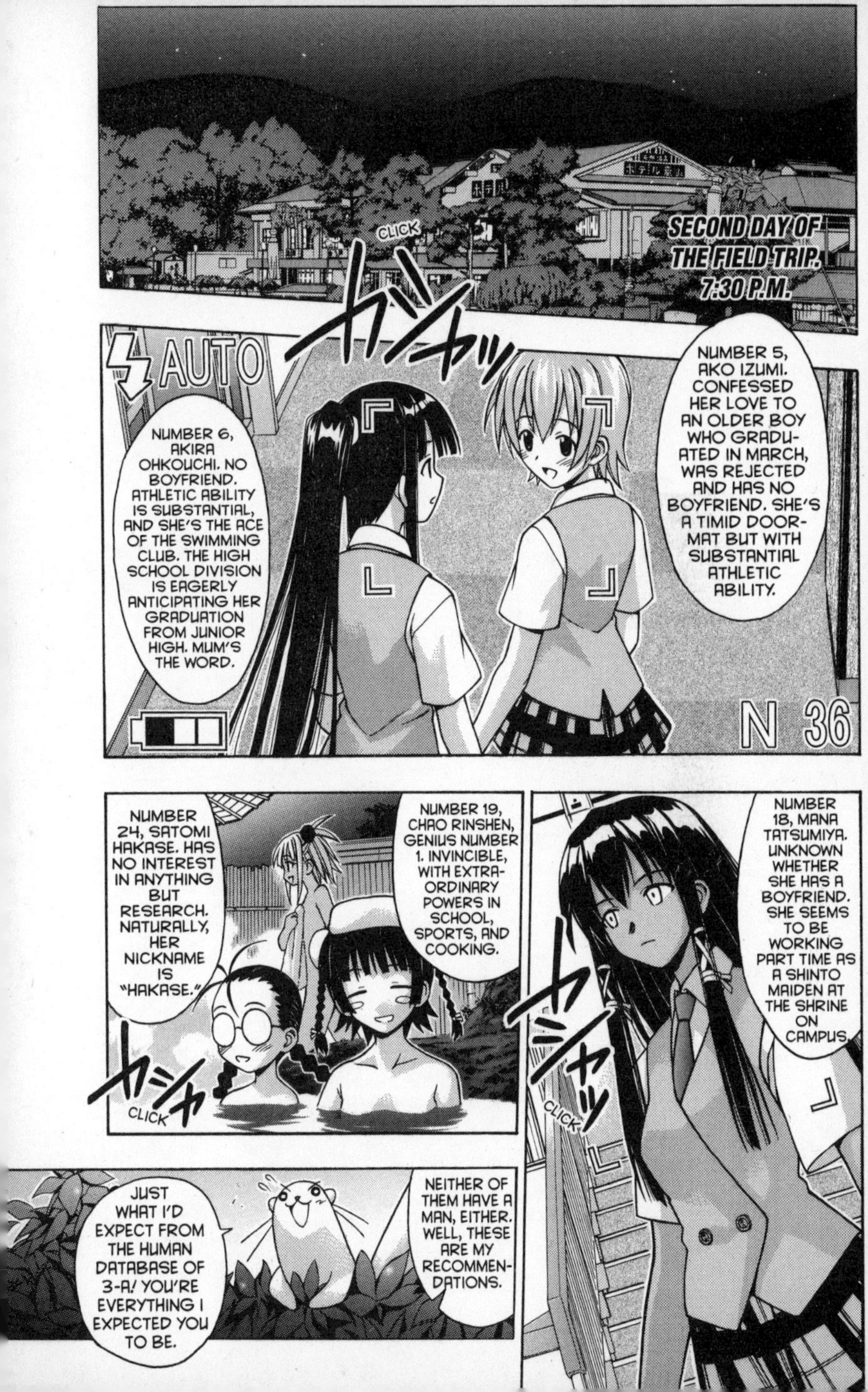
SECOND DAY OF THE FIELD TRIP. 7:30 P.M.
CLICK
カシャッ
AUTO
N 36
NUMBER 5, AKO IZUMI. CONFESSED HER LOVE TO AN OLDER BOY WHO GRADU-ATED IN MARCH, WAS REJECTED AND HAS NO BOYFRIEND. SHE'S A TIMID DOOR-MAT BUT WITH SUBSTANTIAL ATHLETIC ABILITY.
NUMBER 6, AKIRA OHKOUCHI. NO BOYFRIEND. ATHLETIC ABILITY IS SUBSTANTIAL, AND SHE'S THE ACE OF THE SWIMMING CLUB. THE HIGH SCHOOL DIVISION IS EAGERLY ANTICIPATING HER GRADUATION FROM JUNIOR HIGH. MUM'S THE WORD.
NUMBER 18, MANA TATSUMIYA. UNKNOWN WHETHER SHE HAS A BOYFRIEND. SHE SEEMS TO BE WORKING PART TIME AS A SHINTO MAIDEN AT THE SHRINE ON CAMPUS.
カシャッ
CLICK
NUMBER 19, CHAO RINSHEN, GENIUS NUMBER 1. INVINCIBLE, WITH EXTRA-ORDINARY POWERS IN SCHOOL, SPORTS, AND COOKING.
NUMBER 24, SATOMI HAKASE. HAS NO INTEREST IN ANYTHING BUT RESEARCH. NATURALLY, HER NICKNAME IS "HAKASE."
カシャ
CLICK
NEITHER OF THEM HAVE A MAN, EITHER. WELL, THESE ARE MY RECOMMEN-DATIONS.
JUST WHAT I'D EXPECT FROM THE HUMAN DATABASE OF 3-A! YOU'RE EVERYTHING I EXPECTED YOU TO BE.

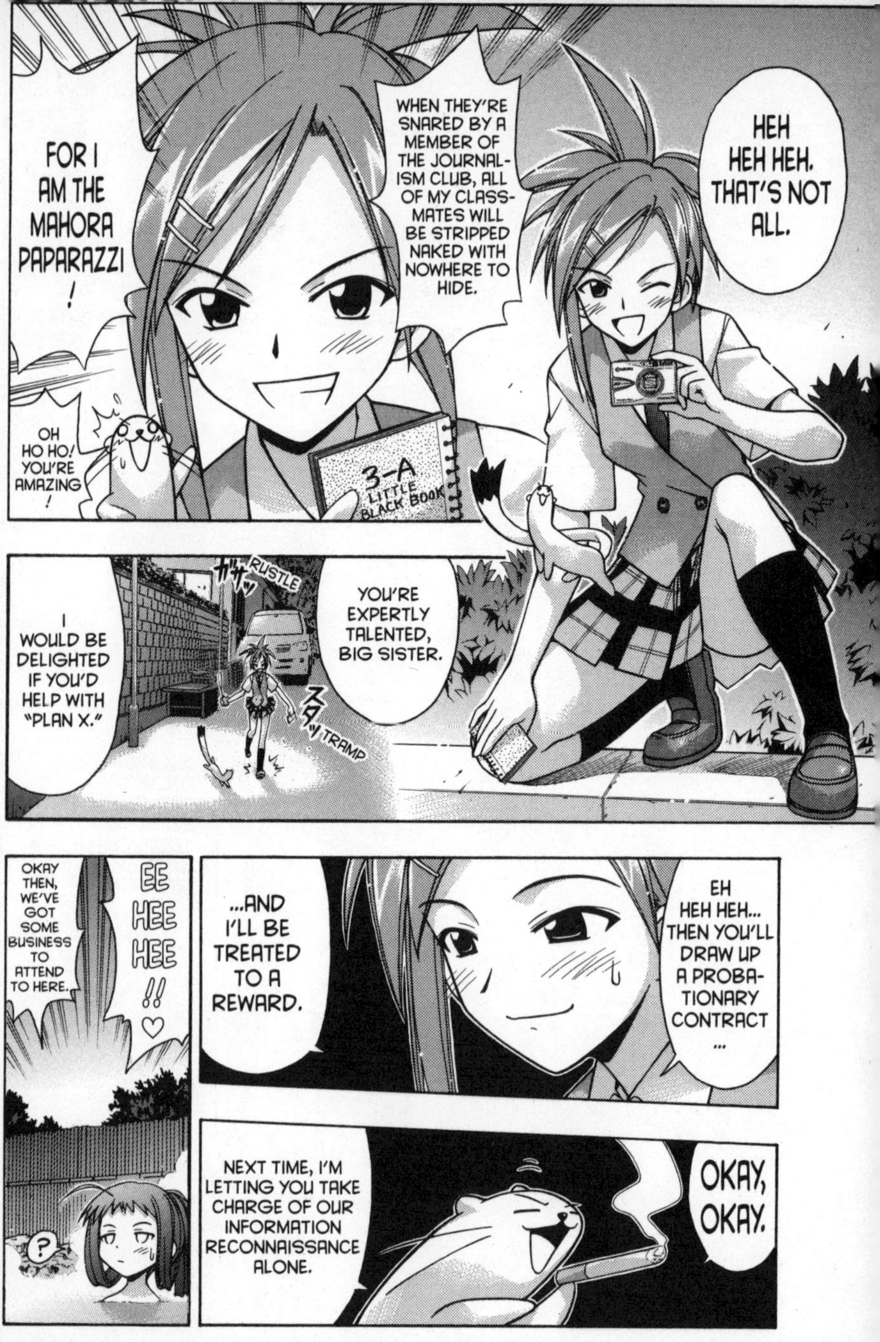
HEH HEH HEH. THAT'S NOT ALL.
WHEN THEY'RE SNARED BY A MEMBER OF THE JOURNALISM CLUB, ALL OF MY CLASSMATES WILL BE STRIPPED NAKED WITH NOWHERE TO HIDE.
FOR I AM THE MAHORA PAPARAZZI!
OH HO HO! YOU'RE AMAZING!
3-A LITTLE BLACK BOOK
YOU'RE EXPERTLY TALENTED, BIG SISTER.
RUSTLE
I WOULD BE DELIGHTED IF YOU'D HELP WITH "PLAN X."
TRAMP
EH HEH HEH... THEN YOU'LL DRAW UP A PROBATIONARY CONTRACT...
...AND I'LL BE TREATED TO A REWARD.
OKAY, OKAY.
NEXT TIME, I'M LETTING YOU TAKE CHARGE OF OUR INFORMATION RECONNAISSANCE ALONE.
EE HEE HEE!! ♡
OKAY THEN, WE'VE GOT SOME BUSINESS TO ATTEND TO HERE.
?

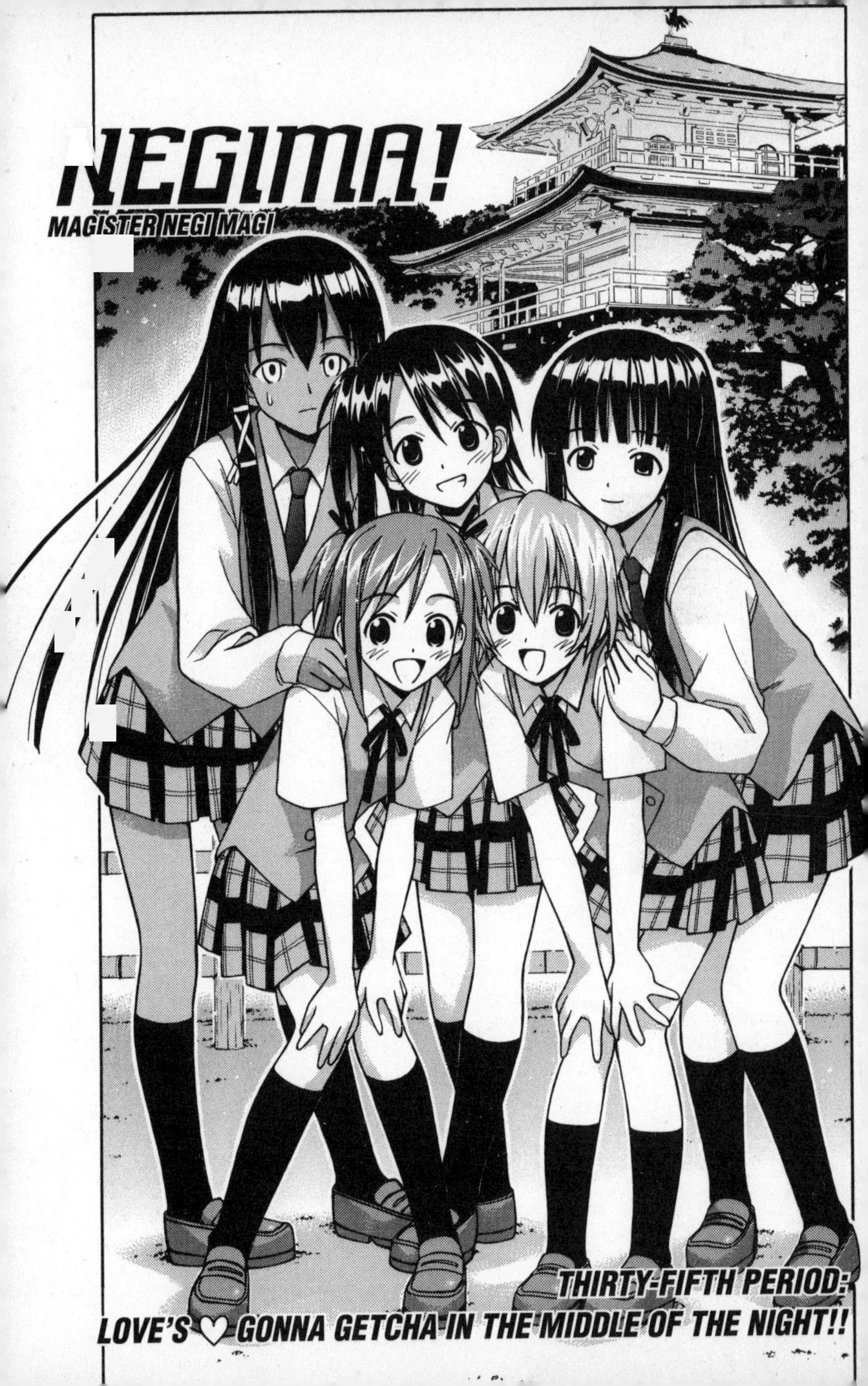
NEGIMA!
MAGISTER NEGI MAGI
THIRTY-FIFTH PERIOD:
LOVE'S ♡ GONNA GETCHA IN THE MIDDLE OF THE NIGHT!!

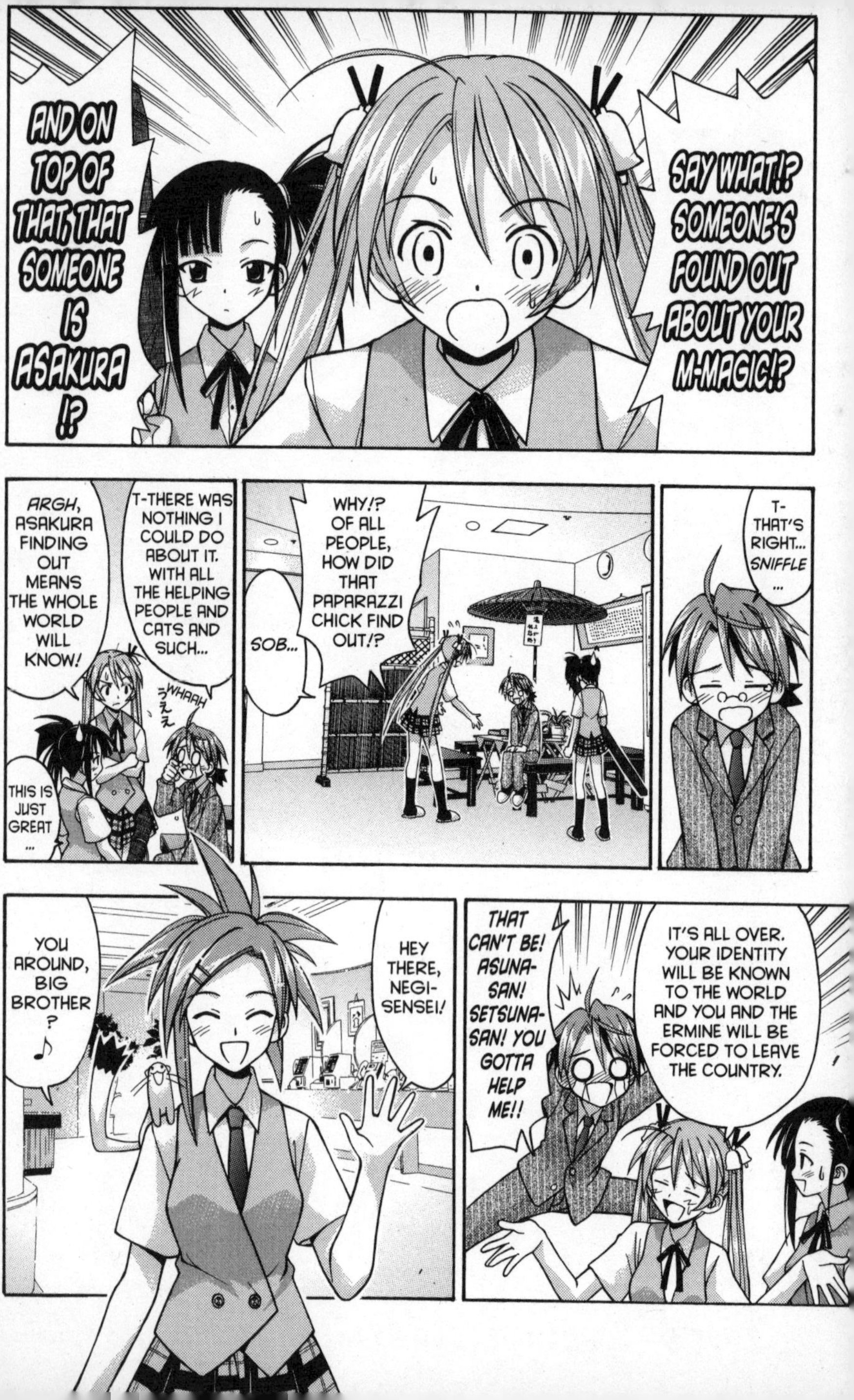
SAY WHAT!? SOMEONE'S FOUND OUT ABOUT YOUR M-MAGIC!?
AND ON TOP OF THAT, THAT SOMEONE IS ASAKURA!?
T- THAT'S RIGHT... SNIFFLE ...
WHY!? OF ALL PEOPLE, HOW DID THAT PAPARAZZI CHICK FIND OUT!?
SOB...
T-THERE WAS NOTHING I COULD DO ABOUT IT. WITH ALL THE HELPING PEOPLE AND CATS AND SUCH...
ARGH, ASAKURA FINDING OUT MEANS THE WHOLE WORLD WILL KNOW!
WHAAH
THIS IS JUST GREAT...
IT'S ALL OVER. YOUR IDENTITY WILL BE KNOWN TO THE WORLD AND YOU AND THE ERMINE WILL BE FORCED TO LEAVE THE COUNTRY.
THAT CAN'T BE! ASUNA-SAN! SETSUNA-SAN! YOU GOTTA HELP ME!!
HEY THERE, NEGI-SENSEI!
YOU AROUND, BIG BROTHER? ♪

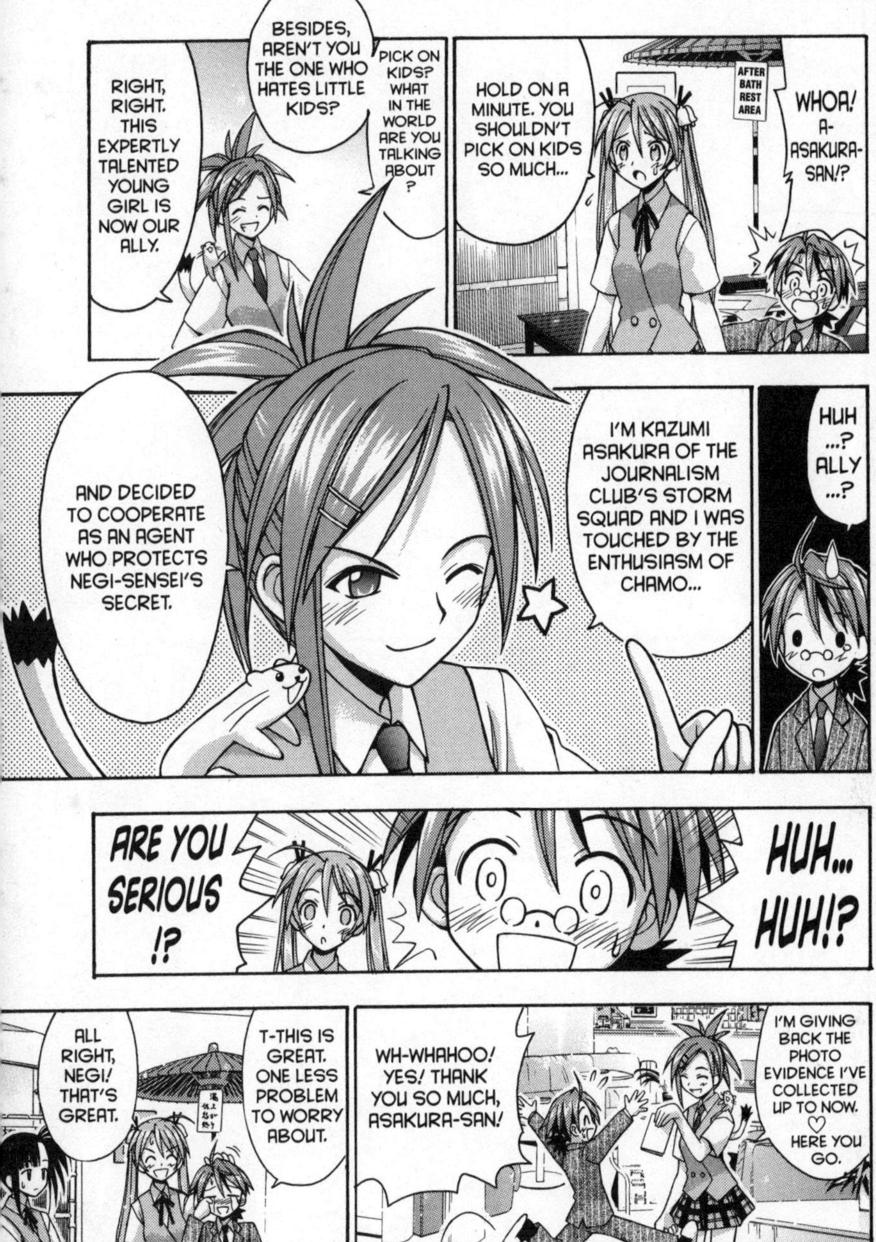
WHOA! A-ASAKURA-SAN!?
AFTER BATH REST AREA
HOLD ON A MINUTE. YOU SHOULDN'T PICK ON KIDS SO MUCH...
PICK ON KIDS? WHAT IN THE WORLD ARE YOU TALKING ABOUT?
BESIDES, AREN'T YOU THE ONE WHO HATES LITTLE KIDS?
RIGHT, RIGHT. THIS EXPERTLY TALENTED YOUNG GIRL IS NOW OUR ALLY.
HUH...? ALLY...?
I'M KAZUMI ASAKURA OF THE JOURNALISM CLUB'S STORM SQUAD AND I WAS TOUCHED BY THE ENTHUSIASM OF CHAMO...
AND DECIDED TO COOPERATE AS AN AGENT WHO PROTECTS NEGI-SENSEI'S SECRET.
HUH... HUH!?
ARE YOU SERIOUS!?
I'M GIVING BACK THE PHOTO EVIDENCE I'VE COLLECTED UP TO NOW. ♡ HERE YOU GO.
WH-WHAHOO! YES! THANK YOU SO MUCH, ASAKURA-SAN!
T-THIS IS GREAT. ONE LESS PROBLEM TO WORRY ABOUT.
ALL RIGHT, NEGI! THAT'S GREAT.

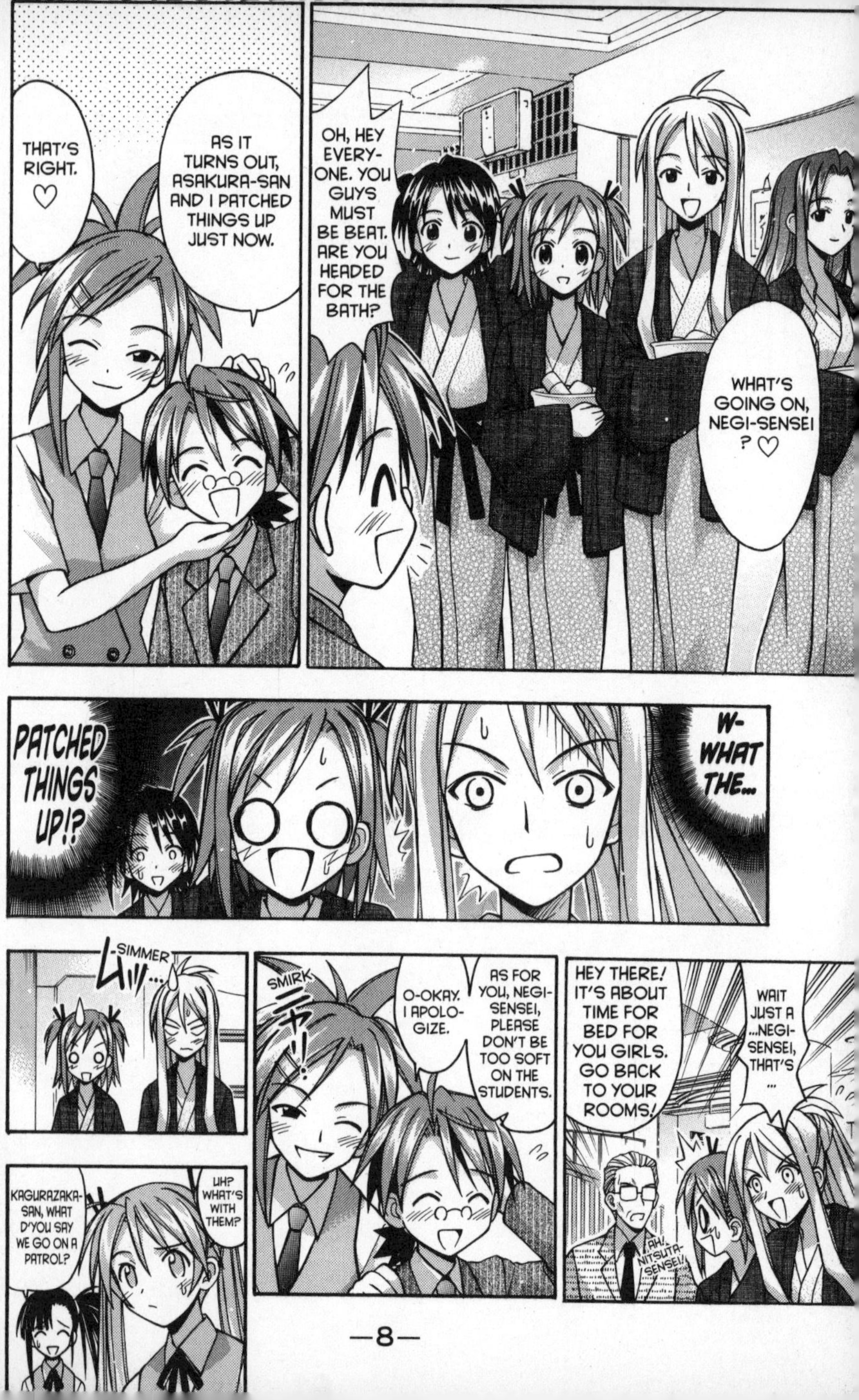
OH, HEY EVERYONE. YOU GUYS MUST BE BEAT. ARE YOU HEADED FOR THE BATH?
WHAT'S GOING ON, NEGI-SENSEI? ♡
AS IT TURNS OUT, ASAKURA-SAN AND I PATCHED THINGS UP JUST NOW.
THAT'S RIGHT. ♡
W-WHAT THE...
PATCHED THINGS UP!?
WAIT JUST A ...NEGI-SENSEI, THAT'S ...
HEY THERE! IT'S ABOUT TIME FOR BED FOR YOU GIRLS. GO BACK TO YOUR ROOMS!
AH! NITSUTA-SENSEI!
AS FOR YOU, NEGI-SENSEI, PLEASE DON'T BE TOO SOFT ON THE STUDENTS.
O-OKAY. I APOLOGIZE.
SMIRK
SIMMER
UH? WHAT'S WITH THEM?
KAGURAZAKA-SAN, WHAT D'YOU SAY WE GO ON A PATROL?

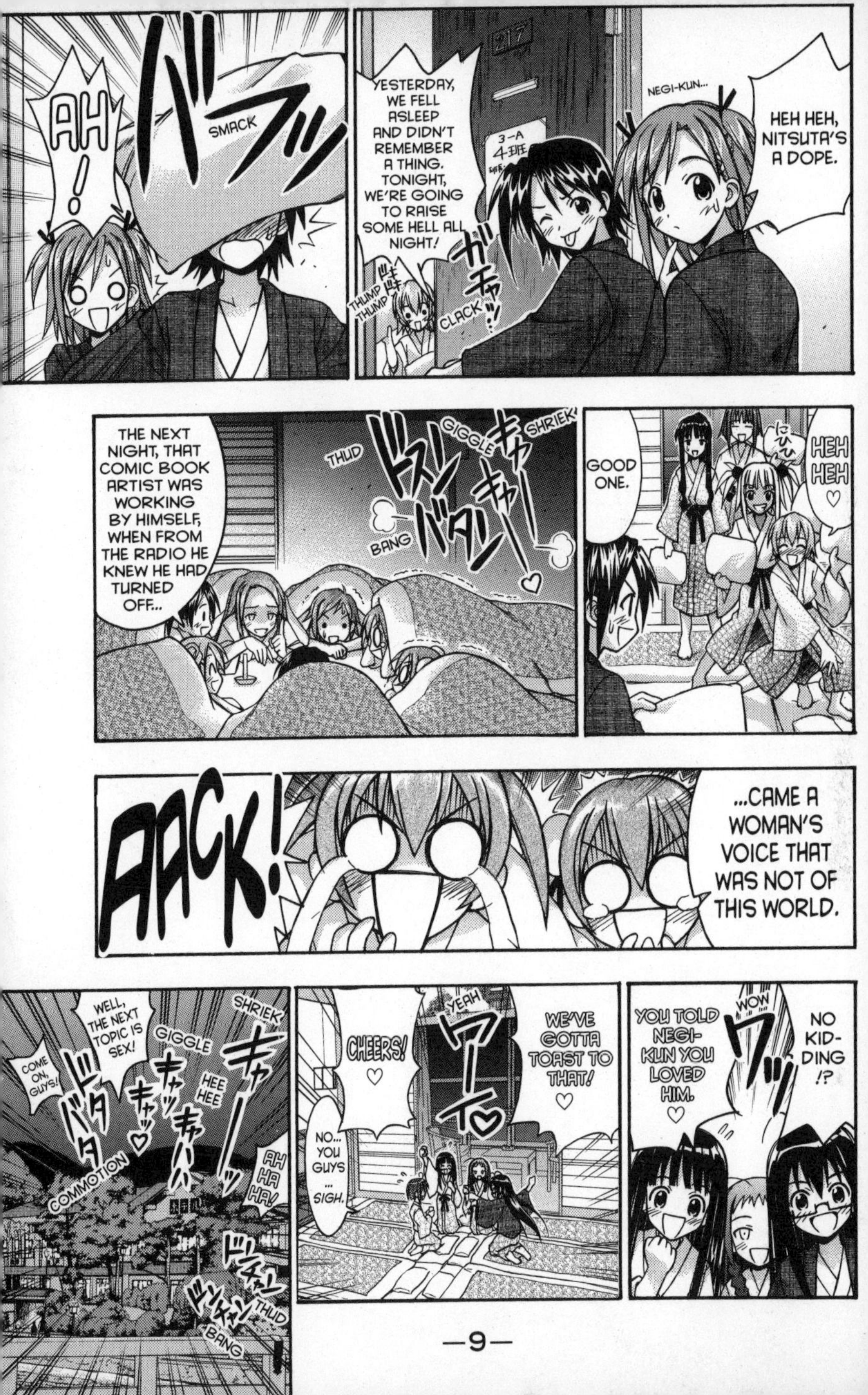
HEH HEH, NITSUTA'S A DOPE.
NEGI-KUN...
YESTERDAY, WE FELL ASLEEP AND DIDN'T REMEMBER A THING. TONIGHT, WE'RE GOING TO RAISE SOME HELL ALL NIGHT!
CLACK
THUMP THUMP
SMACK
AH!
HEH HEH ♡
GOOD ONE.
SHRIEK
GIGGLE
THUD
BANG
THE NEXT NIGHT, THAT COMIC BOOK ARTIST WAS WORKING BY HIMSELF, WHEN FROM THE RADIO HE KNEW HE HAD TURNED OFF...
...CAME A WOMAN'S VOICE THAT WAS NOT OF THIS WORLD.
AACK!
NO KIDDING!?
WOW
YOU TOLD NEGI-KUN YOU LOVED HIM. ♡
WE'VE GOTTA TOAST TO THAT! ♡
YEAH
CHEERS! ♡
NO... YOU GUYS ... SIGH.
SHRIEK
WELL, THE NEXT TOPIC IS SEX!
GIGGLE
HEE HEE
COME ON, GUYS!
AH HA HA!
COMMOTION
THUD
BANG

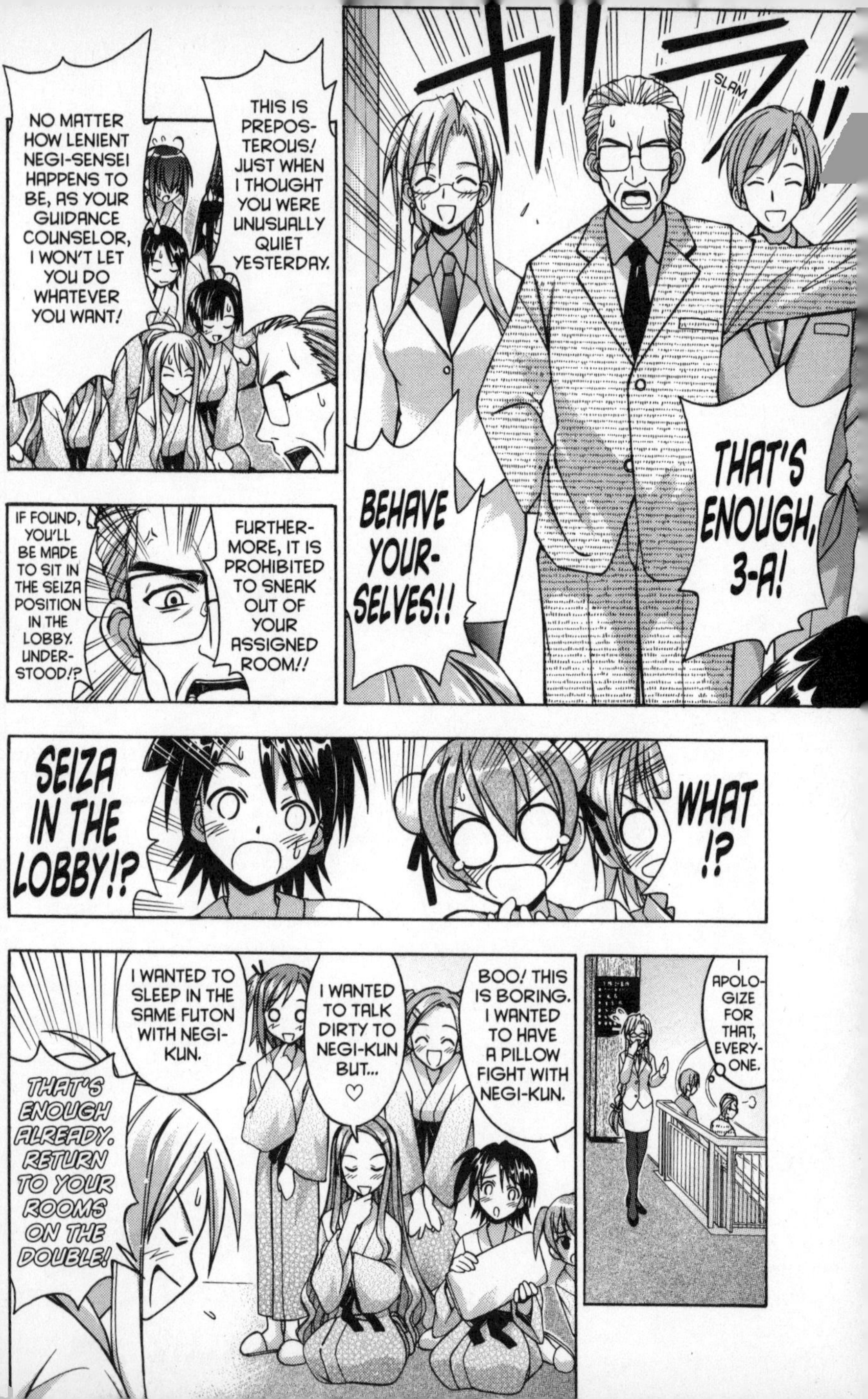
SLAM
THAT'S ENOUGH, 3-A!
BEHAVE YOURSELVES!!
THIS IS PREPOSTEROUS! JUST WHEN I THOUGHT YOU WERE UNUSUALLY QUIET YESTERDAY.
NO MATTER HOW LENIENT NEGI-SENSEI HAPPENS TO BE, AS YOUR GUIDANCE COUNSELOR, I WON'T LET YOU DO WHATEVER YOU WANT!
FURTHERMORE, IT IS PROHIBITED TO SNEAK OUT OF YOUR ASSIGNED ROOM!!
IF FOUND, YOU'LL BE MADE TO SIT IN THE SEIZA POSITION IN THE LOBBY. UNDERSTOOD!?
WHAT!?
SEIZA IN THE LOBBY!?
I APOLOGIZE FOR THAT, EVERYONE.
BOO! THIS IS BORING. I WANTED TO HAVE A PILLOW FIGHT WITH NEGI-KUN.
I WANTED TO TALK DIRTY TO NEGI-KUN BUT... ♡
I WANTED TO SLEEP IN THE SAME FUTON WITH NEGI-KUN.
THAT'S ENOUGH ALREADY. RETURN TO YOUR ROOMS ON THE DOUBLE!

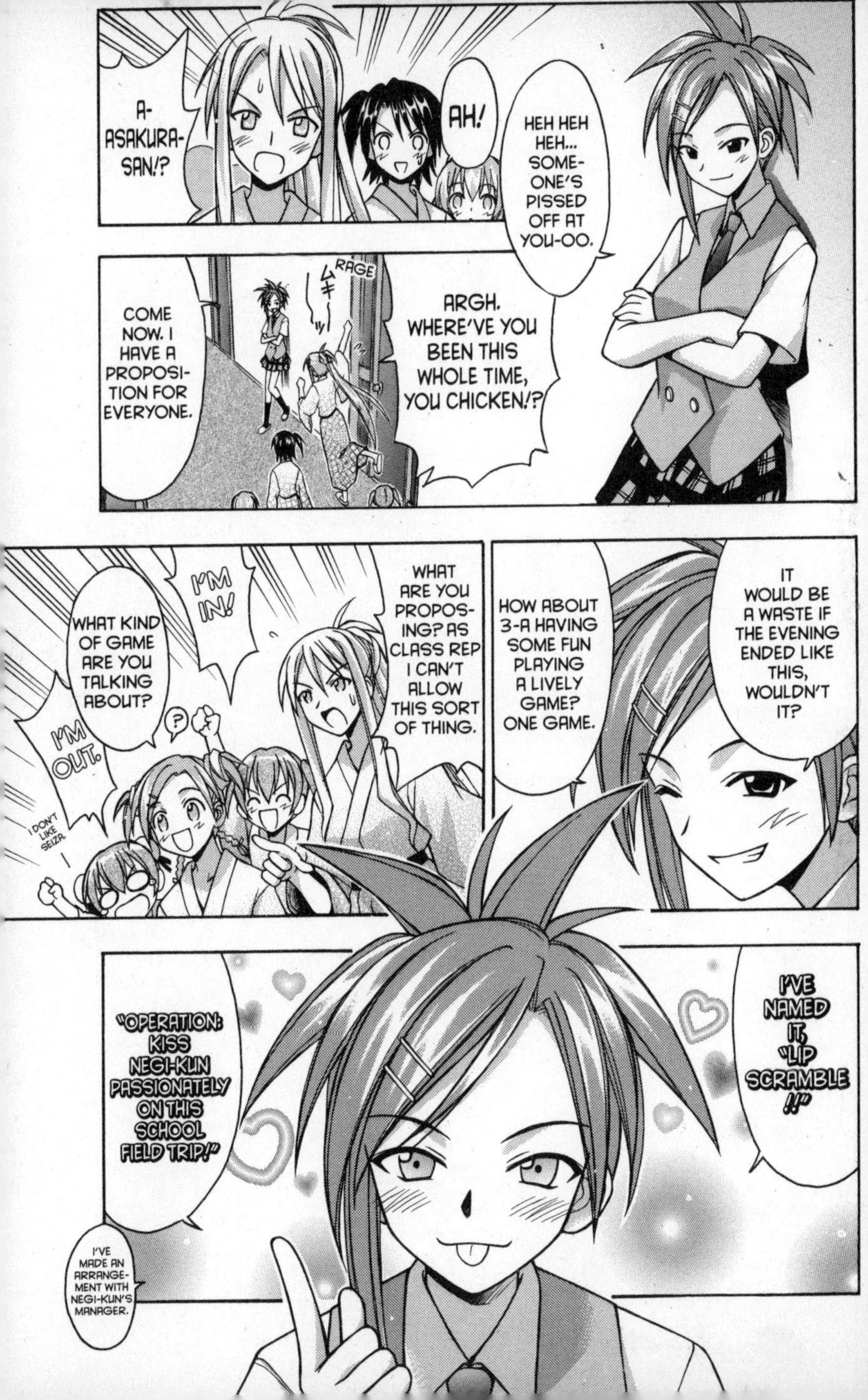
A-ASAKURA-SAN!?
AH!
HEH HEH HEH... SOMEONE'S PISSED OFF AT YOU-OO.
RAGE
ARGH. WHERE'VE YOU BEEN THIS WHOLE TIME, YOU CHICKEN!?
COME NOW. I HAVE A PROPOSITION FOR EVERYONE.
IT WOULD BE A WASTE IF THE EVENING ENDED LIKE THIS, WOULDN'T IT?
HOW ABOUT 3-A HAVING SOME FUN PLAYING A LIVELY GAME? ONE GAME.
WHAT ARE YOU PROPOSING? AS CLASS REP I CAN'T ALLOW THIS SORT OF THING.
I'M IN!
WHAT KIND OF GAME ARE YOU TALKING ABOUT?
I'M OUT.
I DON'T LIKE SEIZA.
I'VE NAMED IT, "LIP SCRAMBLE!!"
"OPERATION: KISS NEGI-KUN PASSIONATELY ON THIS SCHOOL FIELD TRIP!"
I'VE MADE AN ARRANGEMENT WITH NEGI-KUN'S MANAGER.

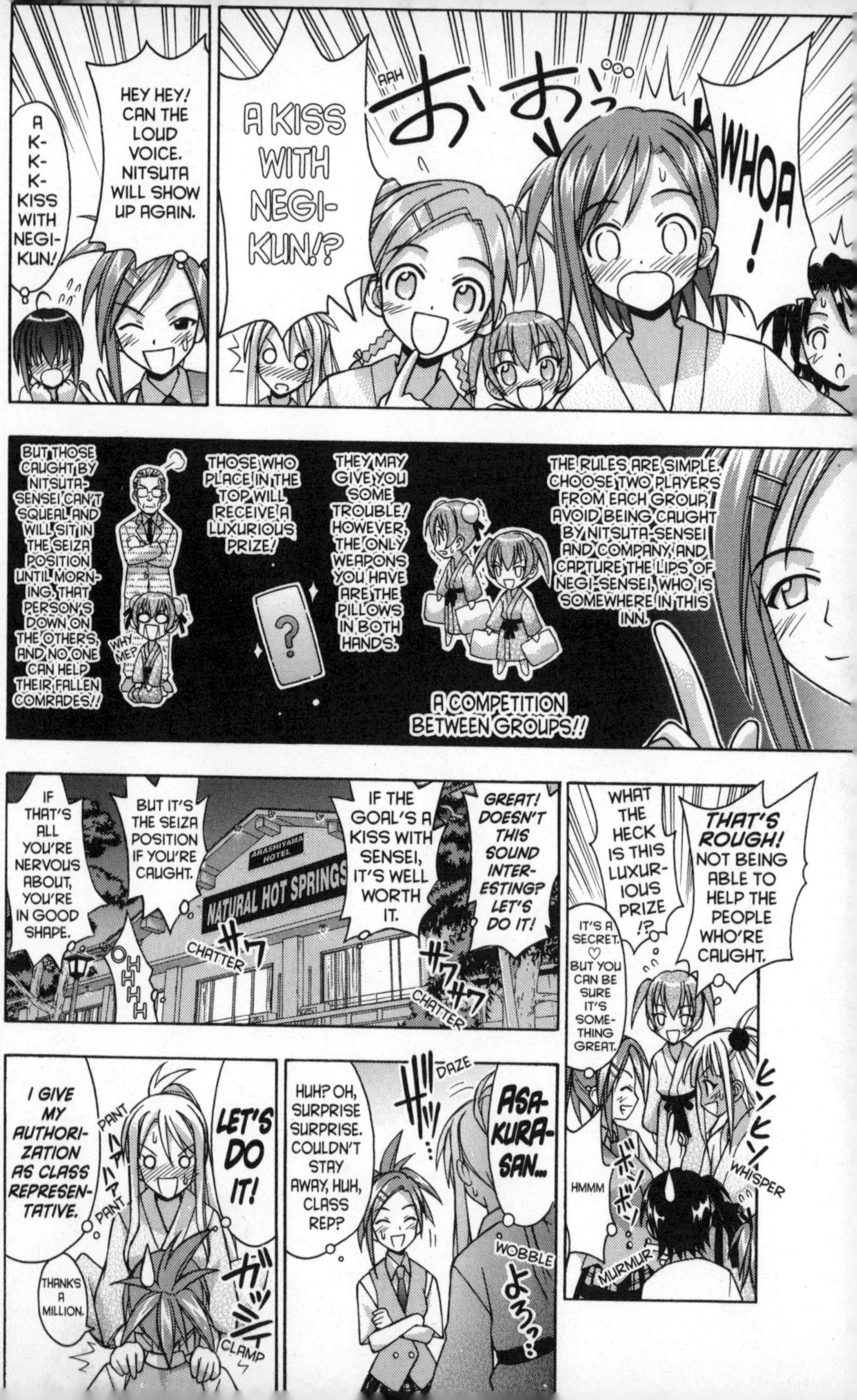
WHOA!
AAH
A KISS WITH NEGI-KUN!?
HEY HEY! CAN THE LOUD VOICE. NITSUTA WILL SHOW UP AGAIN.
A K-K-K-KISS WITH NEGI-KUN!
THE RULES ARE SIMPLE. CHOOSE TWO PLAYERS FROM EACH GROUP, AVOID BEING CAUGHT BY NITSUTA-SENSEI AND COMPANY, AND CAPTURE THE LIPS OF NEGI-SENSEI, WHO IS SOMEWHERE IN THIS INN.
A COMPETITION BETWEEN GROUPS!!
THEY MAY GIVE YOU SOME TROUBLE! HOWEVER, THE ONLY WEAPONS YOU HAVE ARE THE PILLOWS IN BOTH HANDS.
THOSE WHO PLACE IN THE TOP WILL RECEIVE A LUXURIOUS PRIZE!
?
BUT THOSE CAUGHT BY NITSUTA-SENSEI CAN'T SQUEAL AND WILL SIT IN THE SEIZA POSITION UNTIL MORNING. THAT PERSON'S DOWN ON THE OTHERS, AND NO ONE CAN HELP THEIR FALLEN COMRADES!!
WHY ME?
THAT'S ROUGH! NOT BEING ABLE TO HELP THE PEOPLE WHO'RE CAUGHT.
WHAT THE HECK IS THIS LUXURIOUS PRIZE!?
IT'S A SECRET. ♡ BUT YOU CAN BE SURE IT'S SOMETHING GREAT.
WHISPER
HMMM
MURMUR
GREAT! DOESN'T THIS SOUND INTERESTING? LET'S DO IT!
IF THE GOAL'S A KISS WITH SENSEI, IT'S WELL WORTH IT.
BUT IT'S THE SEIZA POSITION IF YOU'RE CAUGHT.
IF THAT'S ALL YOU'RE NERVOUS ABOUT, YOU'RE IN GOOD SHAPE.
ARASHIYAMA HOTEL
NATURAL HOT SPRINGS
CHATTER
CHATTER
OHHHH
DAZE
ASA-KURA-SAN...
HUH? OH, SURPRISE SURPRISE. COULDN'T STAY AWAY, HUH, CLASS REP?
WOBBLE
LET'S DO IT!
I GIVE MY AUTHORIZATION AS CLASS REPRESENTATIVE.
PANT
PANT
THANKS A MILLION.
CLAMP

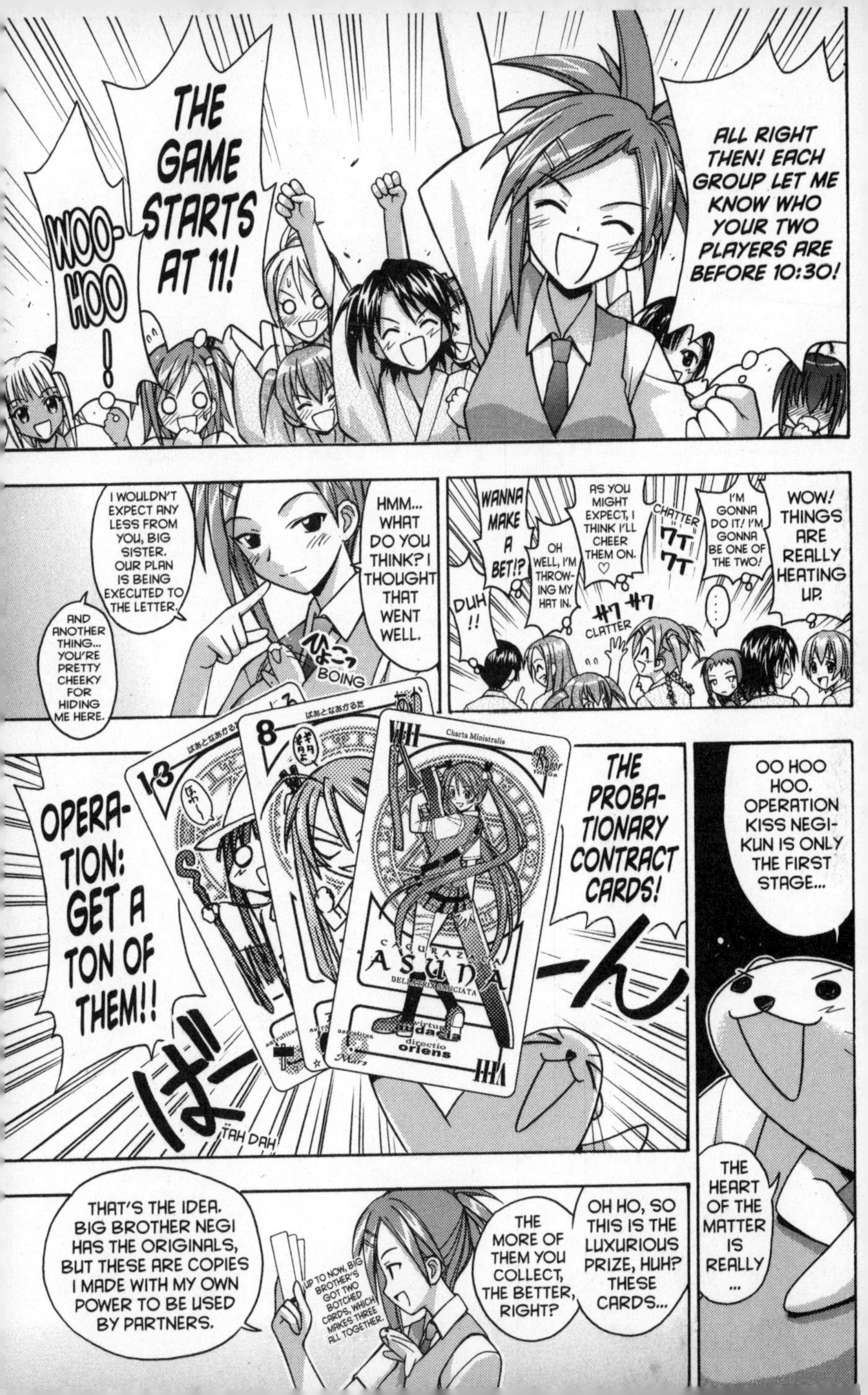
ALL RIGHT THEN! EACH GROUP LET ME KNOW WHO YOUR TWO PLAYERS ARE BEFORE 10:30!
THE GAME STARTS AT 11!
WOO-HOO!
WOW! THINGS ARE REALLY HEATING UP.
I'M GONNA DO IT! I'M GONNA BE ONE OF THE TWO!
...
CHATTER
AS YOU MIGHT EXPECT, I THINK I'LL CHEER THEM ON. ♡
OH WELL, I'M THROWING MY HAT IN.
WANNA MAKE A BET!?
DUH!!
CLATTER
HMM... WHAT DO YOU THINK? I THOUGHT THAT WENT WELL.
I WOULDN'T EXPECT ANY LESS FROM YOU, BIG SISTER. OUR PLAN IS BEING EXECUTED TO THE LETTER.
BOING
AND ANOTHER THING... YOU'RE PRETTY CHEEKY FOR HIDING ME HERE.
OO HOO HOO. OPERATION KISS NEGI-KUN IS ONLY THE FIRST STAGE...
THE HEART OF THE MATTER IS REALLY ...
THE PROBATIONARY CONTRACT CARDS!
OPERATION: GET A TON OF THEM!!
TAH DAH
OH HO, SO THIS IS THE LUXURIOUS PRIZE, HUH? THESE CARDS...
THE MORE OF THEM YOU COLLECT, THE BETTER, RIGHT?
THAT'S THE IDEA. BIG BROTHER NEGI HAS THE ORIGINALS, BUT THESE ARE COPIES I MADE WITH MY OWN POWER TO BE USED BY PARTNERS.
UP TO NOW, BIG BROTHER'S GOT TWO BOTCHED CARDS, WHICH MAKES THREE ALL TOGETHER.

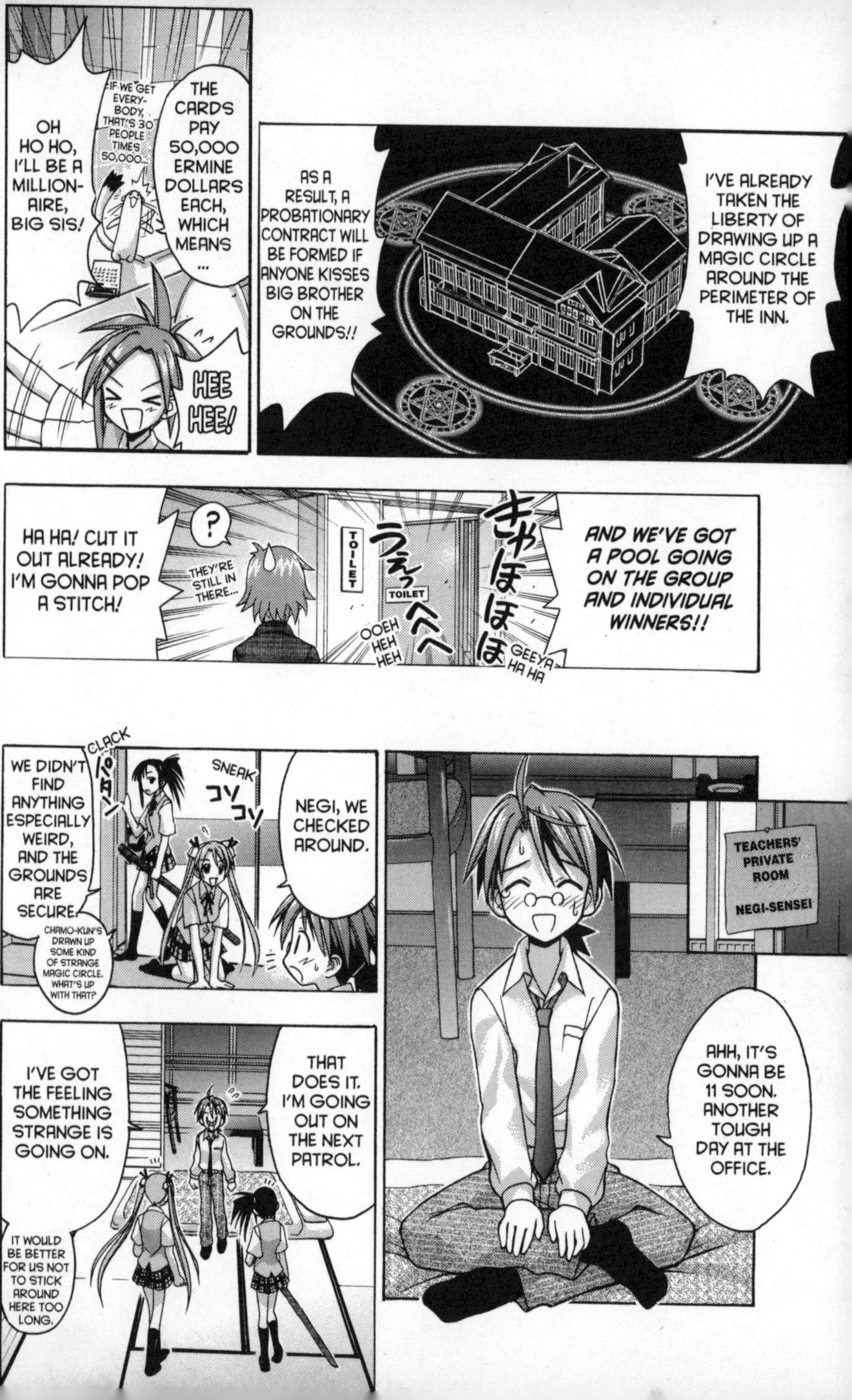
I'VE ALREADY TAKEN THE LIBERTY OF DRAWING UP A MAGIC CIRCLE AROUND THE PERIMETER OF THE INN.
AS A RESULT, A PROBATIONARY CONTRACT WILL BE FORMED IF ANYONE KISSES BIG BROTHER ON THE GROUNDS!!
THE CARDS PAY 50,000 ERMINE DOLLARS EACH, WHICH MEANS ...
IF WE GET EVERYBODY, THAT'S 30 PEOPLE TIMES 50,000...
OH HO HO, I'LL BE A MILLIONAIRE, BIG SIS!
HEE HEE!
AND WE'VE GOT A POOL GOING ON THE GROUP AND INDIVIDUAL WINNERS!!
きゃほほほ
GEEYA HA HA
うえっへへ
OOEH HEH HEH
TOILET
TOILET
THEY'RE STILL IN THERE...
?
HA HA! CUT IT OUT ALREADY! I'M GONNA POP A STITCH!
TEACHERS' PRIVATE ROOM
NEGI-SENSEI
AHH, IT'S GONNA BE 11 SOON. ANOTHER TOUGH DAY AT THE OFFICE.
NEGI, WE CHECKED AROUND.
SNEAK
コソコソ
CLACK
パタン
WE DIDN'T FIND ANYTHING ESPECIALLY WEIRD, AND THE GROUNDS ARE SECURE.
CHAMO-KUN'S DRAWN UP SOME KIND OF STRANGE MAGIC CIRCLE. WHAT'S UP WITH THAT?
THAT DOES IT. I'M GOING OUT ON THE NEXT PATROL.
I'VE GOT THE FEELING SOMETHING STRANGE IS GOING ON.
IT WOULD BE BETTER FOR US NOT TO STICK AROUND HERE TOO LONG.

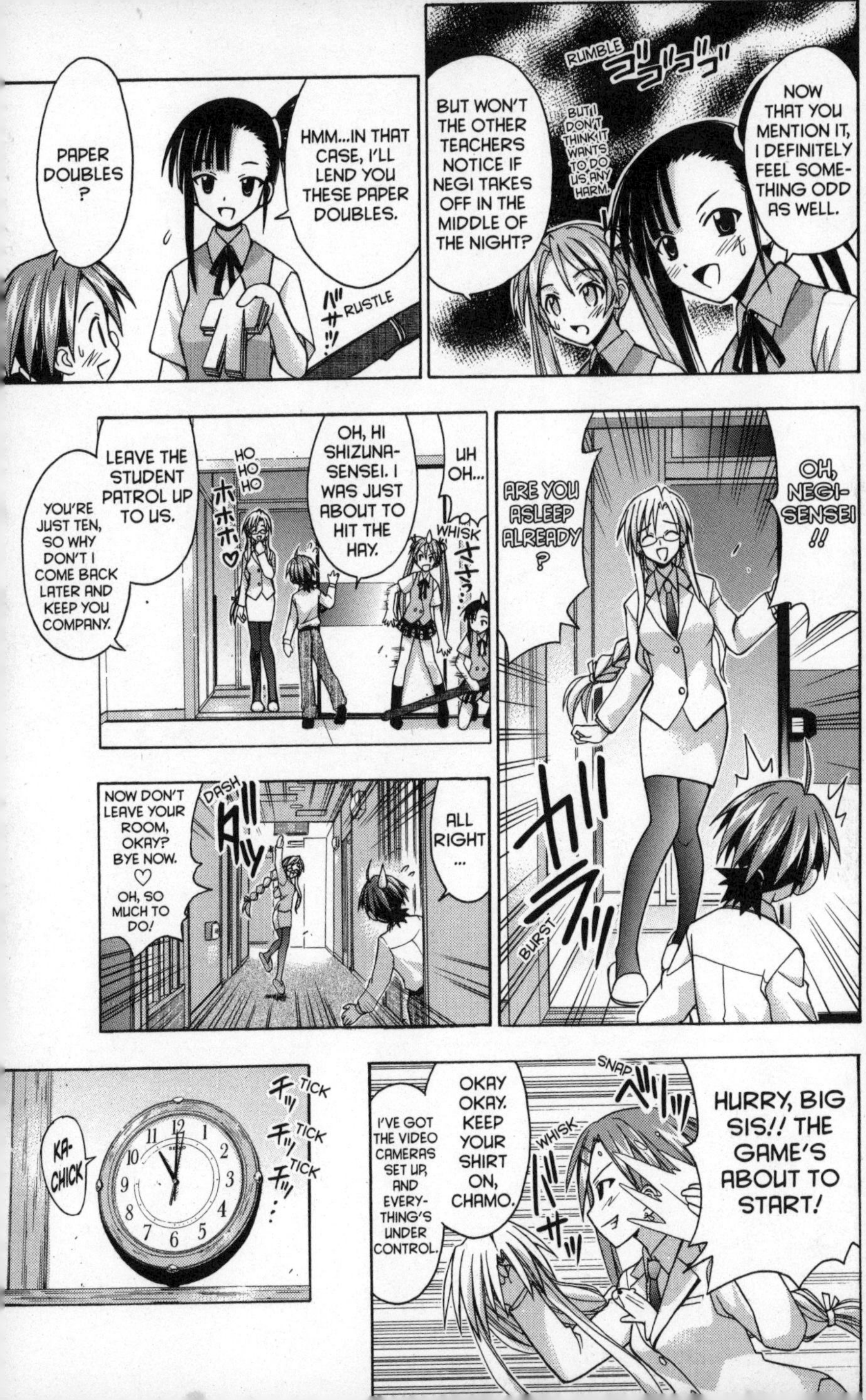
RUMBLE
NOW THAT YOU MENTION IT, I DEFINITELY FEEL SOME-THING ODD AS WELL.
BUT I DON'T THINK IT WANTS TO DO US ANY HARM.
BUT WON'T THE OTHER TEACHERS NOTICE IF NEGI TAKES OFF IN THE MIDDLE OF THE NIGHT?
HMM...IN THAT CASE, I'LL LEND YOU THESE PAPER DOUBLES.
RUSTLE
PAPER DOUBLES ?
OH, NEGI-SENSEI !!
ARE YOU ASLEEP ALREADY ?
BURST
UH OH...
OH, HI SHIZUNA-SENSEI. I WAS JUST ABOUT TO HIT THE HAY.
WHISK
HO HO HO
LEAVE THE STUDENT PATROL UP TO US.
YOU'RE JUST TEN, SO WHY DON'T I COME BACK LATER AND KEEP YOU COMPANY.
ALL RIGHT ...
DASH
NOW DON'T LEAVE YOUR ROOM, OKAY? BYE NOW. ♡
OH, SO MUCH TO DO!
HURRY, BIG SIS!! THE GAME'S ABOUT TO START!
SNAP
WHISK
OKAY OKAY. KEEP YOUR SHIRT ON, CHAMO.
I'VE GOT THE VIDEO CAMERAS SET UP, AND EVERY-THING'S UNDER CONTROL.
TICK
TICK
TICK
KA-CHICK

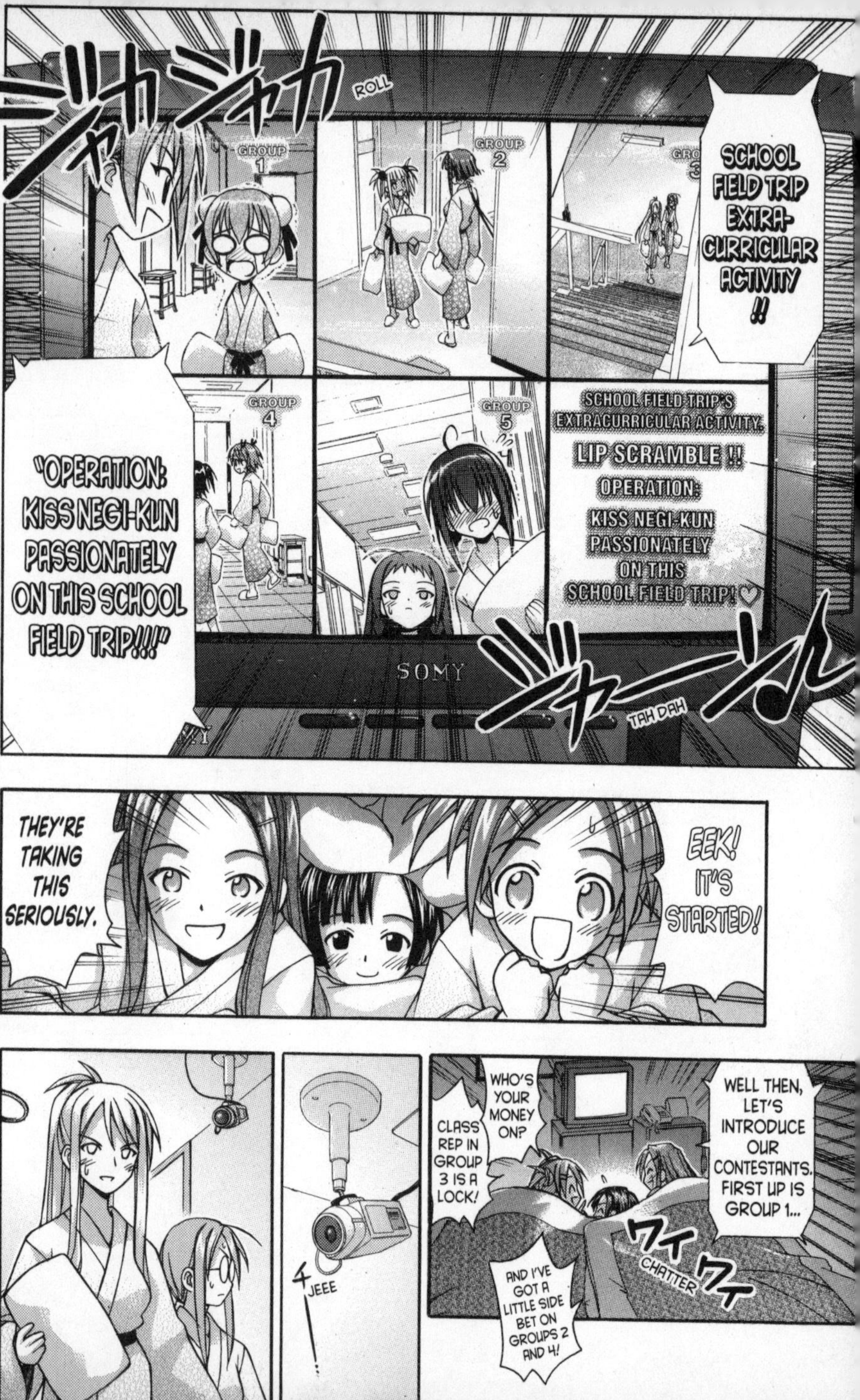
ジャカジャカ
ROLL
SCHOOL FIELD TRIP EXTRA-CURRICULAR ACTIVITY !!
GROUP 1
GROUP 2
GROUP 3
GROUP 4
GROUP 5
SCHOOL FIELD TRIP'S EXTRACURRICULAR ACTIVITY. LIP SCRAMBLE !! OPERATION: KISS NEGI-KUN PASSIONATELY ON THIS SCHOOL FIELD TRIP! ♡
"OPERATION: KISS NEGI-KUN PASSIONATELY ON THIS SCHOOL FIELD TRIP!!!"
SOMY
ジャーン
TAH DAH
EEK! IT'S STARTED!
THEY'RE TAKING THIS SERIOUSLY.
WELL THEN, LET'S INTRODUCE OUR CONTESTANTS. FIRST UP IS GROUP 1...
WHO'S YOUR MONEY ON?
CLASS REP IN GROUP 3 IS A LOCK!
AND I'VE GOT A LITTLE SIDE BET ON GROUPS 2 AND 4!
ワイワイ
CHATTER
JEEE

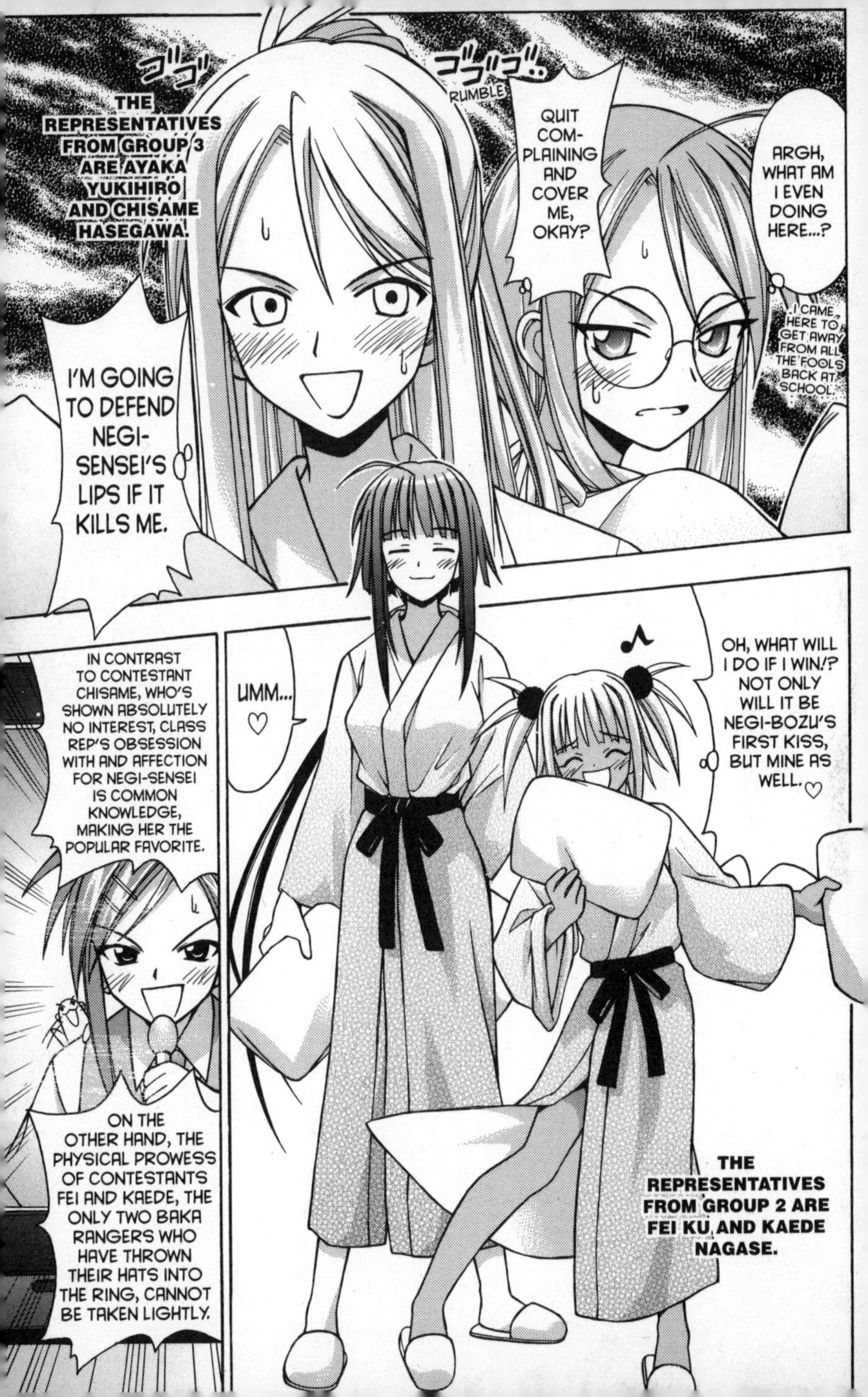
ARGH, WHAT AM I EVEN DOING HERE...?
I CAME HERE TO GET AWAY FROM ALL THE FOOLS BACK AT SCHOOL.
RUMBLE
QUIT COMPLAINING AND COVER ME, OKAY?
THE REPRESENTATIVES FROM GROUP 3 ARE AYAKA YUKIHIRO AND CHISAME HASEGAWA.
I'M GOING TO DEFEND NEGI-SENSEI'S LIPS IF IT KILLS ME.
OH, WHAT WILL I DO IF I WIN!? NOT ONLY WILL IT BE NEGI-BOZU'S FIRST KISS, BUT MINE AS WELL. ♡
UMM... ♡
THE REPRESENTATIVES FROM GROUP 2 ARE FEI KU AND KAEDE NAGASE.
IN CONTRAST TO CONTESTANT CHISAME, WHO'S SHOWN ABSOLUTELY NO INTEREST, CLASS REP'S OBSESSION WITH AND AFFECTION FOR NEGI-SENSEI IS COMMON KNOWLEDGE, MAKING HER THE POPULAR FAVORITE.
ON THE OTHER HAND, THE PHYSICAL PROWESS OF CONTESTANTS FEI AND KAEDE, THE ONLY TWO BAKA RANGERS WHO HAVE THROWN THEIR HATS INTO THE RING, CANNOT BE TAKEN LIGHTLY.

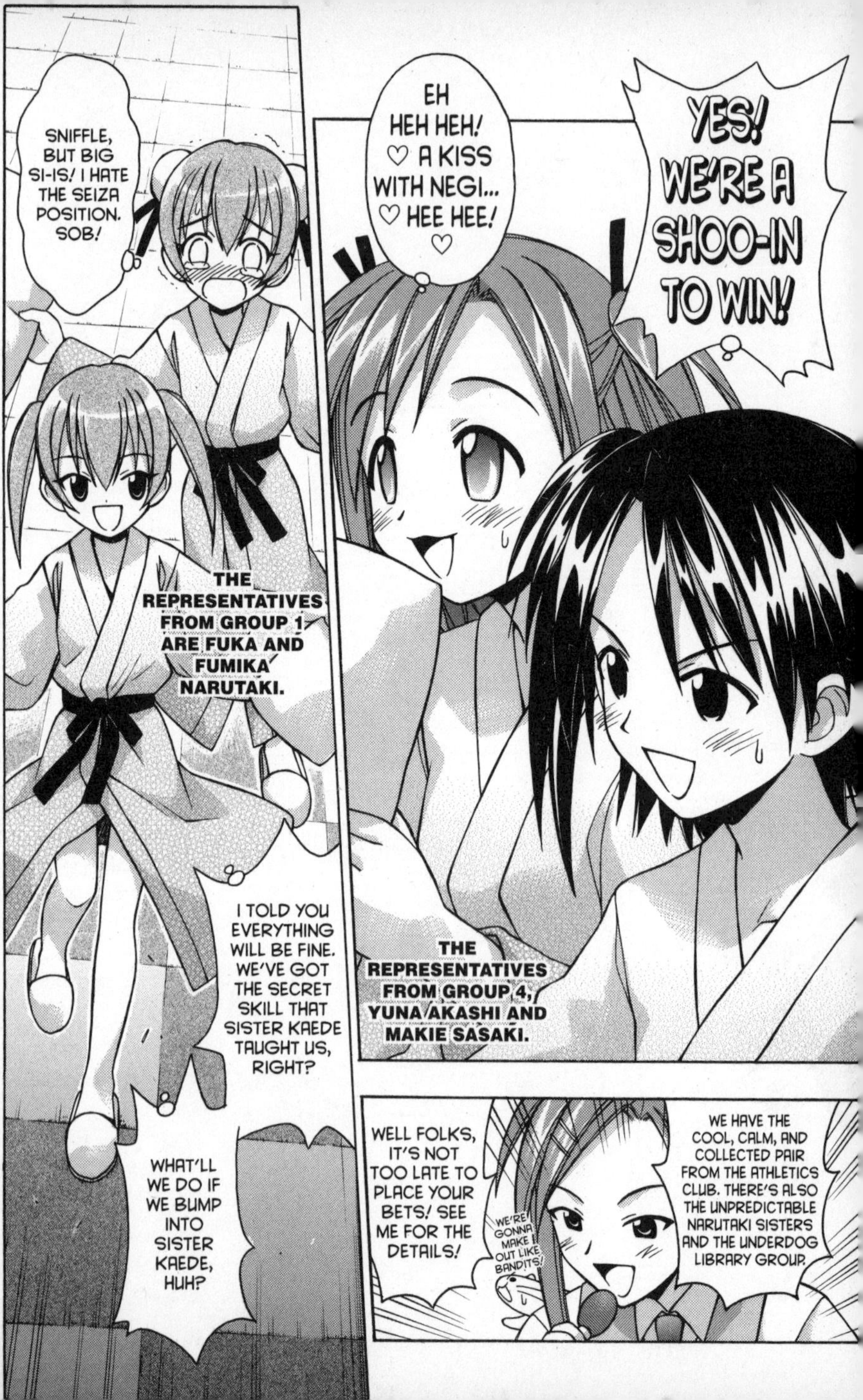
YES! WE'RE A SHOO-IN TO WIN!
EH HEH HEH! ♡ A KISS WITH NEGI... ♡ HEE HEE! ♡
THE REPRESENTATIVES FROM GROUP 4, YUNA AKASHI AND MAKIE SASAKI.
WE HAVE THE COOL, CALM, AND COLLECTED PAIR FROM THE ATHLETICS CLUB. THERE'S ALSO THE UNPREDICTABLE NARUTAKI SISTERS AND THE UNDERDOG LIBRARY GROUP.
WELL FOLKS, IT'S NOT TOO LATE TO PLACE YOUR BETS! SEE ME FOR THE DETAILS!
WE'RE GONNA MAKE OUT LIKE BANDITS!
SNIFFLE, BUT BIG SI-IS! I HATE THE SEIZA POSITION. SOB!
THE REPRESENTATIVES FROM GROUP 1 ARE FUKA AND FUMIKA NARUTAKI.
I TOLD YOU EVERYTHING WILL BE FINE. WE'VE GOT THE SECRET SKILL THAT SISTER KAEDE TAUGHT US, RIGHT?
WHAT'LL WE DO IF WE BUMP INTO SISTER KAEDE, HUH?

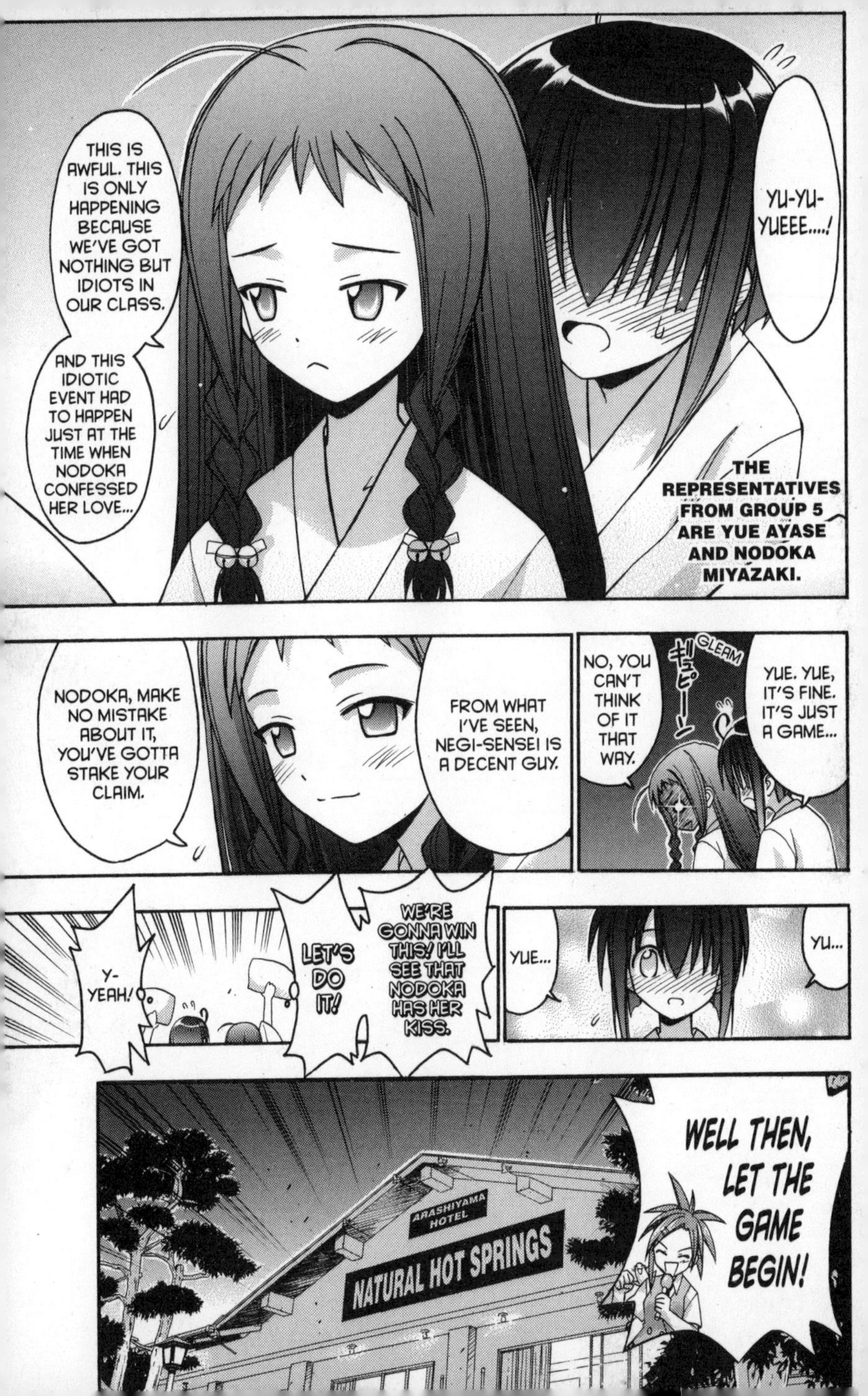

YU-YU-YUEEE....!
THIS IS AWFUL. THIS IS ONLY HAPPENING BECAUSE WE'VE GOT NOTHING BUT IDIOTS IN OUR CLASS.
AND THIS IDIOTIC EVENT HAD TO HAPPEN JUST AT THE TIME WHEN NODOKA CONFESSED HER LOVE...
THE REPRESENTATIVES FROM GROUP 5 ARE YUE AYASE AND NODOKA MIYAZAKI.
YUE. YUE, IT'S FINE. IT'S JUST A GAME...
GLEAM
NO, YOU CAN'T THINK OF IT THAT WAY.
FROM WHAT I'VE SEEN, NEGI-SENSEI IS A DECENT GUY.
NODOKA, MAKE NO MISTAKE ABOUT IT, YOU'VE GOTTA STAKE YOUR CLAIM.
YU...
YUE...
WE'RE GONNA WIN THIS! I'LL SEE THAT NODOKA HAS HER KISS.
LET'S DO IT!
Y-YEAH!
WELL THEN, LET THE GAME BEGIN!
ARASHIYAMA HOTEL
NATURAL HOT SPRINGS

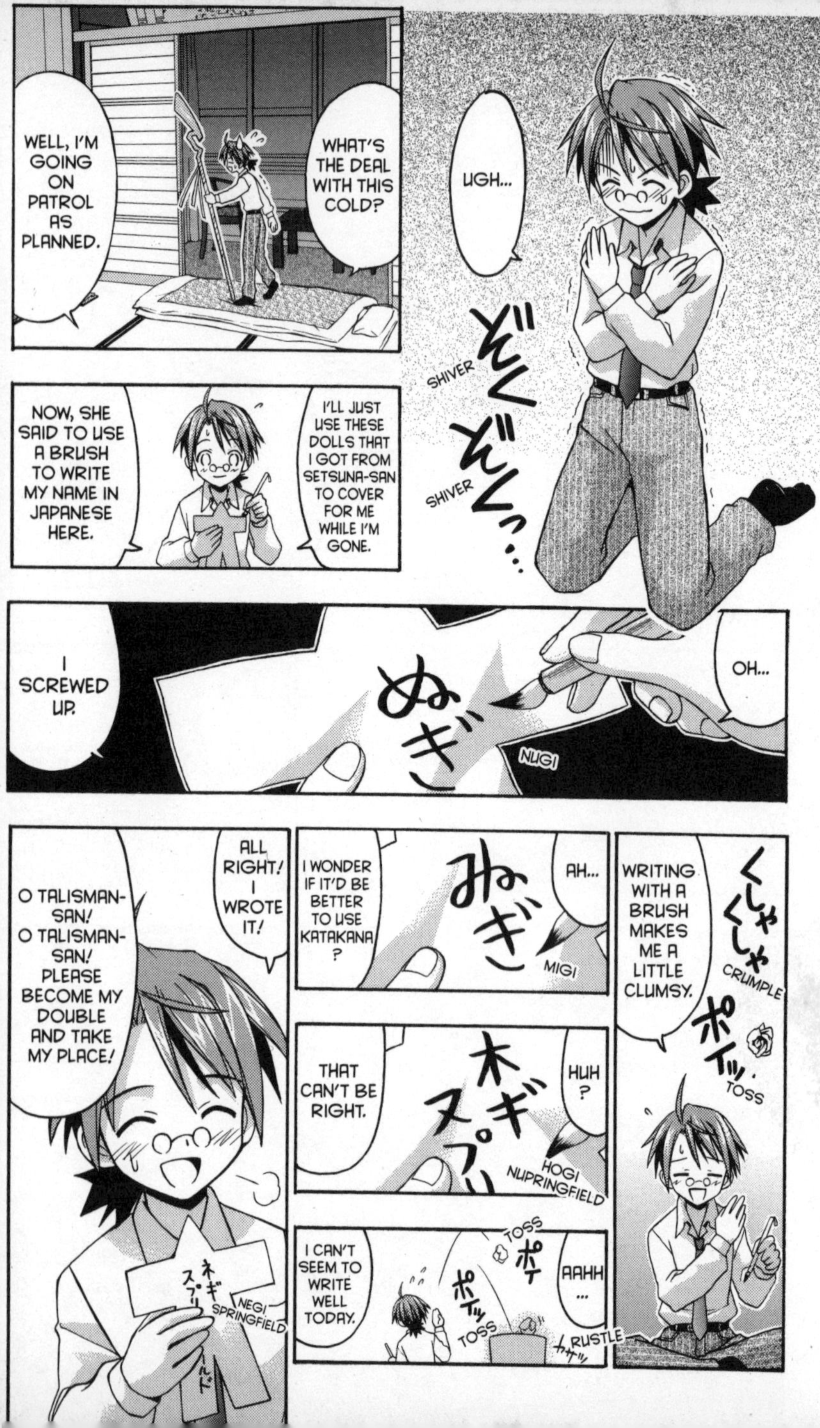
UGH...
ぞくぞくっ...
SHIVER
SHIVER
WHAT'S THE DEAL WITH THIS COLD?
WELL, I'M GOING ON PATROL AS PLANNED.
I'LL JUST USE THESE DOLLS THAT I GOT FROM SETSUNA-SAN TO COVER FOR ME WHILE I'M GONE.
NOW, SHE SAID TO USE A BRUSH TO WRITE MY NAME IN JAPANESE HERE.
OH...
ぬぎ
NUGI
I SCREWED UP.
くしゃくしゃ
CRUMPLE
WRITING WITH A BRUSH MAKES ME A LITTLE CLUMSY.
ポイッ
TOSS
AH...
みぎ
MIGI
I WONDER IF IT'D BE BETTER TO USE KATAKANA?
HUH?
ホギヌプリ
HOGI NUPRINGFIELD
THAT CAN'T BE RIGHT.
AAHH...
ポイ
TOSS
ポイッ
TOSS
カサッ
RUSTLE
I CAN'T SEEM TO WRITE WELL TODAY.
ALL RIGHT! I WROTE IT!
O TALISMAN-SAN! O TALISMAN-SAN! PLEASE BECOME MY DOUBLE AND TAKE MY PLACE!
NEGI SPRINGFIELD

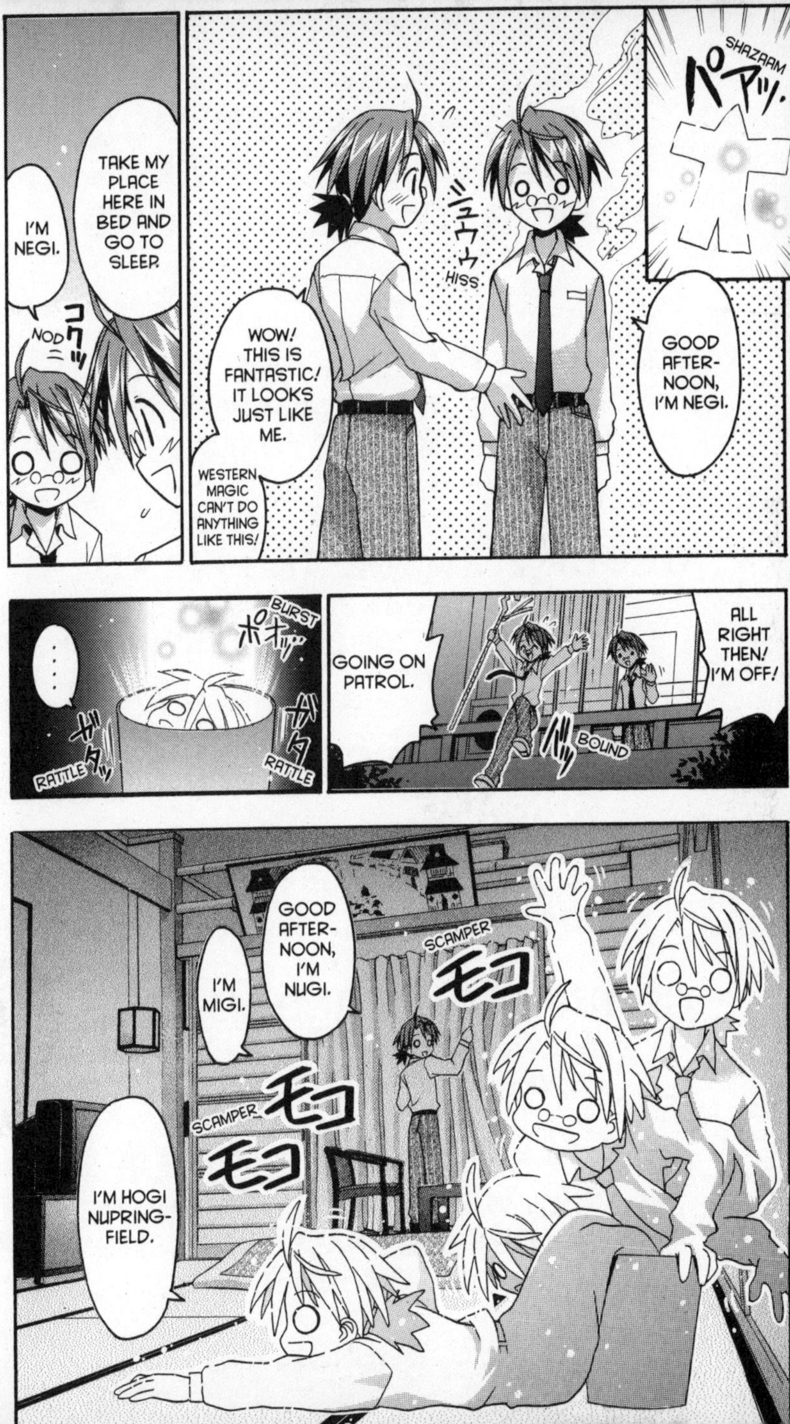
SHAZAAM
パアッ…
GOOD AFTER-NOON, I'M NEGI.
シュウウ
HISS
WOW! THIS IS FANTASTIC! IT LOOKS JUST LIKE ME.
WESTERN MAGIC CAN'T DO ANYTHING LIKE THIS!
TAKE MY PLACE HERE IN BED AND GO TO SLEEP.
I'M NEGI.
コクッ
NOD
ALL RIGHT THEN! I'M OFF!
GOING ON PATROL.
バッ
BOUND
BURST
ポオッ
ガタ
RATTLE
. . . .
ガタッ
RATTLE
GOOD AFTER-NOON, I'M NUGI.
SCAMPER
モコ
I'M MIGI.
SCAMPER
モコ
モコ
I'M HOGI NUPRING-FIELD.

"OPERATION KISS NEGI-KUN PASSIONATELY ON THIS SCHOOL FIELD TRIP" PLAYER INTRODUCTIONS.

GROUP 1: FUMIKA AND FUKA
WE'VE GOT A SECRET PLAN!! IF YOU WANNA ROCK THE BOAT, WE'RE YOUR TEAM!

GROUP 2: KAEDE AND FEI KU
THEIR COMBAT POWERS MAKE THEM THE BIG FAVORITES! BUT DO THEY LACK THE WILL TO WIN?

GROUP 3: CLASS REP AND CHISAME
THERE ARE DOUBTS ABOUT THEIR TEAMWORK, BUT IF THEY CAN WORK TOGETHER THERE'S NO STOPPING THEM.

GROUP 4: YUNA AND MAKIE
WE'VE GOT SUPREME BALANCE!! WE'LL NEVER GIVE AN INCH!!

GROUP 5: NODOKA AND YUE
THEY WANT IT BAD ENOUGH!! THEY'LL TAKE ON THE CHALLENGE USING THEIR INTELLECT AND HEART!!

THIRTY-SIXTH PERIOD: THE LABYRINTH OF LIPS

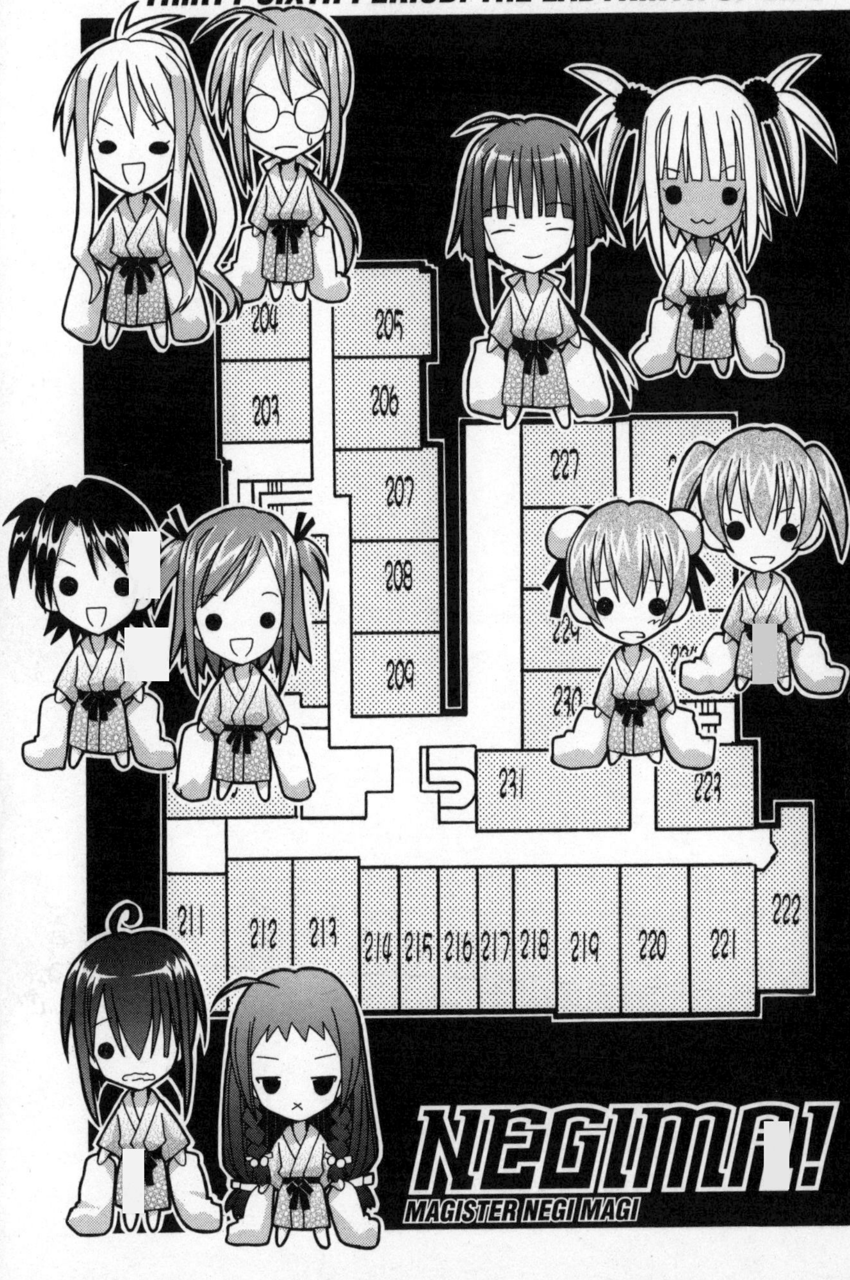
204
205
203
206
227
207
208
224
209
230
231
223
211
212
213
214
215
216
217
218
219
220
221
222
NEGIMA!
MAGISTER NEGI MAGI

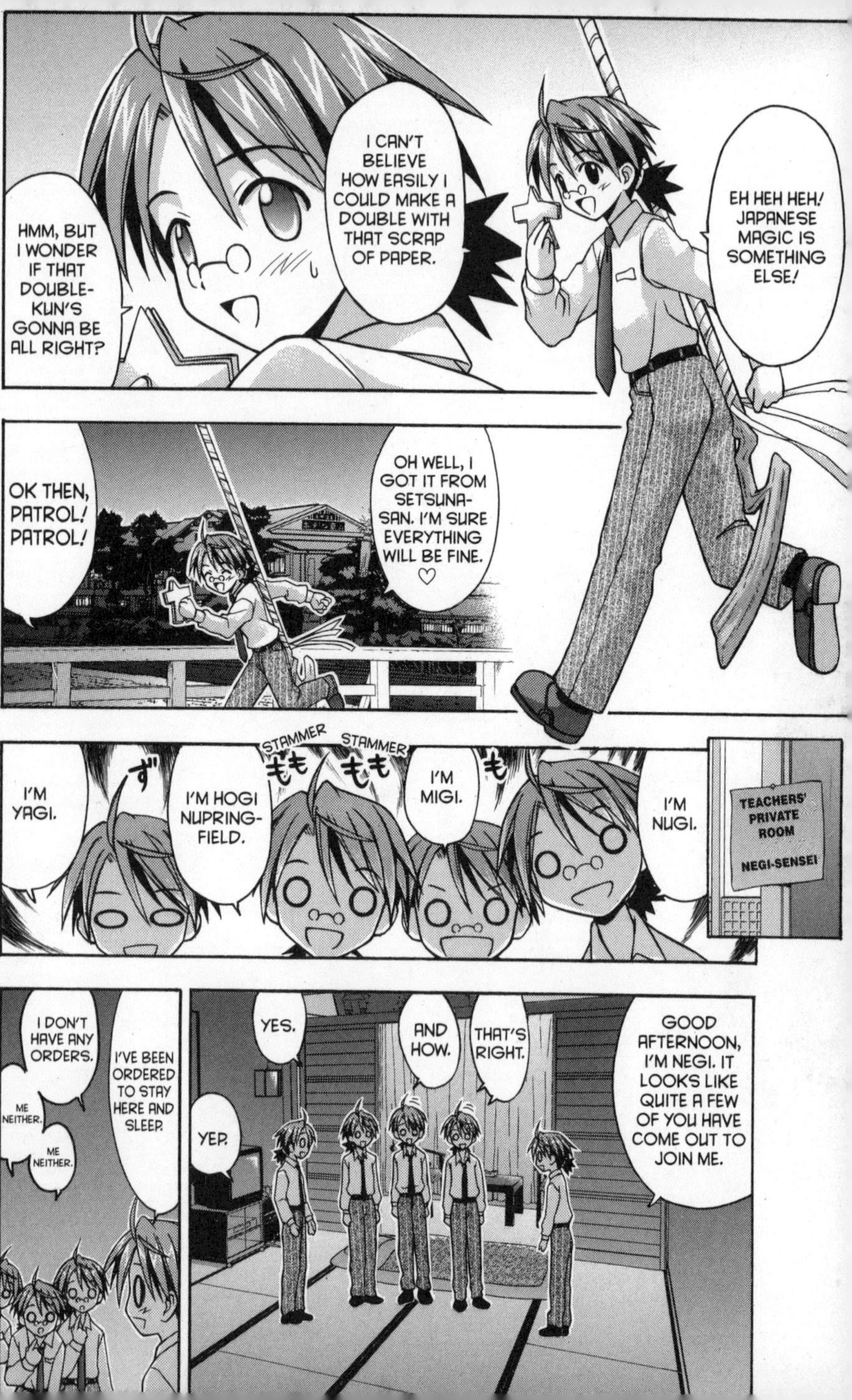
EH HEH HEH! JAPANESE MAGIC IS SOMETHING ELSE!
I CAN'T BELIEVE HOW EASILY I COULD MAKE A DOUBLE WITH THAT SCRAP OF PAPER.
HMM, BUT I WONDER IF THAT DOUBLE-KUN'S GONNA BE ALL RIGHT?
OH WELL, I GOT IT FROM SETSUNA-SAN. I'M SURE EVERYTHING WILL BE FINE. ♡
OK THEN, PATROL! PATROL!
TEACHERS' PRIVATE ROOM
NEGI-SENSEI
I'M NUGI.
I'M MIGI.
STAMMER
STAMMER
I'M HOGI NUPRING-FIELD.
I'M YAGI.
GOOD AFTERNOON, I'M NEGI. IT LOOKS LIKE QUITE A FEW OF YOU HAVE COME OUT TO JOIN ME.
THAT'S RIGHT.
AND HOW.
YES.
YEP.
I'VE BEEN ORDERED TO STAY HERE AND SLEEP.
I DON'T HAVE ANY ORDERS.
ME NEITHER.
ME NEITHER.

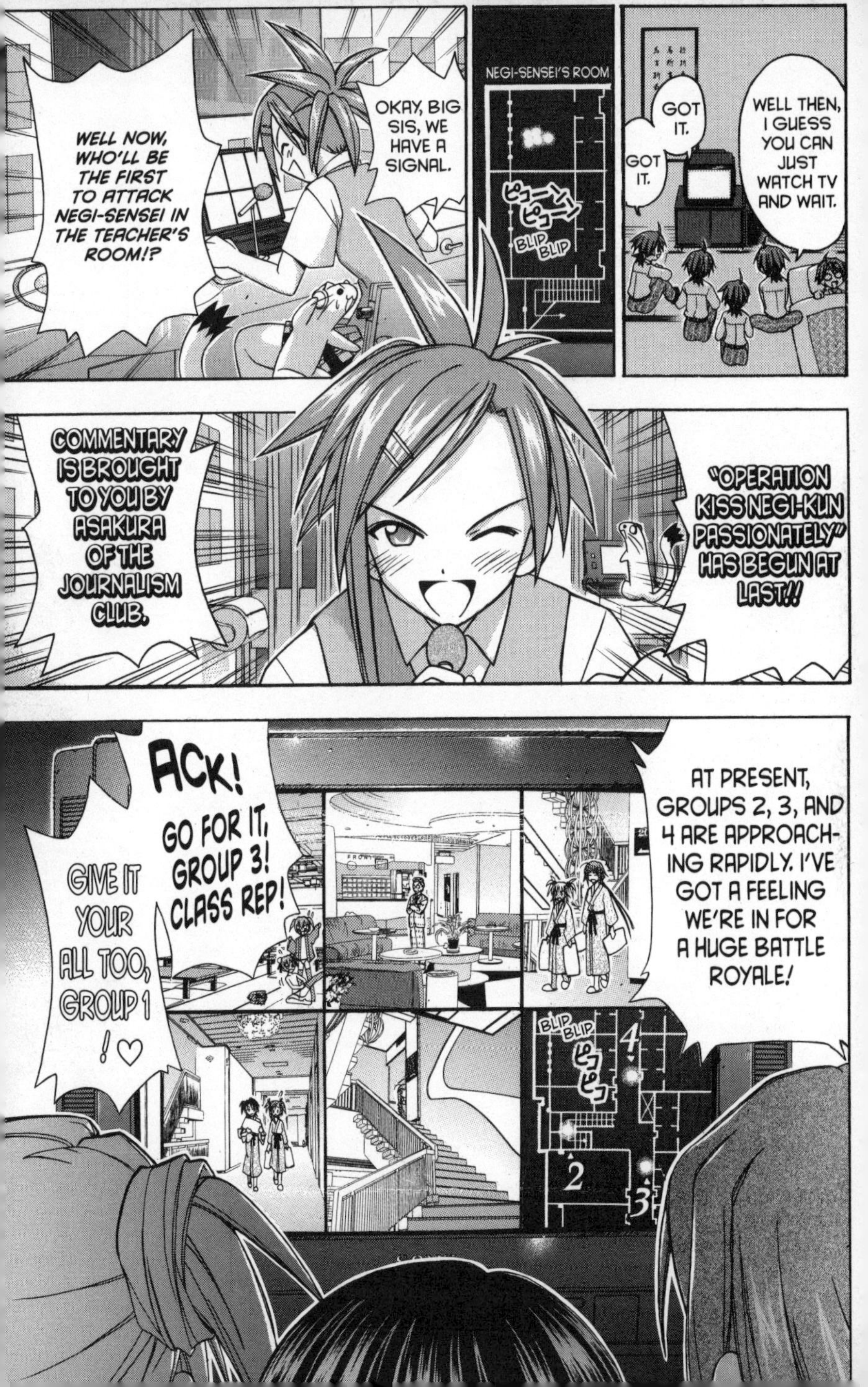
WELL THEN, I GUESS YOU CAN JUST WATCH TV AND WAIT.
GOT IT.
GOT IT.
NEGI-SENSEI'S ROOM
ピコーン ピコーン
BLIP BLIP
OKAY, BIG SIS, WE HAVE A SIGNAL.
WELL NOW, WHO'LL BE THE FIRST TO ATTACK NEGI-SENSEI IN THE TEACHER'S ROOM!?
"OPERATION KISS NEGI-KUN PASSIONATELY" HAS BEGUN AT LAST!!
COMMENTARY IS BROUGHT TO YOU BY ASAKURA OF THE JOURNALISM CLUB.
AT PRESENT, GROUPS 2, 3, AND 4 ARE APPROACHING RAPIDLY. I'VE GOT A FEELING WE'RE IN FOR A HUGE BATTLE ROYALE!
ACK!
GO FOR IT, GROUP 3! CLASS REP!
GIVE IT YOUR ALL TOO, GROUP 1! ♡
BLIP BLIP
ピコピコ
4
2
3

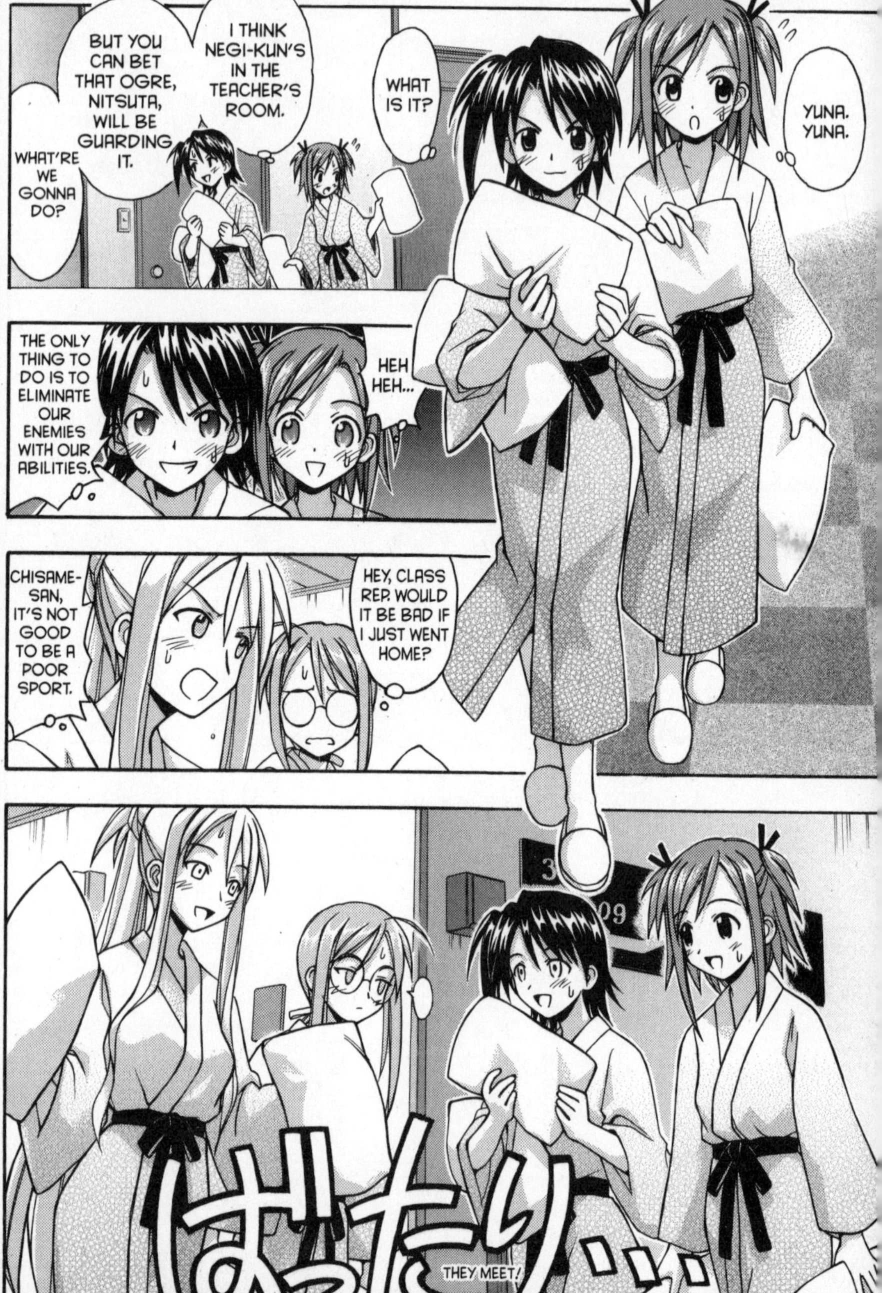
YUNA. YUNA.
WHAT IS IT?
I THINK NEGI-KUN'S IN THE TEACHER'S ROOM.
BUT YOU CAN BET THAT OGRE, NITSUTA, WILL BE GUARDING IT.
WHAT'RE WE GONNA DO?
HEH HEH...
THE ONLY THING TO DO IS TO ELIMINATE OUR ENEMIES WITH OUR ABILITIES.
HEY, CLASS REP. WOULD IT BE BAD IF I JUST WENT HOME?
CHISAME-SAN, IT'S NOT GOOD TO BE A POOR SPORT.
はったり…
THEY MEET!

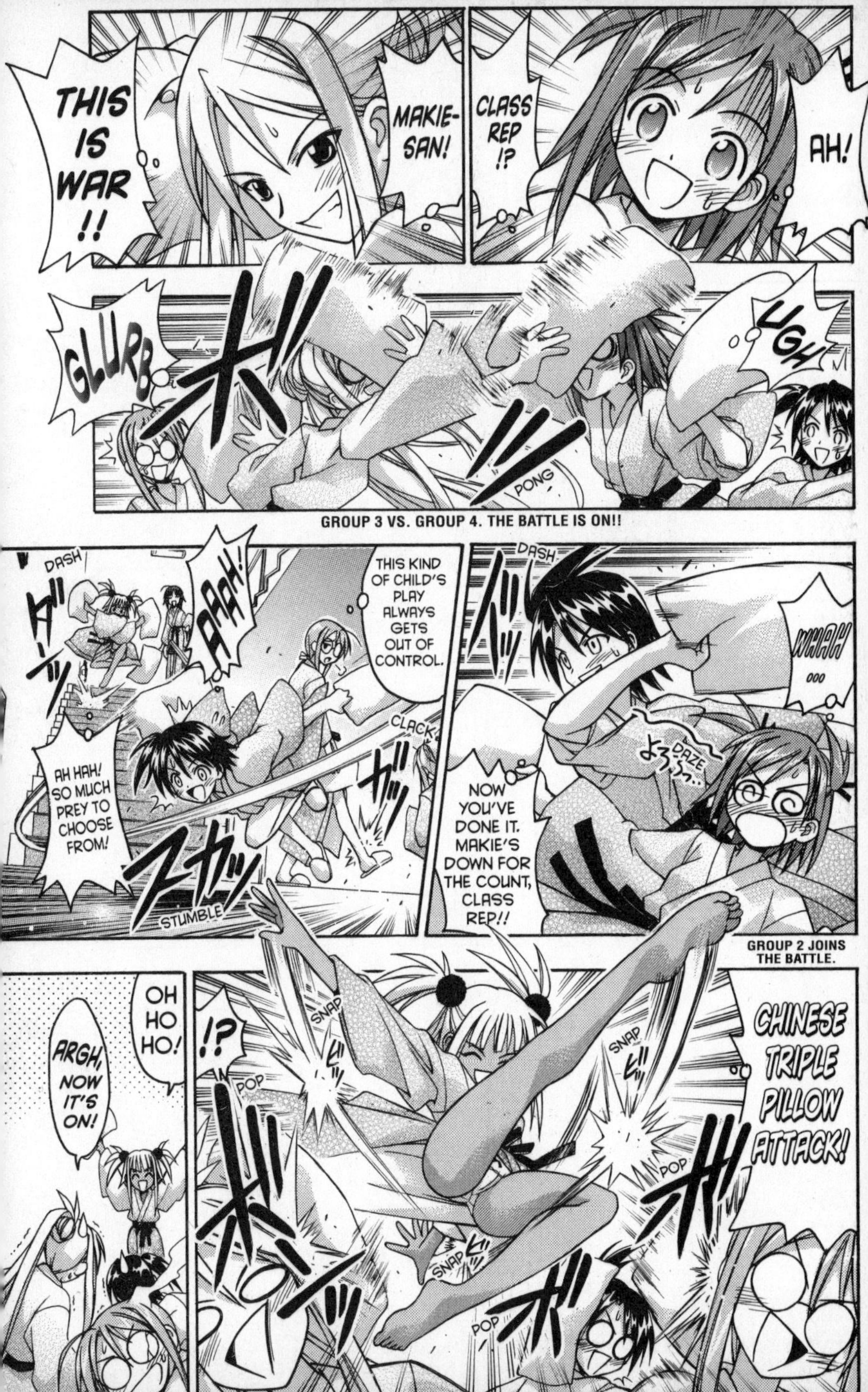
AH!
CLASS REP !?
MAKIE-SAN!
THIS IS WAR !!
UGH
PONG
GLURB
GROUP 3 VS. GROUP 4. THE BATTLE IS ON!!
DASH
WHAAH ...
DAZE
NOW YOU'VE DONE IT. MAKIE'S DOWN FOR THE COUNT, CLASS REP!!
THIS KIND OF CHILD'S PLAY ALWAYS GETS OUT OF CONTROL.
AAAH!
DASH
CLACK
AH HAH! SO MUCH PREY TO CHOOSE FROM!
STUMBLE
GROUP 2 JOINS THE BATTLE.
CHINESE TRIPLE PILLOW ATTACK!
SNAP
SNAP
!?
POP
POP
SNAP
POP
OH HO HO!
ARGH, NOW IT'S ON!

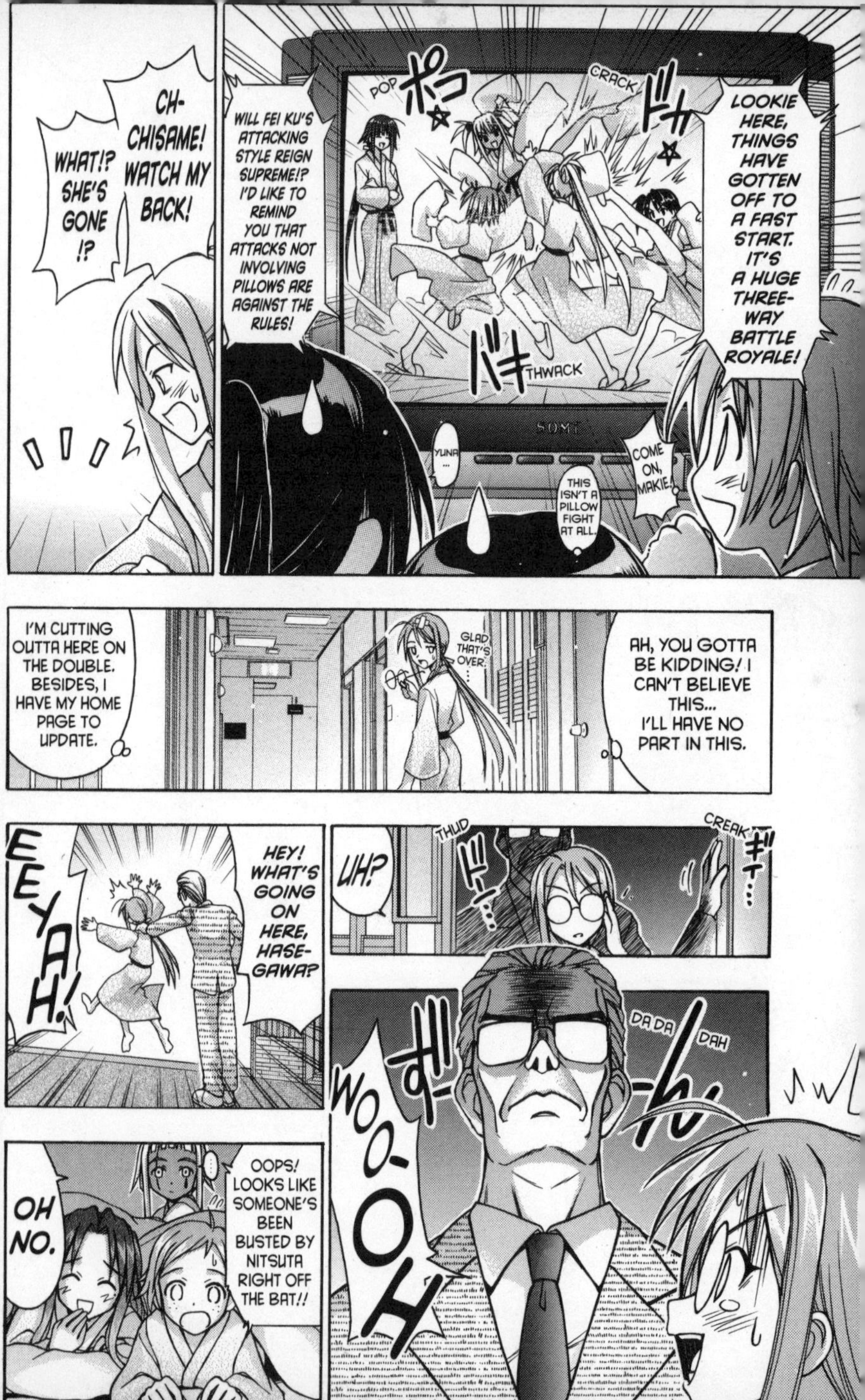
LOOKIE HERE, THINGS HAVE GOTTEN OFF TO A FAST START. IT'S A HUGE THREE-WAY BATTLE ROYALE!
CRACK
POP
WILL FEI KU'S ATTACKING STYLE REIGN SUPREME!? I'D LIKE TO REMIND YOU THAT ATTACKS NOT INVOLVING PILLOWS ARE AGAINST THE RULES!
THWACK
COME ON, MAKIE.
THIS ISN'T A PILLOW FIGHT AT ALL.
YUNA ...
CH-CHISAME! WATCH MY BACK!
WHAT!? SHE'S GONE !?
AH, YOU GOTTA BE KIDDING! I CAN'T BELIEVE THIS... I'LL HAVE NO PART IN THIS.
GLAD THAT'S OVER. ...
I'M CUTTING OUTTA HERE ON THE DOUBLE. BESIDES, I HAVE MY HOME PAGE TO UPDATE.
CREAK
THUD
UH?
DA DA DAH
WOO-OOH
HEY! WHAT'S GOING ON HERE, HASE-GAWA?
EEYAH!
OOPS! LOOKS LIKE SOMEONE'S BEEN BUSTED BY NITSUTA RIGHT OFF THE BAT!!
OH NO.

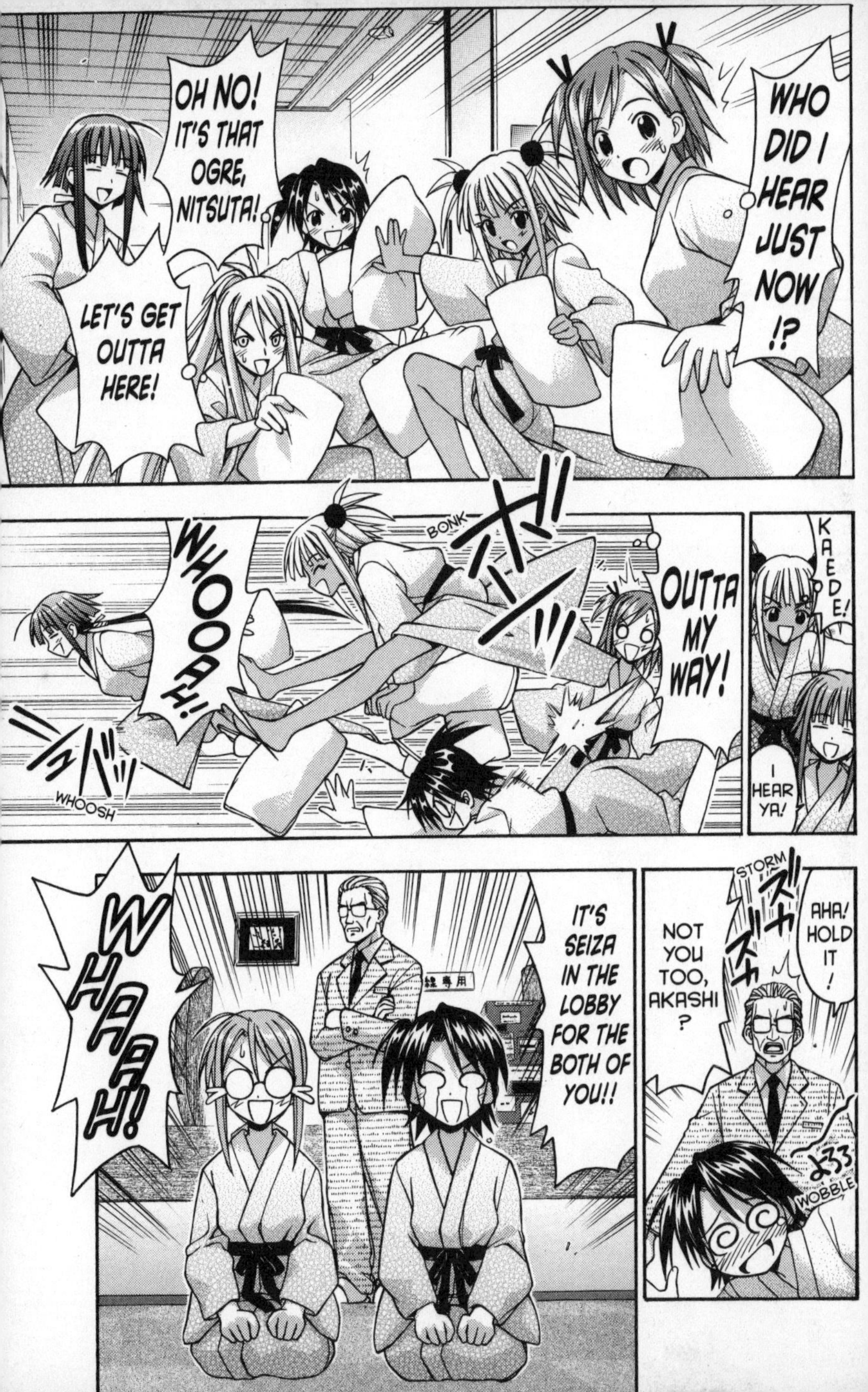
WHO DID I HEAR JUST NOW!?
OH NO! IT'S THAT OGRE, NITSUTA!
LET'S GET OUTTA HERE!
KAEDE!
I HEAR YA!
OUTTA MY WAY!
BONK
WHOOOAAH!!
WHOOSH
STORM
AHA! HOLD IT!
NOT YOU TOO, AKASHI?
WOBBLE
IT'S SEIZA IN THE LOBBY FOR THE BOTH OF YOU!!
WHAAAH!

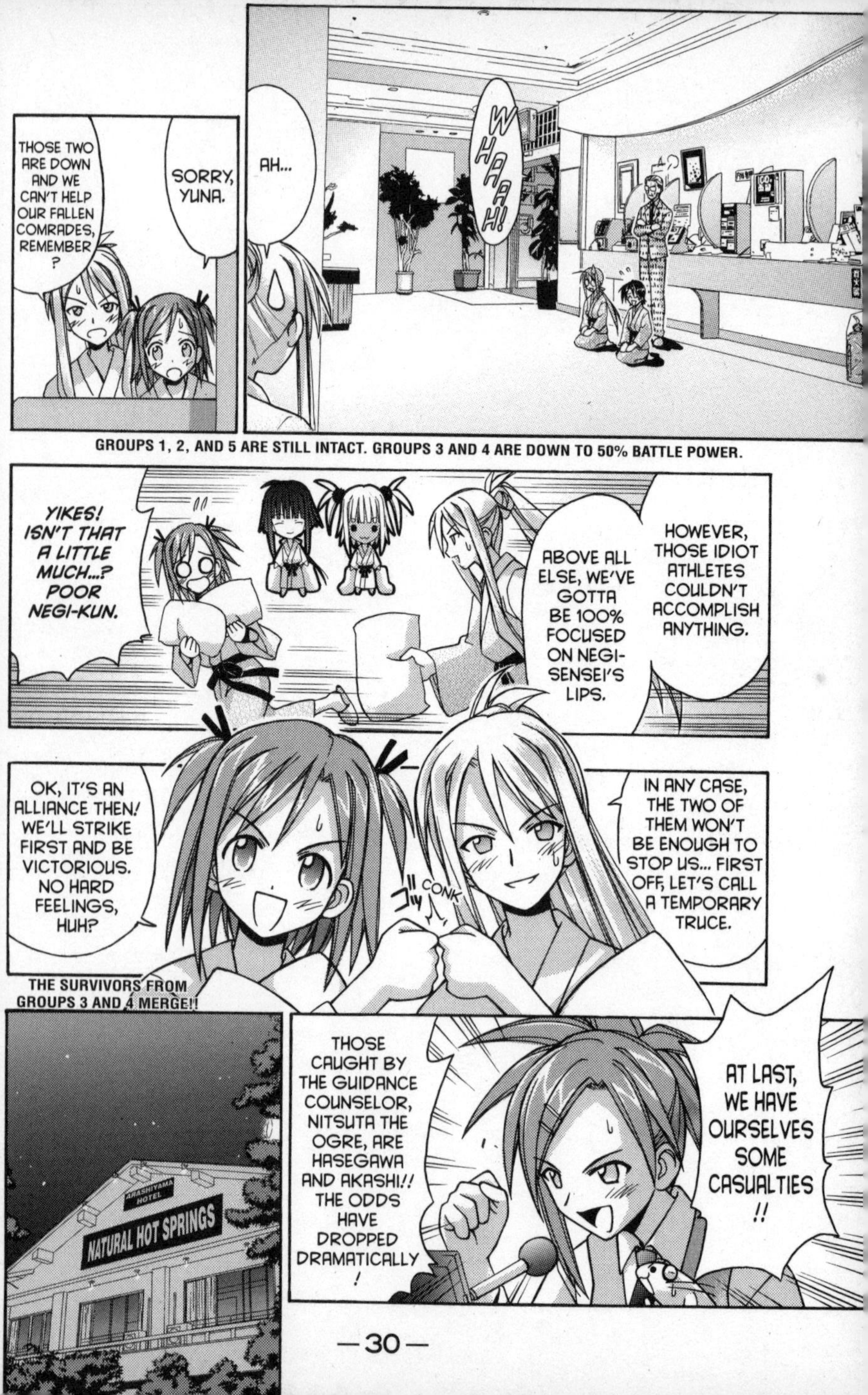
WHAAAH!
AH...
SORRY, YUNA.
THOSE TWO ARE DOWN AND WE CAN'T HELP OUR FALLEN COMRADES, REMEMBER?
GROUPS 1, 2, AND 5 ARE STILL INTACT. GROUPS 3 AND 4 ARE DOWN TO 50% BATTLE POWER.
HOWEVER, THOSE IDIOT ATHLETES COULDN'T ACCOMPLISH ANYTHING.
ABOVE ALL ELSE, WE'VE GOTTA BE 100% FOCUSED ON NEGI-SENSEI'S LIPS.
YIKES! ISN'T THAT A LITTLE MUCH...? POOR NEGI-KUN.
IN ANY CASE, THE TWO OF THEM WON'T BE ENOUGH TO STOP US... FIRST OFF, LET'S CALL A TEMPORARY TRUCE.
CONK
OK, IT'S AN ALLIANCE THEN! WE'LL STRIKE FIRST AND BE VICTORIOUS. NO HARD FEELINGS, HUH?
THE SURVIVORS FROM GROUPS 3 AND 4 MERGE!!
AT LAST, WE HAVE OURSELVES SOME CASUALTIES!!
THOSE CAUGHT BY THE GUIDANCE COUNSELOR, NITSUTA THE OGRE, ARE HASEGAWA AND AKASHI!! THE ODDS HAVE DROPPED DRAMATICALLY!
ARASHIYAMA HOTEL
NATURAL HOT SPRINGS

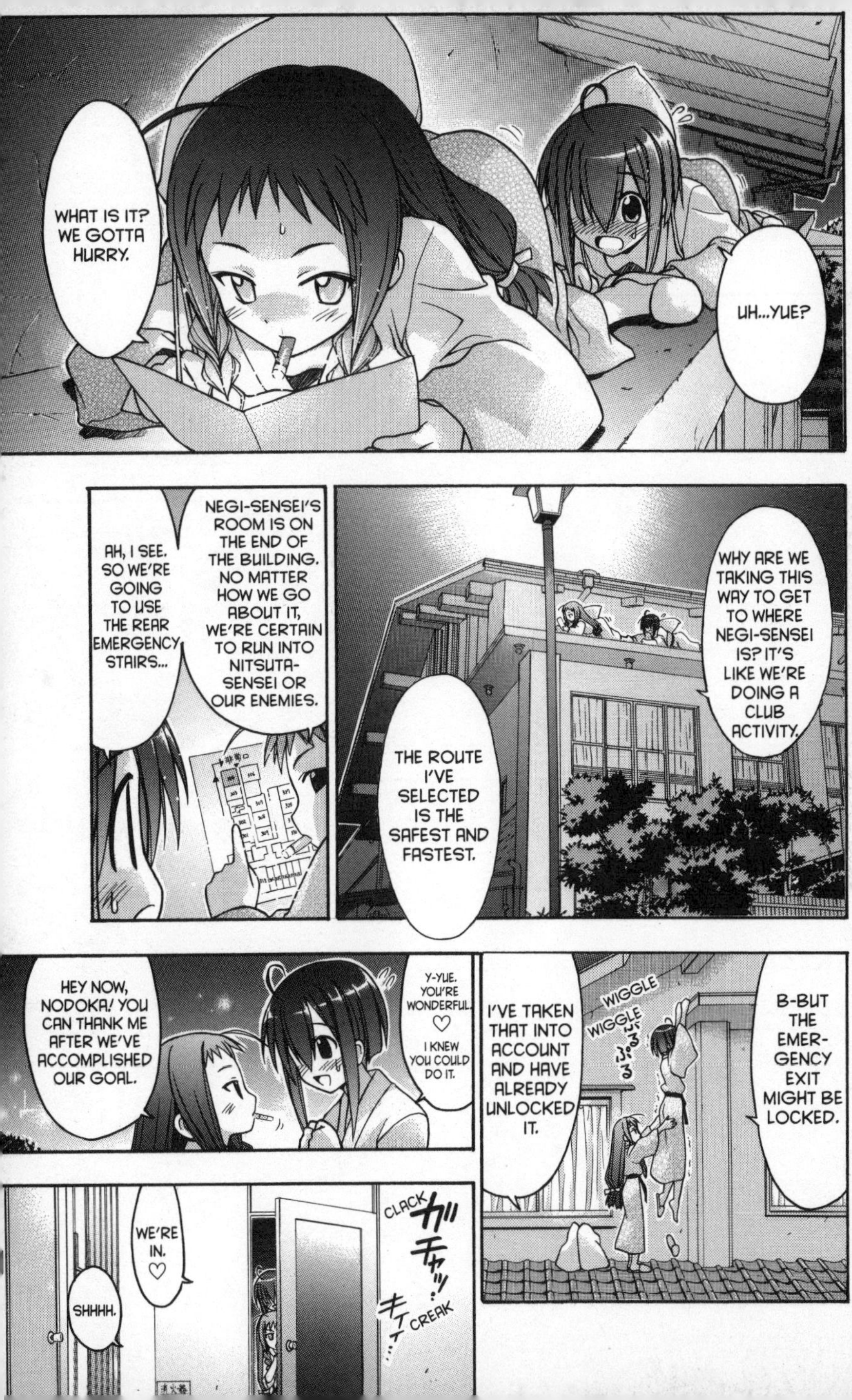
UH...YUE?
WHAT IS IT? WE GOTTA HURRY.
WHY ARE WE TAKING THIS WAY TO GET TO WHERE NEGI-SENSEI IS? IT'S LIKE WE'RE DOING A CLUB ACTIVITY.
THE ROUTE I'VE SELECTED IS THE SAFEST AND FASTEST.
NEGI-SENSEI'S ROOM IS ON THE END OF THE BUILDING. NO MATTER HOW WE GO ABOUT IT, WE'RE CERTAIN TO RUN INTO NITSUTA-SENSEI OR OUR ENEMIES.
AH, I SEE. SO WE'RE GOING TO USE THE REAR EMERGENCY STAIRS...
B-BUT THE EMERGENCY EXIT MIGHT BE LOCKED.
WIGGLE
WIGGLE
I'VE TAKEN THAT INTO ACCOUNT AND HAVE ALREADY UNLOCKED IT.
Y-YUE. YOU'RE WONDERFUL. ♡
I KNEW YOU COULD DO IT.
HEY NOW, NODOKA! YOU CAN THANK ME AFTER WE'VE ACCOMPLISHED OUR GOAL.
CLACK
WE'RE IN. ♡
CREAK
SHHHH.

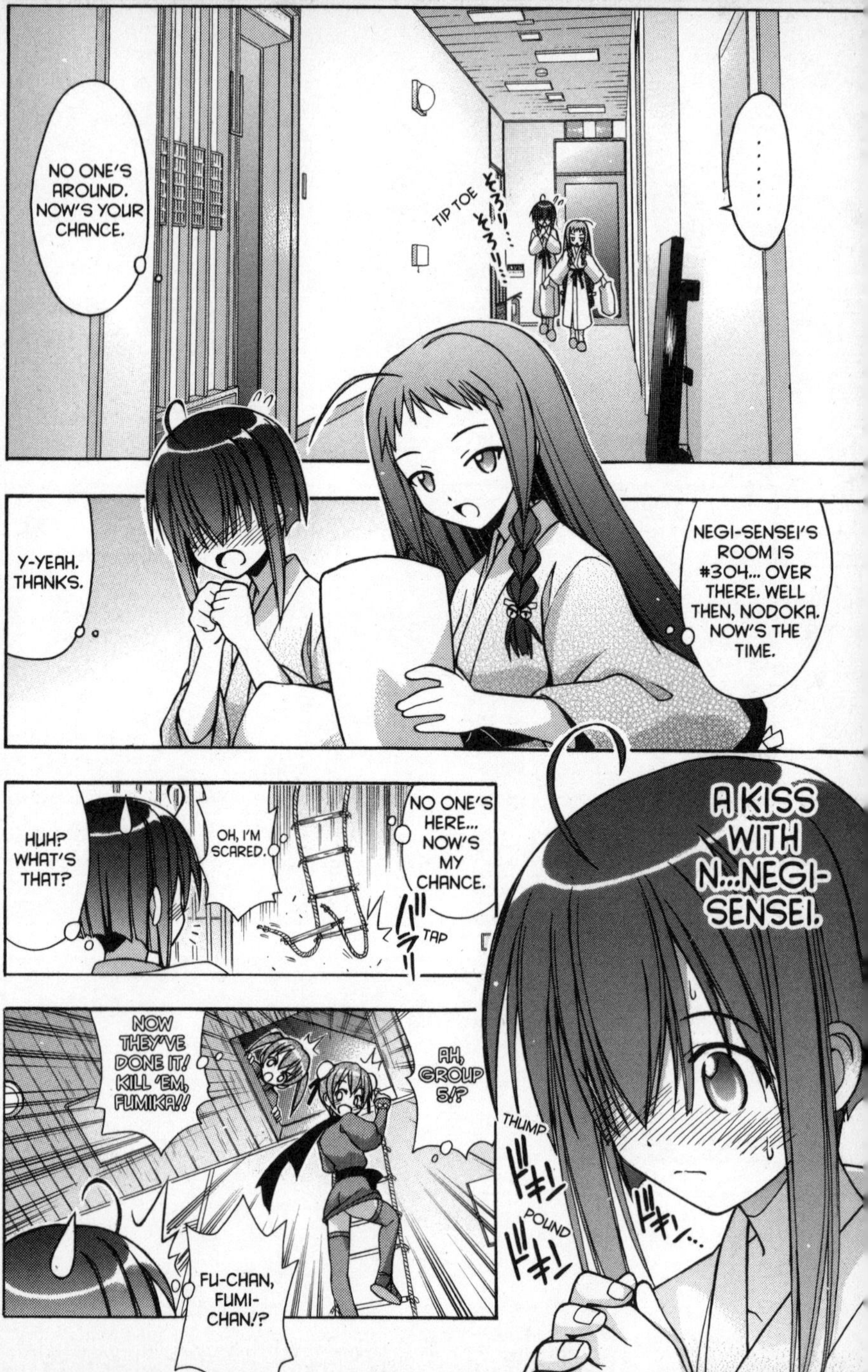
......
TIP TOE
そろり...
そろり...
NO ONE'S AROUND. NOW'S YOUR CHANCE.
NEGI-SENSEI'S ROOM IS #304... OVER THERE. WELL THEN, NODOKA. NOW'S THE TIME.
Y-YEAH. THANKS.
A KISS WITH N...NEGI-SENSEI.
THUMP
ドキン
ドキン...
POUND
ドキン
NO ONE'S HERE... NOW'S MY CHANCE.
OH, I'M SCARED.
HUH? WHAT'S THAT?
バラリ
TAP
AH, GROUP 5!?
NOW THEY'VE DONE IT! KILL 'EM, FUMIKA!!
FU-CHAN, FUMI-CHAN!?

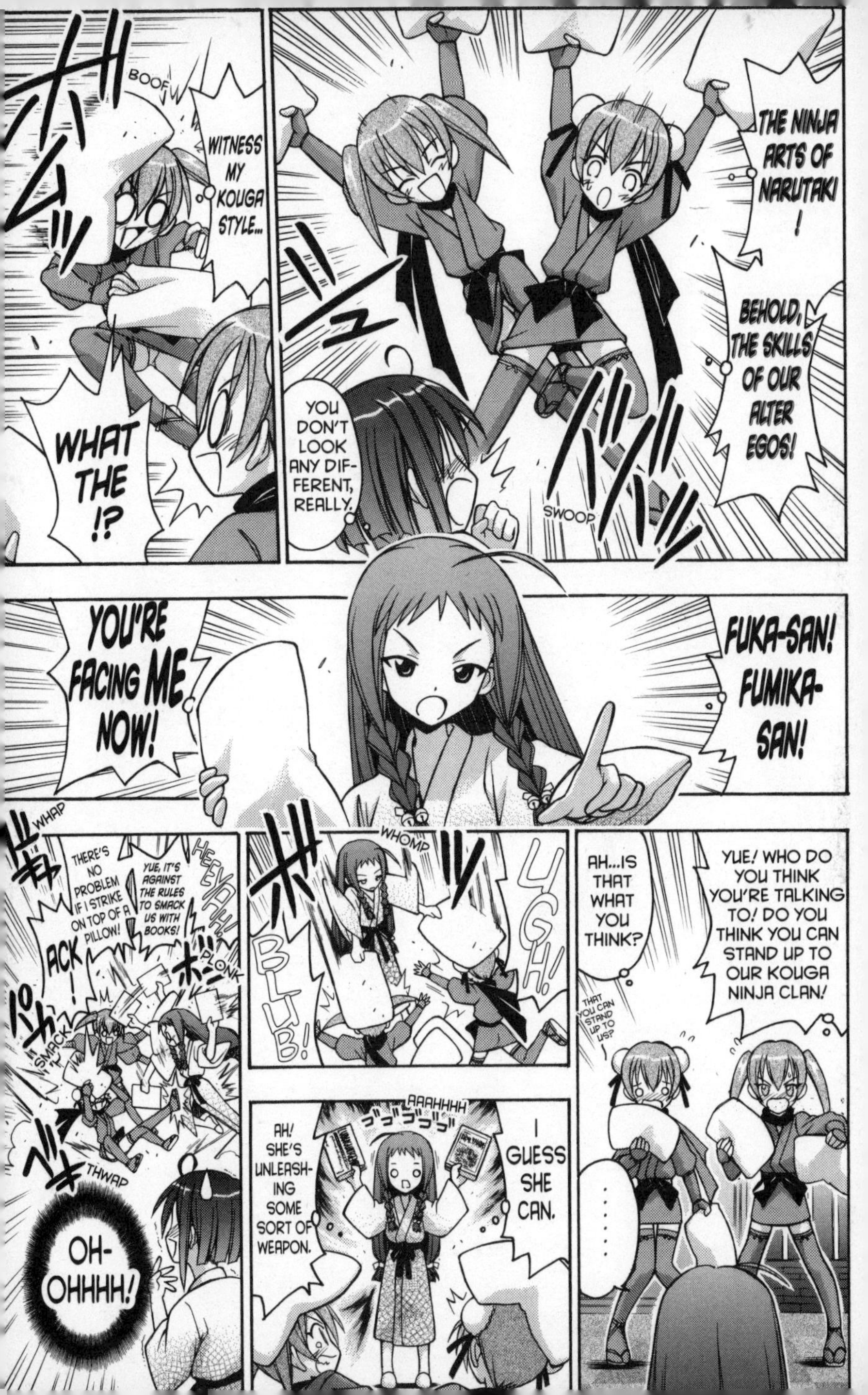
THE NINJA ARTS OF NARUTAKI!
BEHOLD, THE SKILLS OF OUR ALTER EGOS!
YOU DON'T LOOK ANY DIF-FERENT, REALLY.
SWOOP
BOOF
WITNESS MY KOUGA STYLE...
WHAT THE !?
FUKA-SAN! FUMIKA-SAN!
YOU'RE FACING ME NOW!
YUE! WHO DO YOU THINK YOU'RE TALKING TO! DO YOU THINK YOU CAN STAND UP TO OUR KOUGA NINJA CLAN!
AH...IS THAT WHAT YOU THINK?
THAT YOU CAN STAND UP TO US?
......
WHOMP
UGH!
BLUB!
AAAHHHH
I GUESS SHE CAN.
AH! SHE'S UNLEASH-ING SOME SORT OF WEAPON.
WHAP
YUE, IT'S AGAINST THE RULES TO SMACK US WITH BOOKS!
HEEYAH!
THERE'S NO PROBLEM IF I STRIKE ON TOP OF A PILLOW!
PLONK
ACK!
SMACK
THWAP
OH-OHHHH!

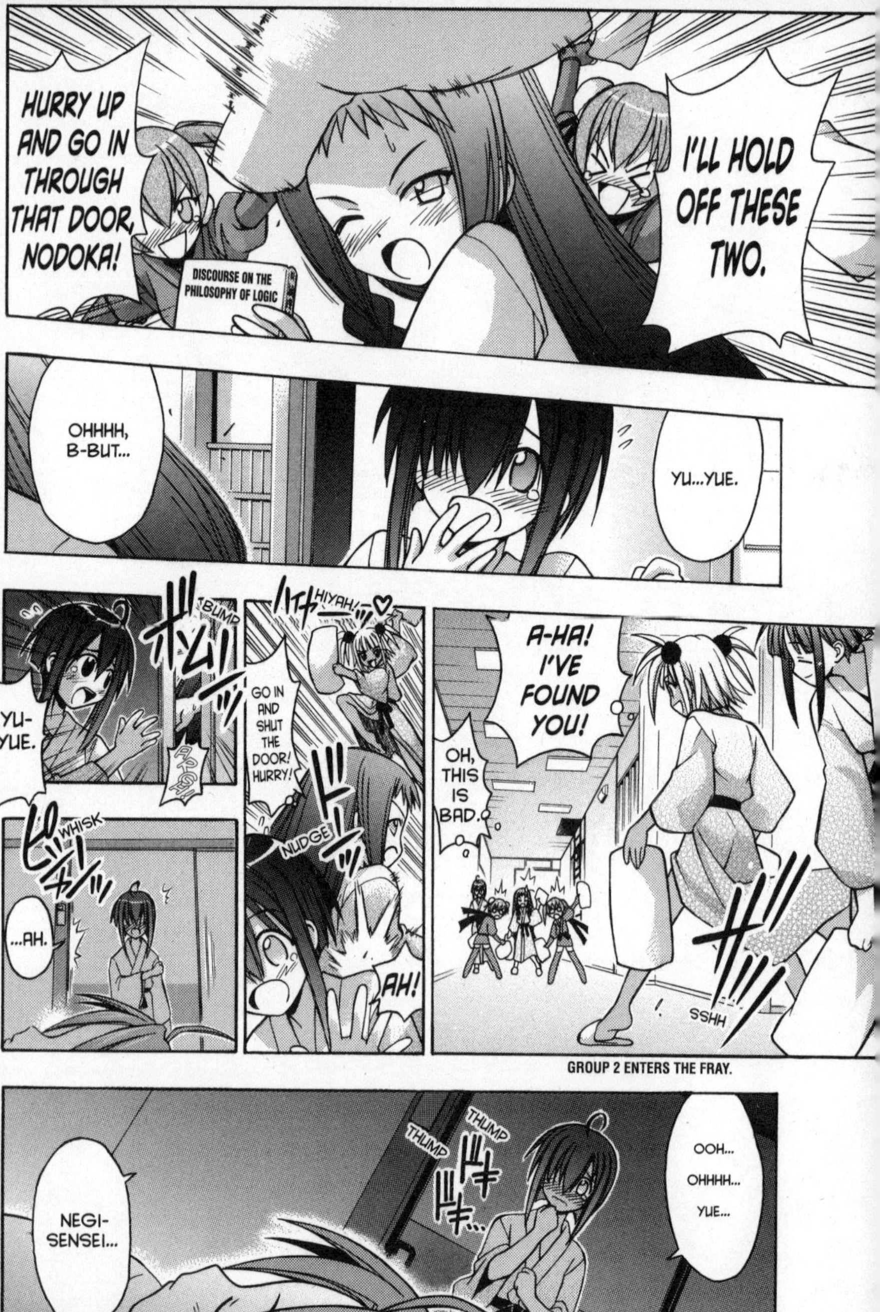
I'LL HOLD OFF THESE TWO.
HURRY UP AND GO IN THROUGH THAT DOOR, NODOKA!
DISCOURSE ON THE PHILOSOPHY OF LOGIC
YU...YUE.
OHHHH, B-BUT...
A-HA! I'VE FOUND YOU!
OH, THIS IS BAD.
SSHH
HIYAH!
GO IN AND SHUT THE DOOR! HURRY!
NUDGE
AH!
BUMP
YU-YUE.
WHISK
...AH.
OOH... OHHHH... YUE...
THUMP
THUMP
NEGI-SENSEI...

GROUP 2 ENTERS THE FRAY.

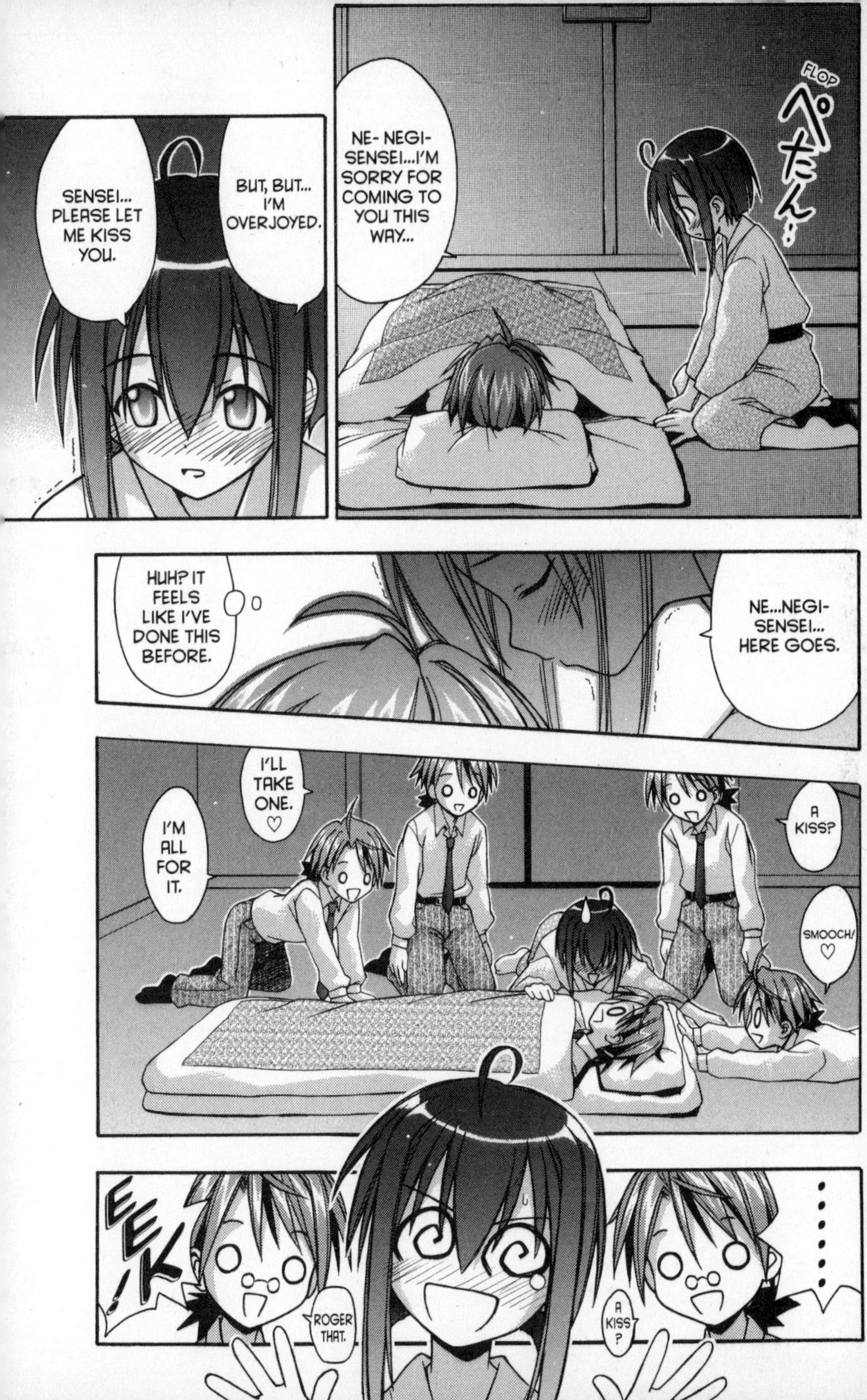
FLOP
ぺたん！
NE- NEGI-SENSEI...I'M SORRY FOR COMING TO YOU THIS WAY...
BUT, BUT... I'M OVERJOYED.
SENSEI... PLEASE LET ME KISS YOU.
NE...NEGI-SENSEI... HERE GOES.
HUH? IT FEELS LIKE I'VE DONE THIS BEFORE.
A KISS?
SMOOCH! ♡
I'LL TAKE ONE. ♡
I'M ALL FOR IT.
......
A KISS?
ROGER THAT.
EEK!

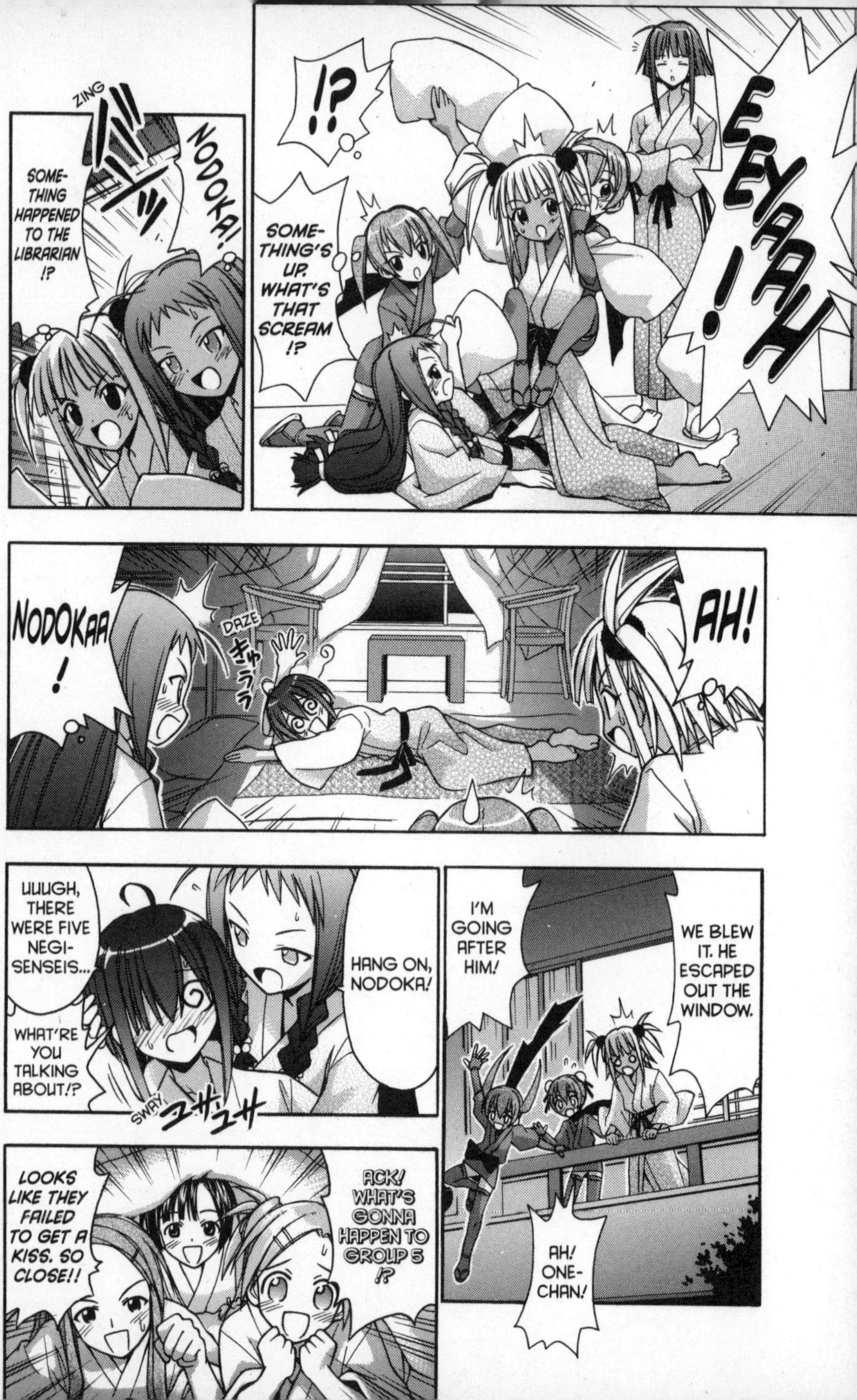
EEYAAAH!
!?
SOMETHING'S UP. WHAT'S THAT SCREAM!?
ZING
NODOKA!
SOMETHING HAPPENED TO THE LIBRARIAN!?
AH!
DAZE
NODOKAA!
WE BLEW IT. HE ESCAPED OUT THE WINDOW.
I'M GOING AFTER HIM!
AH! ONE-CHAN!
HANG ON, NODOKA!
UUUGH, THERE WERE FIVE NEGI-SENSEIS...
WHAT'RE YOU TALKING ABOUT!?
SWAY
ユサユサ
ACK! WHAT'S GONNA HAPPEN TO GROUP 5!?
LOOKS LIKE THEY FAILED TO GET A KISS. SO CLOSE!!

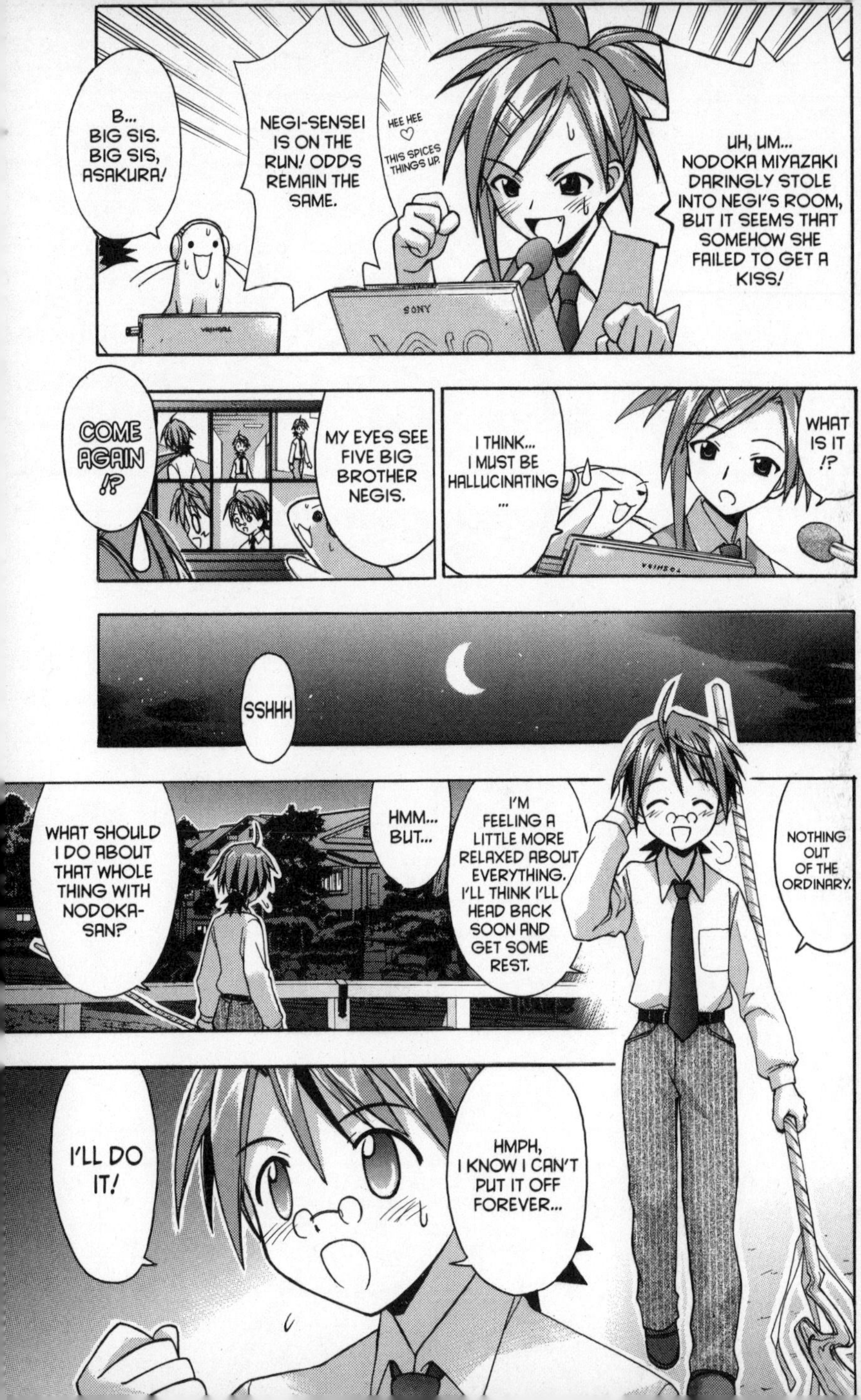
UH, UM... NODOKA MIYAZAKI DARINGLY STOLE INTO NEGI'S ROOM, BUT IT SEEMS THAT SOMEHOW SHE FAILED TO GET A KISS!
HEE HEE ♡ THIS SPICES THINGS UP.
NEGI-SENSEI IS ON THE RUN! ODDS REMAIN THE SAME.
B... BIG SIS. BIG SIS, ASAKURA!
WHAT IS IT !?
I THINK... I MUST BE HALLUCINATING ...
MY EYES SEE FIVE BIG BROTHER NEGIS.
COME AGAIN !?
SSHHH
NOTHING OUT OF THE ORDINARY.
I'M FEELING A LITTLE MORE RELAXED ABOUT EVERYTHING. I'LL THINK I'LL HEAD BACK SOON AND GET SOME REST.
HMM... BUT...
WHAT SHOULD I DO ABOUT THAT WHOLE THING WITH NODOKA-SAN?
HMPH, I KNOW I CAN'T PUT IT OFF FOREVER...
I'LL DO IT!

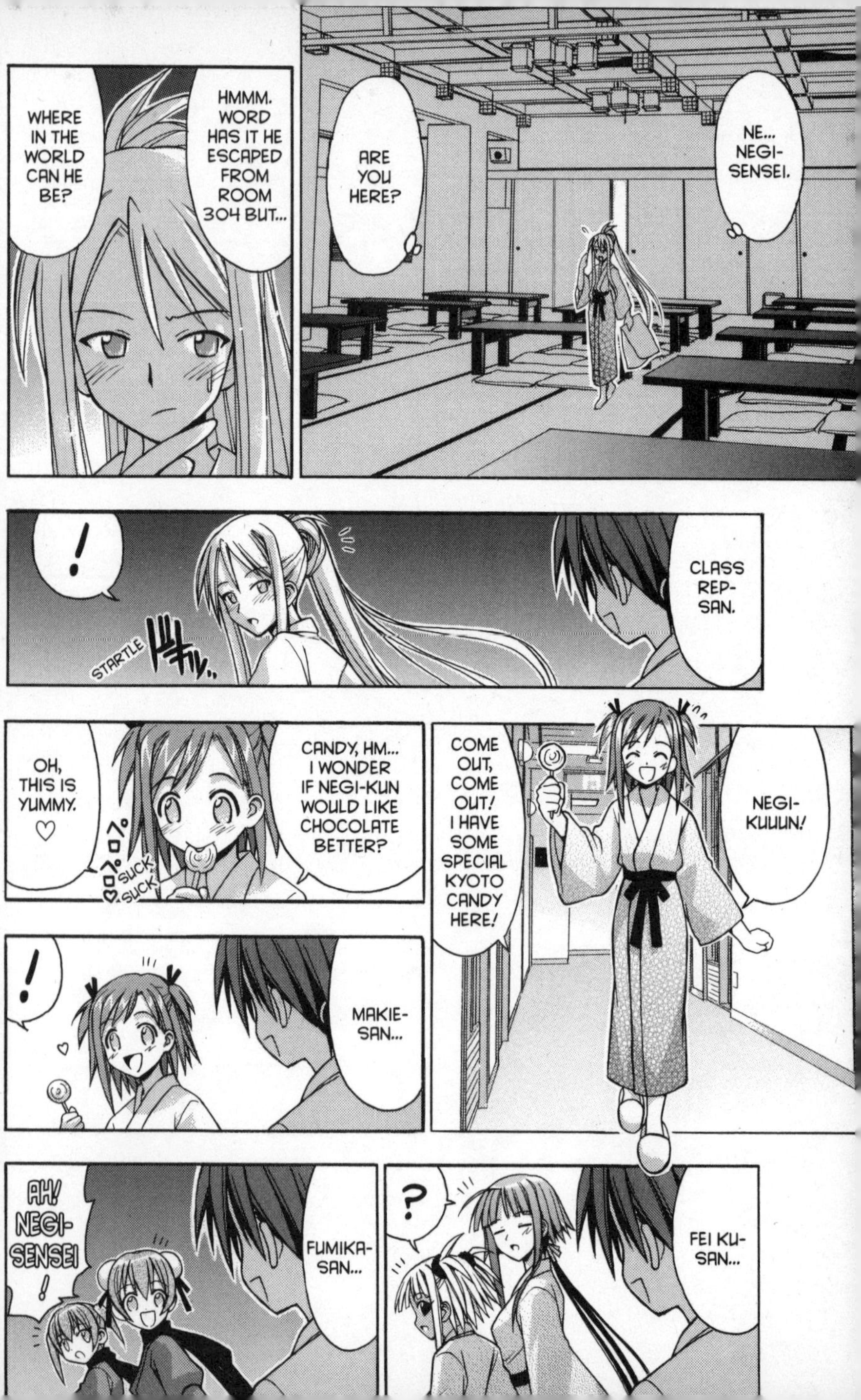
NE... NEGI-SENSEI.
ARE YOU HERE?
HMMM. WORD HAS IT HE ESCAPED FROM ROOM 304 BUT...
WHERE IN THE WORLD CAN HE BE?
CLASS REP-SAN.
!
STARTLE
NEGI-KUUUN!
COME OUT, COME OUT! I HAVE SOME SPECIAL KYOTO CANDY HERE!
CANDY, HM... I WONDER IF NEGI-KUN WOULD LIKE CHOCOLATE BETTER?
OH, THIS IS YUMMY. ♡
SUCK SUCK
MAKIE-SAN...
!
FEI KU-SAN...
?
FUMIKA-SAN...
AH! NEGI-SENSEI!

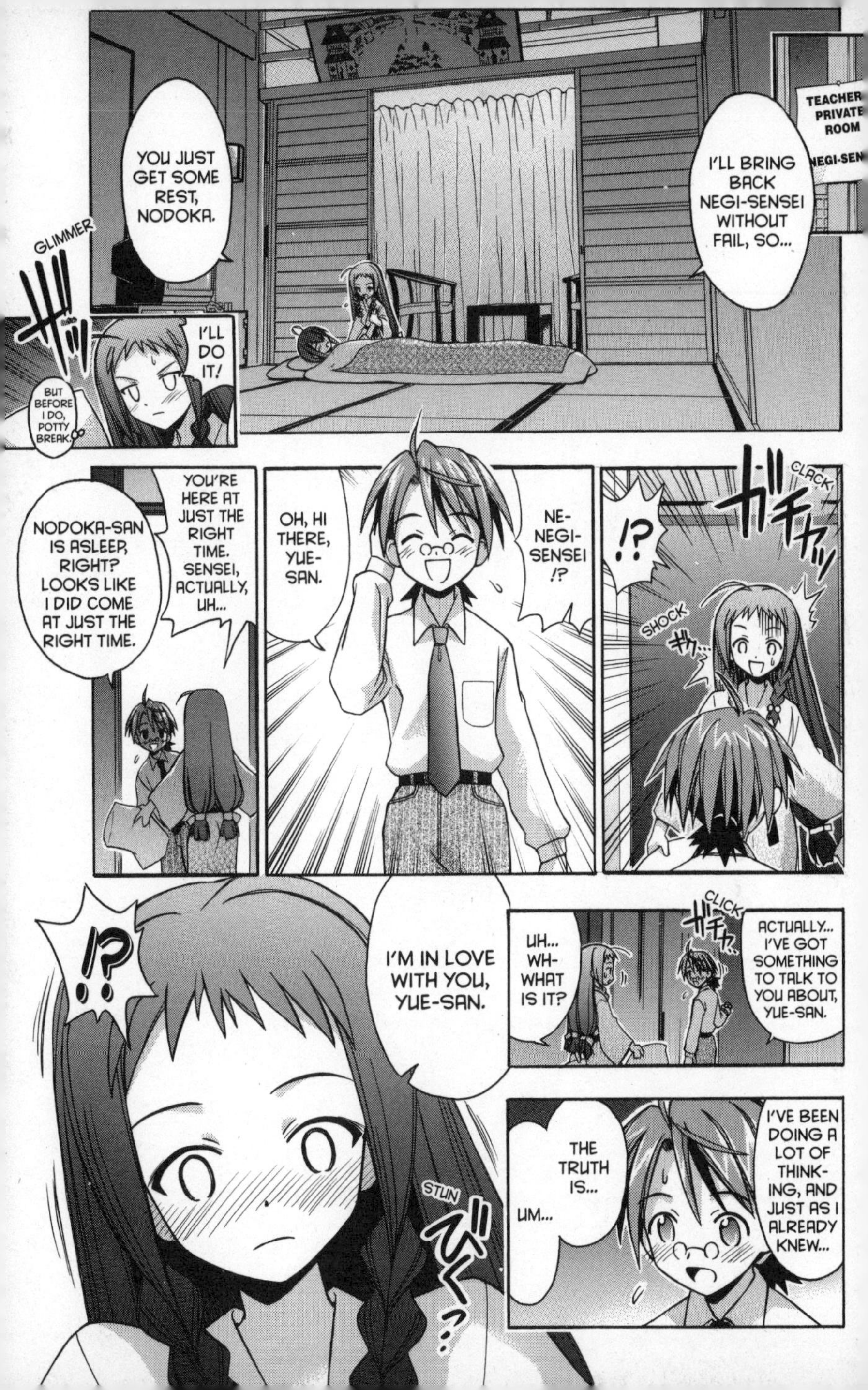
TEACHER PRIVATE ROOM
NEGI-SEN
I'LL BRING BACK NEGI-SENSEI WITHOUT FAIL, SO...
YOU JUST GET SOME REST, NODOKA.
GLIMMER
I'LL DO IT!
BUT BEFORE I DO, POTTY BREAK.
CLACK!
!?
SHOCK
NE-NEGI-SENSEI!?
OH, HI THERE, YUE-SAN.
YOU'RE HERE AT JUST THE RIGHT TIME. SENSEI, ACTUALLY, UH...
NODOKA-SAN IS ASLEEP, RIGHT? LOOKS LIKE I DID COME AT JUST THE RIGHT TIME.
CLICK
ACTUALLY... I'VE GOT SOMETHING TO TALK TO YOU ABOUT, YUE-SAN.
UH... WH-WHAT IS IT?
I'VE BEEN DOING A LOT OF THINK-ING, AND JUST AS I ALREADY KNEW...
THE TRUTH IS...
UM...
I'M IN LOVE WITH YOU, YUE-SAN.
!?
STUN

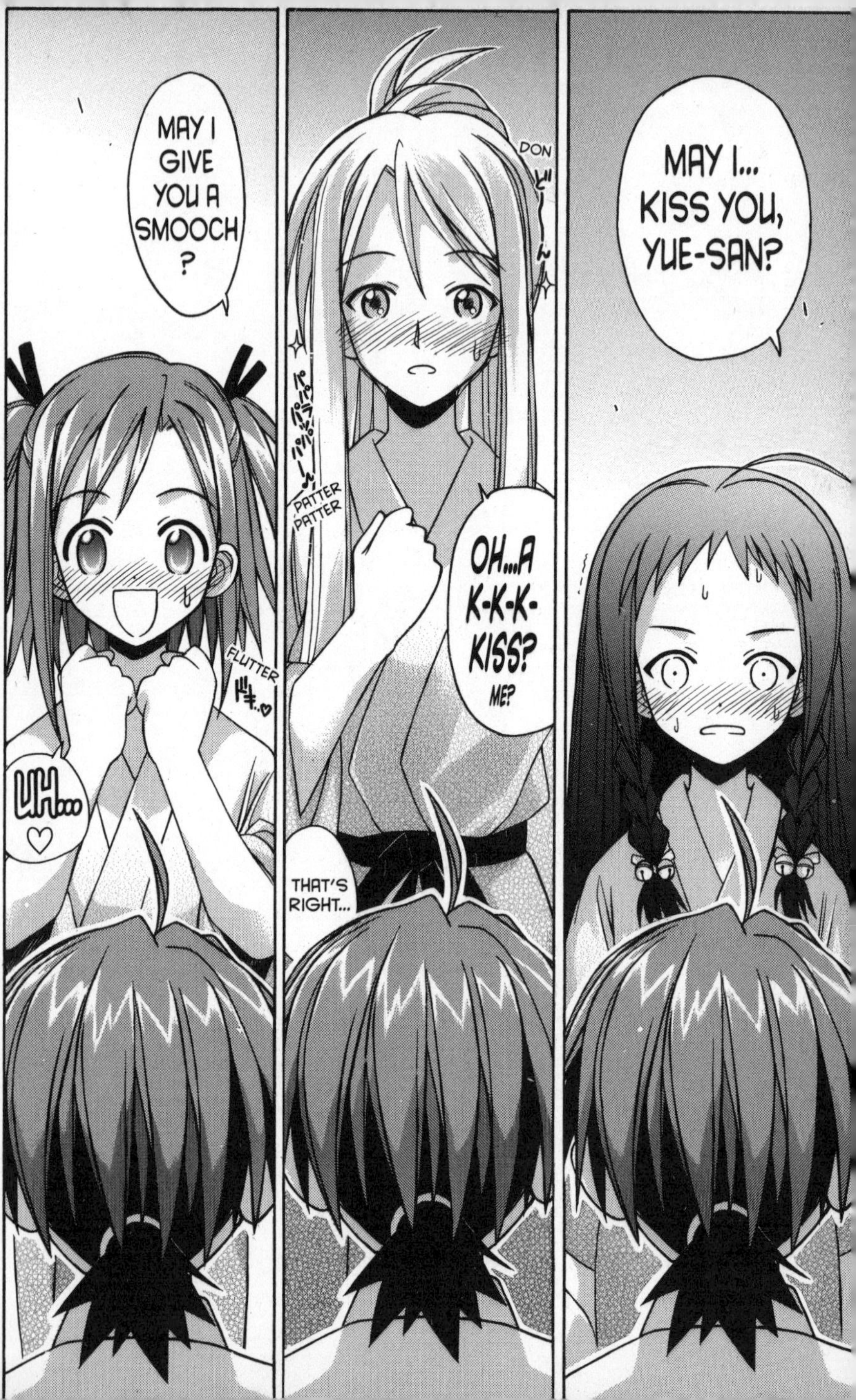
MAY I... KISS YOU, YUE-SAN?
DON
OH...A K-K-K-KISS?
ME?
PATTER PATTER
THAT'S RIGHT...
MAY I GIVE YOU A SMOOCH?
FLUTTER
ドキ..♡
UH... ♡

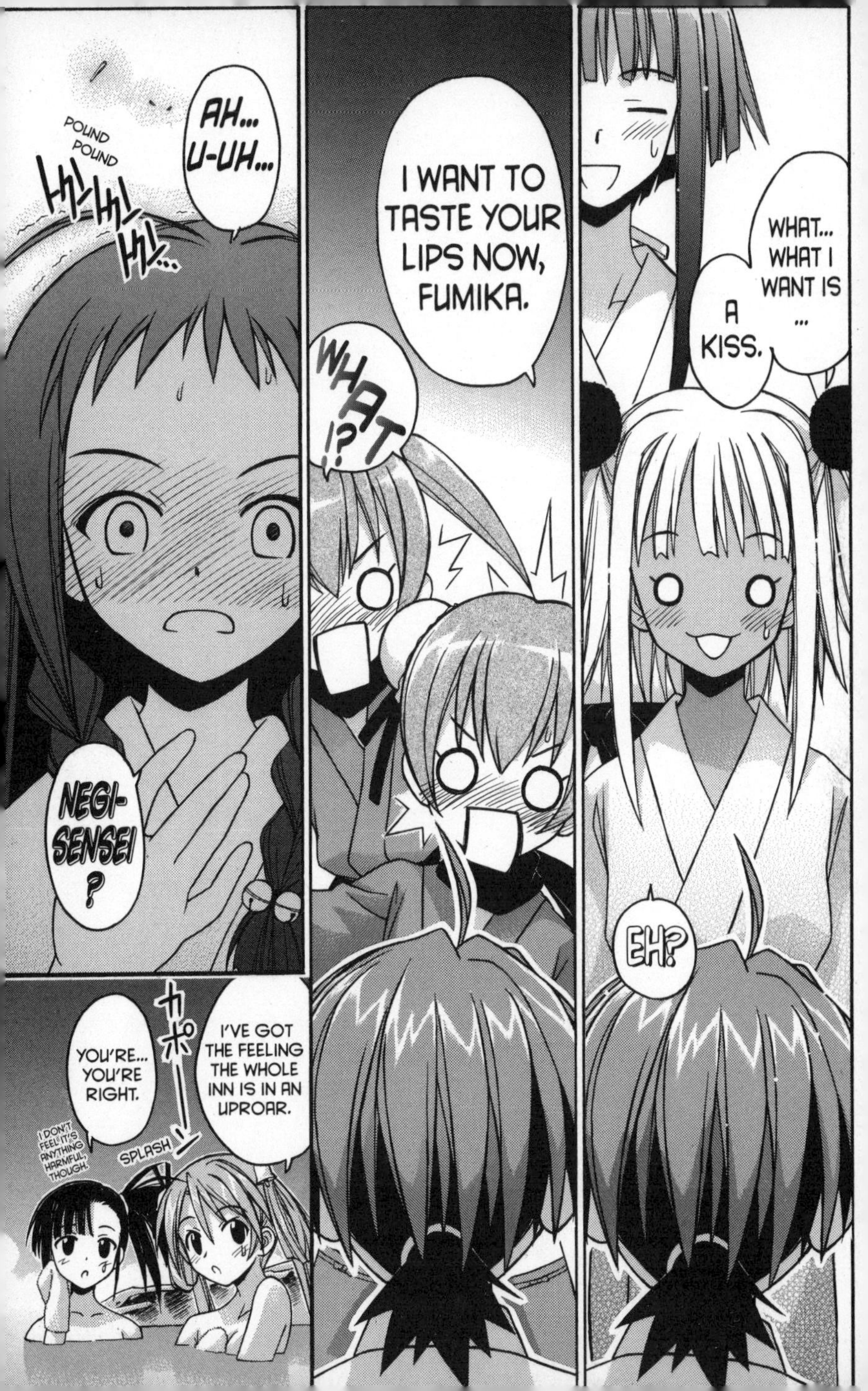
WHAT... WHAT I WANT IS ...
A KISS.
EH?
I WANT TO TASTE YOUR LIPS NOW, FUMIKA.
WHAT!?
AH... U-UH...
POUND POUND
NEGI-SENSEI?
I'VE GOT THE FEELING THE WHOLE INN IS IN AN UPROAR.
SPLASH
YOU'RE... YOU'RE RIGHT.
I DON'T FEEL IT'S ANYTHING HARMFUL, THOUGH.

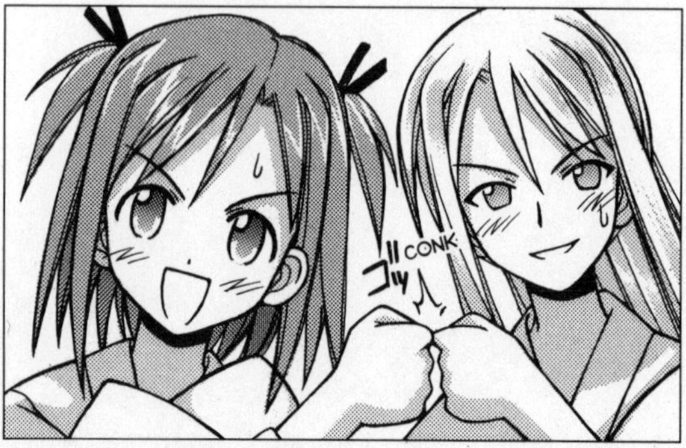
CONK
ゴッ

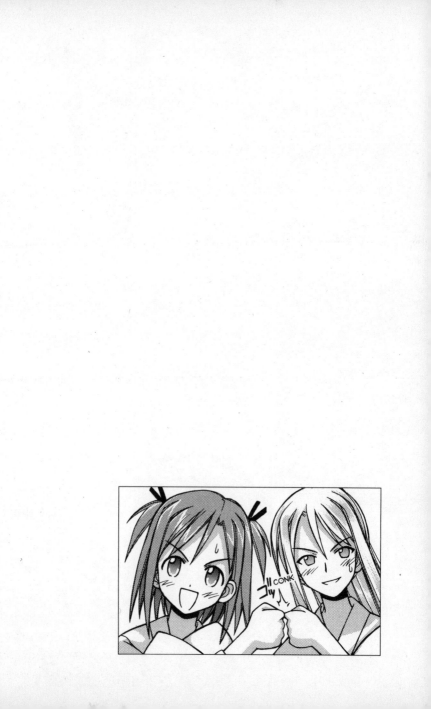

NEGIMA!

MAGISTER NEGI MAGI

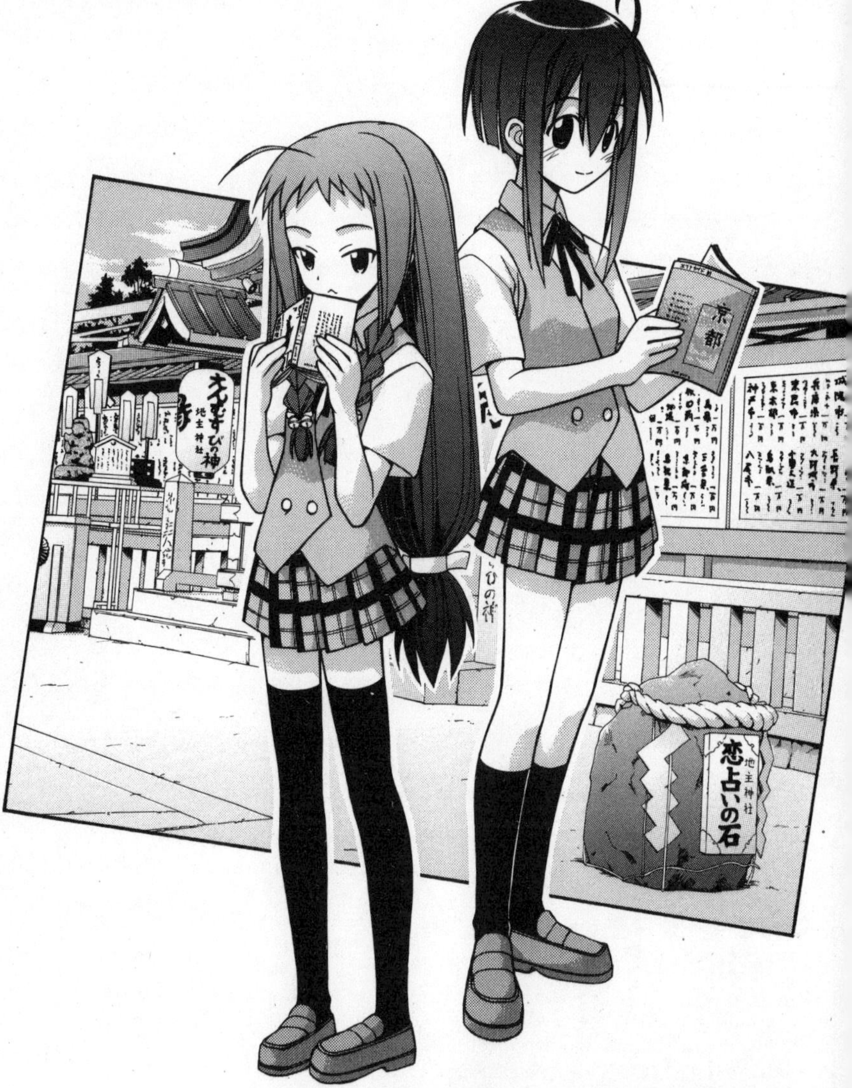
京都
地主神社
恋占いの石

THIRTY-SEVENTH PERIOD:
WHO DOES NEGI'S KISS BELONG TO!?

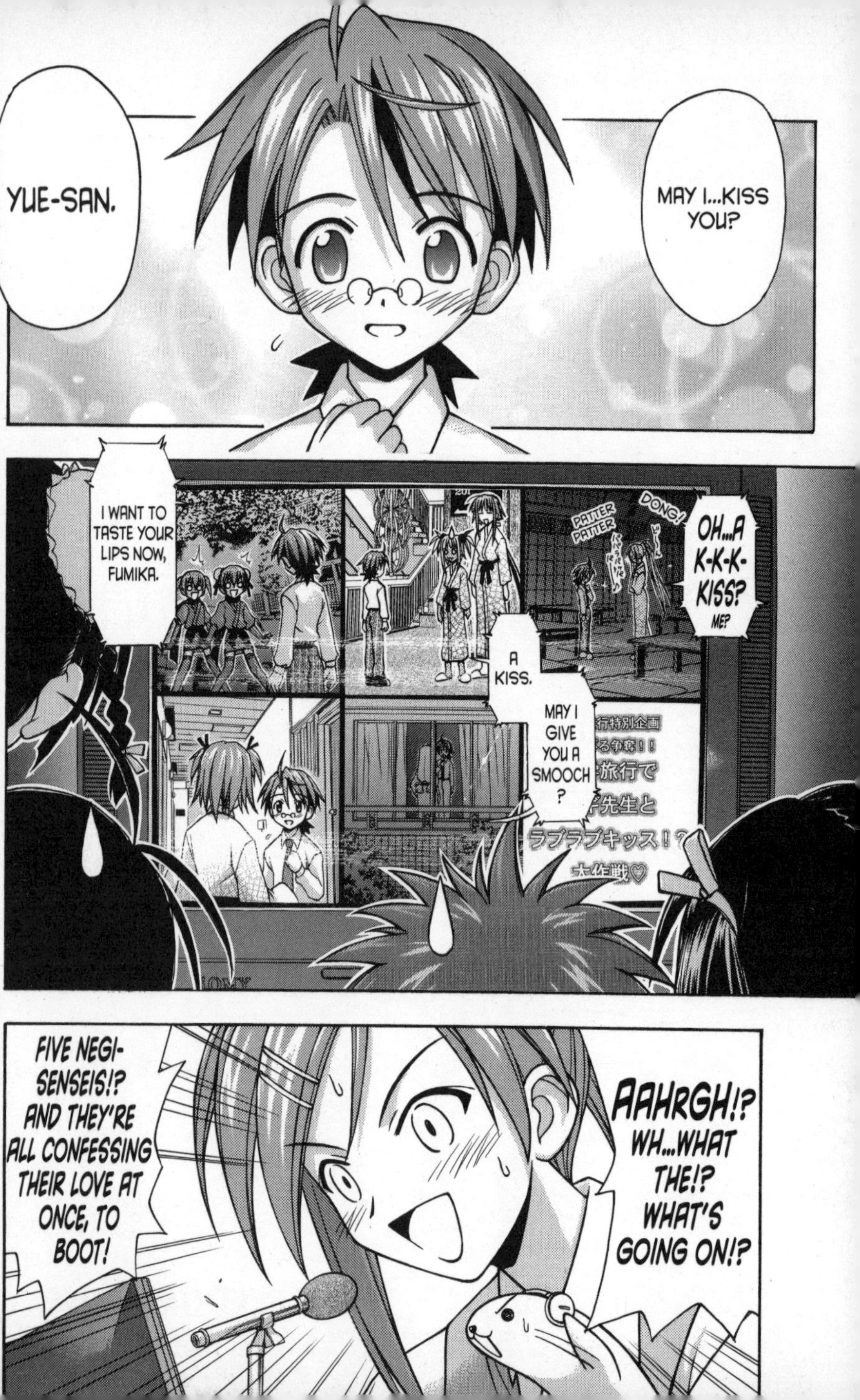
YUE-SAN.
MAY I...KISS YOU?
DONG!
PATTER PATTER
OH...A K-K-K-KISS? ME?
A KISS.
MAY I GIVE YOU A SMOOCH?
ラブラブキッス！？
I WANT TO TASTE YOUR LIPS NOW, FUMIKA.
AAHRGH!? WH...WHAT THE!? WHAT'S GOING ON!?
FIVE NEGI-SENSEIS!? AND THEY'RE ALL CONFESSING THEIR LOVE AT ONCE, TO BOOT!

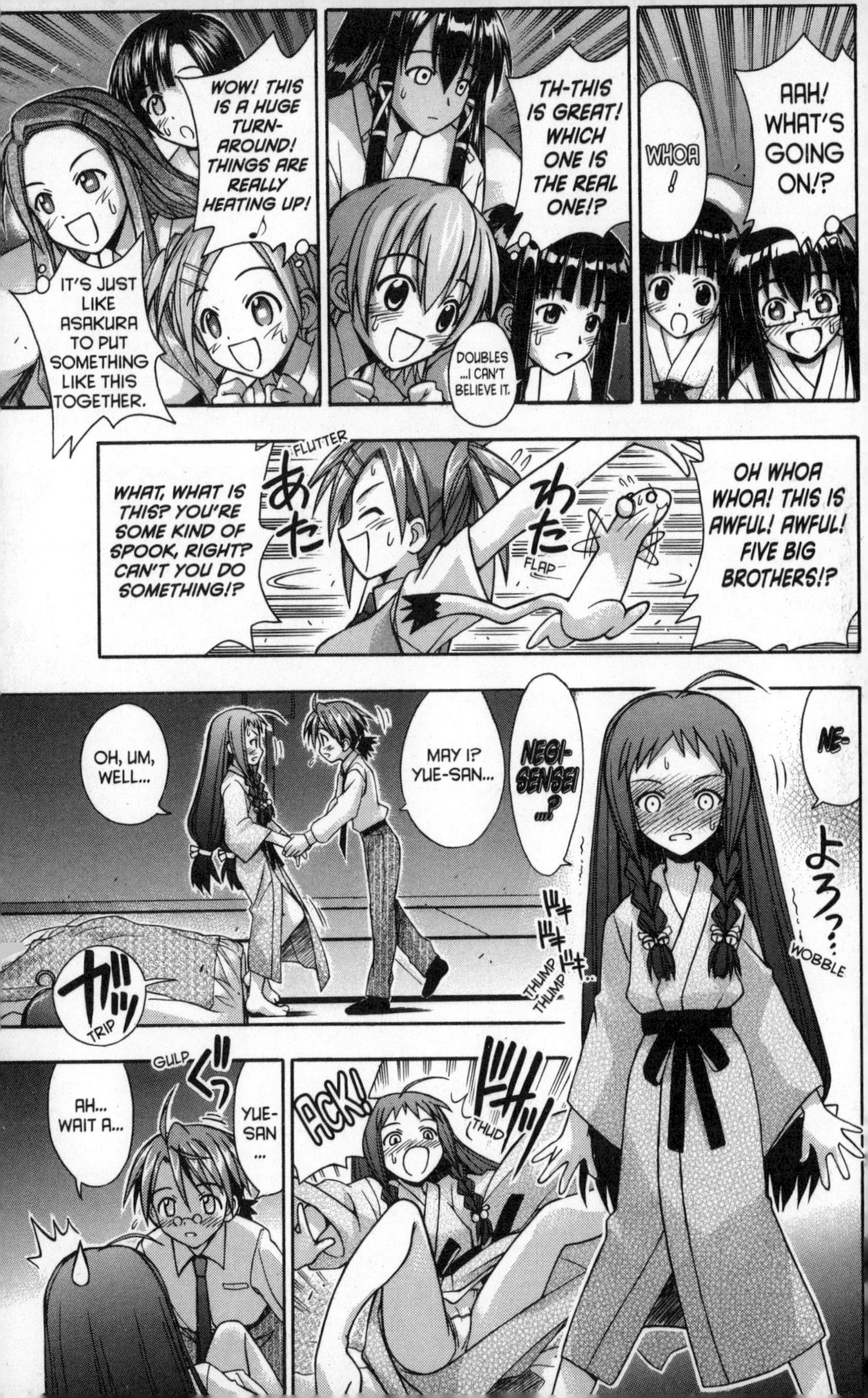
AAH! WHAT'S GOING ON!?
WHOA!
TH-THIS IS GREAT! WHICH ONE IS THE REAL ONE!?
DOUBLES ...I CAN'T BELIEVE IT.
WOW! THIS IS A HUGE TURN-AROUND! THINGS ARE REALLY HEATING UP! ♪
IT'S JUST LIKE ASAKURA TO PUT SOMETHING LIKE THIS TOGETHER.
OH WHOA WHOA! THIS IS AWFUL! AWFUL! FIVE BIG BROTHERS!?
わた
FLAP
あた
FLUTTER
WHAT, WHAT IS THIS? YOU'RE SOME KIND OF SPOOK, RIGHT? CAN'T YOU DO SOMETHING!?
NE-
よろっ
WOBBLE
NEGI-SENSEI ...?
ドキドキドキ...
THUMP THUMP
MAY I? YUE-SAN...
OH, UM, WELL...
ガッ
TRIP
ドサッ
THUD
ACK!
YUE-SAN ...
ぐっ
GULP
AH... WAIT A...

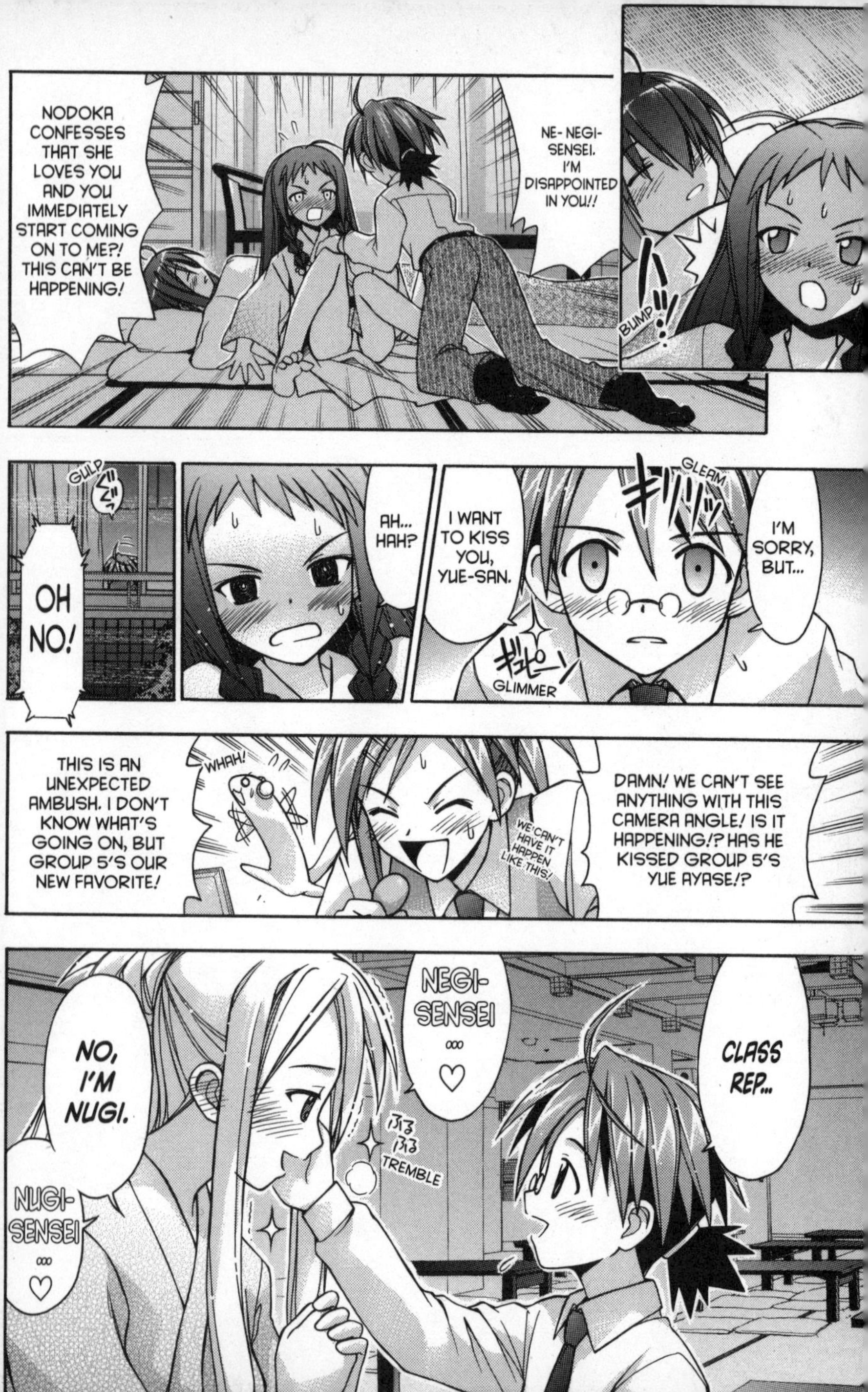
BUMP
NE- NEGI-SENSEI. I'M DISAPPOINTED IN YOU!!
NODOKA CONFESSES THAT SHE LOVES YOU AND YOU IMMEDIATELY START COMING ON TO ME?! THIS CAN'T BE HAPPENING!
GLEAM
I'M SORRY, BUT...
GLIMMER
I WANT TO KISS YOU, YUE-SAN.
AH... HAH?
GULP
OH NO!
DAMN! WE CAN'T SEE ANYTHING WITH THIS CAMERA ANGLE! IS IT HAPPENING!? HAS HE KISSED GROUP 5'S YUE AYASE!?
WE CAN'T HAVE IT HAPPEN LIKE THIS!
WHAH!
THIS IS AN UNEXPECTED AMBUSH. I DON'T KNOW WHAT'S GOING ON, BUT GROUP 5'S OUR NEW FAVORITE!
CLASS REP...
NEGI-SENSEI... ♡
TREMBLE
NO, I'M NUGI.
NUGI-SENSEI... ♡

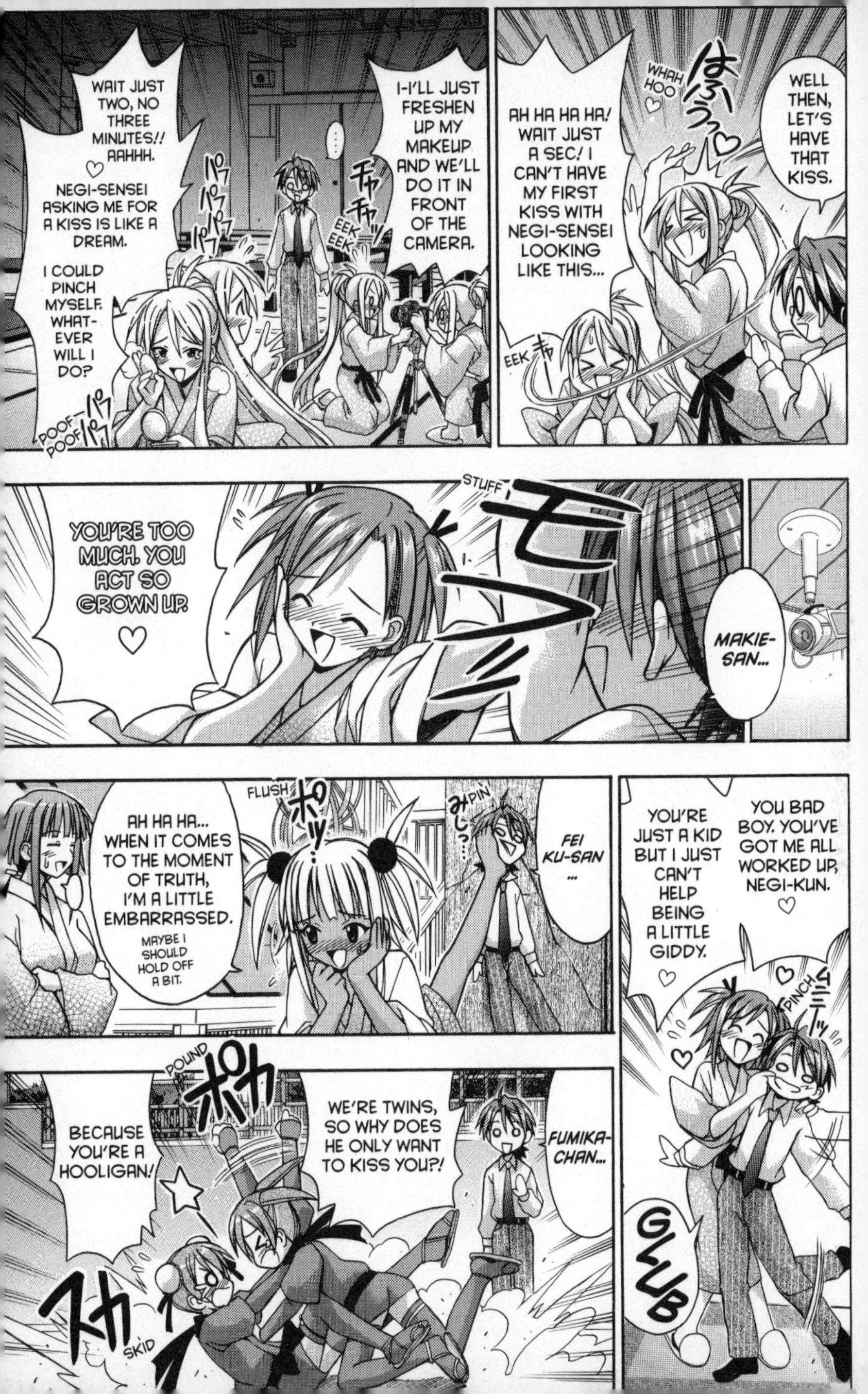
WELL THEN, LET'S HAVE THAT KISS.
WHAH HOO
AH HA HA HA! WAIT JUST A SEC! I CAN'T HAVE MY FIRST KISS WITH NEGI-SENSEI LOOKING LIKE THIS...
EEK
キャ
I-I'LL JUST FRESHEN UP MY MAKEUP AND WE'LL DO IT IN FRONT OF THE CAMERA.
EEK EEK
キャキャッ
...
WAIT JUST TWO, NO THREE MINUTES!! AAHHH.
NEGI-SENSEI ASKING ME FOR A KISS IS LIKE A DREAM.
I COULD PINCH MYSELF. WHATEVER WILL I DO?
パフパフパフパフ
POOF POOF
パフパフ
MAKIE-SAN...
STUFF
モフ
YOU'RE TOO MUCH. YOU ACT SO GROWN UP.
YOU BAD BOY. YOU'VE GOT ME ALL WORKED UP, NEGI-KUN.
YOU'RE JUST A KID BUT I JUST CAN'T HELP BEING A LITTLE GIDDY.
PINCH
ムニーッ
GLUB
FEI KU-SAN ...
PIN
みしっ
FLUSH
ポッ
AH HA HA... WHEN IT COMES TO THE MOMENT OF TRUTH, I'M A LITTLE EMBARRASSED.
MAYBE I SHOULD HOLD OFF A BIT.
FUMIKA-CHAN...
WE'RE TWINS, SO WHY DOES HE ONLY WANT TO KISS YOU?!
POUND
ポカ
BECAUSE YOU'RE A HOOLIGAN!
スカ
SKID

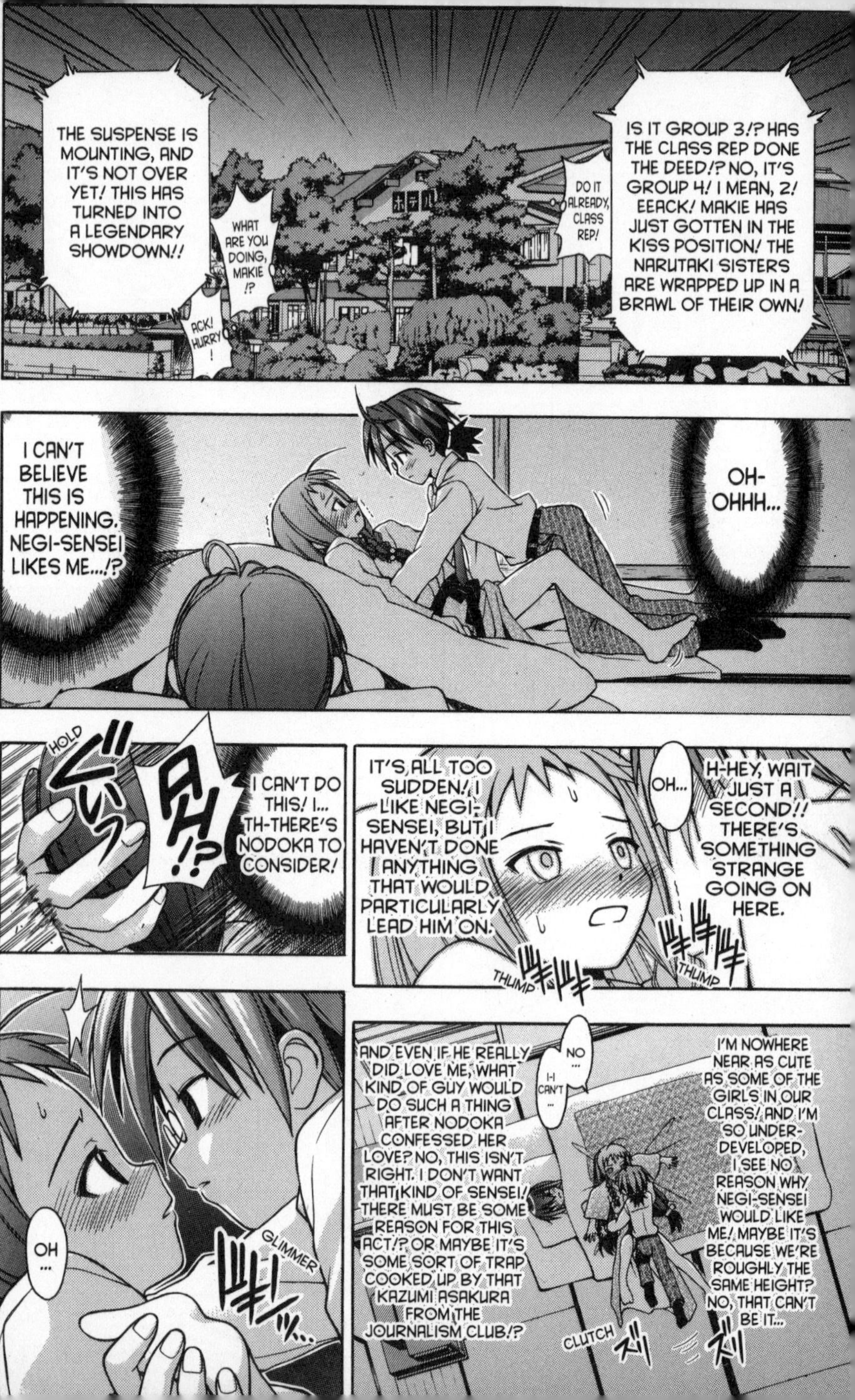
IS IT GROUP 3!? HAS THE CLASS REP DONE THE DEED!? NO, IT'S GROUP 4! I MEAN, 2! EEACK! MAKIE HAS JUST GOTTEN IN THE KISS POSITION! THE NARUTAKI SISTERS ARE WRAPPED UP IN A BRAWL OF THEIR OWN!
DO IT ALREADY, CLASS REP!
WHAT ARE YOU DOING, MAKIE !?
ACK! HURRY !
THE SUSPENSE IS MOUNTING, AND IT'S NOT OVER YET! THIS HAS TURNED INTO A LEGENDARY SHOWDOWN!!
OH- OHHH...
I CAN'T BELIEVE THIS IS HAPPENING. NEGI-SENSEI LIKES ME...!?
H-HEY, WAIT JUST A SECOND!! THERE'S SOMETHING STRANGE GOING ON HERE.
OH...
IT'S ALL TOO SUDDEN! I LIKE NEGI-SENSEI, BUT I HAVEN'T DONE ANYTHING THAT WOULD PARTICULARLY LEAD HIM ON.
THUMP
THUMP
I CAN'T DO THIS! I... TH-THERE'S NODOKA TO CONSIDER!
AH!!?
HOLD
I'M NOWHERE NEAR AS CUTE AS SOME OF THE GIRLS IN OUR CLASS! AND I'M SO UNDER-DEVELOPED, I SEE NO REASON WHY NEGI-SENSEI WOULD LIKE ME! MAYBE IT'S BECAUSE WE'RE ROUGHLY THE SAME HEIGHT? NO, THAT CAN'T BE IT...
NO ...
I-I CAN'T ...
AND EVEN IF HE REALLY DID LOVE ME, WHAT KIND OF GUY WOULD DO SUCH A THING AFTER NODOKA CONFESSED HER LOVE? NO, THIS ISN'T RIGHT. I DON'T WANT THAT KIND OF SENSEI! THERE MUST BE SOME REASON FOR THIS ACT!? OR MAYBE IT'S SOME SORT OF TRAP COOKED UP BY THAT KAZUMI ASAKURA FROM THE JOURNALISM CLUB!?
CLUTCH
GLIMMER
OH ...

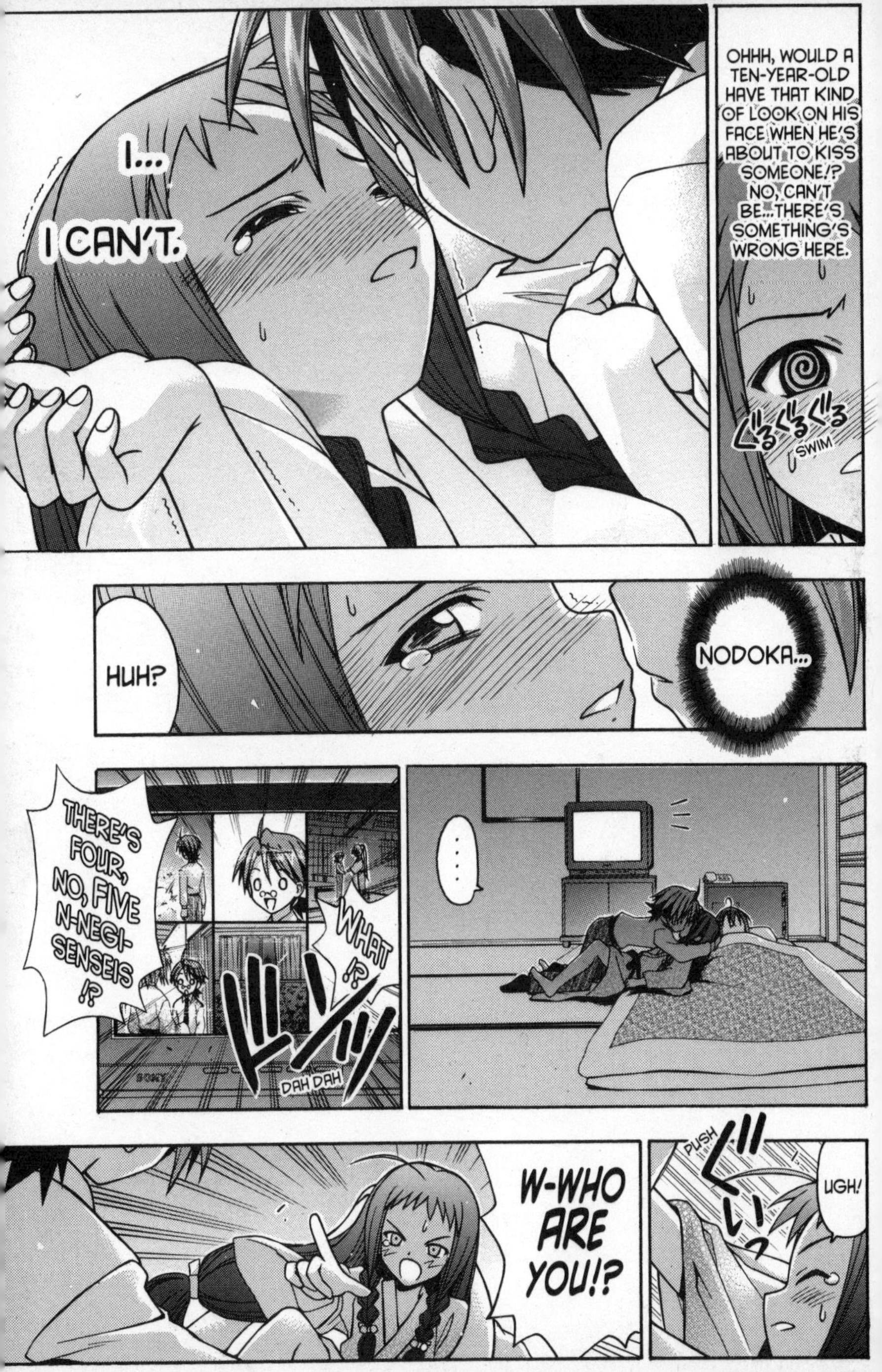
OHHH, WOULD A TEN-YEAR-OLD HAVE THAT KIND OF LOOK ON HIS FACE WHEN HE'S ABOUT TO KISS SOMEONE!? NO, CAN'T BE...THERE'S SOMETHING'S WRONG HERE.
ぐるぐるぐる
SWIM
I...
I CAN'T.
NODOKA...
HUH?
...
THERE'S FOUR, NO, FIVE N-NEGI-SENSEIS!?
WHAT!?
ドンッ
DAH DAH
PUSH
ぐいっ
UGH!
W-WHO ARE YOU!?

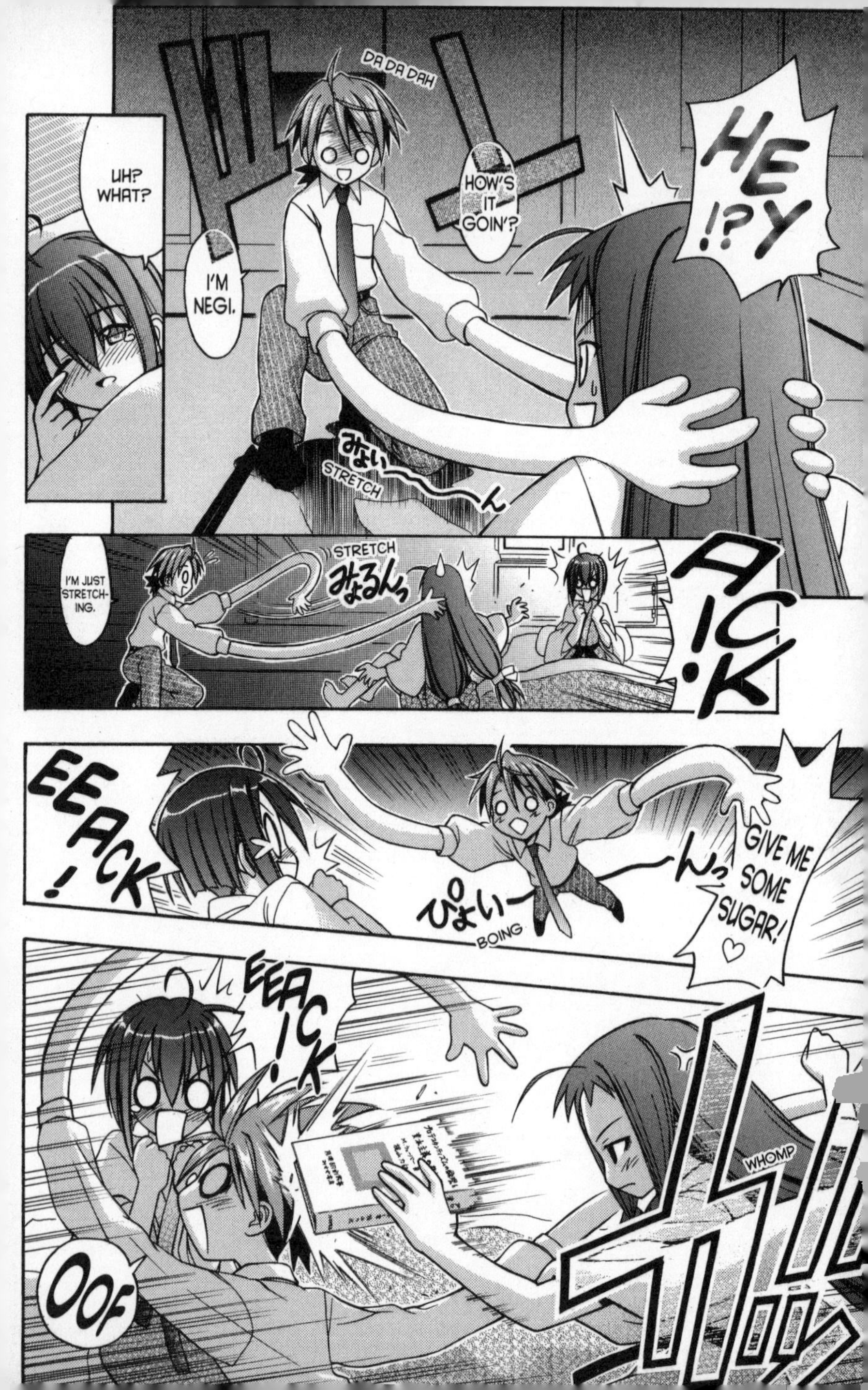
HEY!?
DA DA DAH
HOW'S IT GOIN'?
I'M NEGI.
みょい〜〜ん
STRETCH
UH? WHAT?
ACK!
STRETCH
みょるんっ
I'M JUST STRETCHING.
GIVE ME SOME SUGAR! ♥
ぴょい〜んっ
BOING
EEACK!
WHOMP
EEACK!
OOF

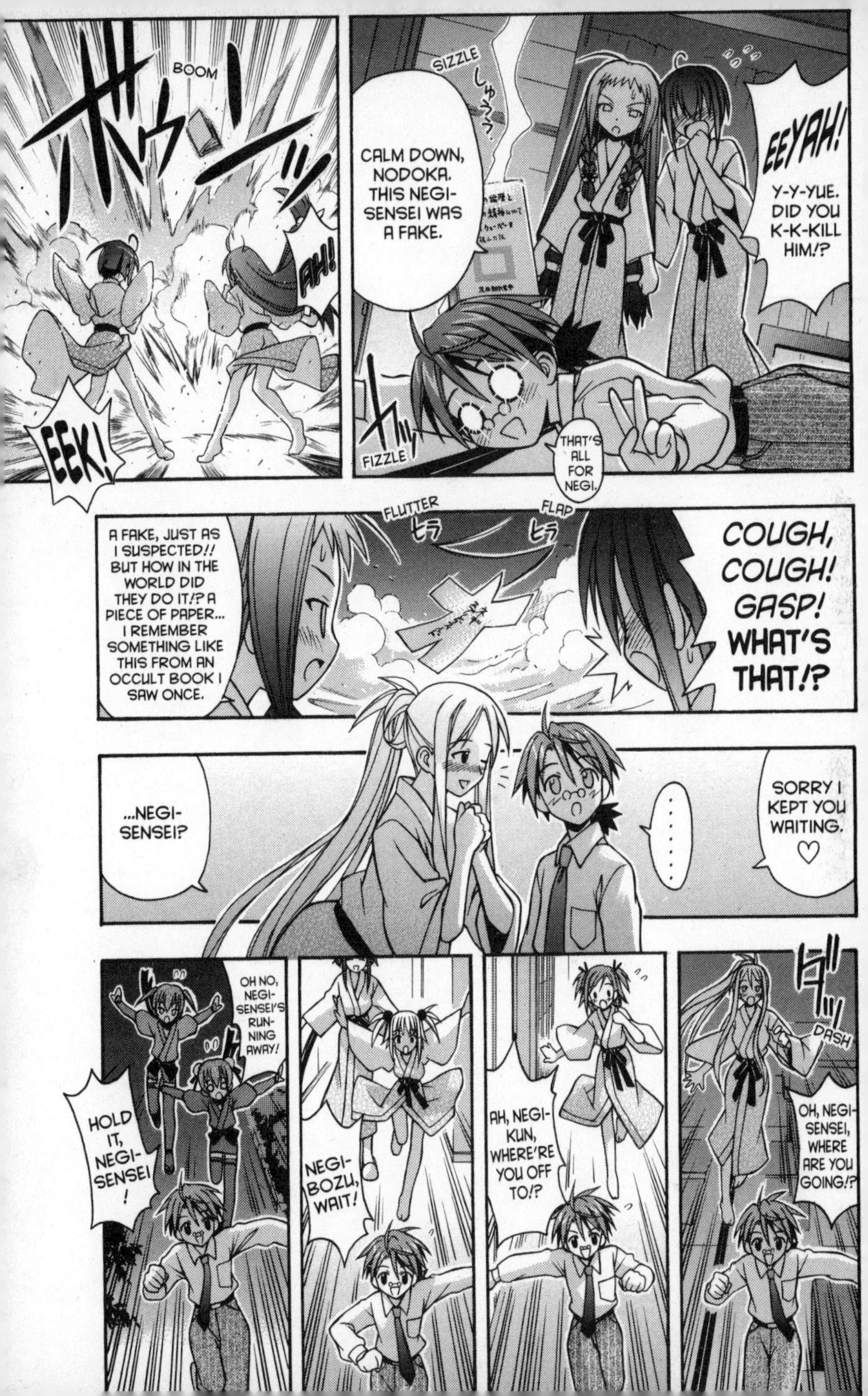
SIZZLE
EEYAH!
Y-Y-YUE. DID YOU K-K-KILL HIM!?
CALM DOWN, NODOKA. THIS NEGI-SENSEI WAS A FAKE.
FIZZLE
THAT'S ALL FOR NEGI.
BOOM
AH!
EEK!
COUGH, COUGH! GASP! WHAT'S THAT!?
FLAP ヒラ
FLUTTER ヒラ
A FAKE, JUST AS I SUSPECTED!! BUT HOW IN THE WORLD DID THEY DO IT!? A PIECE OF PAPER... I REMEMBER SOMETHING LIKE THIS FROM AN OCCULT BOOK I SAW ONCE.
SORRY I KEPT YOU WAITING. ♡
......
...NEGI-SENSEI?
DASH
OH, NEGI-SENSEI, WHERE ARE YOU GOING!?
AH, NEGI-KUN, WHERE'RE YOU OFF TO!?
NEGI-BOZU, WAIT!
OH NO, NEGI-SENSEI'S RUNNING AWAY!
HOLD IT, NEGI-SENSEI!

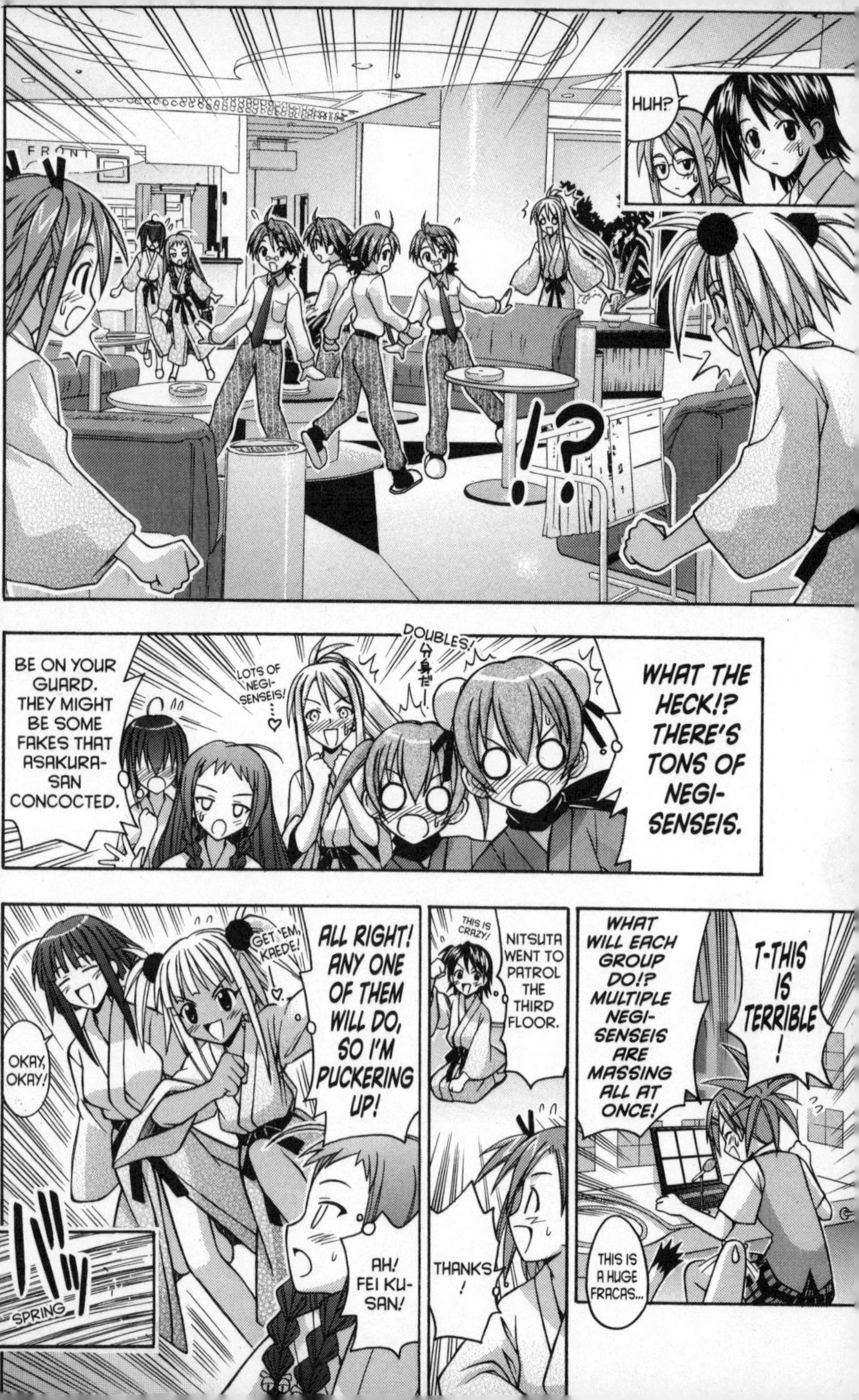
HUH?
FRONT
!?
WHAT THE HECK!? THERE'S TONS OF NEGI-SENSEIS.
DOUBLES! 分身だ!
LOTS OF NEGI-SENSEIS! ♡
BE ON YOUR GUARD. THEY MIGHT BE SOME FAKES THAT ASAKURA-SAN CONCOCTED.
T-THIS IS TERRIBLE!
WHAT WILL EACH GROUP DO!? MULTIPLE NEGI-SENSEIS ARE MASSING ALL AT ONCE!
THIS IS A HUGE FRACAS...
THIS IS CRAZY!
NITSUTA WENT TO PATROL THE THIRD FLOOR.
THANKS!
ALL RIGHT! ANY ONE OF THEM WILL DO, SO I'M PUCKERING UP!
GET 'EM, KAEDE! ♡
OKAY, OKAY!
AH! FEI KU-SAN!
SPRING

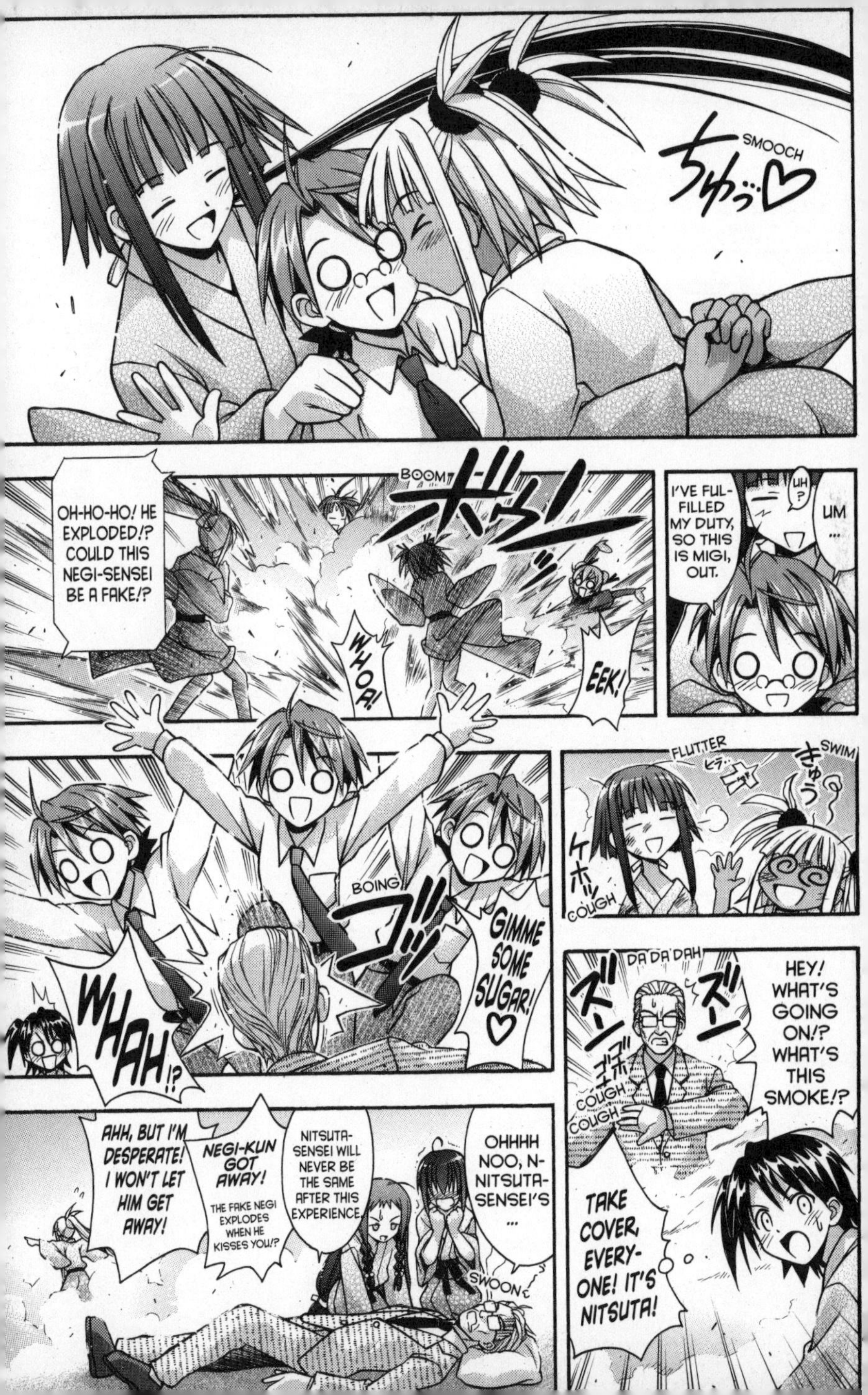
SMOOCH
UH?
UM ...
I'VE FULFILLED MY DUTY, SO THIS IS MIGI, OUT.
BOOM
EEK!
WHOA!
OH-HO-HO! HE EXPLODED!? COULD THIS NEGI-SENSEI BE A FAKE!?
FLUTTER
SWIM
COUGH
BOING
GIMME SOME SUGAR! ♡
WHAH!?
DA DA DAH
HEY! WHAT'S GOING ON!? WHAT'S THIS SMOKE!?
COUGH COUGH
TAKE COVER, EVERYONE! IT'S NITSUTA!
OHHHH NOO, N-NITSUTA-SENSEI'S ...
SWOON
NITSUTA-SENSEI WILL NEVER BE THE SAME AFTER THIS EXPERIENCE.
NEGI-KUN GOT AWAY!
THE FAKE NEGI EXPLODES WHEN HE KISSES YOU!?
AHH, BUT I'M DESPERATE! I WON'T LET HIM GET AWAY!

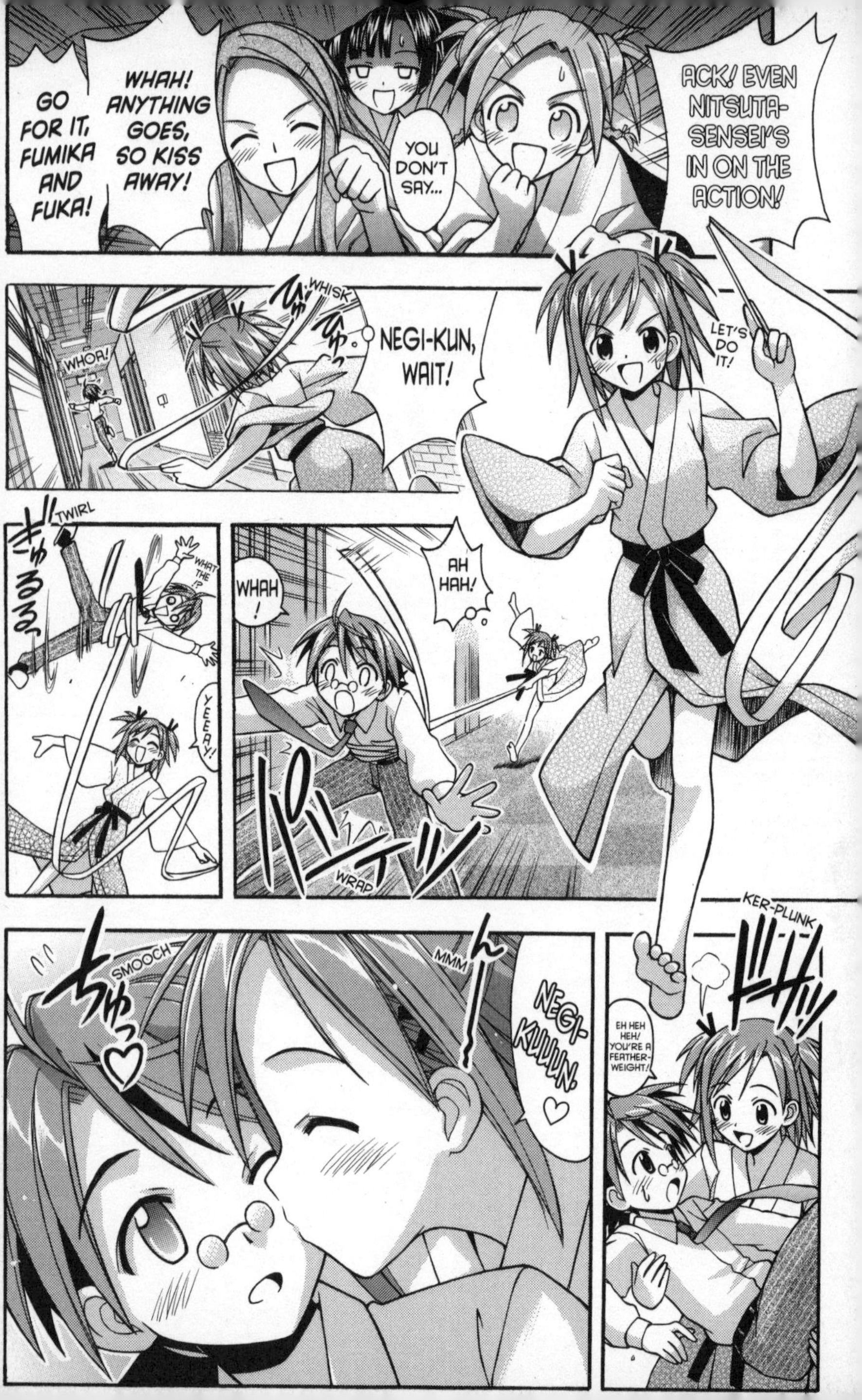
ACK! EVEN NITSUTA-SENSEI'S IN ON THE ACTION!
YOU DON'T SAY...
WHAH! ANYTHING GOES, SO KISS AWAY!
GO FOR IT, FUMIKA AND FUKA!
LET'S DO IT!
NEGI-KUN, WAIT!
WHISK
WHOA!
AH HAH!
WHAH!
WRAP
TWIRL
WHAT THE !?
YEEEAY!
KER-PLUNK
EH HEH HEH! YOU'RE A FEATHER-WEIGHT!
NEGI-KUUUN.
MMM
SMOOCH

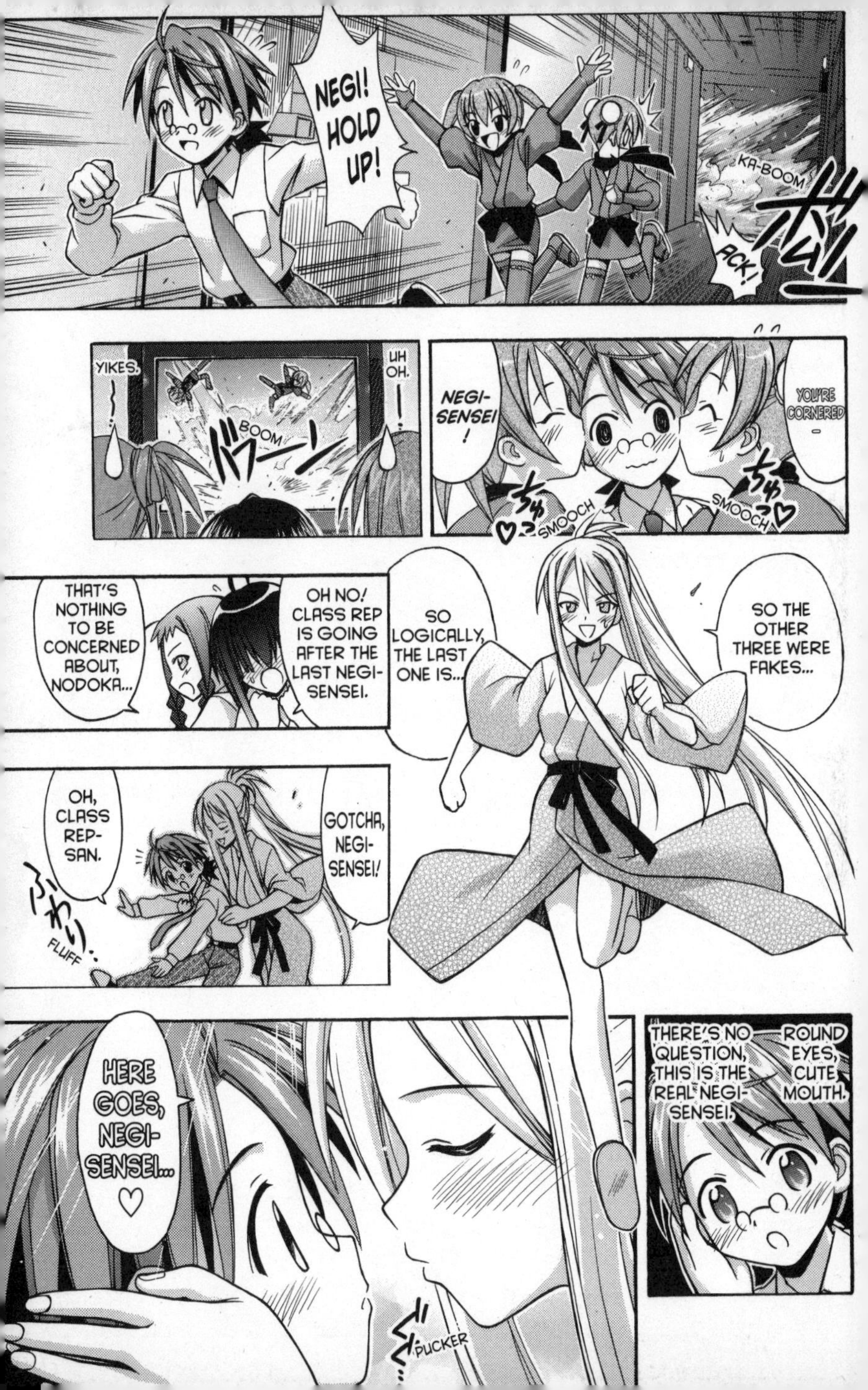
KA-BOOM
ACK!
NEGI! HOLD UP!
YOU'RE CORNERED—
SMOOCH
NEGI-SENSEI!
SMOOCH
UH OH.
BOOM
YIKES.
SO THE OTHER THREE WERE FAKES...
SO LOGICALLY, THE LAST ONE IS...
OH NO! CLASS REP IS GOING AFTER THE LAST NEGI-SENSEI.
THAT'S NOTHING TO BE CONCERNED ABOUT, NODOKA...
GOTCHA, NEGI-SENSEI!
OH, CLASS REP-SAN.
FLUFF
ROUND EYES, CUTE MOUTH.
THERE'S NO QUESTION, THIS IS THE REAL NEGI-SENSEI.
HERE GOES, NEGI-SENSEI... ♥
PUCKER

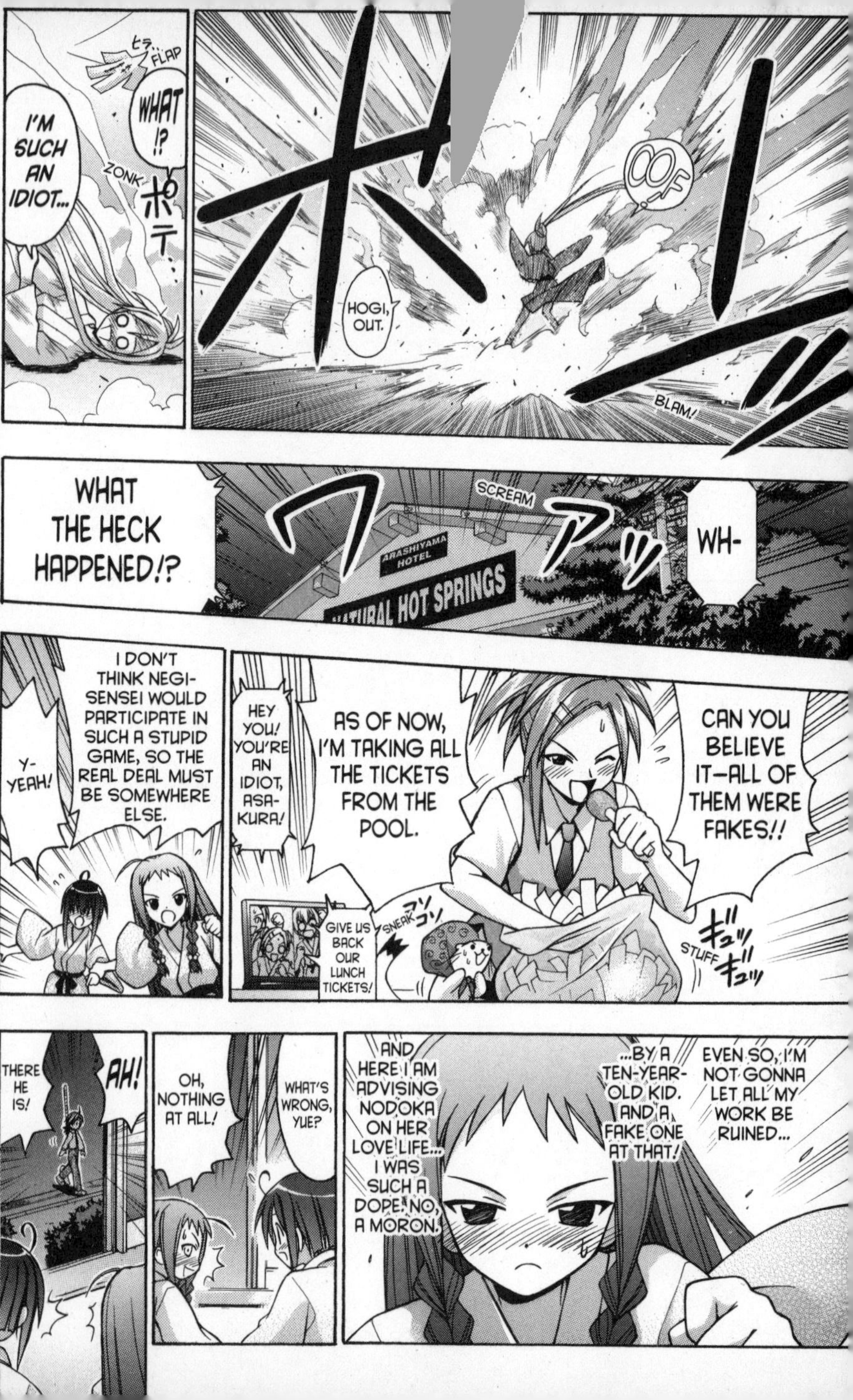
OOF
HOGI, OUT.
BLAM!
ヒラ... FLAP
WHAT !?
I'M SUCH AN IDIOT...
ZONK ポテ
WH-
SCREAM
ARASHIYAMA HOTEL
NATURAL HOT SPRINGS
WHAT THE HECK HAPPENED!?
CAN YOU BELIEVE IT—ALL OF THEM WERE FAKES!!
AS OF NOW, I'M TAKING ALL THE TICKETS FROM THE POOL.
HEY YOU! YOU'RE AN IDIOT, ASA-KURA!
STUFF
SNEAK
GIVE US BACK OUR LUNCH TICKETS!
I DON'T THINK NEGI-SENSEI WOULD PARTICIPATE IN SUCH A STUPID GAME, SO THE REAL DEAL MUST BE SOMEWHERE ELSE.
Y-YEAH!
EVEN SO, I'M NOT GONNA LET ALL MY WORK BE RUINED...
...BY A TEN-YEAR-OLD KID. AND A FAKE ONE AT THAT!
AND HERE I AM ADVISING NODOKA ON HER LOVE LIFE... I WAS SUCH A DOPE. NO, A MORON.
WHAT'S WRONG, YUE?
OH, NOTHING AT ALL!
AH!
THERE HE IS!

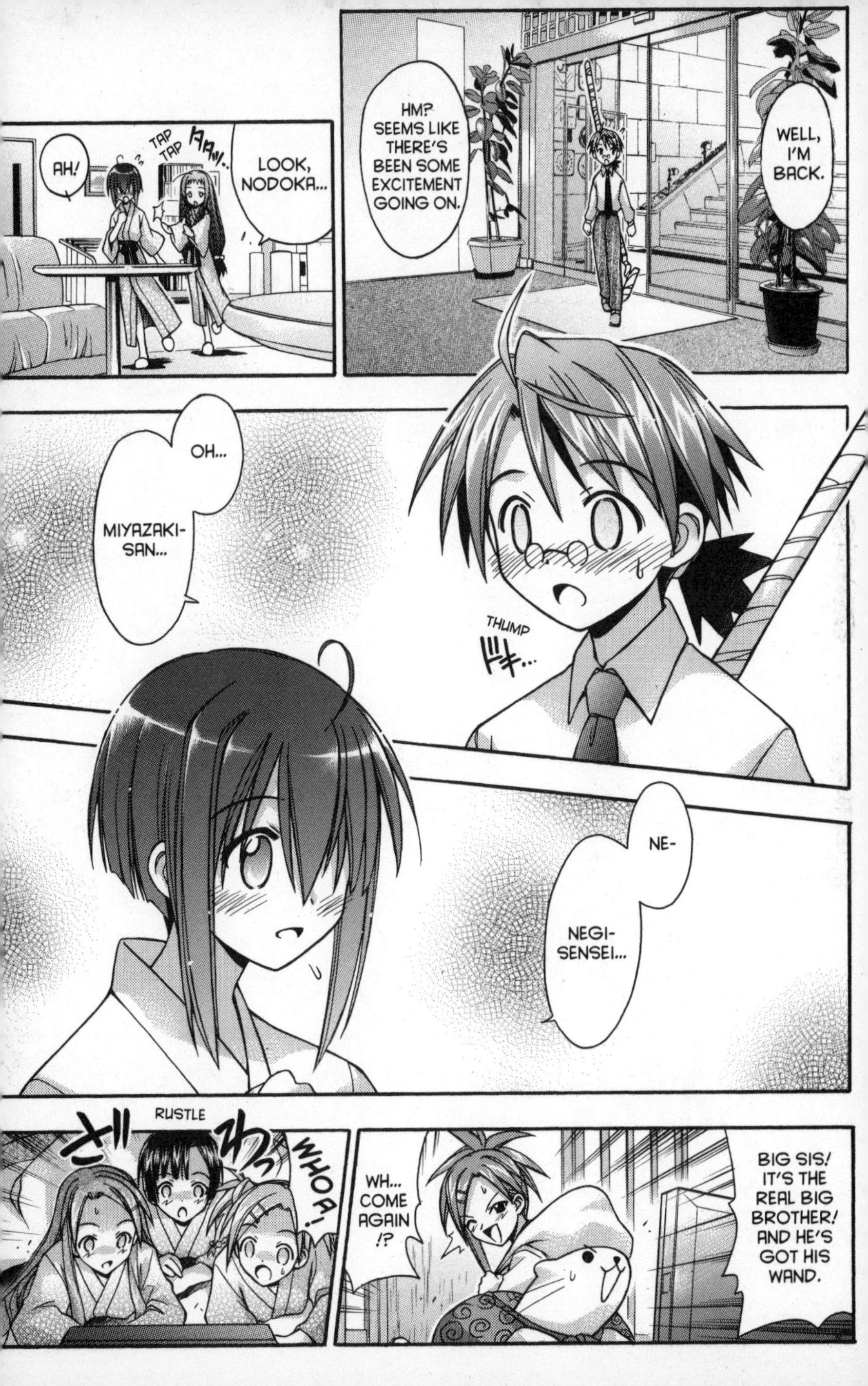
WELL, I'M BACK.
HM? SEEMS LIKE THERE'S BEEN SOME EXCITEMENT GOING ON.
LOOK, NODOKA...
TAP TAP
AH!
THUMP
OH...
MIYAZAKI-SAN...
NE-
NEGI-SENSEI...
BIG SIS! IT'S THE REAL BIG BROTHER! AND HE'S GOT HIS WAND.
WH... COME AGAIN!?
RUSTLE
WHOA!

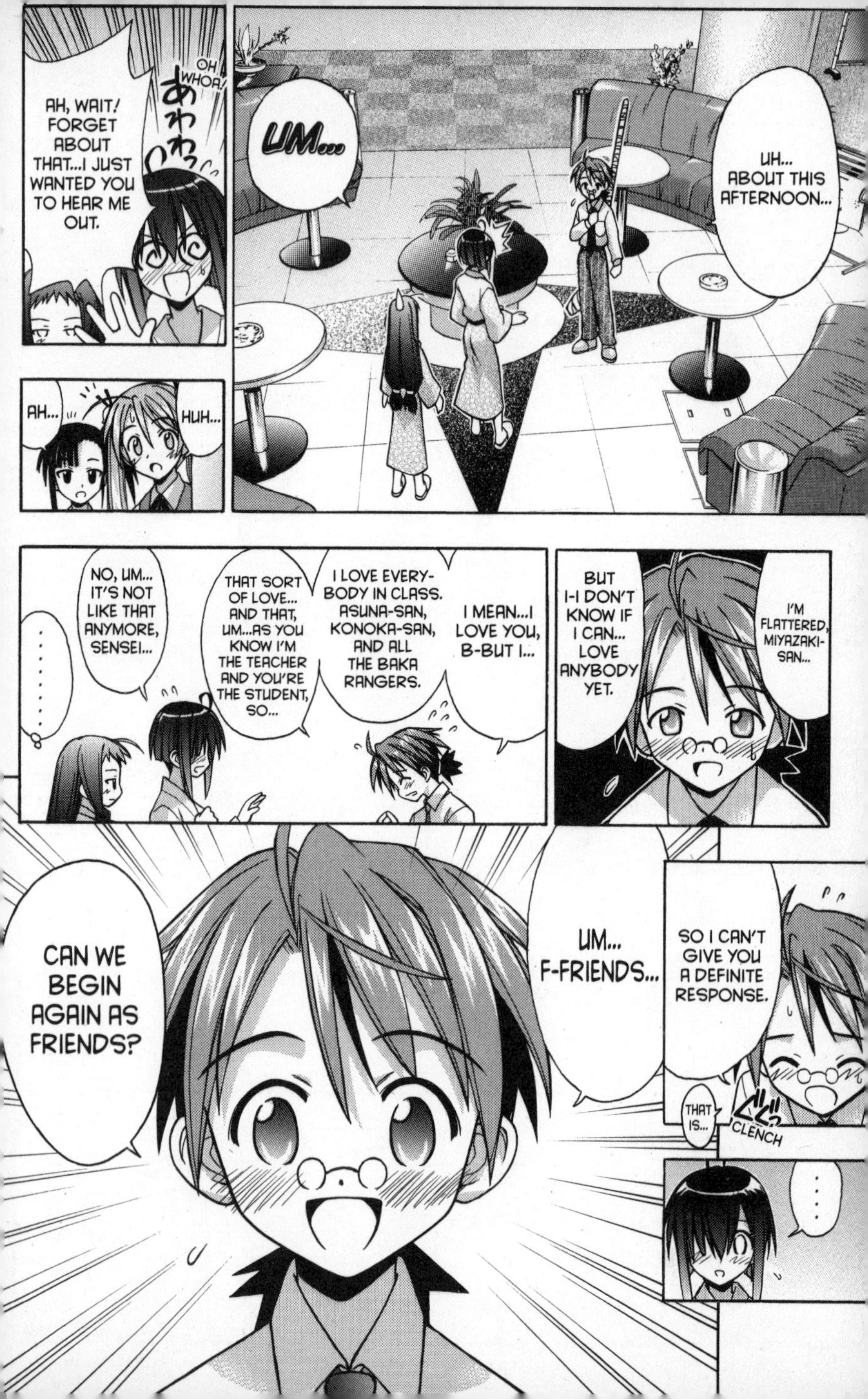
UH... ABOUT THIS AFTERNOON...
UM...
OH WHOA!
あわわっ
AH, WAIT! FORGET ABOUT THAT...I JUST WANTED YOU TO HEAR ME OUT.
HUH...
AH...
I'M FLATTERED, MIYAZAKI-SAN...
BUT I-I DON'T KNOW IF I CAN... LOVE ANYBODY YET.
I MEAN...I LOVE YOU, B-BUT I...
I LOVE EVERY-BODY IN CLASS. ASUNA-SAN, KONOKA-SAN, AND ALL THE BAKA RANGERS.
THAT SORT OF LOVE... AND THAT, UM...AS YOU KNOW I'M THE TEACHER AND YOU'RE THE STUDENT, SO...
NO, UM... IT'S NOT LIKE THAT ANYMORE, SENSEI...
......
SO I CAN'T GIVE YOU A DEFINITE RESPONSE.
THAT IS...
ぐぐっ
CLENCH
....
UM... F-FRIENDS...
CAN WE BEGIN AGAIN AS FRIENDS?

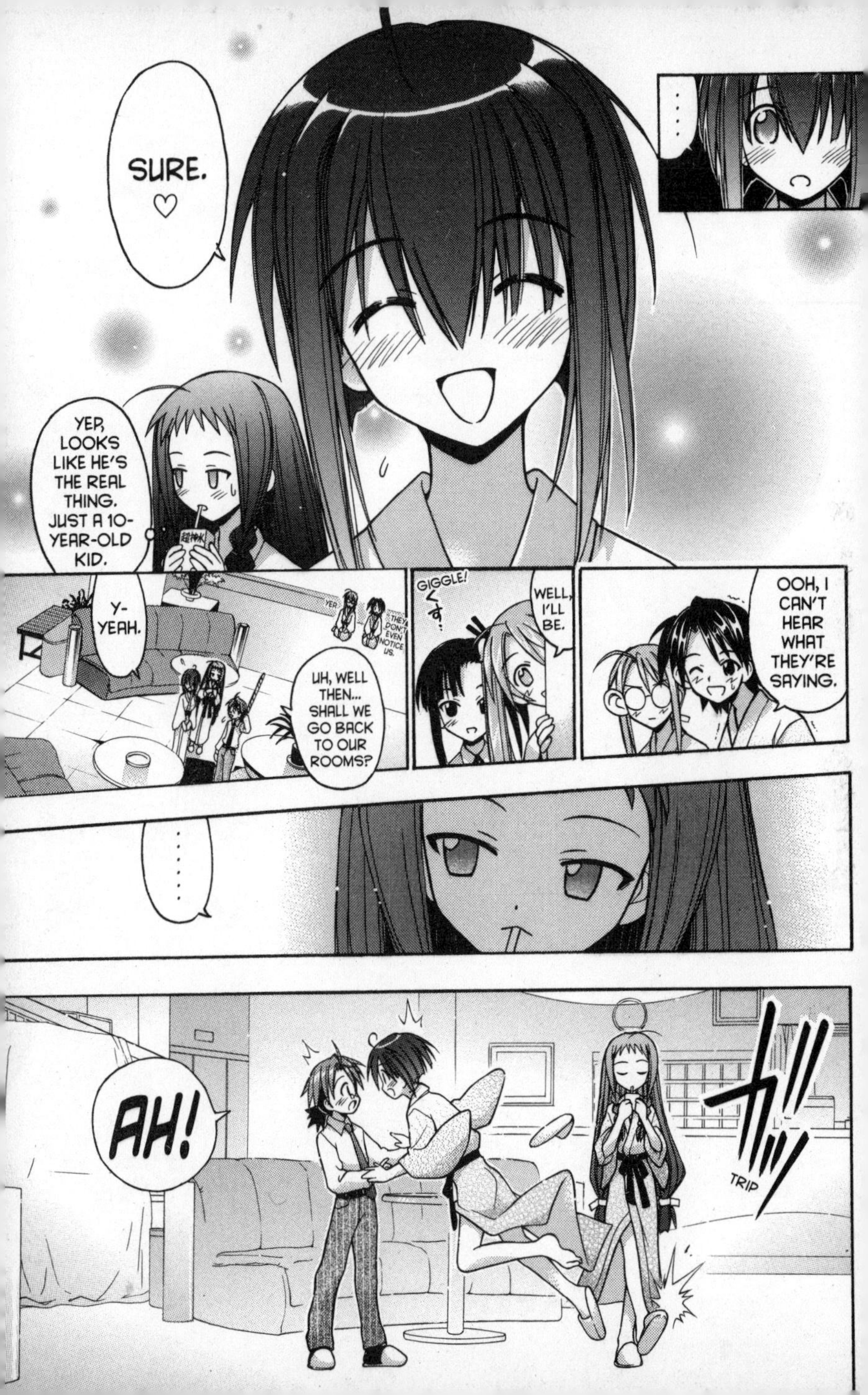
......
SURE. ♡
YEP, LOOKS LIKE HE'S THE REAL THING. JUST A 10-YEAR-OLD KID.
OOH, I CAN'T HEAR WHAT THEY'RE SAYING.
GIGGLE! くす
WELL, I'LL BE.
YEP.
THEY DON'T EVEN NOTICE US.
UH, WELL THEN... SHALL WE GO BACK TO OUR ROOMS?
Y-YEAH.
......
TRIP
AH!

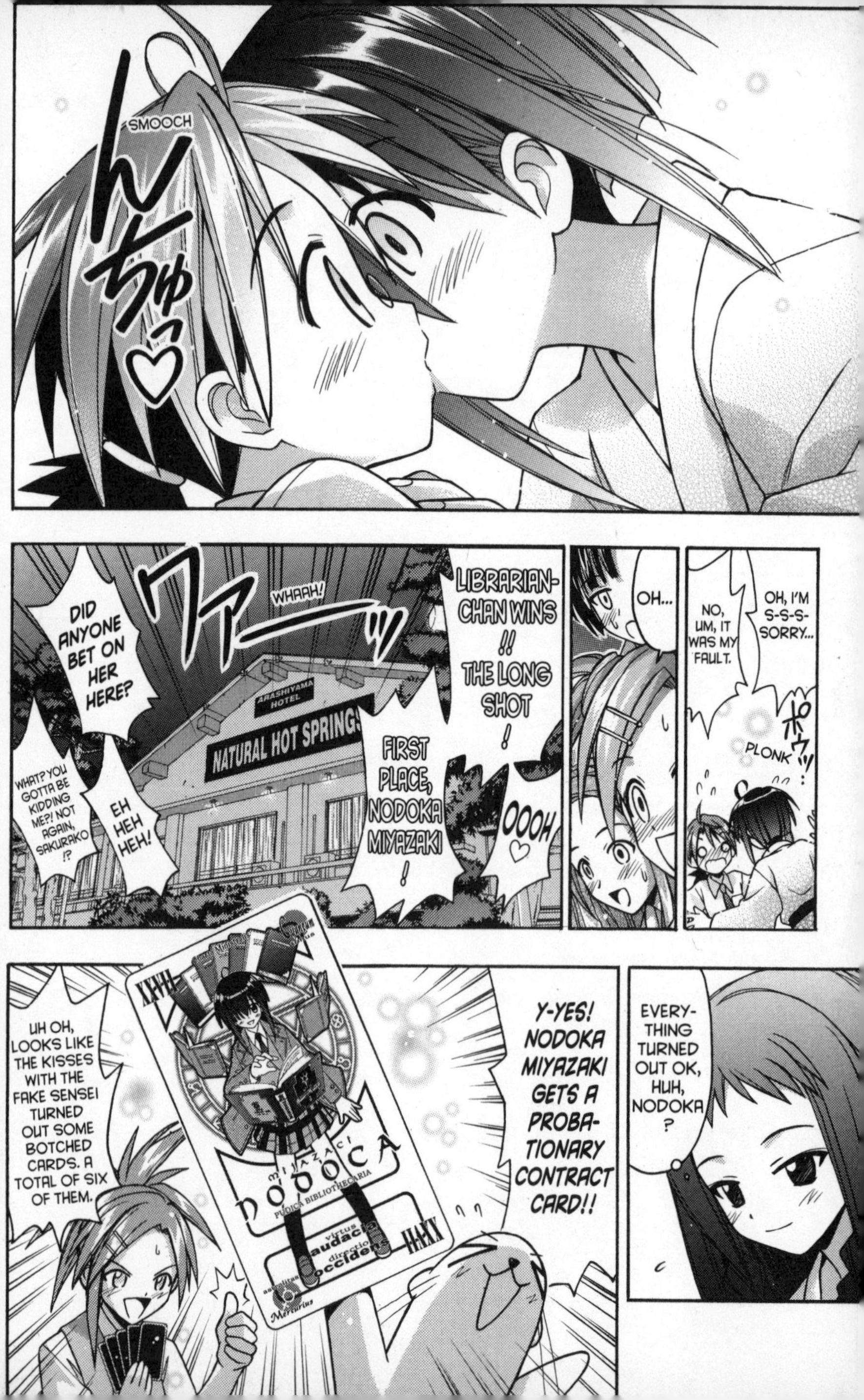
SMOOCH
んちゅっ♡
OH, I'M S-S-S-SORRY...
NO, UM, IT WAS MY FAULT.
ポウッ
PLONK
OH...
OOOH ♡
LIBRARIAN-CHAN WINS!! THE LONG SHOT!
FIRST PLACE, NODOKA MIYAZAKI!
ワァーッ
WHAAH!
DID ANYONE BET ON HER HERE?
ARASHIYAMA HOTEL
NATURAL HOT SPRINGS
EH HEH HEH!
WHAT? YOU GOTTA BE KIDDING ME?! NOT AGAIN, SAKURAKO!?
EVERY-THING TURNED OUT OK, HUH, NODOKA?
Y-YES! NODOKA MIYAZAKI GETS A PROBA-TIONARY CONTRACT CARD!!
NODOCA
PUDICA BIBLIOTHECARIA
virtus audacia
directio occidens
Mercurius
UH OH, LOOKS LIKE THE KISSES WITH THE FAKE SENSEI TURNED OUT SOME BOTCHED CARDS. A TOTAL OF SIX OF THEM.

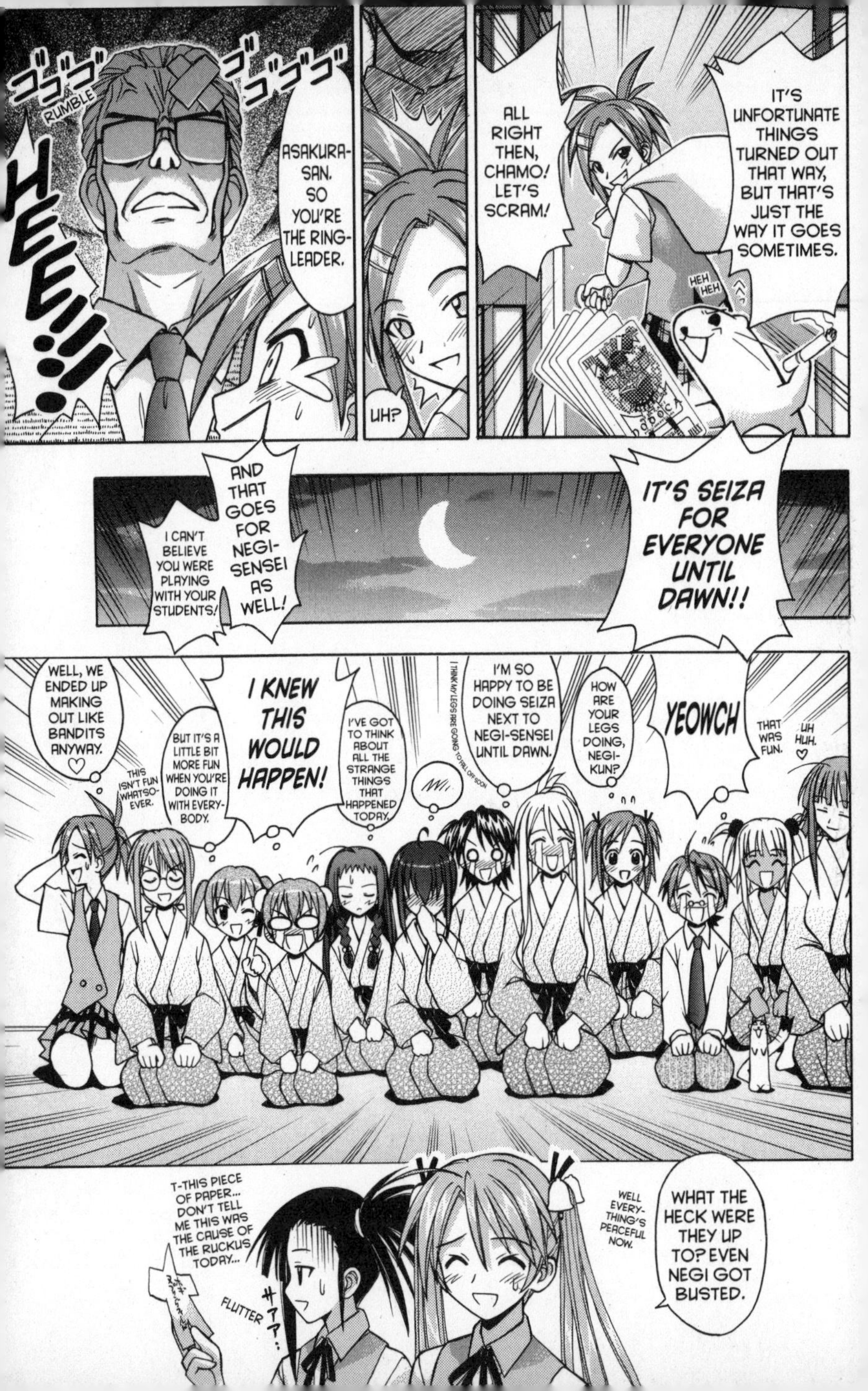
IT'S UNFORTUNATE THINGS TURNED OUT THAT WAY, BUT THAT'S JUST THE WAY IT GOES SOMETIMES.
ALL RIGHT THEN, CHAMO! LET'S SCRAM!
HEH HEH
UH?
ASAKURA-SAN. SO YOU'RE THE RING-LEADER.
ゴゴゴ
ゴゴゴ
RUMBLE
HEEE!!!!
IT'S SEIZA FOR EVERYONE UNTIL DAWN!!
AND THAT GOES FOR NEGI-SENSEI AS WELL!
I CAN'T BELIEVE YOU WERE PLAYING WITH YOUR STUDENTS!
UH HUH. ♡
THAT WAS FUN.
YEOWCH
HOW ARE YOUR LEGS DOING, NEGI-KUN?
I'M SO HAPPY TO BE DOING SEIZA NEXT TO NEGI-SENSEI UNTIL DAWN.
I THINK MY LEGS ARE GOING TO FALL OFF SOON
I'VE GOT TO THINK ABOUT ALL THE STRANGE THINGS THAT HAPPENED TODAY.
I KNEW THIS WOULD HAPPEN!
BUT IT'S A LITTLE BIT MORE FUN WHEN YOU'RE DOING IT WITH EVERY-BODY.
THIS ISN'T FUN WHATSO-EVER.
WELL, WE ENDED UP MAKING OUT LIKE BANDITS ANYWAY. ♡
WHAT THE HECK WERE THEY UP TO? EVEN NEGI GOT BUSTED.
WELL EVERY-THING'S PEACEFUL NOW.
T-THIS PIECE OF PAPER... DON'T TELL ME THIS WAS THE CAUSE OF THE RUCKUS TODAY...
サァ…
FLUTTER

3-A SCHOOL FIELD TRIP'S GROUPS 4 AND 5

GROUP 4
(GROUP LEADER)
YUNA AKASHI

AKO IZUMI
AKIRA OHKOUCHI
MAKIE SASAKI
MANA TATSUMIYA

GROUP 5
(GROUP LEADER)
ASUNA KAGURAZAKA

YUE AYASE
KONOKA KONOE
HARUNA SAOTOME
SETSUNA SAKURAZAKI
NODOKA MIYAZAKI

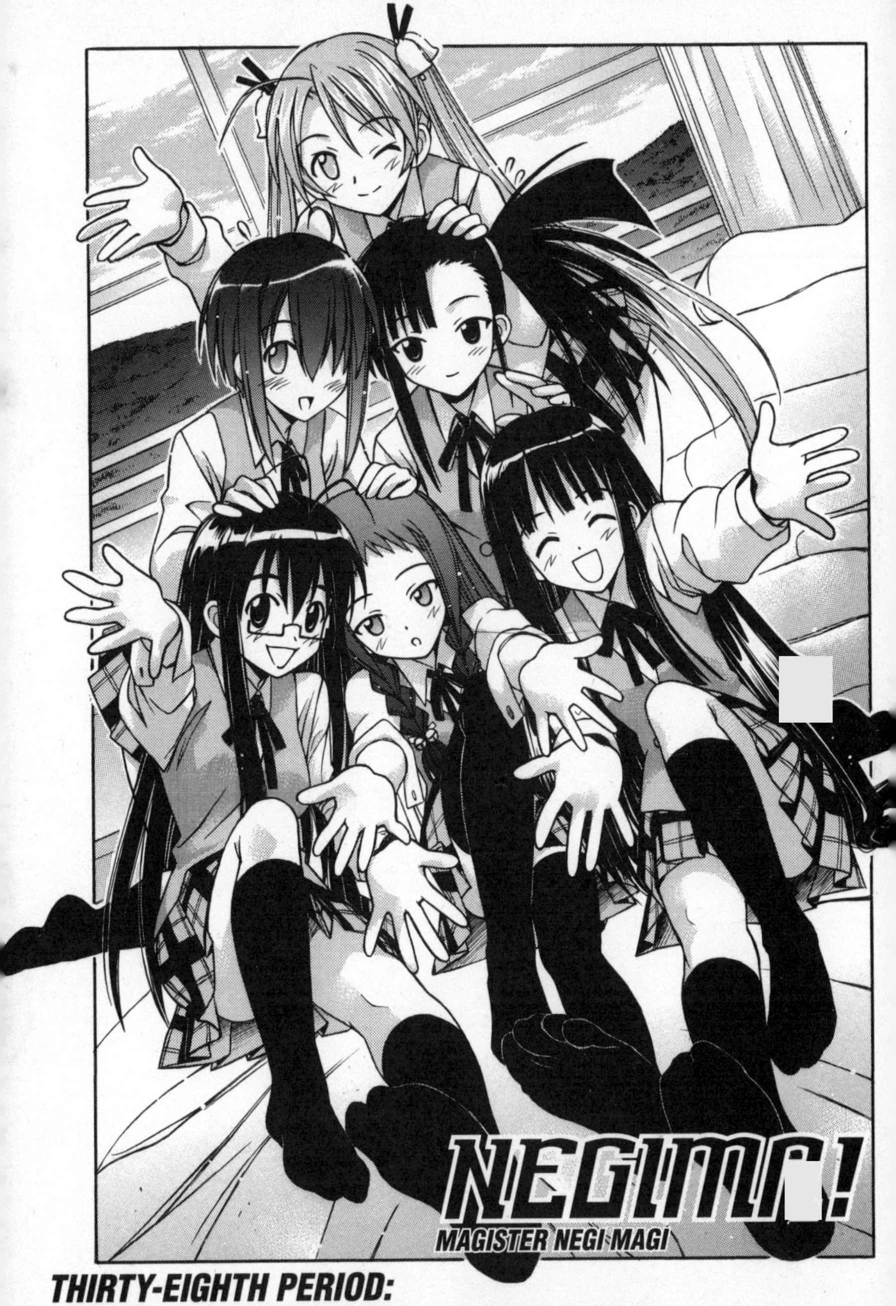
NEGIMA!
MAGISTER NEGI MAGI

THIRTY-EIGHTH PERIOD:
NODOKA AND THE SECRET PICTURE DIARY

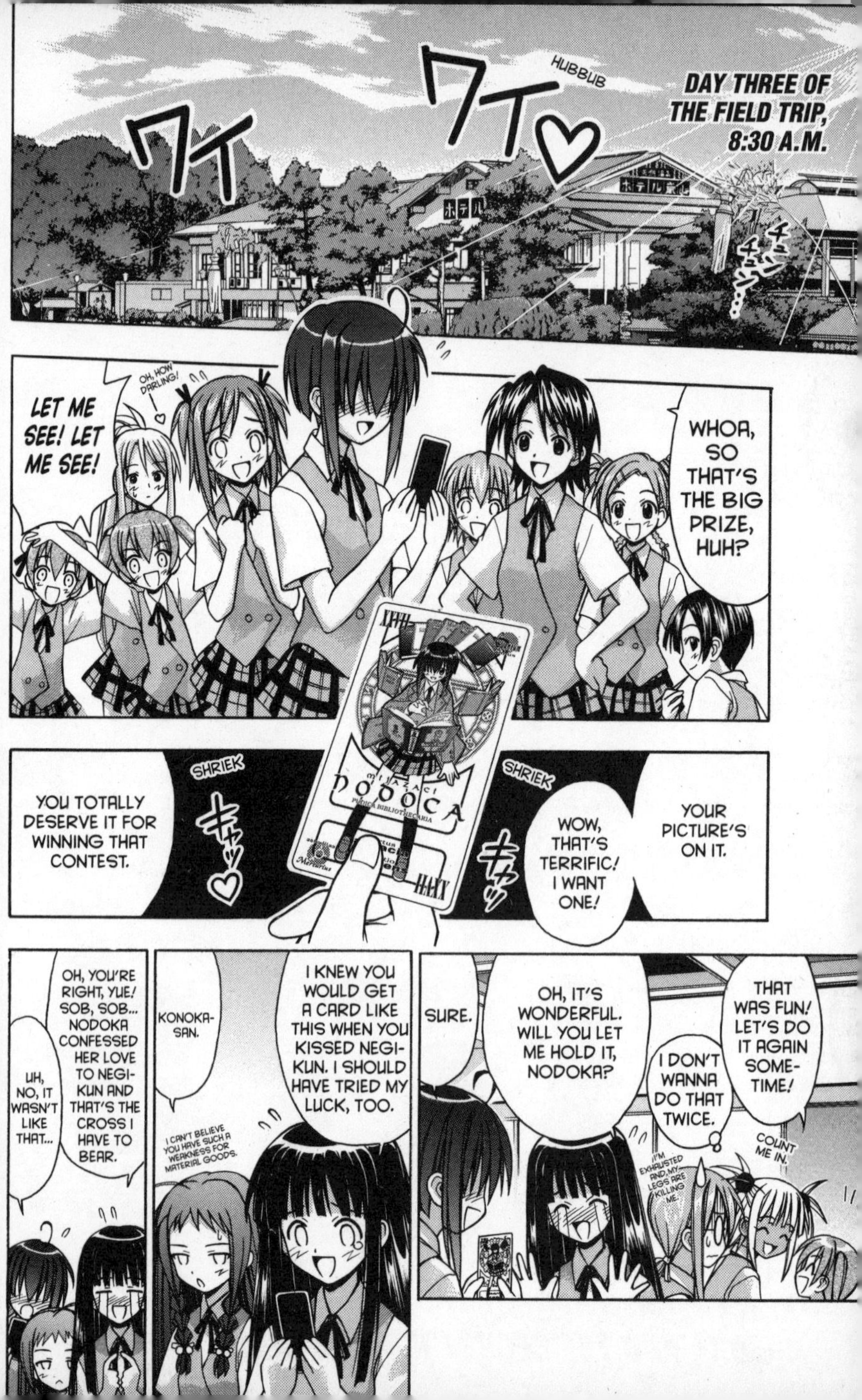
DAY THREE OF THE FIELD TRIP, 8:30 A.M.
HUBBUB
ワイ ワイ♡
チュン チュン…
WHOA, SO THAT'S THE BIG PRIZE, HUH?
OH, HOW DARLING! ♡
LET ME SEE! LET ME SEE!
YOUR PICTURE'S ON IT.
WOW, THAT'S TERRIFIC! I WANT ONE!
SHRIEK
キャッ
NODOCA
SHRIEK
キャッ♡
YOU TOTALLY DESERVE IT FOR WINNING THAT CONTEST.
THAT WAS FUN! LET'S DO IT AGAIN SOME- TIME!
I DON'T WANNA DO THAT TWICE.
COUNT ME IN.
I'M EXHAUSTED AND MY LEGS ARE KILLING ME.
OH, IT'S WONDERFUL. WILL YOU LET ME HOLD IT, NODOKA?
SURE.
I KNEW YOU WOULD GET A CARD LIKE THIS WHEN YOU KISSED NEGI-KUN. I SHOULD HAVE TRIED MY LUCK, TOO.
KONOKA-SAN.
I CAN'T BELIEVE YOU HAVE SUCH A WEAKNESS FOR MATERIAL GOODS.
OH, YOU'RE RIGHT, YUE! SOB, SOB... NODOKA CONFESSED HER LOVE TO NEGI-KUN AND THAT'S THE CROSS I HAVE TO BEAR.
UH, NO, IT WASN'T LIKE THAT...

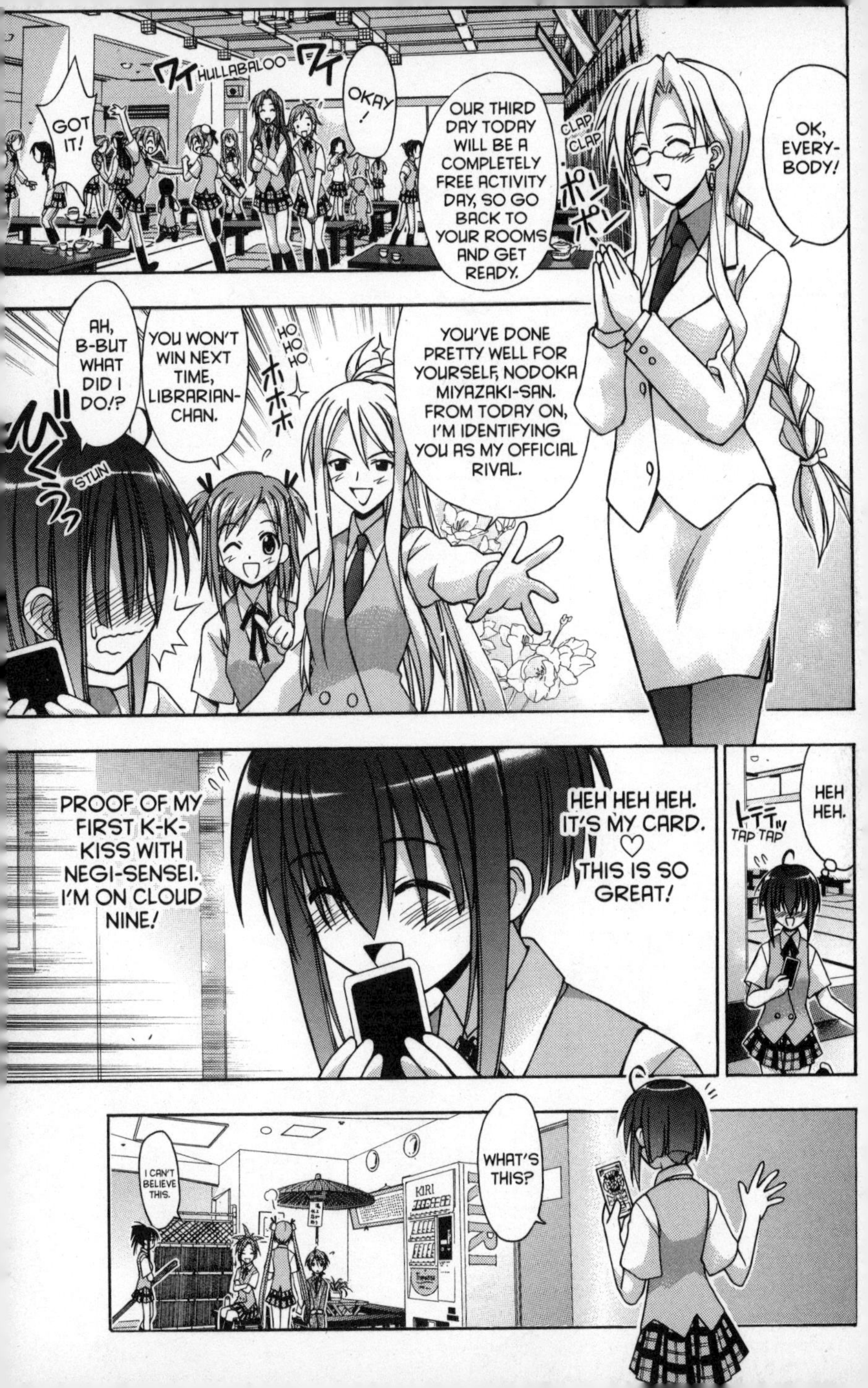
OK, EVERY-BODY!
CLAP CLAP
OUR THIRD DAY TODAY WILL BE A COMPLETELY FREE ACTIVITY DAY, SO GO BACK TO YOUR ROOMS AND GET READY.
OKAY!
HULLABALOO
GOT IT!
YOU'VE DONE PRETTY WELL FOR YOURSELF, NODOKA MIYAZAKI-SAN. FROM TODAY ON, I'M IDENTIFYING YOU AS MY OFFICIAL RIVAL.
HO HO HO
YOU WON'T WIN NEXT TIME, LIBRARIAN-CHAN.
AH, B-BUT WHAT DID I DO!?
STUN
HEH HEH.
TAP TAP
HEH HEH HEH. IT'S MY CARD. ♡ THIS IS SO GREAT!
PROOF OF MY FIRST K-K-KISS WITH NEGI-SENSEI. I'M ON CLOUD NINE!
WHAT'S THIS?
I CAN'T BELIEVE THIS.
KIRI

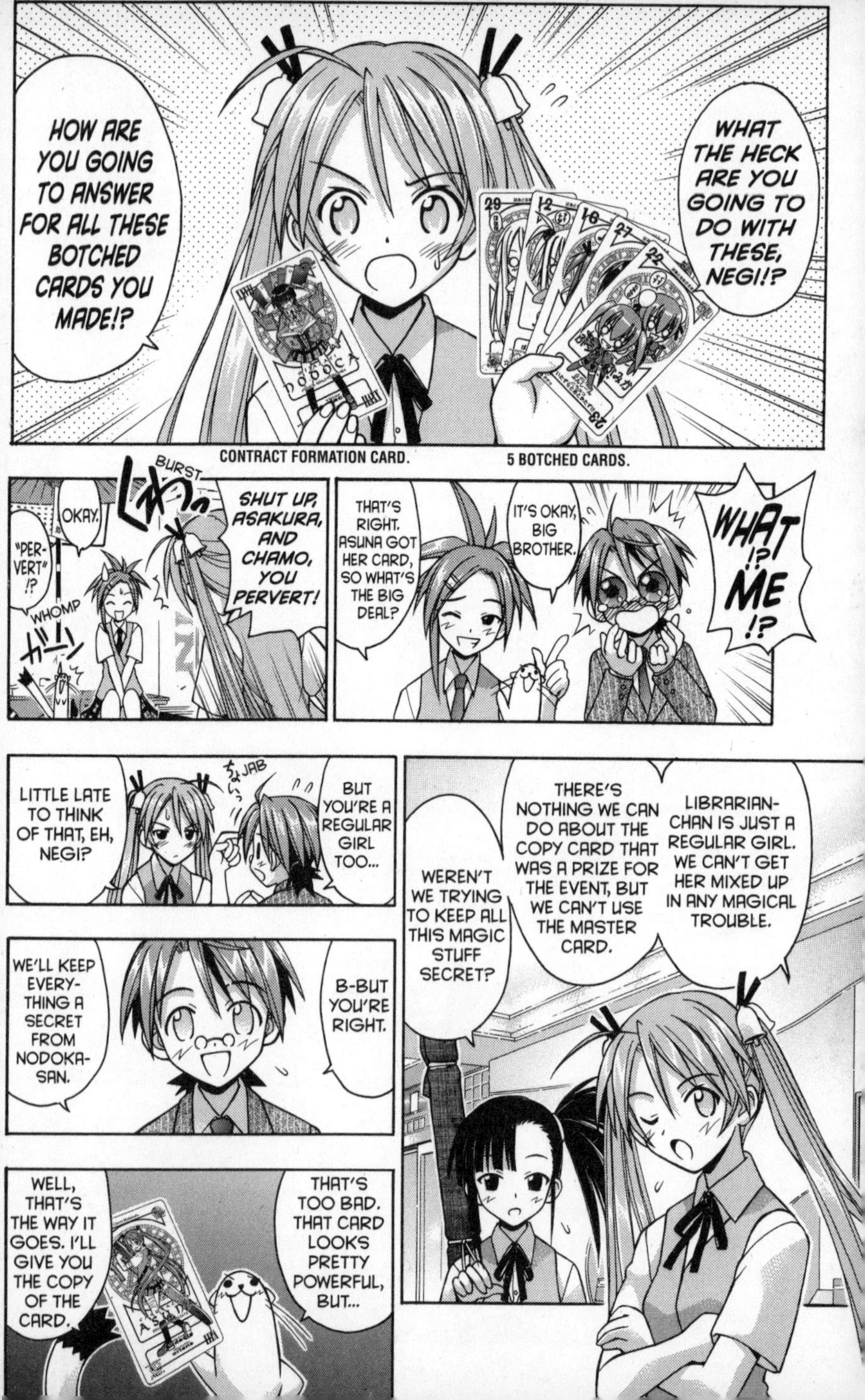
WHAT THE HECK ARE YOU GOING TO DO WITH THESE, NEGI!?
HOW ARE YOU GOING TO ANSWER FOR ALL THESE BOTCHED CARDS YOU MADE!?
5 BOTCHED CARDS.
CONTRACT FORMATION CARD.
WHAT!? ME!?
IT'S OKAY, BIG BROTHER.
THAT'S RIGHT. ASUNA GOT HER CARD, SO WHAT'S THE BIG DEAL?
SHUT UP, ASAKURA, AND CHAMO, YOU PERVERT!
BURST
OKAY.
"PER-VERT"!?
WHOMP
LIBRARIAN-CHAN IS JUST A REGULAR GIRL. WE CAN'T GET HER MIXED UP IN ANY MAGICAL TROUBLE.
THERE'S NOTHING WE CAN DO ABOUT THE COPY CARD THAT WAS A PRIZE FOR THE EVENT, BUT WE CAN'T USE THE MASTER CARD.
WEREN'T WE TRYING TO KEEP ALL THIS MAGIC STUFF SECRET?
BUT YOU'RE A REGULAR GIRL TOO...
JAB
LITTLE LATE TO THINK OF THAT, EH, NEGI?
B-BUT YOU'RE RIGHT.
WE'LL KEEP EVERY-THING A SECRET FROM NODOKA-SAN.
THAT'S TOO BAD. THAT CARD LOOKS PRETTY POWERFUL, BUT...
WELL, THAT'S THE WAY IT GOES. I'LL GIVE YOU THE COPY OF THE CARD.

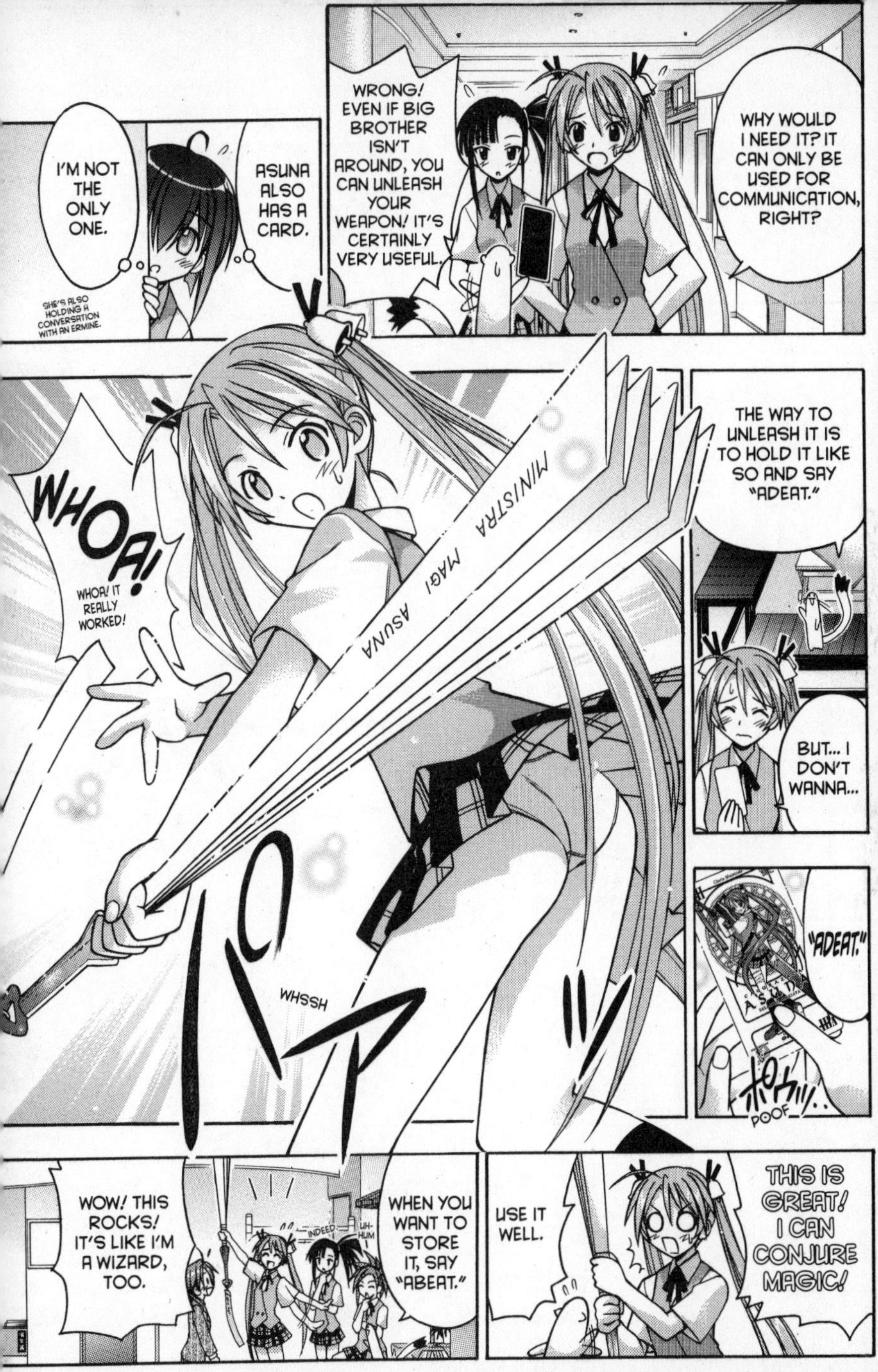
WHY WOULD I NEED IT? IT CAN ONLY BE USED FOR COMMUNICATION, RIGHT?
WRONG! EVEN IF BIG BROTHER ISN'T AROUND, YOU CAN UNLEASH YOUR WEAPON! IT'S CERTAINLY VERY USEFUL.
ASUNA ALSO HAS A CARD.
I'M NOT THE ONLY ONE.
SHE'S ALSO HOLDING A CONVERSATION WITH AN ERMINE.
THE WAY TO UNLEASH IT IS TO HOLD IT LIKE SO AND SAY "ADEAT."
BUT... I DON'T WANNA...
"ADEAT."
POOF
MINISTRA MAGI ASUNA
WHSSH
WHOA!
WHOA! IT REALLY WORKED!
THIS IS GREAT! I CAN CONJURE MAGIC!
USE IT WELL.
WHEN YOU WANT TO STORE IT, SAY "ABEAT."
WOW! THIS ROCKS! IT'S LIKE I'M A WIZARD, TOO.
INDEED
UH-HUM

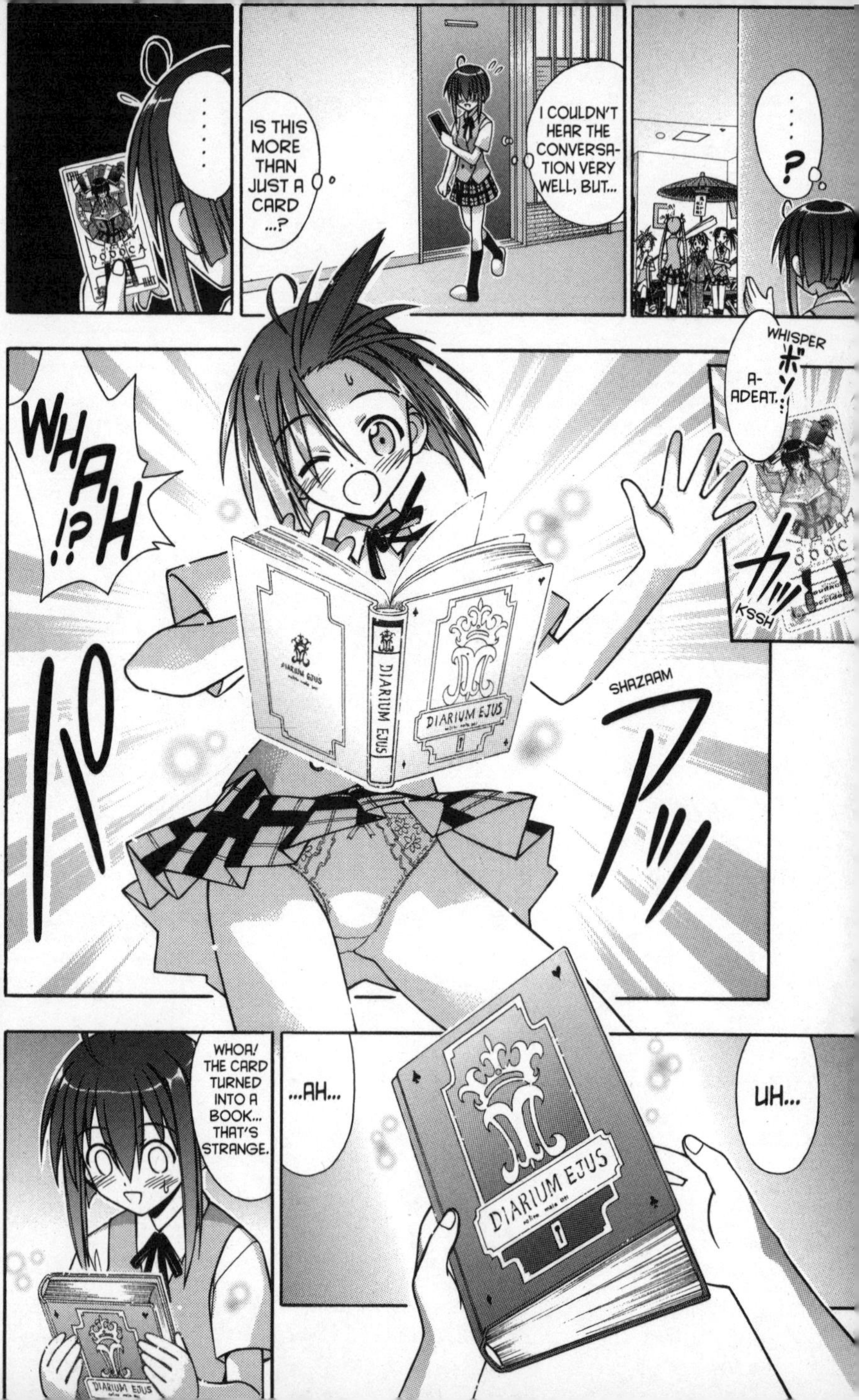
......
?
I COULDN'T HEAR THE CONVERSATION VERY WELL, BUT...
IS THIS MORE THAN JUST A CARD ...?
......
WHISPER
A-ADEAT...
KSSH
SHAZAAM
WHAH!?H
DIARIUM EJUS
DIARIUM EJUS
UH...
...AH...
DIARIUM EJUS
WHOA! THE CARD TURNED INTO A BOOK... THAT'S STRANGE.
DIARIUM EJUS

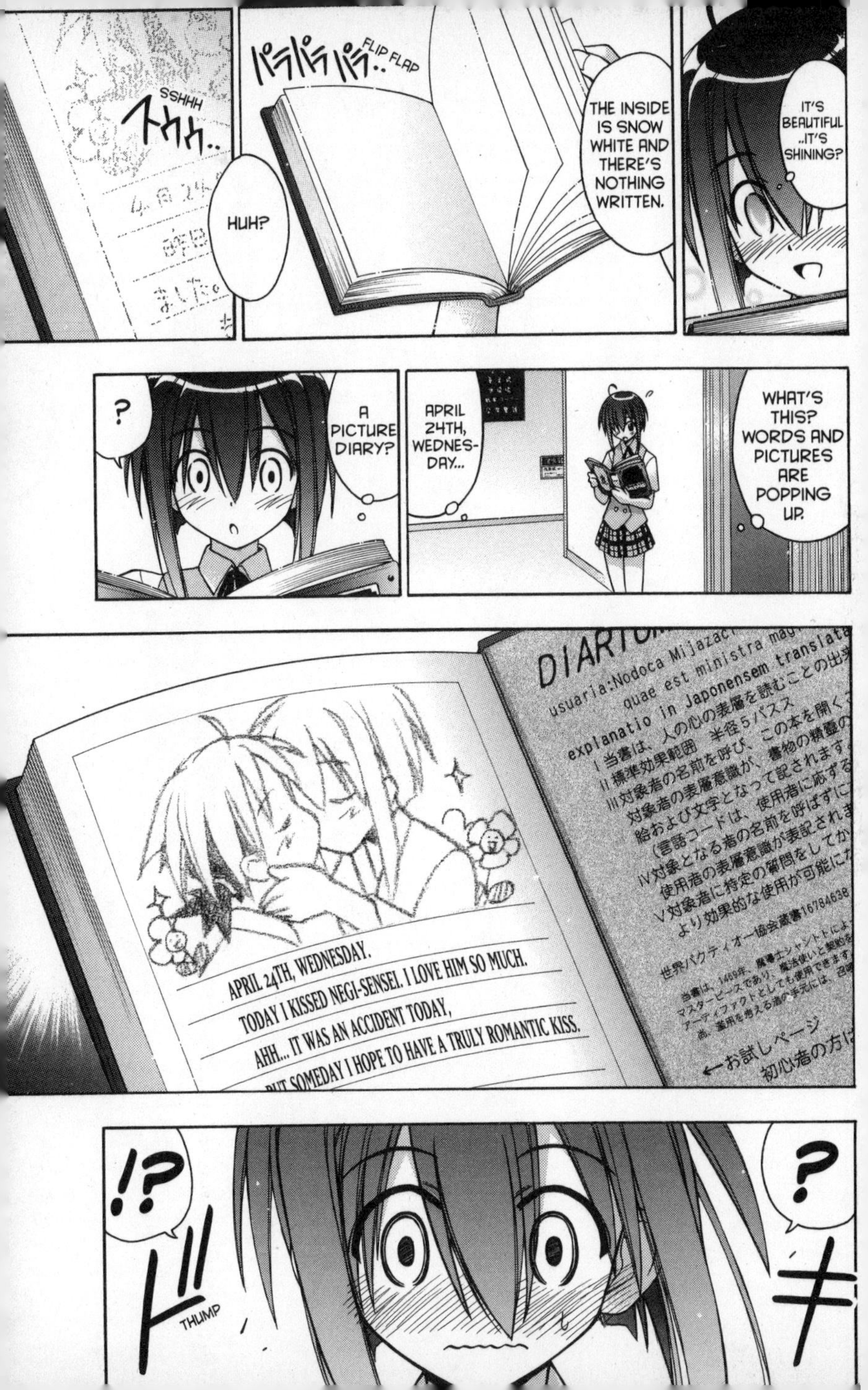
IT'S BEAUTIFUL ..IT'S SHINING?
THE INSIDE IS SNOW WHITE AND THERE'S NOTHING WRITTEN.
パラパラパラ.. FLIP FLAP
HUH?
スゥゥ.. SSHHH
WHAT'S THIS? WORDS AND PICTURES ARE POPPING UP.
APRIL 24TH, WEDNES-DAY...
A PICTURE DIARY?
?
usuaria:Nodoca Mijazaci
quae est ministra mag
explanatio in Japonensem translat
←お試しページ
初心者の方は
APRIL 24TH, WEDNESDAY.
TODAY I KISSED NEGI-SENSEI. I LOVE HIM SO MUCH.
AHH... IT WAS AN ACCIDENT TODAY,
BUT SOMEDAY I HOPE TO HAVE A TRULY ROMANTIC KISS.
?
キ
!?
ド!! THUMP

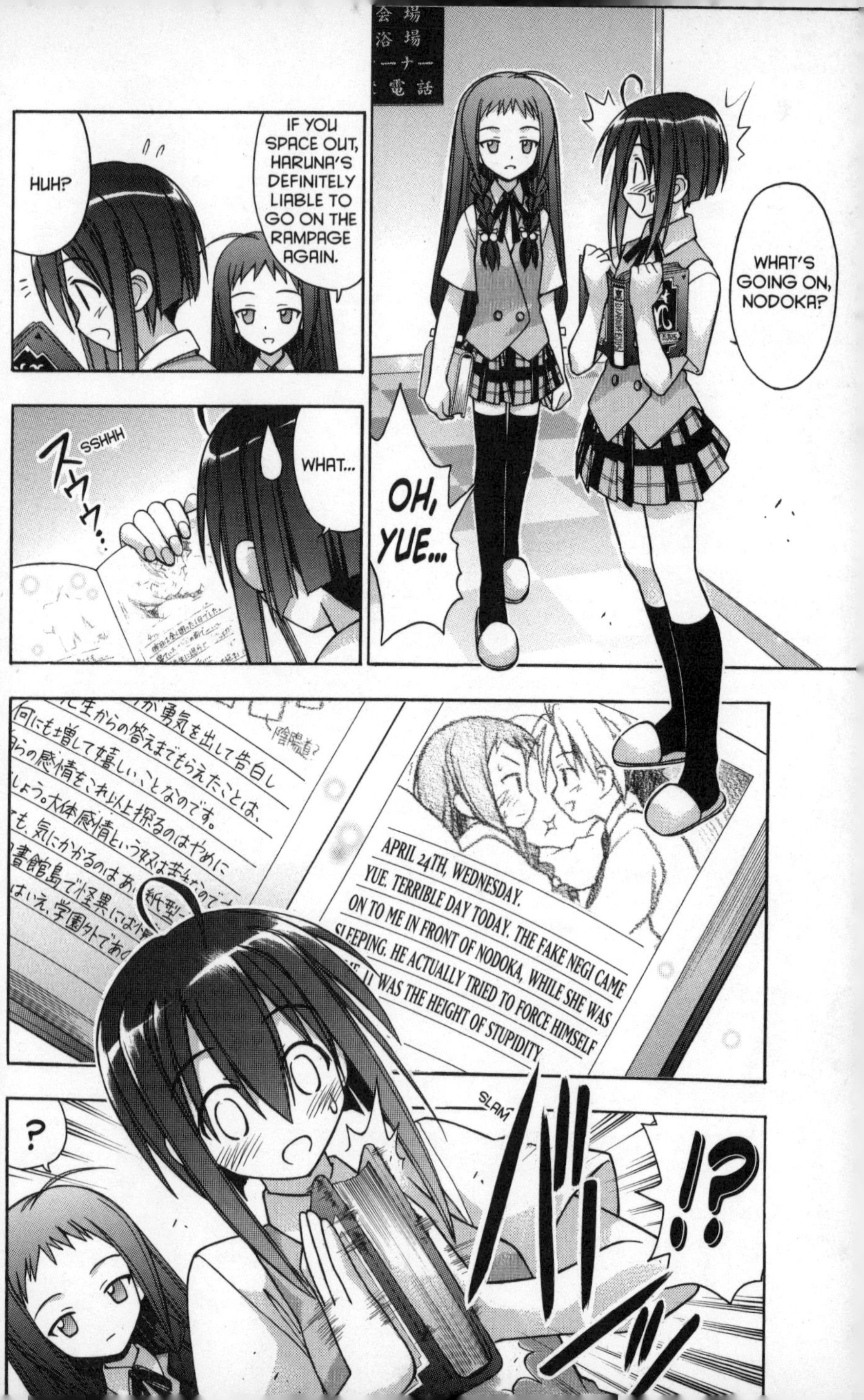
WHAT'S GOING ON, NODOKA?
OH, YUE...
IF YOU SPACE OUT, HARUNA'S DEFINITELY LIABLE TO GO ON THE RAMPAGE AGAIN.
HUH?
WHAT...
SSHHH
APRIL 24TH, WEDNESDAY.
YUE. TERRIBLE DAY TODAY. THE FAKE NEGI CAME
ON TO ME IN FRONT OF NODOKA, WHILE SHE WAS
SLEEPING. HE ACTUALLY TRIED TO FORCE HIMSELF
IT WAS THE HEIGHT OF STUPIDITY
SLAM
!?
?

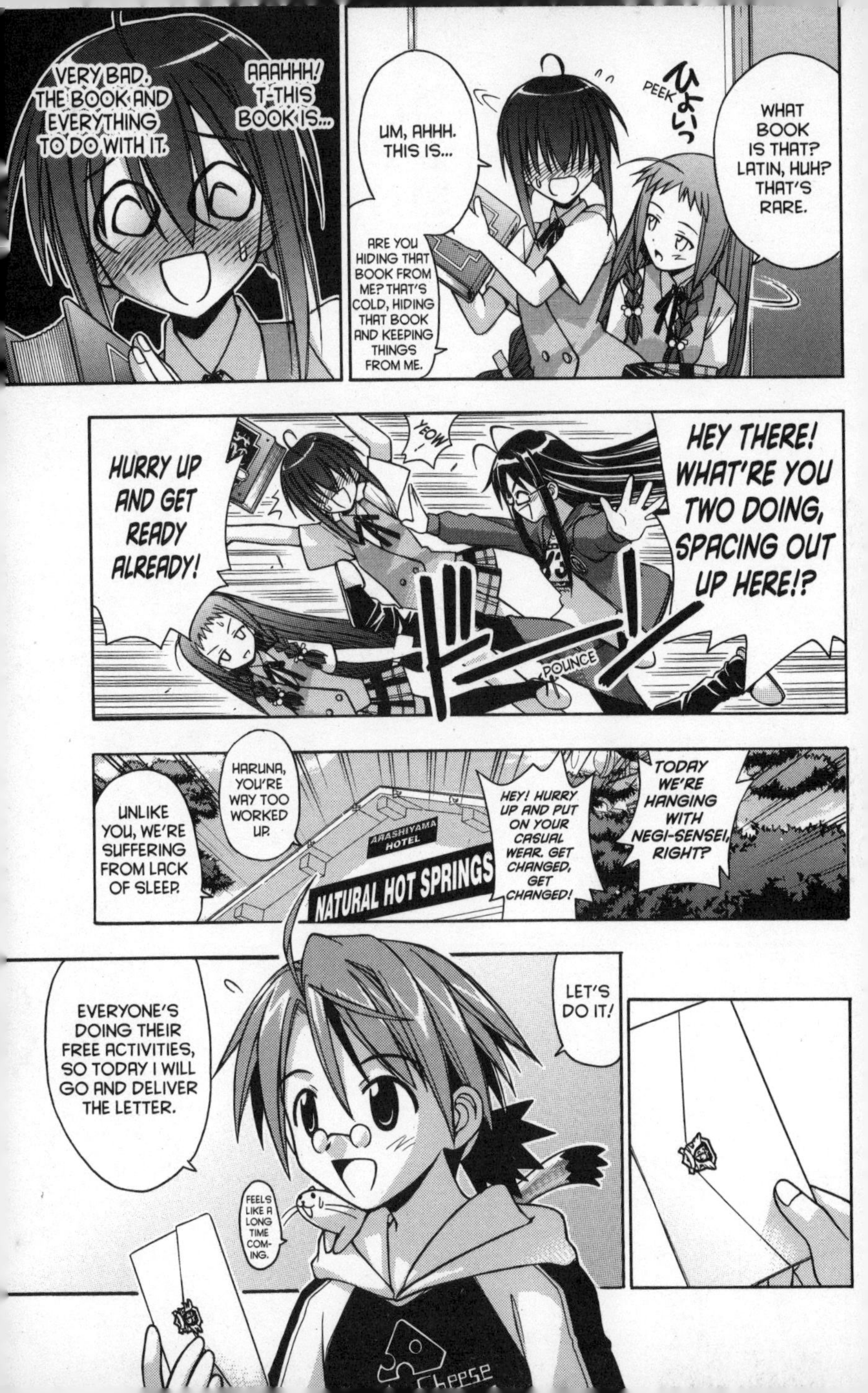

WHAT BOOK IS THAT? LATIN, HUH? THAT'S RARE.
ひょいっ
PEEK
UM, AHHH. THIS IS...
ARE YOU HIDING THAT BOOK FROM ME? THAT'S COLD, HIDING THAT BOOK AND KEEPING THINGS FROM ME.
AAAHHH! T-THIS BOOK IS...
VERY BAD. THE BOOK AND EVERYTHING TO DO WITH IT.
HEY THERE! WHAT'RE YOU TWO DOING, SPACING OUT UP HERE!?
YEOW
HURRY UP AND GET READY ALREADY!
POUNCE
TODAY WE'RE HANGING WITH NEGI-SENSEI, RIGHT?
HEY! HURRY UP AND PUT ON YOUR CASUAL WEAR. GET CHANGED, GET CHANGED!
ARASHIYAMA HOTEL
NATURAL HOT SPRINGS
HARUNA, YOU'RE WAY TOO WORKED UP.
UNLIKE YOU, WE'RE SUFFERING FROM LACK OF SLEEP.
LET'S DO IT!
EVERYONE'S DOING THEIR FREE ACTIVITIES, SO TODAY I WILL GO AND DELIVER THE LETTER.
FEELS LIKE A LONG TIME COMING.
Cheese

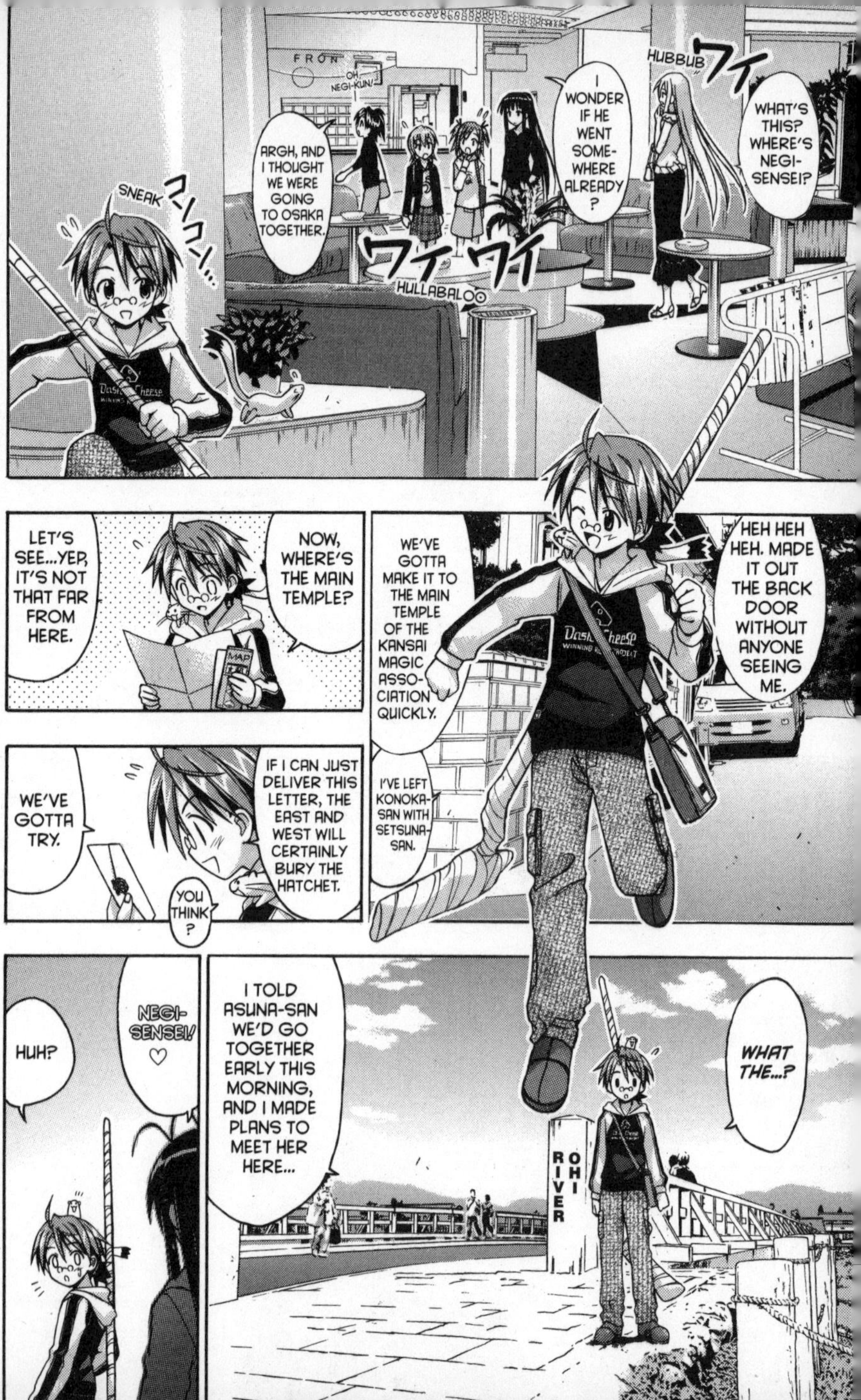

HUBBUB ワイ
WHAT'S THIS? WHERE'S NEGI-SENSEI?
I WONDER IF HE WENT SOMEWHERE ALREADY?
OH, NEGI-KUN!
ARGH, AND I THOUGHT WE WERE GOING TO OSAKA TOGETHER.
ワイワイ
HULLABALOO
SNEAK コソコソ...
HEH HEH HEH. MADE IT OUT THE BACK DOOR WITHOUT ANYONE SEEING ME.
WE'VE GOTTA MAKE IT TO THE MAIN TEMPLE OF THE KANSAI MAGIC ASSOCIATION QUICKLY.
I'VE LEFT KONOKA-SAN WITH SETSUNA-SAN.
NOW, WHERE'S THE MAIN TEMPLE?
LET'S SEE...YEP, IT'S NOT THAT FAR FROM HERE.
MAP
IF I CAN JUST DELIVER THIS LETTER, THE EAST AND WEST WILL CERTAINLY BURY THE HATCHET.
WE'VE GOTTA TRY.
YOU THINK?
WHAT THE...?
OHI RIVER
I TOLD ASUNA-SAN WE'D GO TOGETHER EARLY THIS MORNING, AND I MADE PLANS TO MEET HER HERE...
NEGI-SENSEI! ♡
HUH?

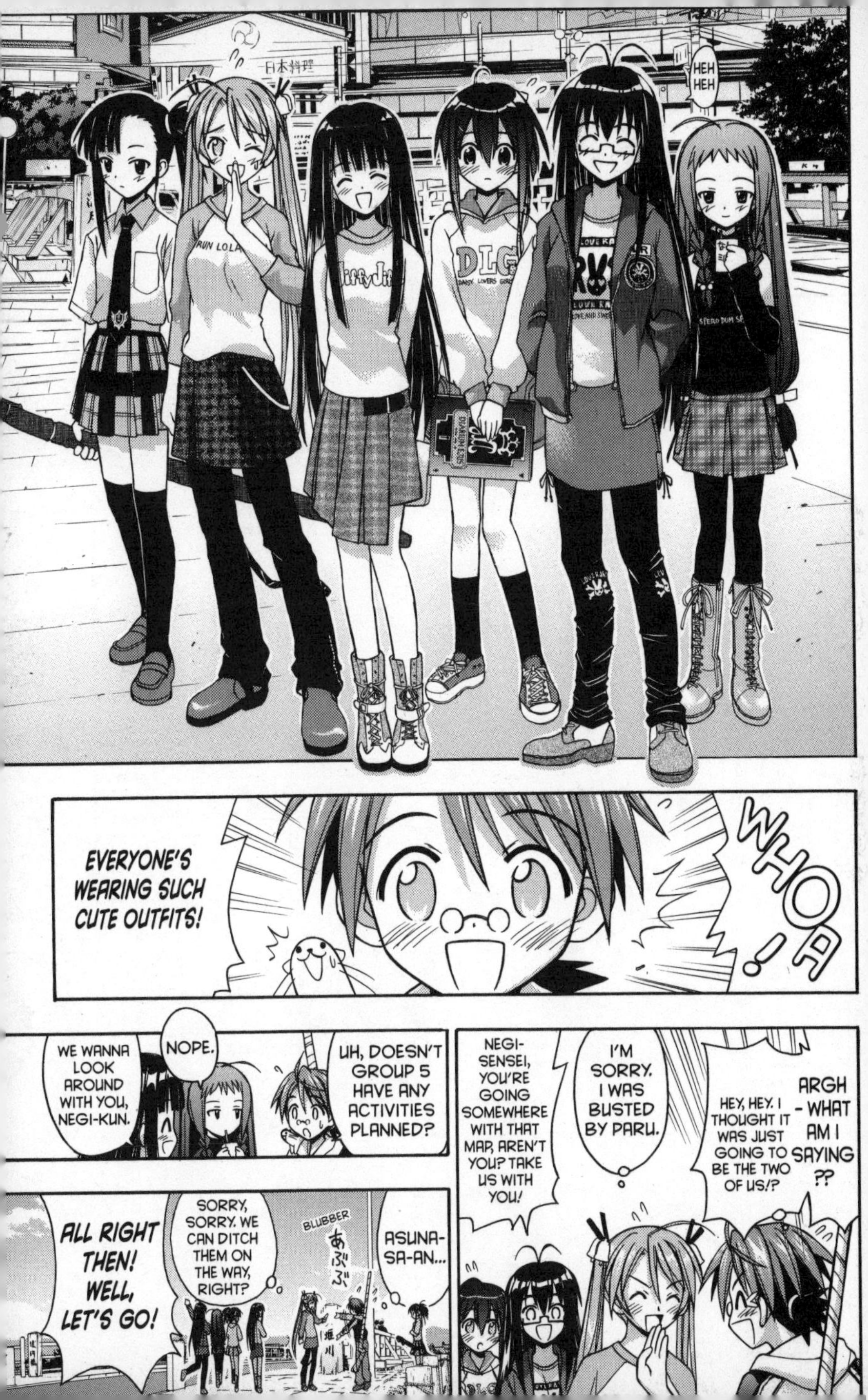
日本料理
HEH HEH
RUN LOLA
DLG
DAISY LOVERS GIRLS
WHOA!
EVERYONE'S WEARING SUCH CUTE OUTFITS!
ARGH - WHAT AM I SAYING ??
HEY, HEY. I THOUGHT IT WAS JUST GOING TO BE THE TWO OF US!?
I'M SORRY. I WAS BUSTED BY PARU.
NEGI-SENSEI, YOU'RE GOING SOMEWHERE WITH THAT MAP, AREN'T YOU? TAKE US WITH YOU!
UH, DOESN'T GROUP 5 HAVE ANY ACTIVITIES PLANNED?
NOPE.
WE WANNA LOOK AROUND WITH YOU, NEGI-KUN.
ASUNA-SA-AN...
BLUBBER
あぶぶ
SORRY, SORRY. WE CAN DITCH THEM ON THE WAY, RIGHT?
ALL RIGHT THEN! WELL, LET'S GO!

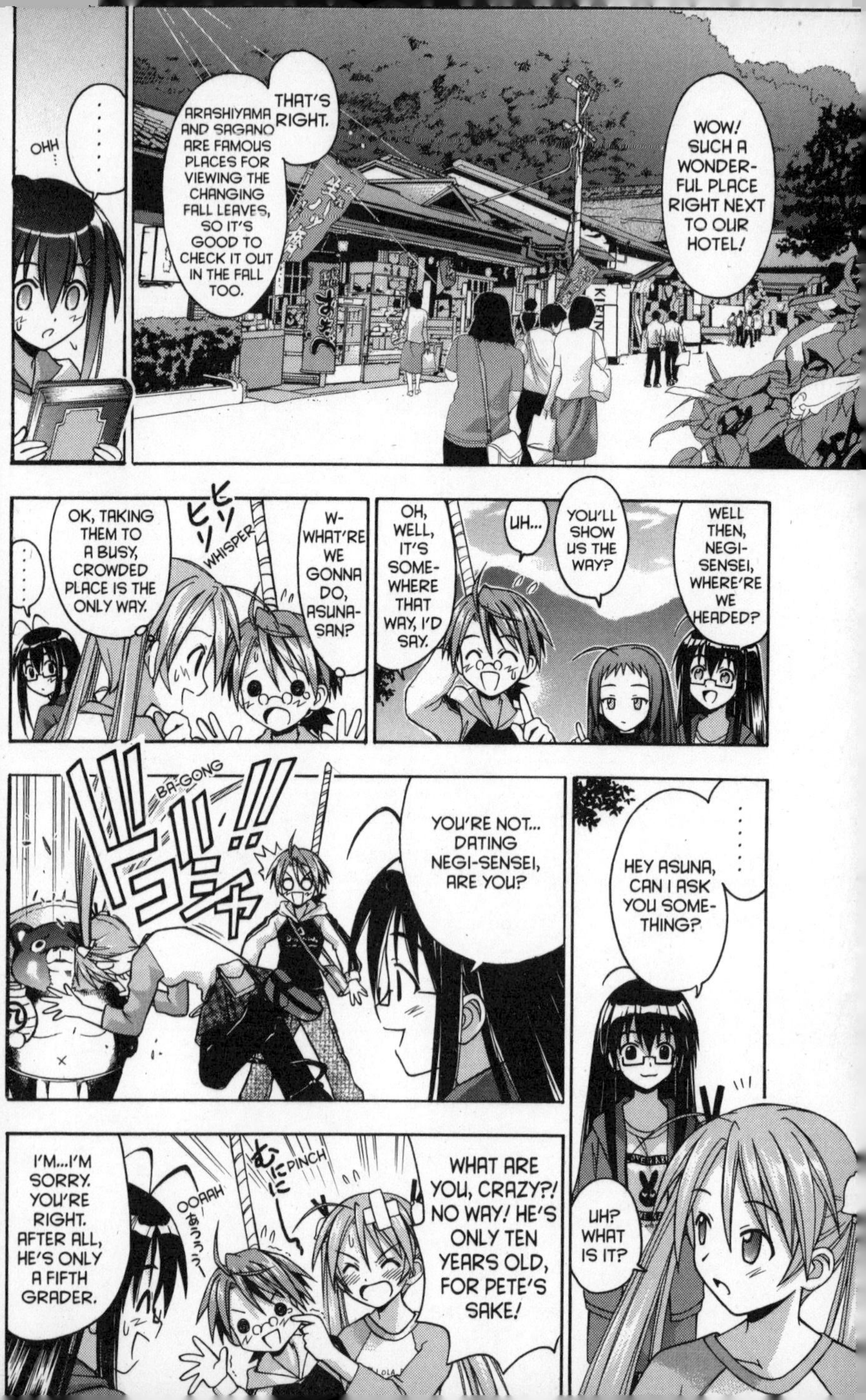
WOW! SUCH A WONDER-FUL PLACE RIGHT NEXT TO OUR HOTEL!
THAT'S RIGHT.
ARASHIYAMA AND SAGANO ARE FAMOUS PLACES FOR VIEWING THE CHANGING FALL LEAVES, SO IT'S GOOD TO CHECK IT OUT IN THE FALL TOO.
......
OHH...
WELL THEN, NEGI-SENSEI, WHERE'RE WE HEADED?
YOU'LL SHOW US THE WAY?
UH...
OH, WELL, IT'S SOME-WHERE THAT WAY, I'D SAY.
W-WHAT'RE WE GONNA DO, ASUNA-SAN?
ヒソ ヒソ
WHISPER
OK, TAKING THEM TO A BUSY, CROWDED PLACE IS THE ONLY WAY.
......
......
HEY ASUNA, CAN I ASK YOU SOME-THING?
UH? WHAT IS IT?
YOU'RE NOT... DATING NEGI-SENSEI, ARE YOU?
BA-GONG
WHAT ARE YOU, CRAZY?! NO WAY! HE'S ONLY TEN YEARS OLD, FOR PETE'S SAKE!
PINCH
OOAAH
I'M...I'M SORRY. YOU'RE RIGHT. AFTER ALL, HE'S ONLY A FIFTH GRADER.

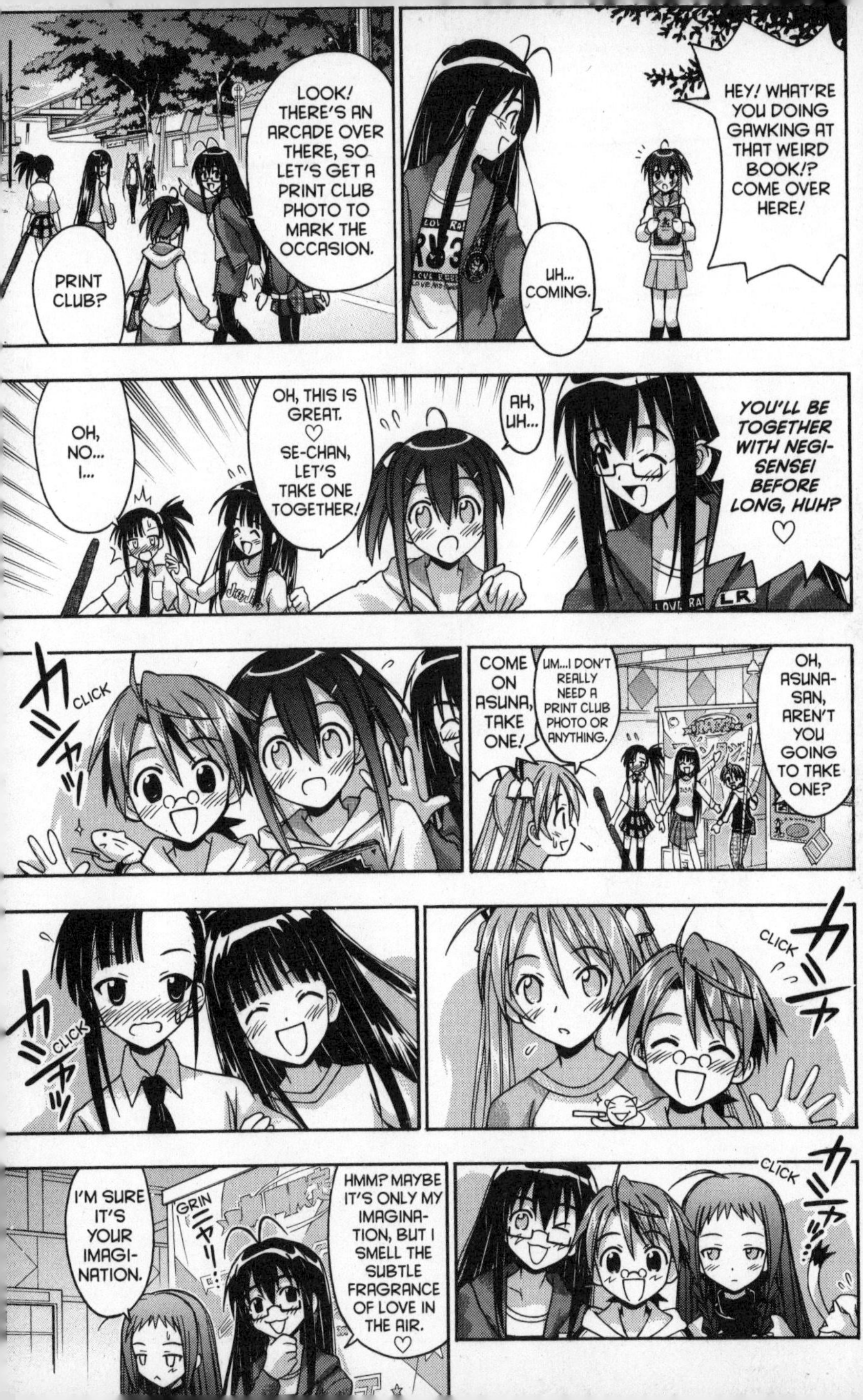
HEY! WHAT'RE YOU DOING GAWKING AT THAT WEIRD BOOK!? COME OVER HERE!
UH... COMING.
LOOK! THERE'S AN ARCADE OVER THERE, SO LET'S GET A PRINT CLUB PHOTO TO MARK THE OCCASION.
PRINT CLUB?
YOU'LL BE TOGETHER WITH NEGI-SENSEI BEFORE LONG, HUH? ♡
AH, UH...
OH, THIS IS GREAT. ♡ SE-CHAN, LET'S TAKE ONE TOGETHER!
OH, NO... I...
OH, ASUNA-SAN, AREN'T YOU GOING TO TAKE ONE?
UM...I DON'T REALLY NEED A PRINT CLUB PHOTO OR ANYTHING.
COME ON ASUNA, TAKE ONE!
CLICK
CLICK
CLICK
CLICK
HMM? MAYBE IT'S ONLY MY IMAGINATION, BUT I SMELL THE SUBTLE FRAGRANCE OF LOVE IN THE AIR. ♡
GRIN
I'M SURE IT'S YOUR IMAGINATION.

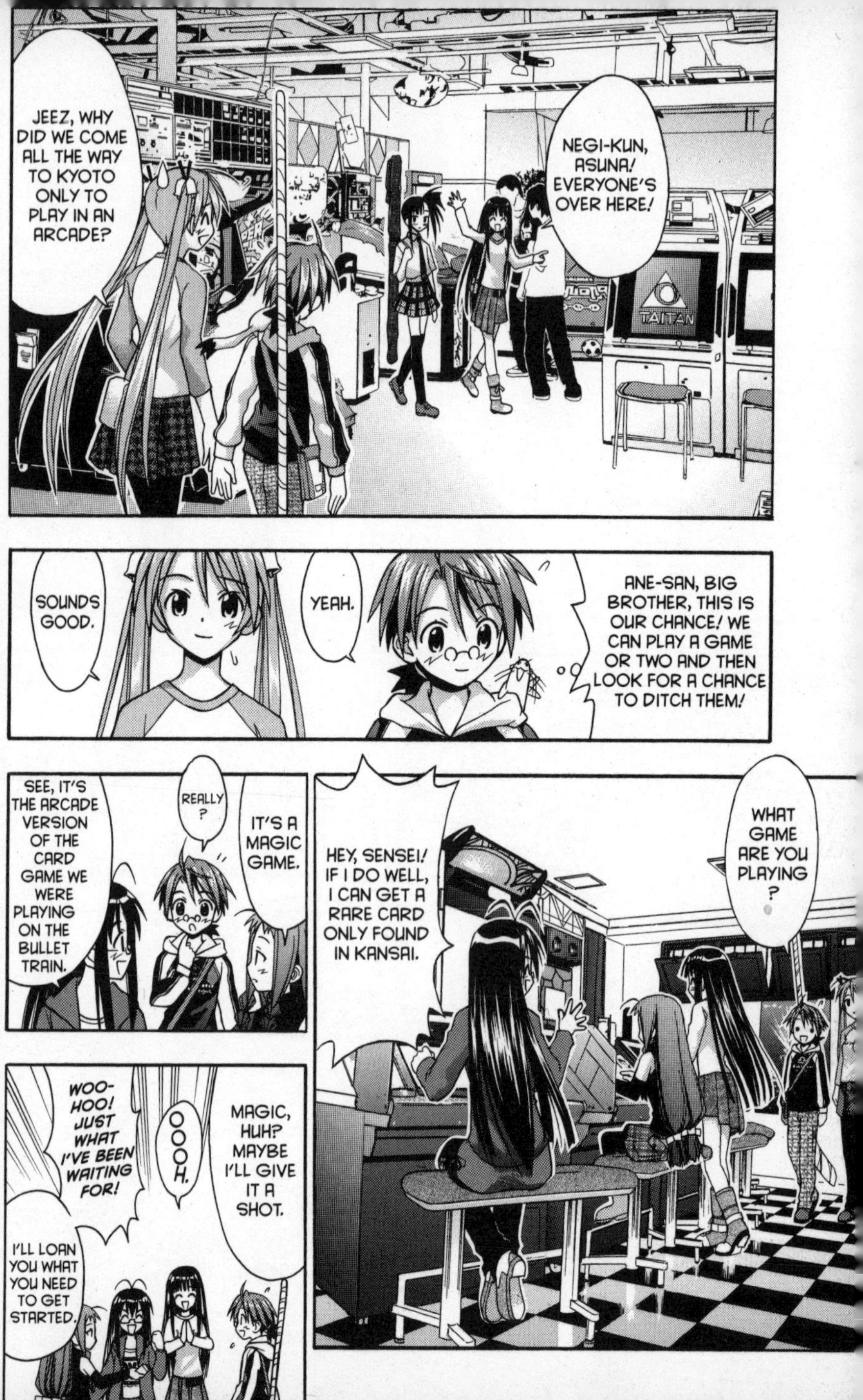
NEGI-KUN, ASUNA! EVERYONE'S OVER HERE!
JEEZ, WHY DID WE COME ALL THE WAY TO KYOTO ONLY TO PLAY IN AN ARCADE?
TAITAN
ANE-SAN, BIG BROTHER, THIS IS OUR CHANCE! WE CAN PLAY A GAME OR TWO AND THEN LOOK FOR A CHANCE TO DITCH THEM!
YEAH.
SOUNDS GOOD.
WHAT GAME ARE YOU PLAYING?
HEY, SENSEI! IF I DO WELL, I CAN GET A RARE CARD ONLY FOUND IN KANSAI.
IT'S A MAGIC GAME.
REALLY?
SEE, IT'S THE ARCADE VERSION OF THE CARD GAME WE WERE PLAYING ON THE BULLET TRAIN.
MAGIC, HUH? MAYBE I'LL GIVE IT A SHOT.
OOOH.
WOO-HOO! JUST WHAT I'VE BEEN WAITING FOR!
I'LL LOAN YOU WHAT YOU NEED TO GET STARTED.

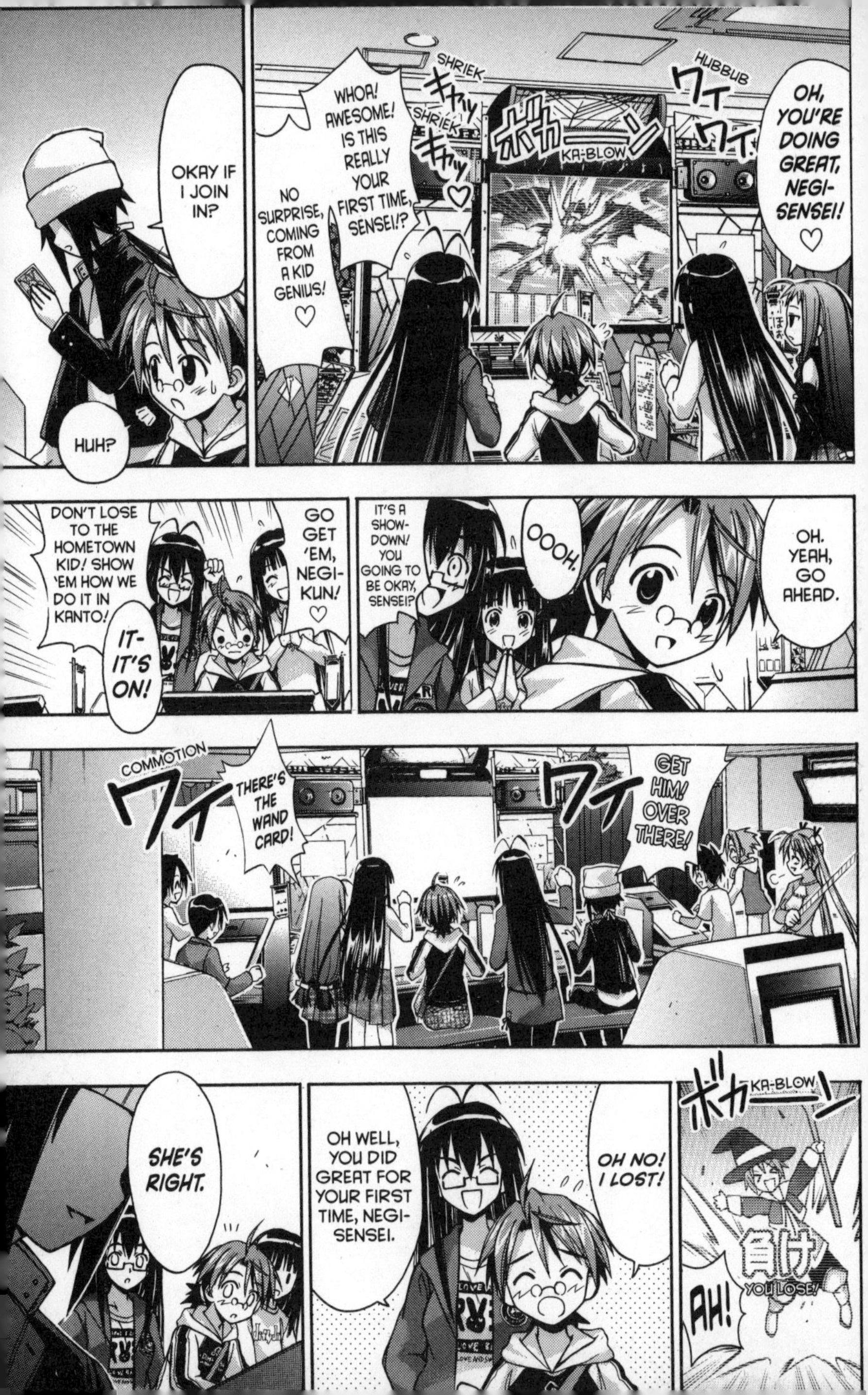
HUBBUB ワイ ワイ
OH, YOU'RE DOING GREAT, NEGI-SENSEI! ♡
KA-BLOW ボカーン
SHRIEK キャッ SHRIEK キャッ ♡
WHOA! AWESOME! IS THIS REALLY YOUR FIRST TIME, SENSEI!?
NO SURPRISE, COMING FROM A KID GENIUS! ♡
OKAY IF I JOIN IN?
HUH?
OH. YEAH, GO AHEAD.
OOOH.
IT'S A SHOWDOWN! YOU GOING TO BE OKAY, SENSEI!?
GO GET 'EM, NEGI-KUN! ♡
DON'T LOSE TO THE HOMETOWN KID! SHOW 'EM HOW WE DO IT IN KANTO!
IT-IT'S ON!
GET HIM! OVER THERE!
ワイ
THERE'S THE WAND CARD!
COMMOTION ワイ
KA-BLOW ボカーン
負け YOU LOSE!
AH!
OH NO! I LOST!
OH WELL, YOU DID GREAT FOR YOUR FIRST TIME, NEGI-SENSEI.
SHE'S RIGHT.

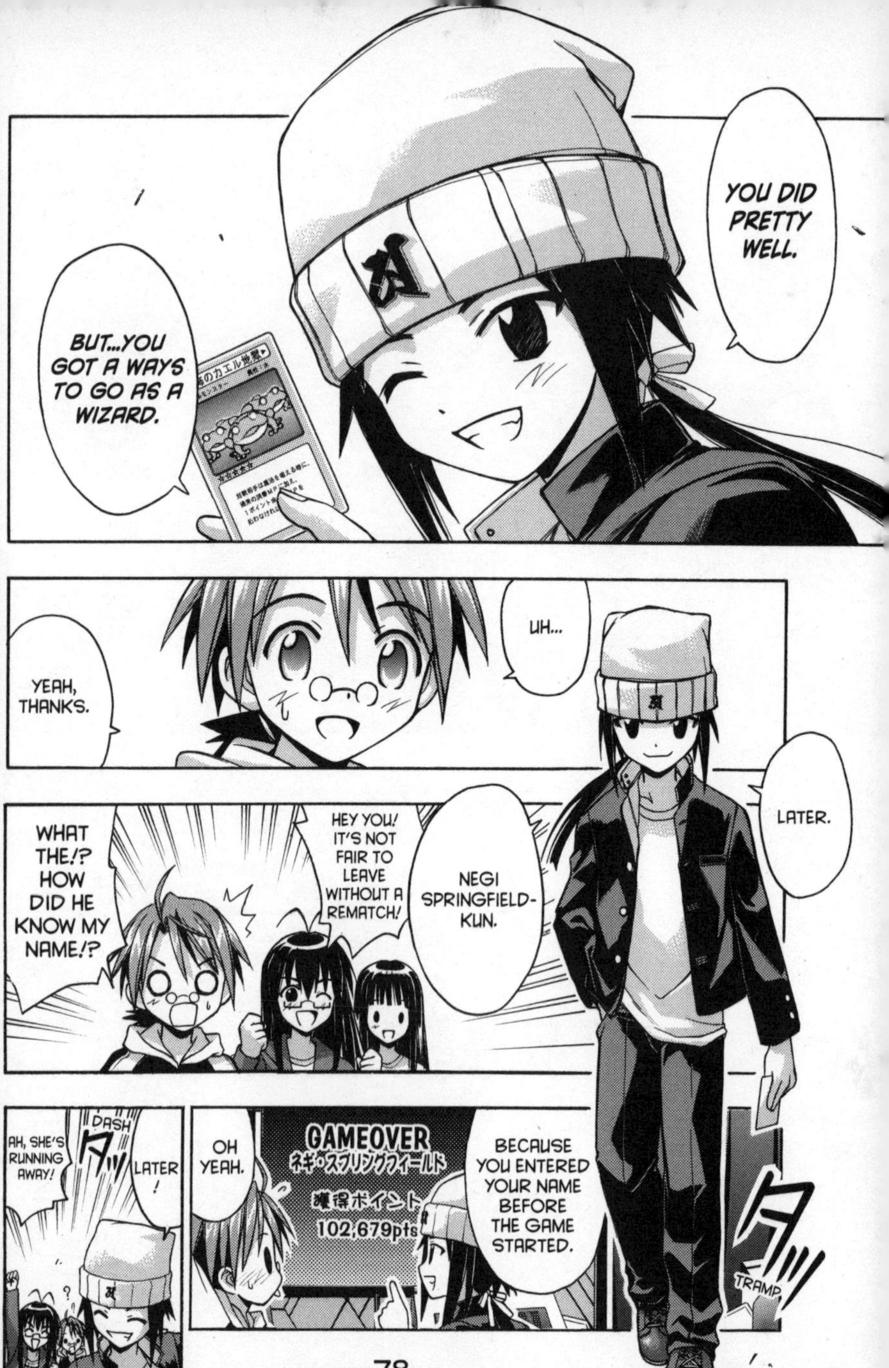
YOU DID PRETTY WELL.
BUT...YOU GOT A WAYS TO GO AS A WIZARD.
UH...
YEAH, THANKS.
LATER.
NEGI SPRINGFIELD-KUN.
HEY YOU! IT'S NOT FAIR TO LEAVE WITHOUT A REMATCH!
WHAT THE!? HOW DID HE KNOW MY NAME!?
TRAMP
BECAUSE YOU ENTERED YOUR NAME BEFORE THE GAME STARTED.
GAMEOVER
ネギ・スプリングフィールド
獲得ポイント
102,679pts
OH YEAH.
LATER!
DASH
AH, SHE'S RUNNING AWAY!

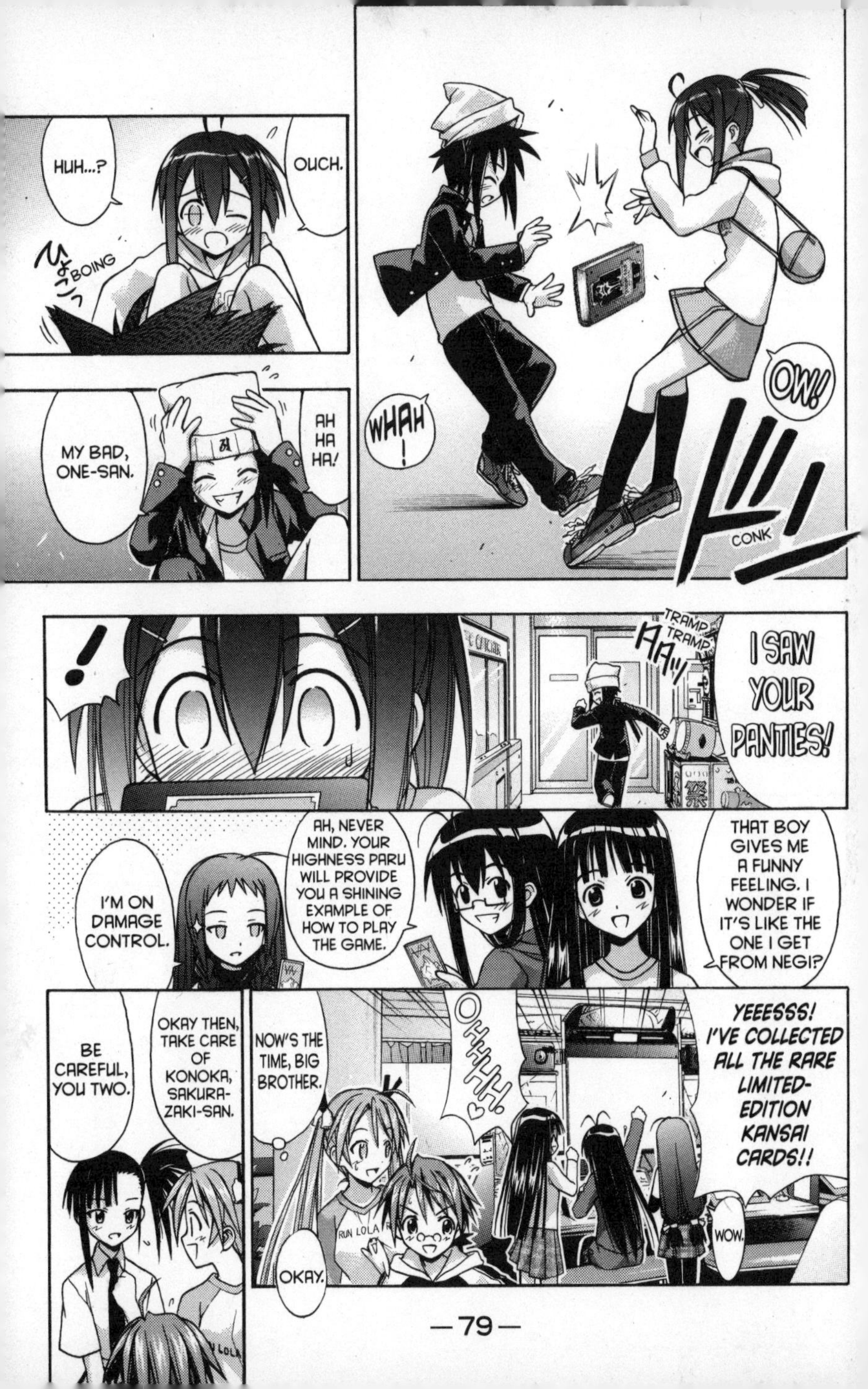
OW!!
WHAH!
CONK
OUCH.
HUH...?
BOING
AH HA HA!
MY BAD, ONE-SAN.
I SAW YOUR PANTIES!
TRAMP TRAMP
!
THAT BOY GIVES ME A FUNNY FEELING. I WONDER IF IT'S LIKE THE ONE I GET FROM NEGI?
AH, NEVER MIND. YOUR HIGHNESS PARU WILL PROVIDE YOU A SHINING EXAMPLE OF HOW TO PLAY THE GAME.
I'M ON DAMAGE CONTROL.
YEEESSS! I'VE COLLECTED ALL THE RARE LIMITED-EDITION KANSAI CARDS!!
OHHHH.
NOW'S THE TIME, BIG BROTHER.
WOW.
OKAY.
OKAY THEN, TAKE CARE OF KONOKA, SAKURAZAKI-SAN.
BE CAREFUL, YOU TWO.

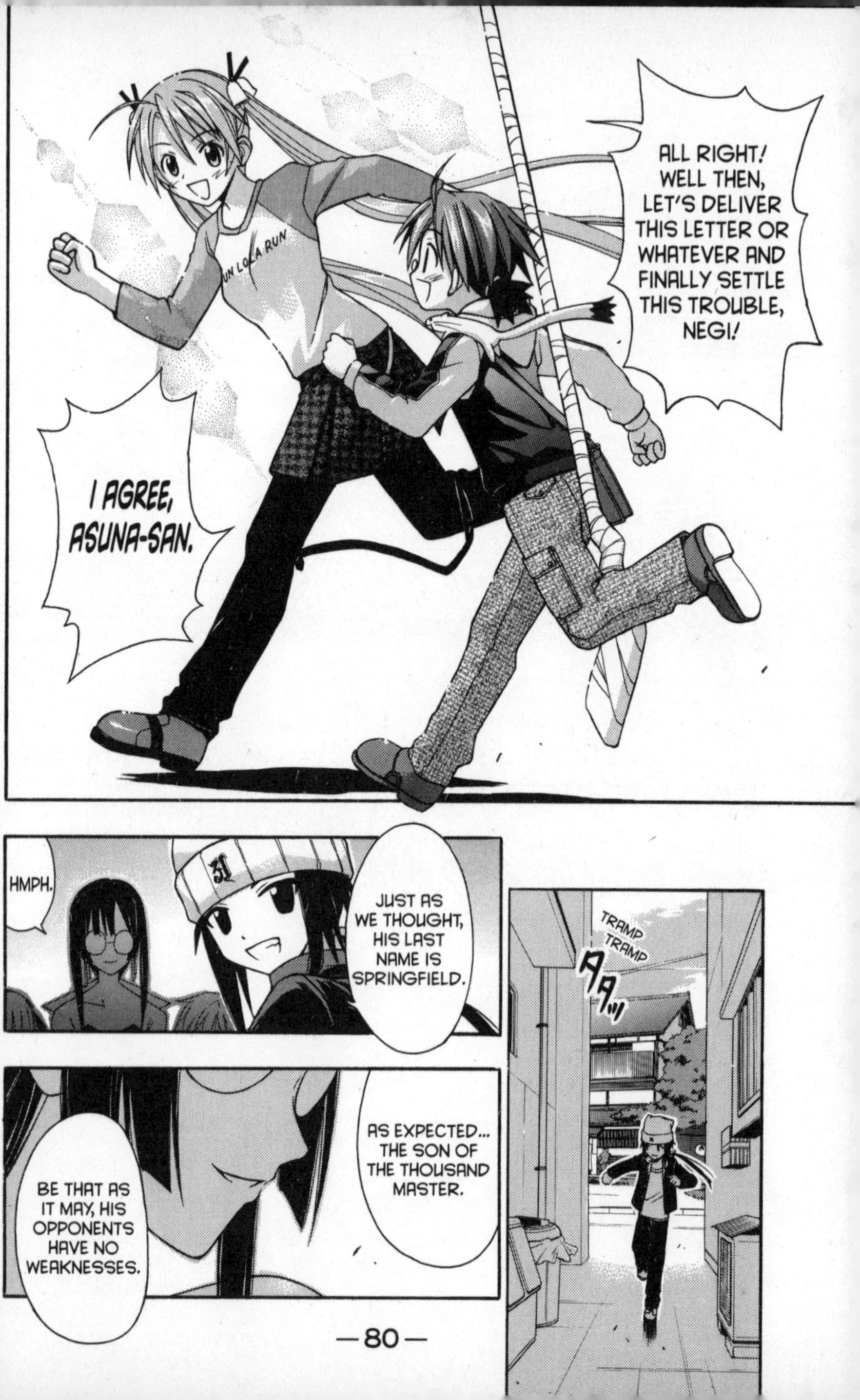
ALL RIGHT! WELL THEN, LET'S DELIVER THIS LETTER OR WHATEVER AND FINALLY SETTLE THIS TROUBLE, NEGI!
UN LOLA RUN
I AGREE, ASUNA-SAN.
TRAMP TRAMP
タタッ
JUST AS WE THOUGHT, HIS LAST NAME IS SPRINGFIELD.
HMPH.
AS EXPECTED... THE SON OF THE THOUSAND MASTER.
BE THAT AS IT MAY, HIS OPPONENTS HAVE NO WEAKNESSES.

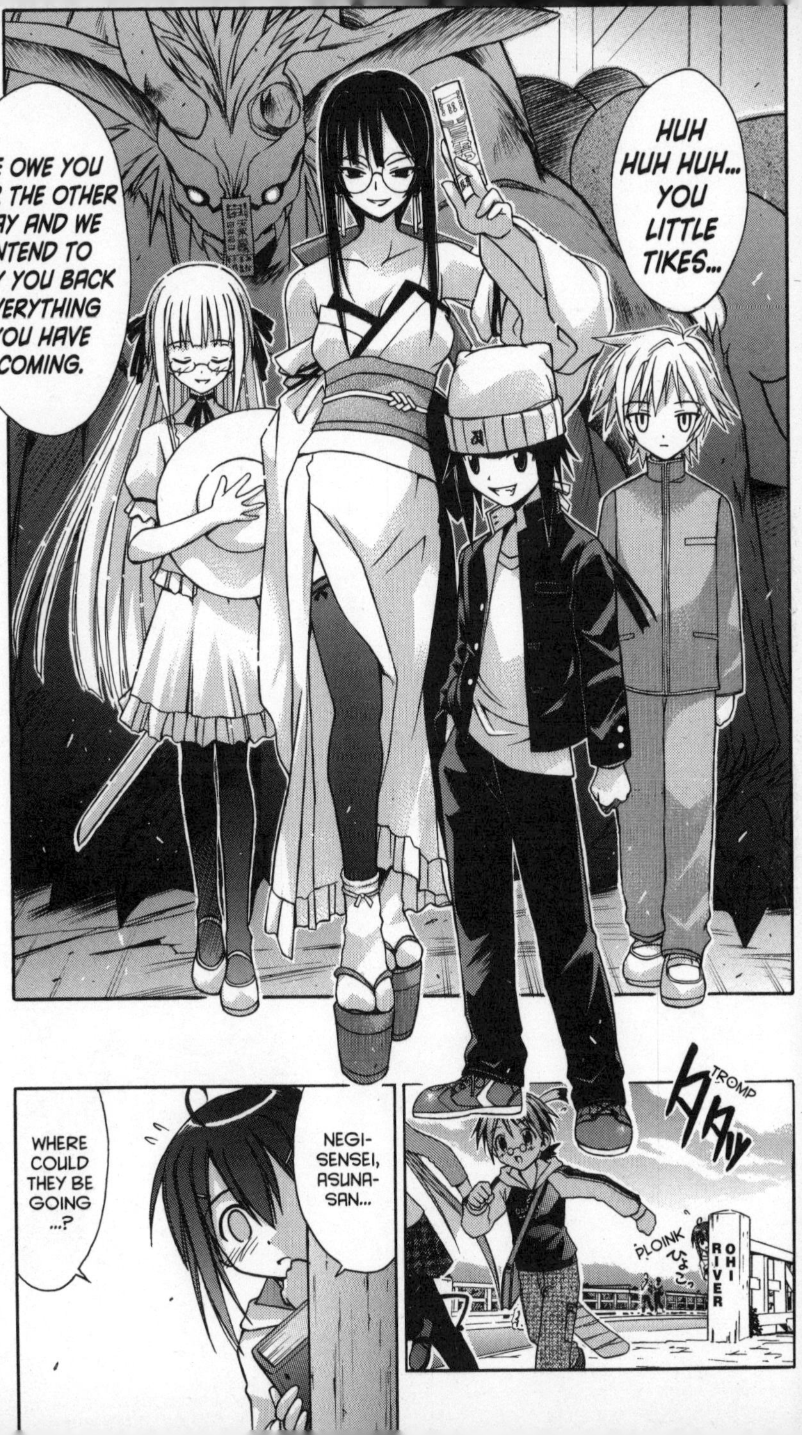
HUH HUH HUH... YOU LITTLE TIKES...
WE OWE YOU FOR THE OTHER DAY AND WE INTEND TO PAY YOU BACK EVERYTHING YOU HAVE COMING.
TROMP
PLOINK
ひょこっ
OHI RIVER
NEGI-SENSEI, ASUNA-SAN...
WHERE COULD THEY BE GOING ...?

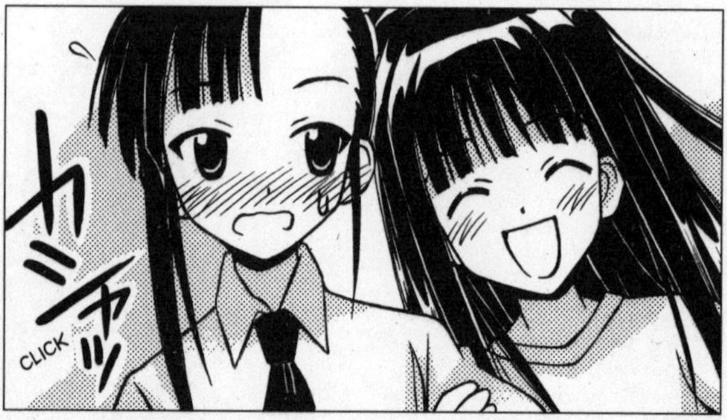
カシャッ
CLICK

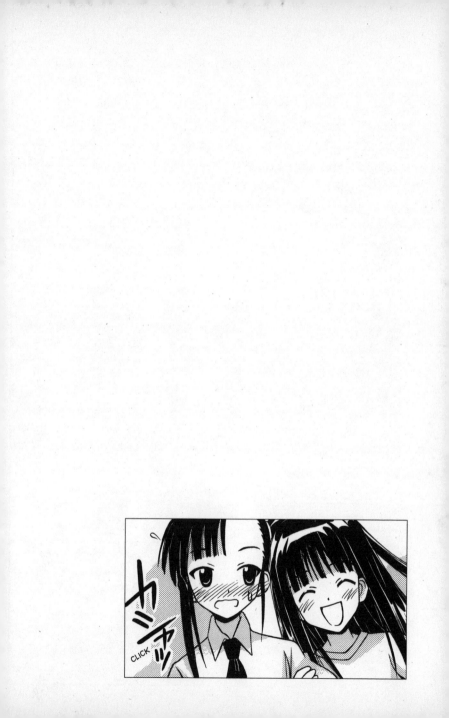

SHRIEK
SHRIEK

RUCKUS

THE MOST IMPORTANT THING IS TO LET HER LIVE IN PEACE LIKE SHE IS NOW.

OF COURSE, KONOKA-OJOU-SAMA KNOWS NOTHING OF HER DANGER...

SINCE SHE'S COME TO MAHORA ACADEMY, SHE'S MADE A LOT OF FRIENDS AND BECOME A LOT CHEERIER.

SHE LOOKS HAPPY...

WHEN WE GET BACK TO THE ACADEMY, NO MATTER WHAT HAPPENS, I MUST PROTECT HER SECRETLY FROM THE SHADOWS.

WE'VE BECOME A LITTLE TOO CLOSE ON THIS SCHOOL FIELD TRIP.

OM.

BUT I CAN'T HELP WORRYING.

IN THE MEANTIME, I THINK THOSE TWO WILL BE ALL RIGHT.

XXVII

Charta Ministralis

Cyaneum
tonus

mIjAZACI
NODOCA
PUDICA BIBLIOTHECARIA

virtus
audacia
directio
occidens

astralitas
Mercurius

II-XX

NEGIMA!
MAGISTER NEGI MAGI

THIRTY-NINTH PERIOD:
THE DAZZLING WHIRLING LOOP SURVIVAL

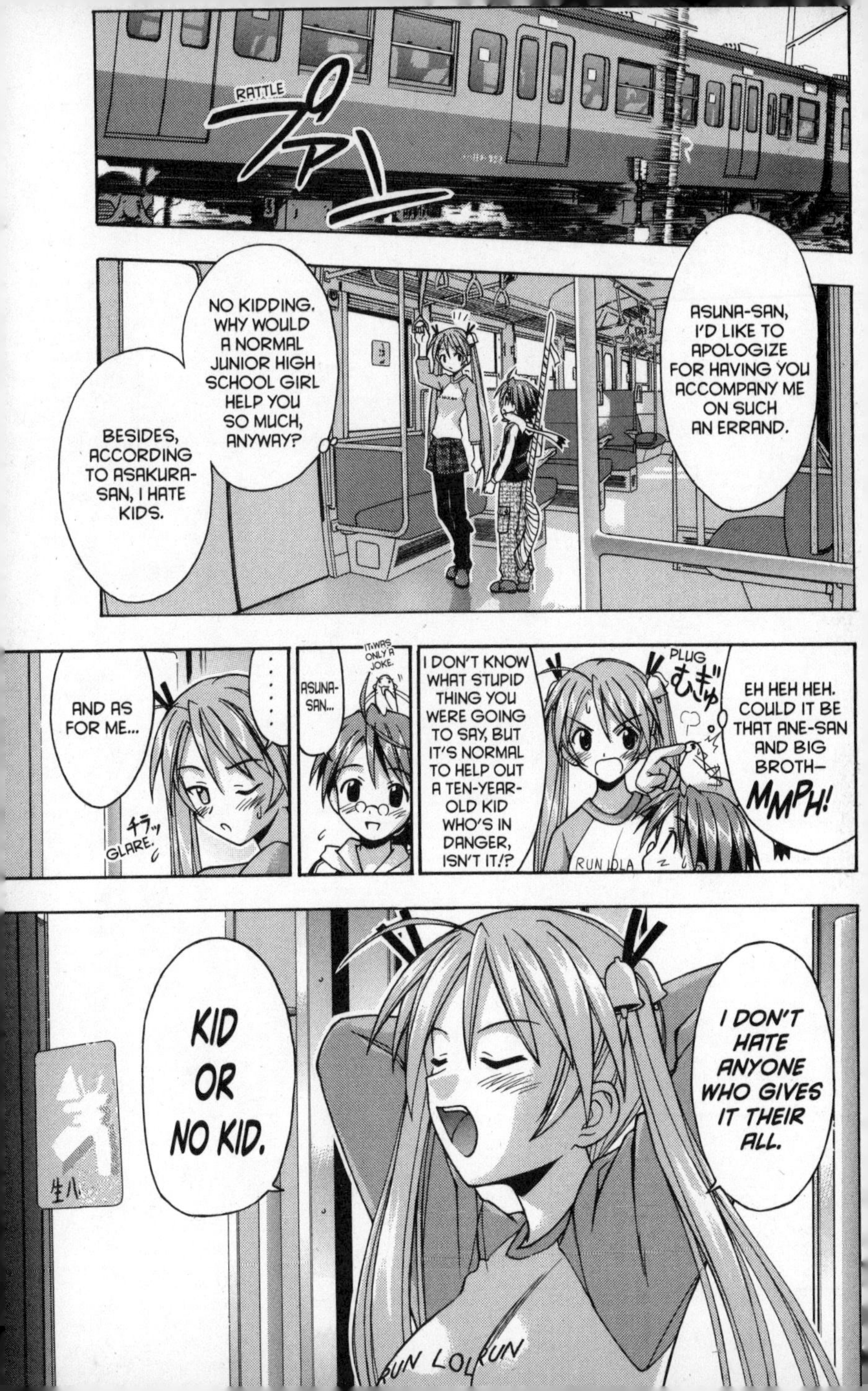
RATTLE
ASUNA-SAN, I'D LIKE TO APOLOGIZE FOR HAVING YOU ACCOMPANY ME ON SUCH AN ERRAND.
NO KIDDING. WHY WOULD A NORMAL JUNIOR HIGH SCHOOL GIRL HELP YOU SO MUCH, ANYWAY?
BESIDES, ACCORDING TO ASAKURA-SAN, I HATE KIDS.
EH HEH HEH. COULD IT BE THAT ANE-SAN AND BIG BROTH—MMPH!
PLUG
I DON'T KNOW WHAT STUPID THING YOU WERE GOING TO SAY, BUT IT'S NORMAL TO HELP OUT A TEN-YEAR-OLD KID WHO'S IN DANGER, ISN'T IT!?
IT WAS ONLY A JOKE.
ASUNA-SAN...
......
AND AS FOR ME...
GLARE
I DON'T HATE ANYONE WHO GIVES IT THEIR ALL.
KID OR NO KID.

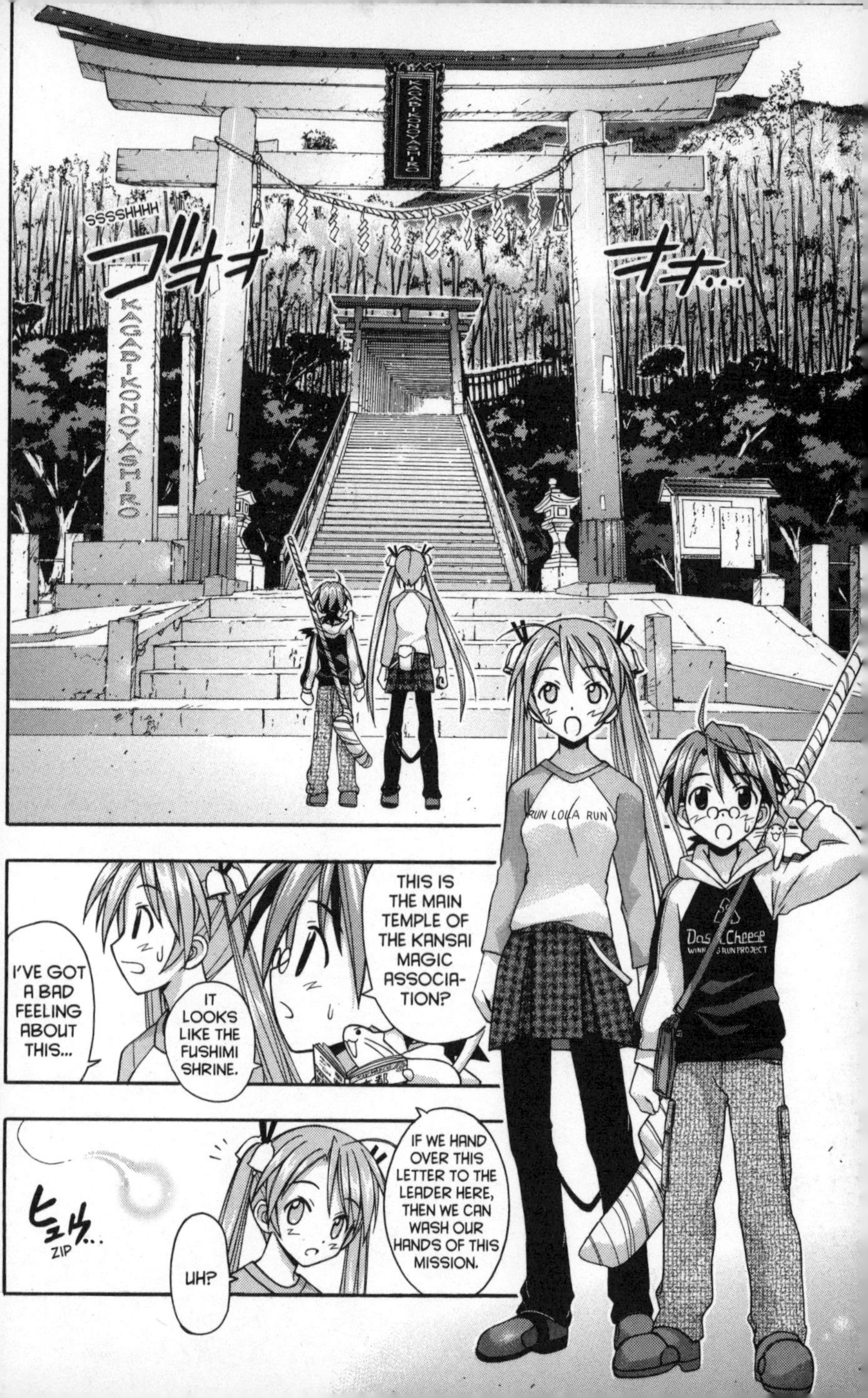
SSSSHHHH
RUN LOLA RUN
THIS IS THE MAIN TEMPLE OF THE KANSAI MAGIC ASSOCIATION?
IT LOOKS LIKE THE FUSHIMI SHRINE.
I'VE GOT A BAD FEELING ABOUT THIS...
IF WE HAND OVER THIS LETTER TO THE LEADER HERE, THEN WE CAN WASH OUR HANDS OF THIS MISSION.
UH?
ZIP

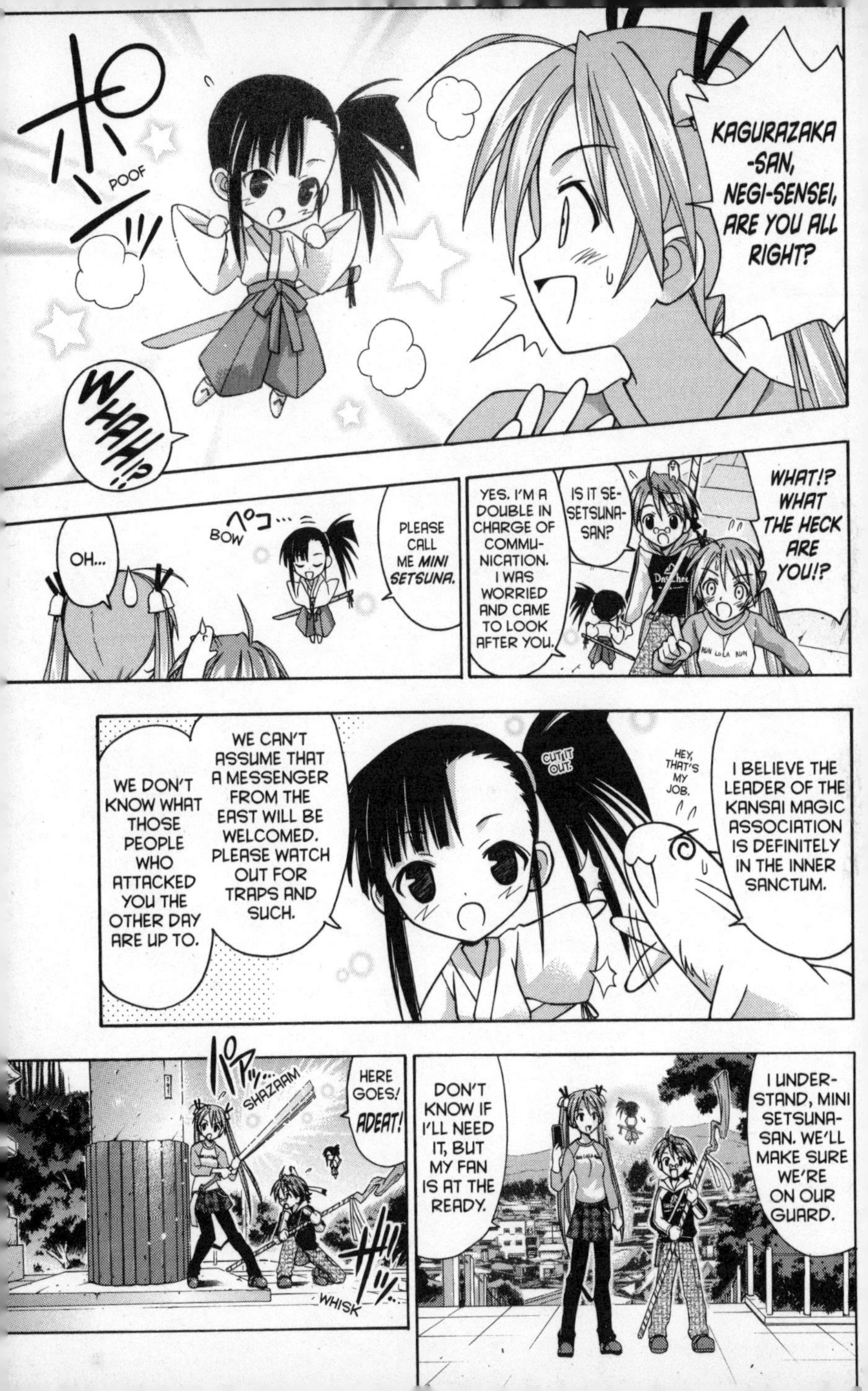
KAGURAZAKA-SAN, NEGI-SENSEI, ARE YOU ALL RIGHT?
POOF
WHAH!?
WHAT!? WHAT THE HECK ARE YOU!?
IS IT SE-SETSUNA-SAN?
YES. I'M A DOUBLE IN CHARGE OF COMMUNICATION. I WAS WORRIED AND CAME TO LOOK AFTER YOU.
PLEASE CALL ME *MINI SETSUNA.*
BOW
OH...
I BELIEVE THE LEADER OF THE KANSAI MAGIC ASSOCIATION IS DEFINITELY IN THE INNER SANCTUM.
HEY, THAT'S MY JOB.
CUT IT OUT.
WE CAN'T ASSUME THAT A MESSENGER FROM THE EAST WILL BE WELCOMED. PLEASE WATCH OUT FOR TRAPS AND SUCH.
WE DON'T KNOW WHAT THOSE PEOPLE WHO ATTACKED YOU THE OTHER DAY ARE UP TO.
I UNDERSTAND, MINI SETSUNA-SAN. WE'LL MAKE SURE WE'RE ON OUR GUARD.
DON'T KNOW IF I'LL NEED IT, BUT MY FAN IS AT THE READY.
HERE GOES! ADEAT!
SHAZAAM
WHISK

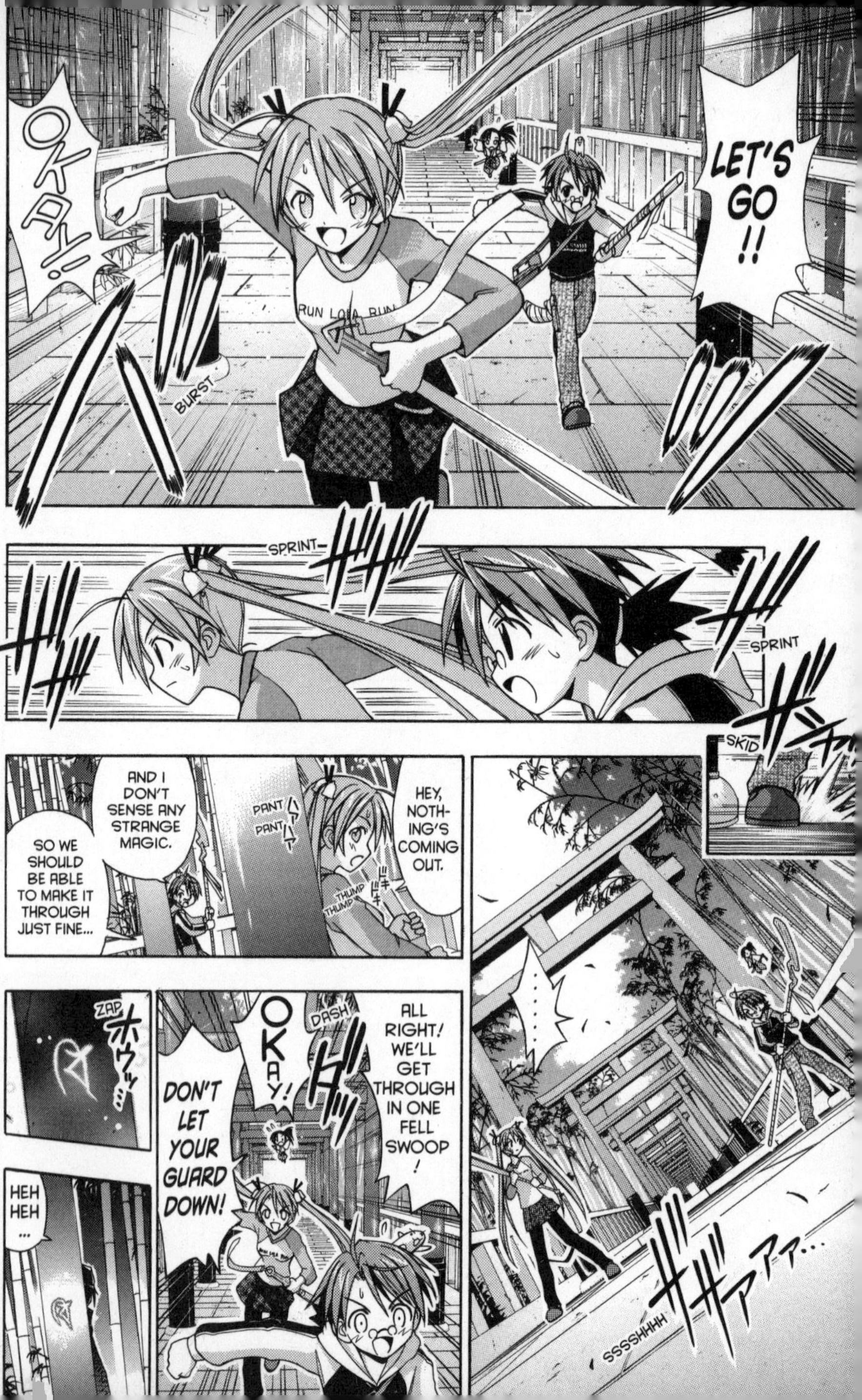
LET'S GO!!
OKAY!
BURST
SPRINT
SPRINT
SKID
...
SSSSHHHH
HEY, NOTHING'S COMING OUT.
PANT PANT
THUMP THUMP
AND I DON'T SENSE ANY STRANGE MAGIC.
SO WE SHOULD BE ABLE TO MAKE IT THROUGH JUST FINE...
ALL RIGHT! WE'LL GET THROUGH IN ONE FELL SWOOP!
DASH
OKAY!
DON'T LET YOUR GUARD DOWN!
ZAP
HEH HEH...

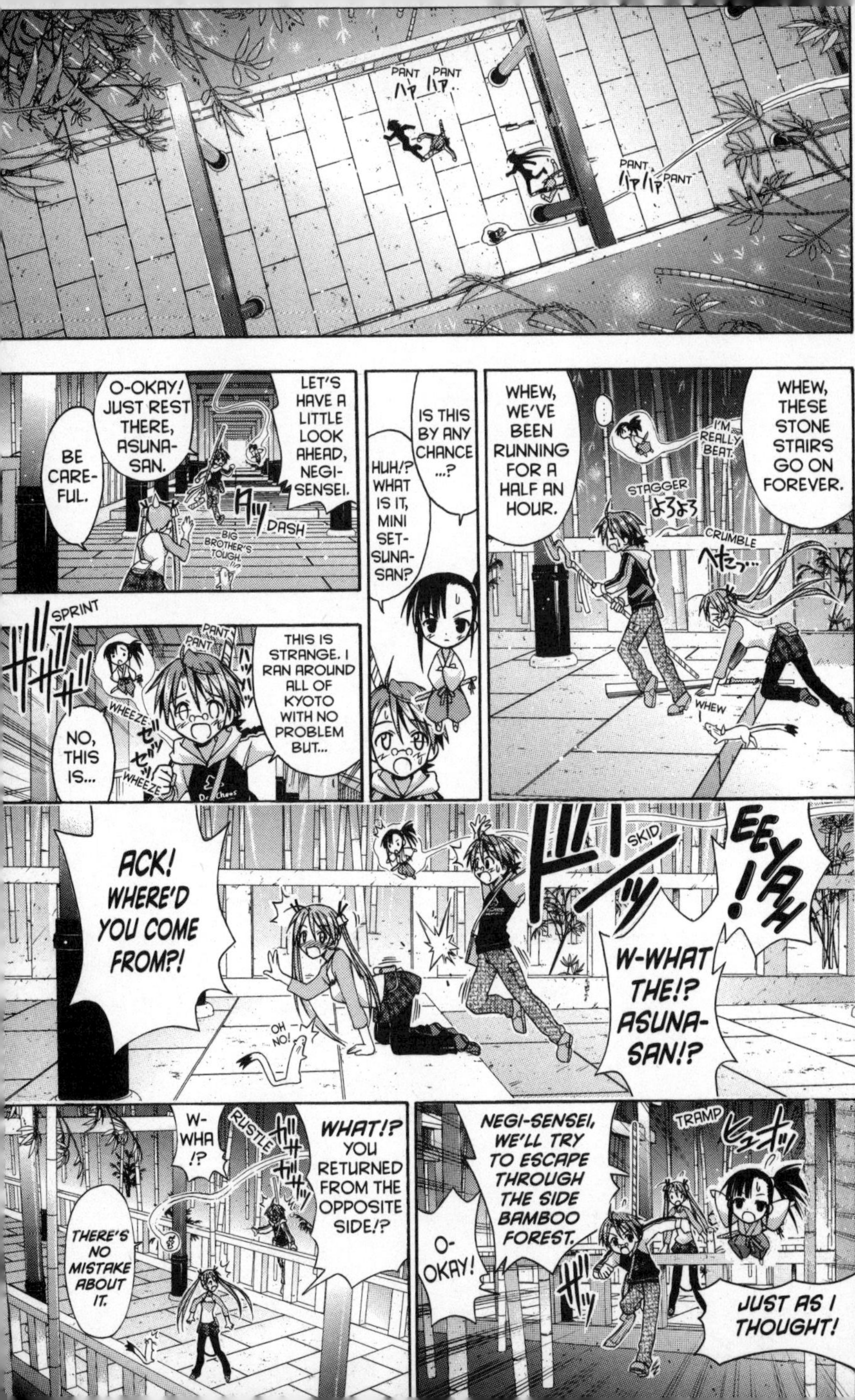
PANT PANT
ハァ ハァ
PANT PANT
ハァハァ
WHEW, THESE STONE STAIRS GO ON FOREVER.
I'M REALLY BEAT.
WHEW, WE'VE BEEN RUNNING FOR A HALF AN HOUR.
...
STAGGER
よろよろ
CRUMBLE
WHEW
IS THIS BY ANY CHANCE ...?
HUH!? WHAT IS IT, MINI SETSUNA-SAN?
LET'S HAVE A LITTLE LOOK AHEAD, NEGI-SENSEI.
O-OKAY! JUST REST THERE, ASUNA-SAN.
BE CARE-FUL.
DASH
BIG BROTHER'S TOUGH.
THIS IS STRANGE. I RAN AROUND ALL OF KYOTO WITH NO PROBLEM BUT...
PANT PANT
SPRINT
WHEEZE
WHEEZE
NO, THIS IS...
EEYAAH!
SKID
W-WHAT THE!? ASUNA-SAN!?
ACK! WHERE'D YOU COME FROM?!
OH NO!
TRAMP
NEGI-SENSEI, WE'LL TRY TO ESCAPE THROUGH THE SIDE BAMBOO FOREST.
JUST AS I THOUGHT!
O-OKAY!
WHAT!? YOU RETURNED FROM THE OPPOSITE SIDE!?
RUSTLE
W-WHA!?
THERE'S NO MISTAKE ABOUT IT.

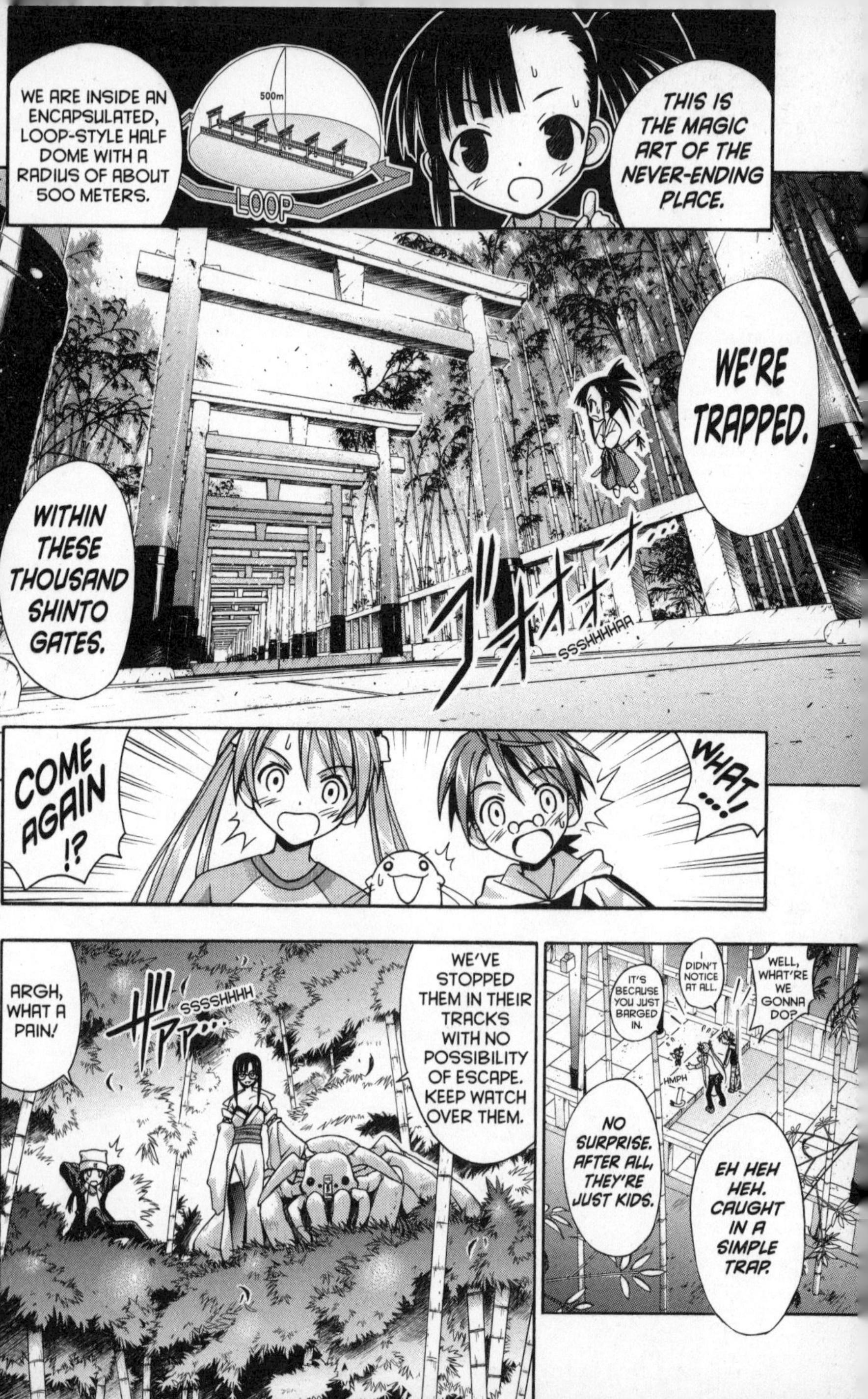
THIS IS THE MAGIC ART OF THE NEVER-ENDING PLACE.
WE ARE INSIDE AN ENCAPSULATED, LOOP-STYLE HALF DOME WITH A RADIUS OF ABOUT 500 METERS.
500m
LOOP
WE'RE TRAPPED.
WITHIN THESE THOUSAND SHINTO GATES.
SSSHHHHAA
WHAT...!
COME AGAIN!?
WELL, WHAT'RE WE GONNA DO?
I DIDN'T NOTICE AT ALL.
IT'S BECAUSE YOU JUST BARGED IN.
HMPH
EH HEH HEH. CAUGHT IN A SIMPLE TRAP.
NO SURPRISE. AFTER ALL, THEY'RE JUST KIDS.
WE'VE STOPPED THEM IN THEIR TRACKS WITH NO POSSIBILITY OF ESCAPE. KEEP WATCH OVER THEM.
SSSSHHHH
ARGH, WHAT A PAIN!

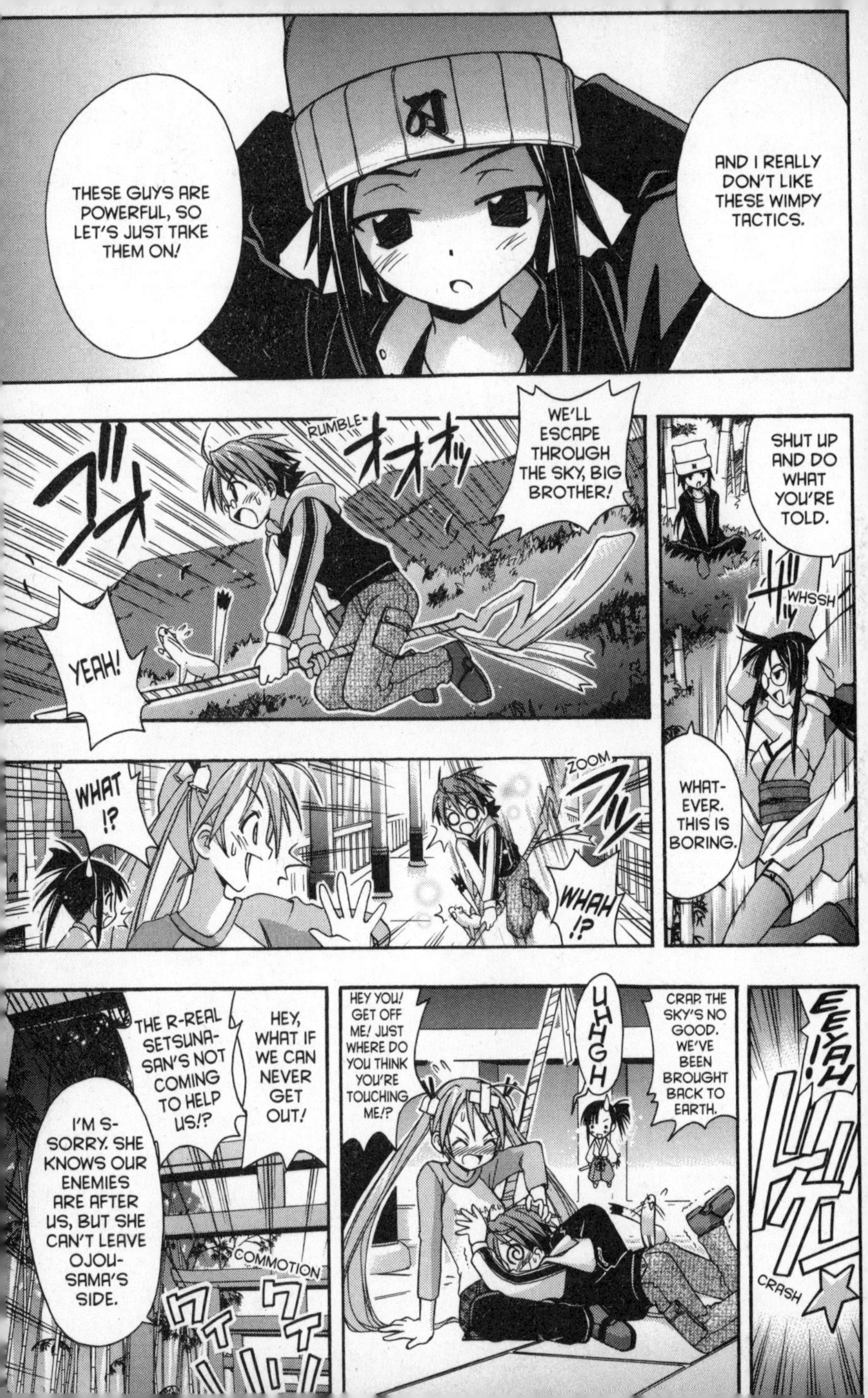
AND I REALLY DON'T LIKE THESE WIMPY TACTICS.
THESE GUYS ARE POWERFUL, SO LET'S JUST TAKE THEM ON!
SHUT UP AND DO WHAT YOU'RE TOLD.
WHSSH
WHAT-EVER. THIS IS BORING.
WE'LL ESCAPE THROUGH THE SKY, BIG BROTHER!
RUMBLE
YEAH!
ZOOM
WHAH!?
WHAT!?
EEYAH!
CRASH
CRAP. THE SKY'S NO GOOD. WE'VE BEEN BROUGHT BACK TO EARTH.
UHHGH
HEY YOU! GET OFF ME! JUST WHERE DO YOU THINK YOU'RE TOUCHING ME!?
HEY, WHAT IF WE CAN NEVER GET OUT!
THE R-REAL SETSUNA-SAN'S NOT COMING TO HELP US!?
I'M S-SORRY. SHE KNOWS OUR ENEMIES ARE AFTER US, BUT SHE CAN'T LEAVE OJOU-SAMA'S SIDE.
COMMOTION

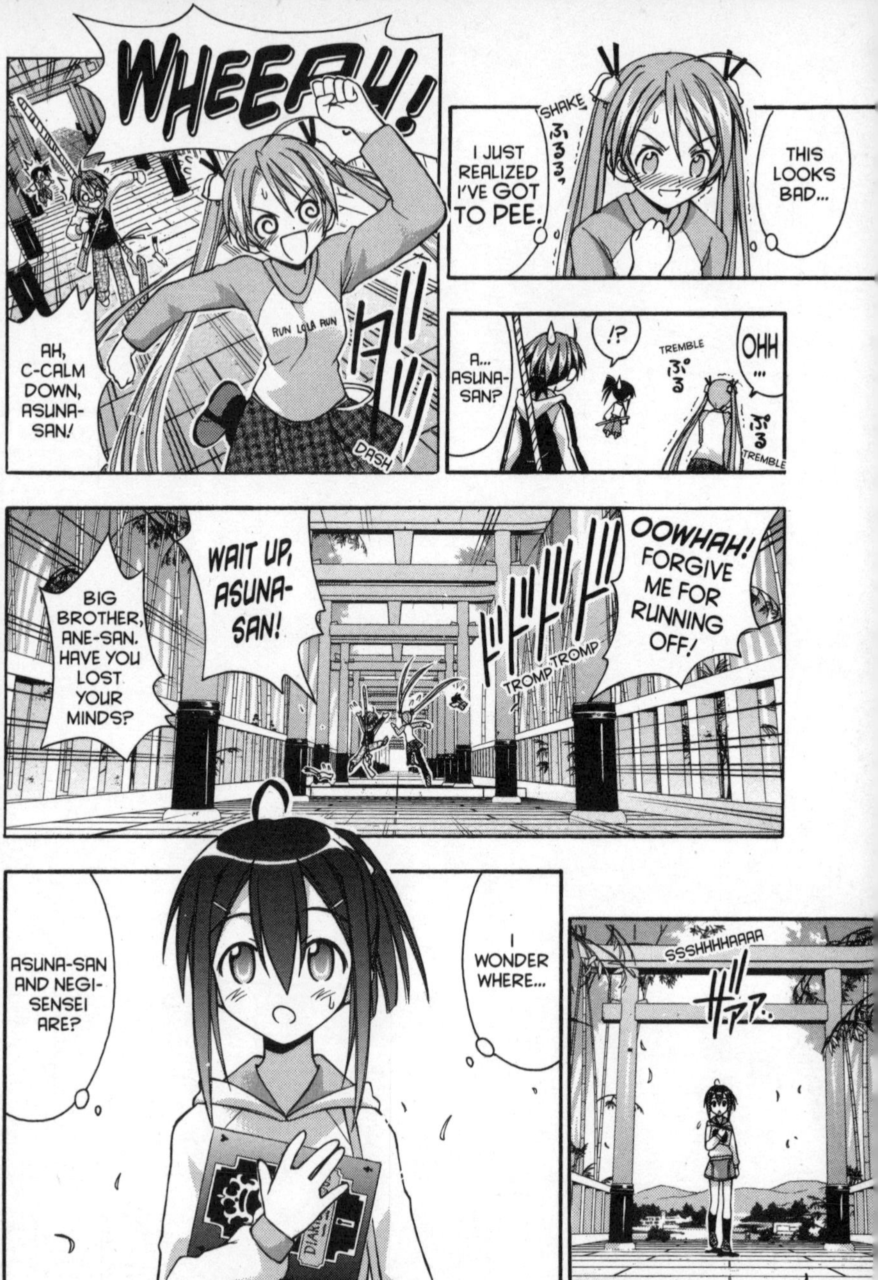
THIS LOOKS BAD...
SHAKE ふるるっ
I JUST REALIZED I'VE GOT TO PEE.
OHH ...
TREMBLE ぷる
!?
A... ASUNA-SAN?
ぷる TREMBLE
WHEEAY!
ダッ DASH
RUN LOLA RUN
AH, C-CALM DOWN, ASUNA-SAN!
OOWHAH! FORGIVE ME FOR RUNNING OFF!
ドドドド TROMP TROMP
WAIT UP, ASUNA-SAN!
BIG BROTHER, ANE-SAN. HAVE YOU LOST YOUR MINDS?
SSSHHHHAAAA ザアア..
I WONDER WHERE...
ASUNA-SAN AND NEGI-SENSEI ARE?

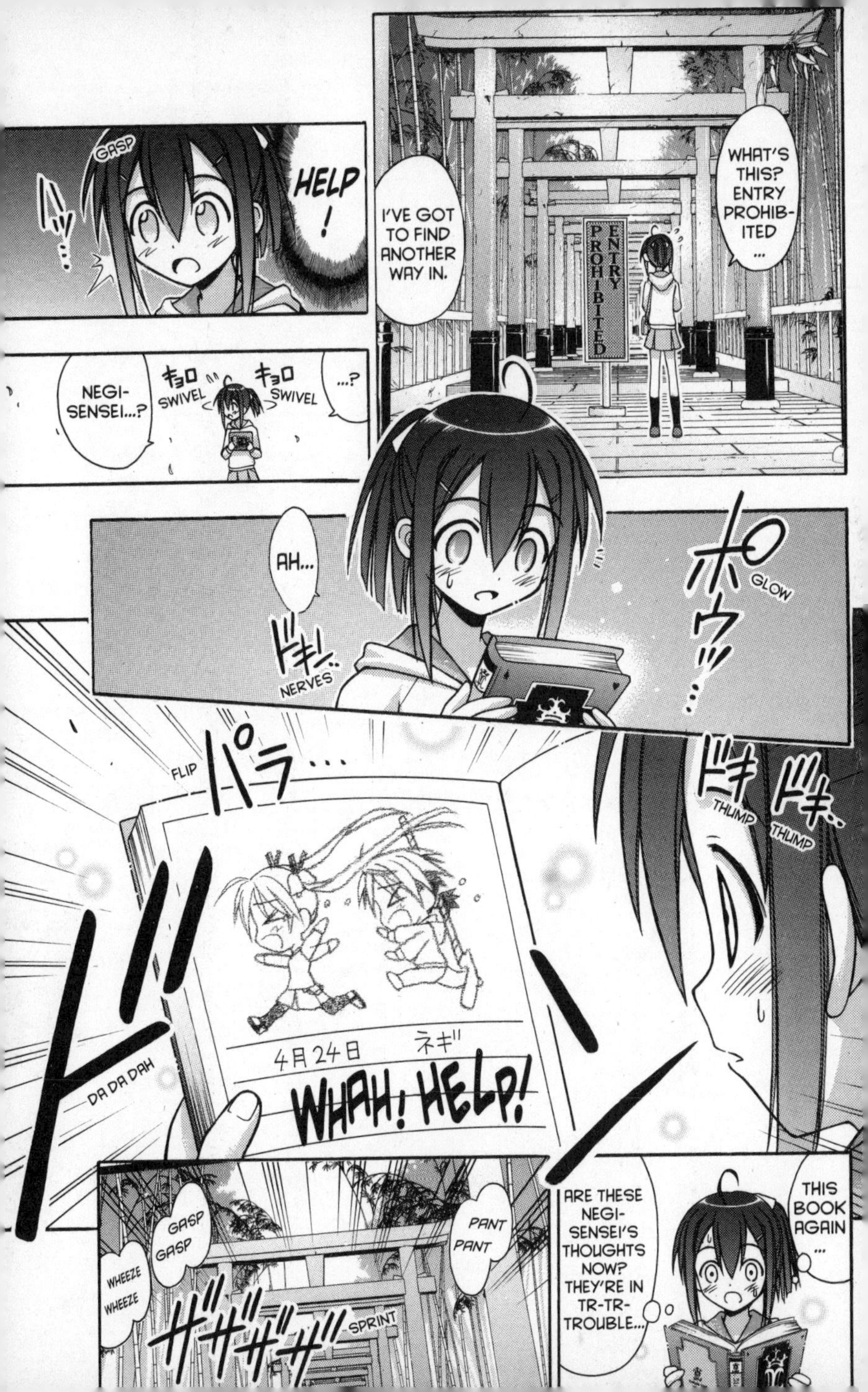
WHAT'S THIS? ENTRY PROHIBITED ...
ENTRY PROHIBITED
I'VE GOT TO FIND ANOTHER WAY IN.
HELP!
GASP
...?
キョロ SWIVEL
キョロ SWIVEL
NEGI-SENSEI...?
ポウッ... GLOW
AH...
ドキン... NERVES
ドキ THUMP
ドキ... THUMP
パラ... FLIP
4月24日 ネギ
WHAH! HELP!
DA DA DAH
THIS BOOK AGAIN ...
ARE THESE NEGI-SENSEI'S THOUGHTS NOW? THEY'RE IN TR-TR-TROUBLE...
PANT PANT
GASP GASP
WHEEZE WHEEZE
ザザザザ SPRINT

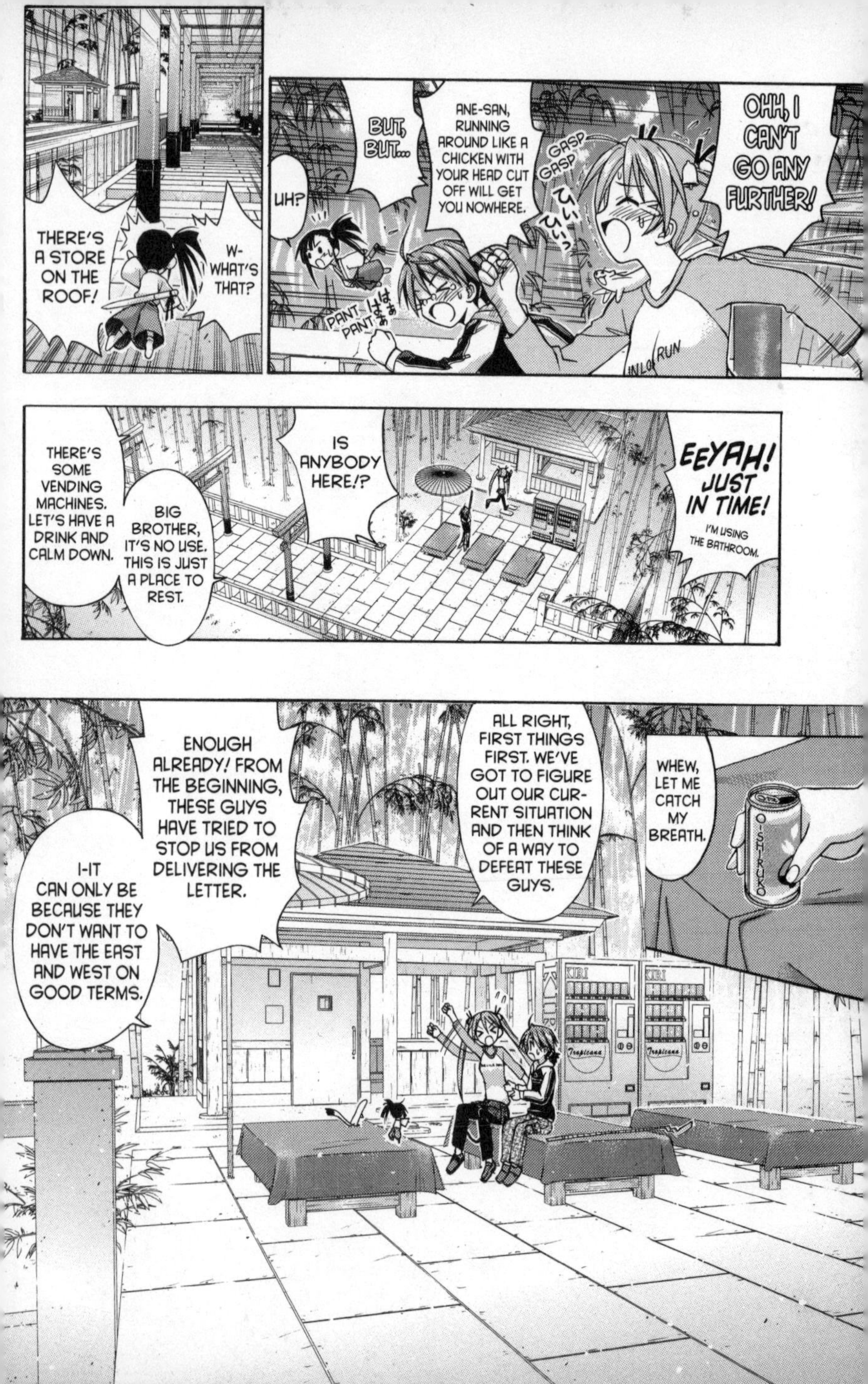
OHH, I CAN'T GO ANY FURTHER!
GASP GASP
ひぃ ひぃっ
ANE-SAN, RUNNING AROUND LIKE A CHICKEN WITH YOUR HEAD CUT OFF WILL GET YOU NOWHERE.
BUT, BUT...
PANT PANT
はぁ はぁ
UH?
W-WHAT'S THAT?
THERE'S A STORE ON THE ROOF!
EEYAH! JUST IN TIME!
I'M USING THE BATHROOM.
IS ANYBODY HERE!?
BIG BROTHER, IT'S NO USE. THIS IS JUST A PLACE TO REST.
THERE'S SOME VENDING MACHINES. LET'S HAVE A DRINK AND CALM DOWN.
WHEW, LET ME CATCH MY BREATH.
OISHIRUKO
ALL RIGHT, FIRST THINGS FIRST. WE'VE GOT TO FIGURE OUT OUR CURRENT SITUATION AND THEN THINK OF A WAY TO DEFEAT THESE GUYS.
ENOUGH ALREADY! FROM THE BEGINNING, THESE GUYS HAVE TRIED TO STOP US FROM DELIVERING THE LETTER.
I-IT CAN ONLY BE BECAUSE THEY DON'T WANT TO HAVE THE EAST AND WEST ON GOOD TERMS.
KIRI
KIRI

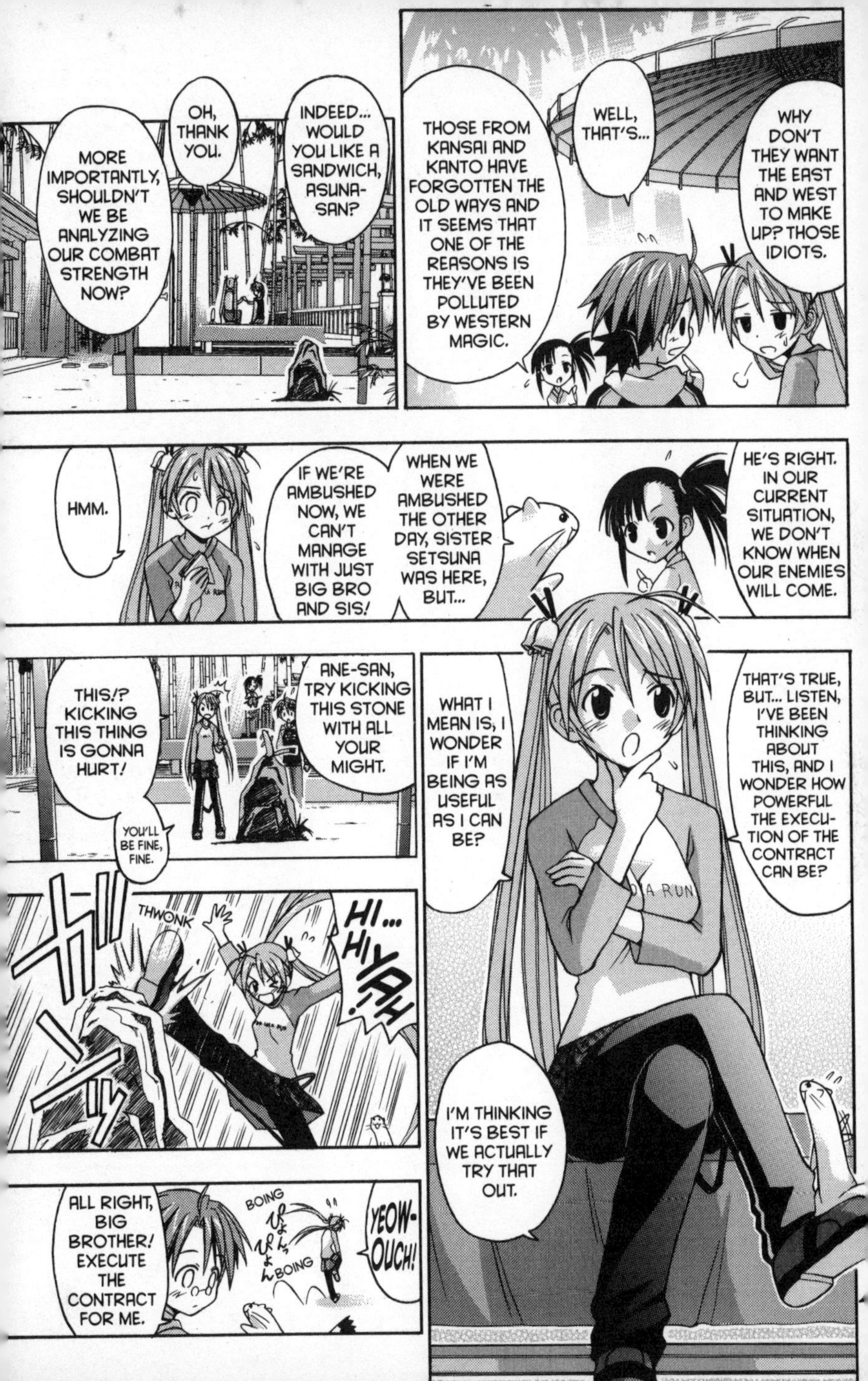
WHY DON'T THEY WANT THE EAST AND WEST TO MAKE UP? THOSE IDIOTS.
WELL, THAT'S...
THOSE FROM KANSAI AND KANTO HAVE FORGOTTEN THE OLD WAYS AND IT SEEMS THAT ONE OF THE REASONS IS THEY'VE BEEN POLLUTED BY WESTERN MAGIC.
INDEED... WOULD YOU LIKE A SANDWICH, ASUNA-SAN?
OH, THANK YOU.
MORE IMPORTANTLY, SHOULDN'T WE BE ANALYZING OUR COMBAT STRENGTH NOW?
HE'S RIGHT. IN OUR CURRENT SITUATION, WE DON'T KNOW WHEN OUR ENEMIES WILL COME.
WHEN WE WERE AMBUSHED THE OTHER DAY, SISTER SETSUNA WAS HERE, BUT...
IF WE'RE AMBUSHED NOW, WE CAN'T MANAGE WITH JUST BIG BRO AND SIS!
HMM.
THAT'S TRUE, BUT... LISTEN, I'VE BEEN THINKING ABOUT THIS, AND I WONDER HOW POWERFUL THE EXECUTION OF THE CONTRACT CAN BE?
WHAT I MEAN IS, I WONDER IF I'M BEING AS USEFUL AS I CAN BE?
I'M THINKING IT'S BEST IF WE ACTUALLY TRY THAT OUT.
ANE-SAN, TRY KICKING THIS STONE WITH ALL YOUR MIGHT.
THIS!? KICKING THIS THING IS GONNA HURT!
YOU'LL BE FINE, FINE.
HI... HIYAH!
THWONK
YEOW-OUCH!
BOING
BOING
ALL RIGHT, BIG BROTHER! EXECUTE THE CONTRACT FOR ME.

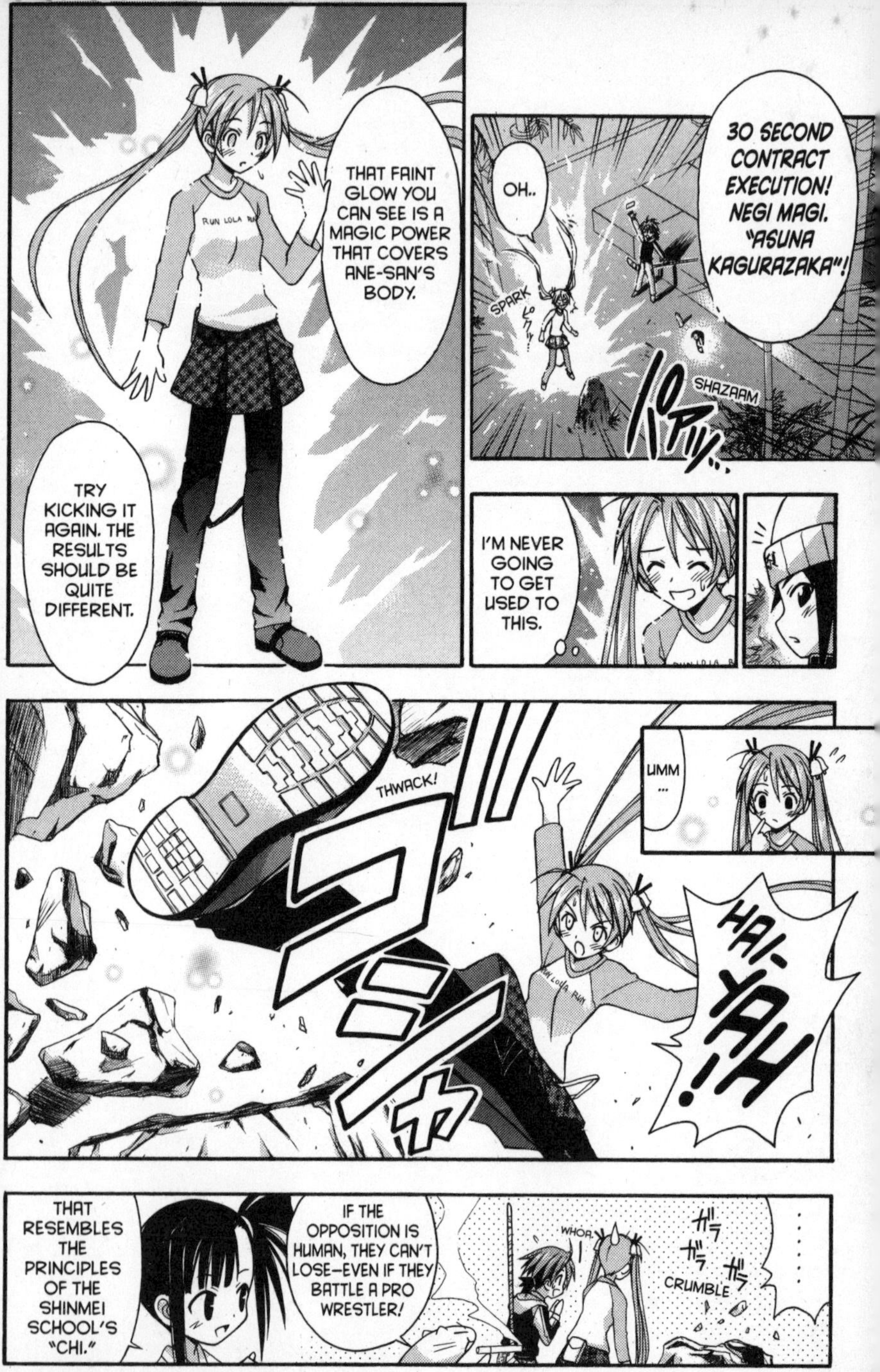
30 SECOND CONTRACT EXECUTION! NEGI MAGI. "ASUNA KAGURAZAKA"!
OH..
SPARK
SHAZAAM
I'M NEVER GOING TO GET USED TO THIS.
THAT FAINT GLOW YOU CAN SEE IS A MAGIC POWER THAT COVERS ANE-SAN'S BODY.
TRY KICKING IT AGAIN. THE RESULTS SHOULD BE QUITE DIFFERENT.
UMM ...
HAI-YAH!!
THWACK!
.....
CRUMBLE
WHOA!
IF THE OPPOSITION IS HUMAN, THEY CAN'T LOSE—EVEN IF THEY BATTLE A PRO WRESTLER!
THAT RESEMBLES THE PRINCIPLES OF THE SHINMEI SCHOOL'S "CHI."

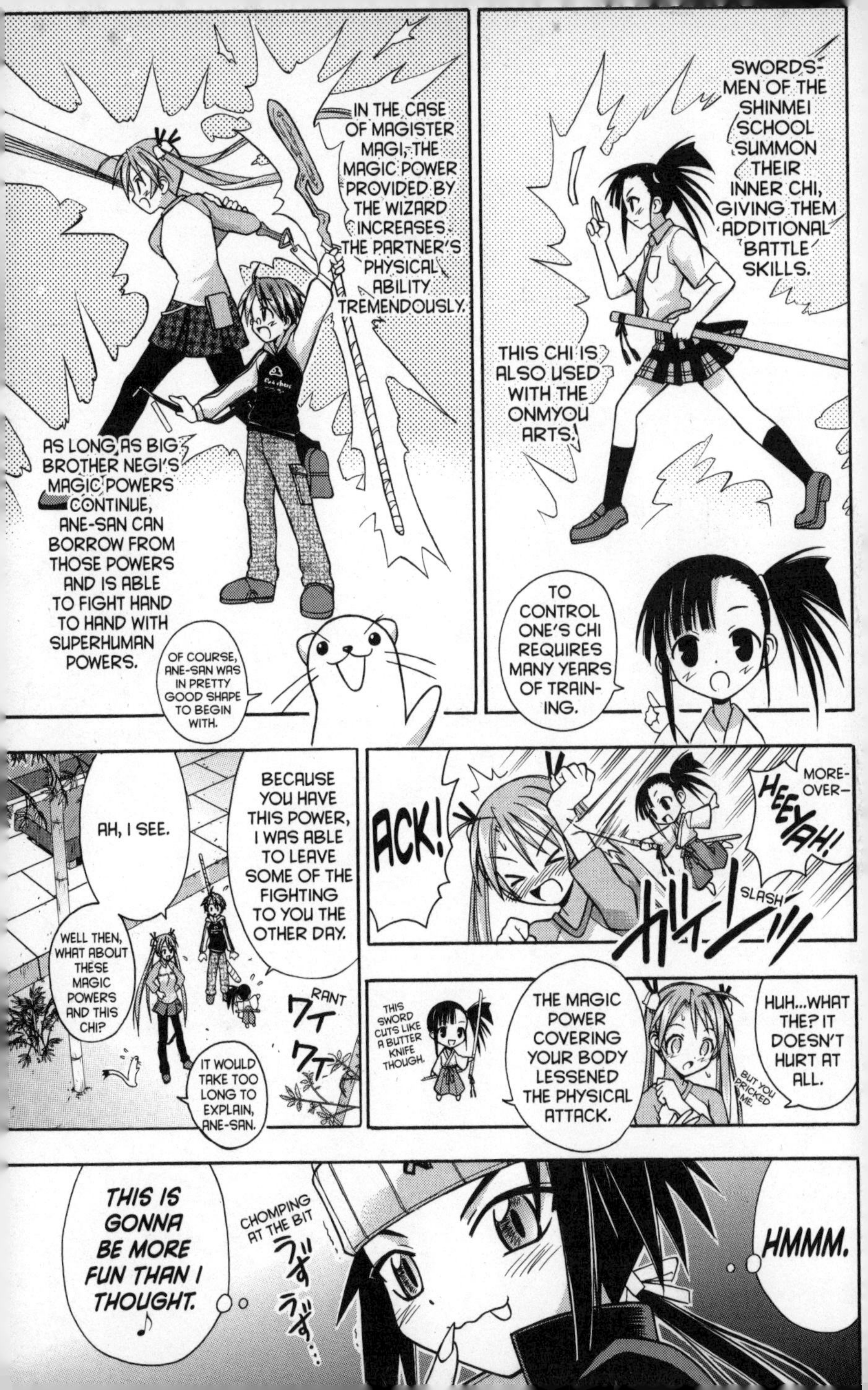
SWORDS-MEN OF THE SHINMEI SCHOOL SUMMON THEIR INNER CHI, GIVING THEM ADDITIONAL BATTLE SKILLS.
THIS CHI IS ALSO USED WITH THE ONMYOU ARTS.
TO CONTROL ONE'S CHI REQUIRES MANY YEARS OF TRAIN-ING.
IN THE CASE OF MAGISTER MAGI, THE MAGIC POWER PROVIDED BY THE WIZARD INCREASES THE PARTNER'S PHYSICAL ABILITY TREMENDOUSLY.
AS LONG AS BIG BROTHER NEGI'S MAGIC POWERS CONTINUE, ANE-SAN CAN BORROW FROM THOSE POWERS AND IS ABLE TO FIGHT HAND TO HAND WITH SUPERHUMAN POWERS.
OF COURSE, ANE-SAN WAS IN PRETTY GOOD SHAPE TO BEGIN WITH.
MORE-OVER—
HEEYAH!
ACK!
SLASH
HUH...WHAT THE? IT DOESN'T HURT AT ALL.
BUT YOU PRICKED ME.
THE MAGIC POWER COVERING YOUR BODY LESSENED THE PHYSICAL ATTACK.
THIS SWORD CUTS LIKE A BUTTER KNIFE THOUGH.
BECAUSE YOU HAVE THIS POWER, I WAS ABLE TO LEAVE SOME OF THE FIGHTING TO YOU THE OTHER DAY.
AH, I SEE.
RANT
ワイワイ
WELL THEN, WHAT ABOUT THESE MAGIC POWERS AND THIS CHI?
IT WOULD TAKE TOO LONG TO EXPLAIN, ANE-SAN.
HMMM.
CHOMPING AT THE BIT
うずうず...
THIS IS GONNA BE MORE FUN THAN I THOUGHT. ♪

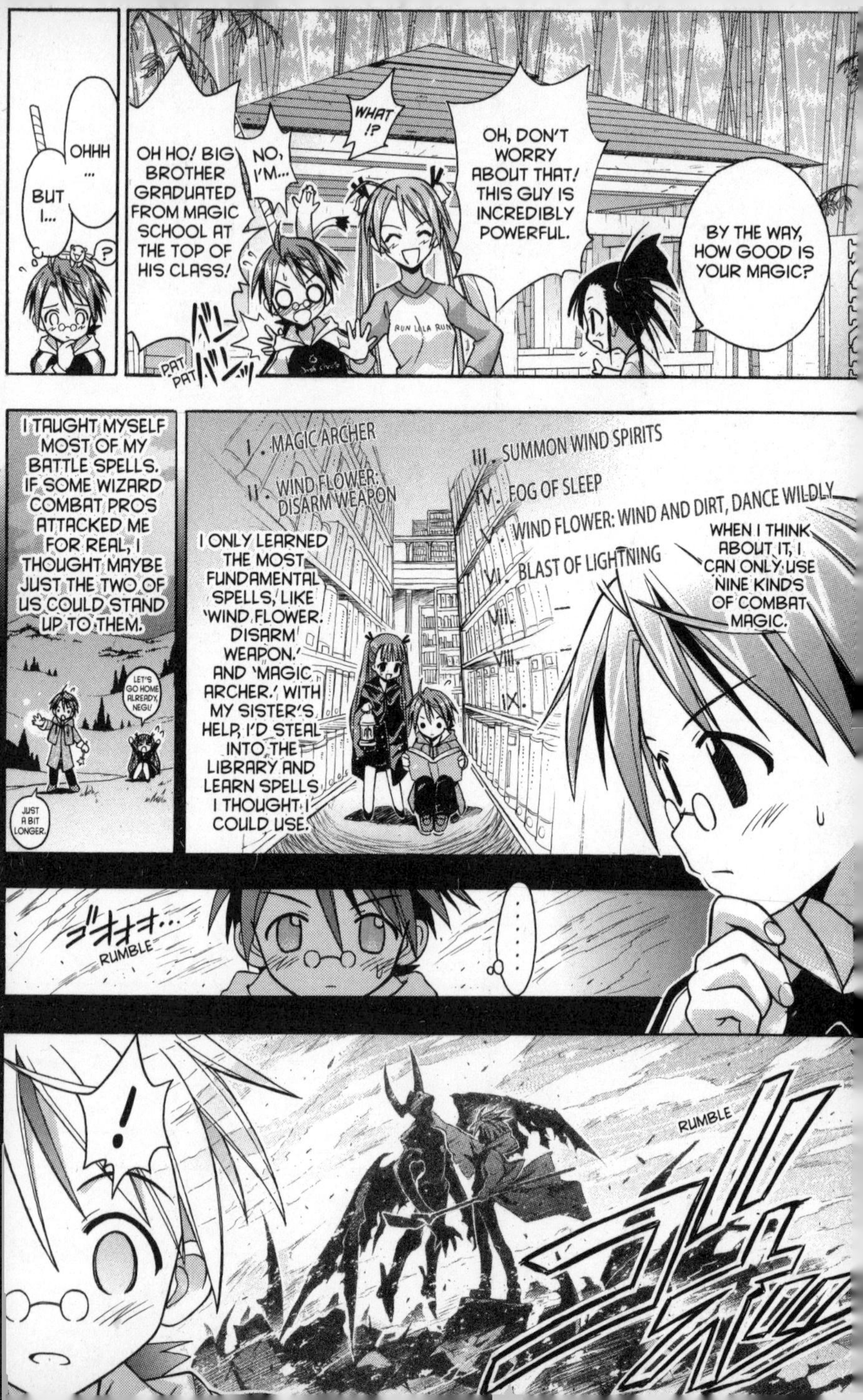
BY THE WAY, HOW GOOD IS YOUR MAGIC?
OH, DON'T WORRY ABOUT THAT! THIS GUY IS INCREDIBLY POWERFUL.
WHAT !?
NO, I'M...
OH HO! BIG BROTHER GRADUATED FROM MAGIC SCHOOL AT THE TOP OF HIS CLASS!
PAT PAT
OHHH ... BUT I...
?
WHEN I THINK ABOUT IT, I CAN ONLY USE NINE KINDS OF COMBAT MAGIC.
I. MAGIC ARCHER
II. WIND FLOWER: DISARM WEAPON
III. SUMMON WIND SPIRITS
IV. FOG OF SLEEP
V. WIND FLOWER: WIND AND DIRT, DANCE WILDLY
VI. BLAST OF LIGHTNING
VII. —
VIII. —
IX. —
I ONLY LEARNED THE MOST FUNDAMENTAL SPELLS, LIKE 'WIND FLOWER. DISARM WEAPON.' AND 'MAGIC ARCHER.' WITH MY SISTER'S HELP, I'D STEAL INTO THE LIBRARY AND LEARN SPELLS I THOUGHT I COULD USE.
I TAUGHT MYSELF MOST OF MY BATTLE SPELLS. IF SOME WIZARD COMBAT PROS ATTACKED ME FOR REAL, I THOUGHT MAYBE JUST THE TWO OF US COULD STAND UP TO THEM.
LET'S GO HOME ALREADY, NEGI!
JUST A BIT LONGER.
...
RUMBLE
!
RUMBLE

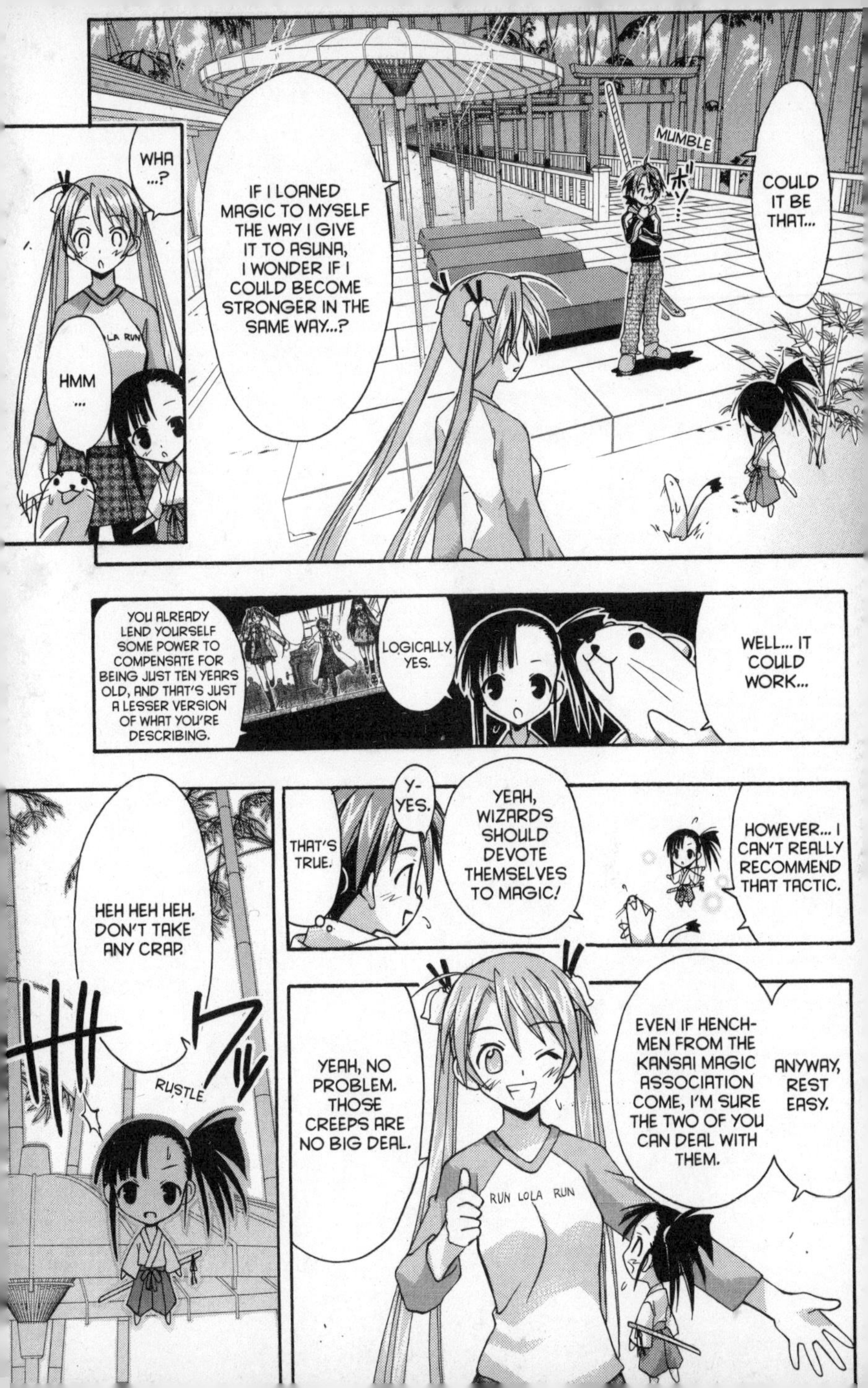
COULD IT BE THAT...
MUMBLE
IF I LOANED MAGIC TO MYSELF THE WAY I GIVE IT TO ASUNA, I WONDER IF I COULD BECOME STRONGER IN THE SAME WAY...?
WHA ...?
HMM ...
WELL... IT COULD WORK...
LOGICALLY, YES.
YOU ALREADY LEND YOURSELF SOME POWER TO COMPENSATE FOR BEING JUST TEN YEARS OLD, AND THAT'S JUST A LESSER VERSION OF WHAT YOU'RE DESCRIBING.
HOWEVER... I CAN'T REALLY RECOMMEND THAT TACTIC.
YEAH, WIZARDS SHOULD DEVOTE THEMSELVES TO MAGIC!
Y- YES.
THAT'S TRUE.
ANYWAY, REST EASY.
EVEN IF HENCH- MEN FROM THE KANSAI MAGIC ASSOCIATION COME, I'M SURE THE TWO OF YOU CAN DEAL WITH THEM.
YEAH, NO PROBLEM. THOSE CREEPS ARE NO BIG DEAL.
RUN LOLA RUN
HEH HEH HEH. DON'T TAKE ANY CRAP.
RUSTLE

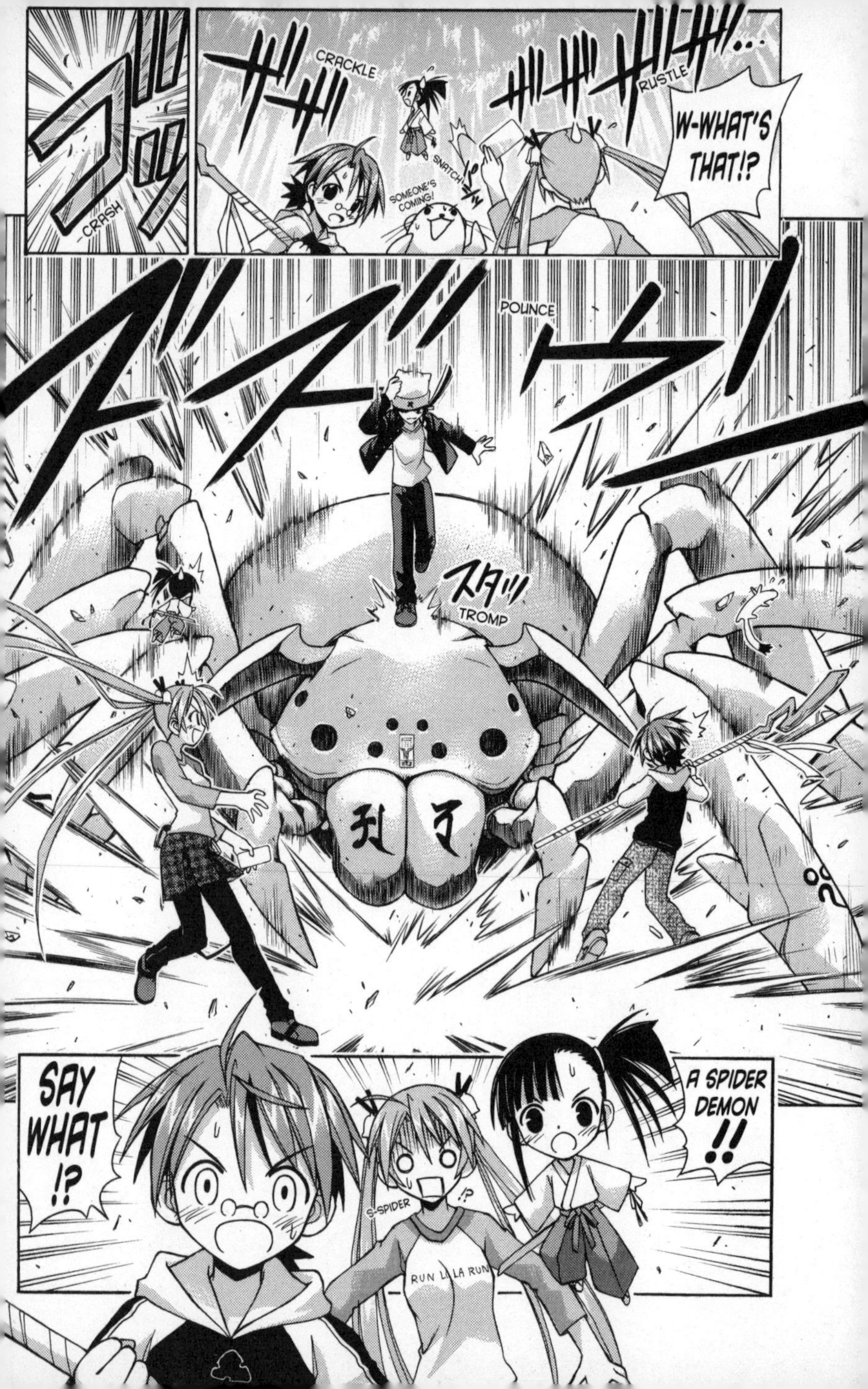

W-WHAT'S THAT!?
RUSTLE
SNATCH
CRACKLE
SOMEONE'S COMING!
CRASH
POUNCE
スタッ
TROMP
A SPIDER DEMON !!
!?
S-SPIDER
SAY WHAT !?

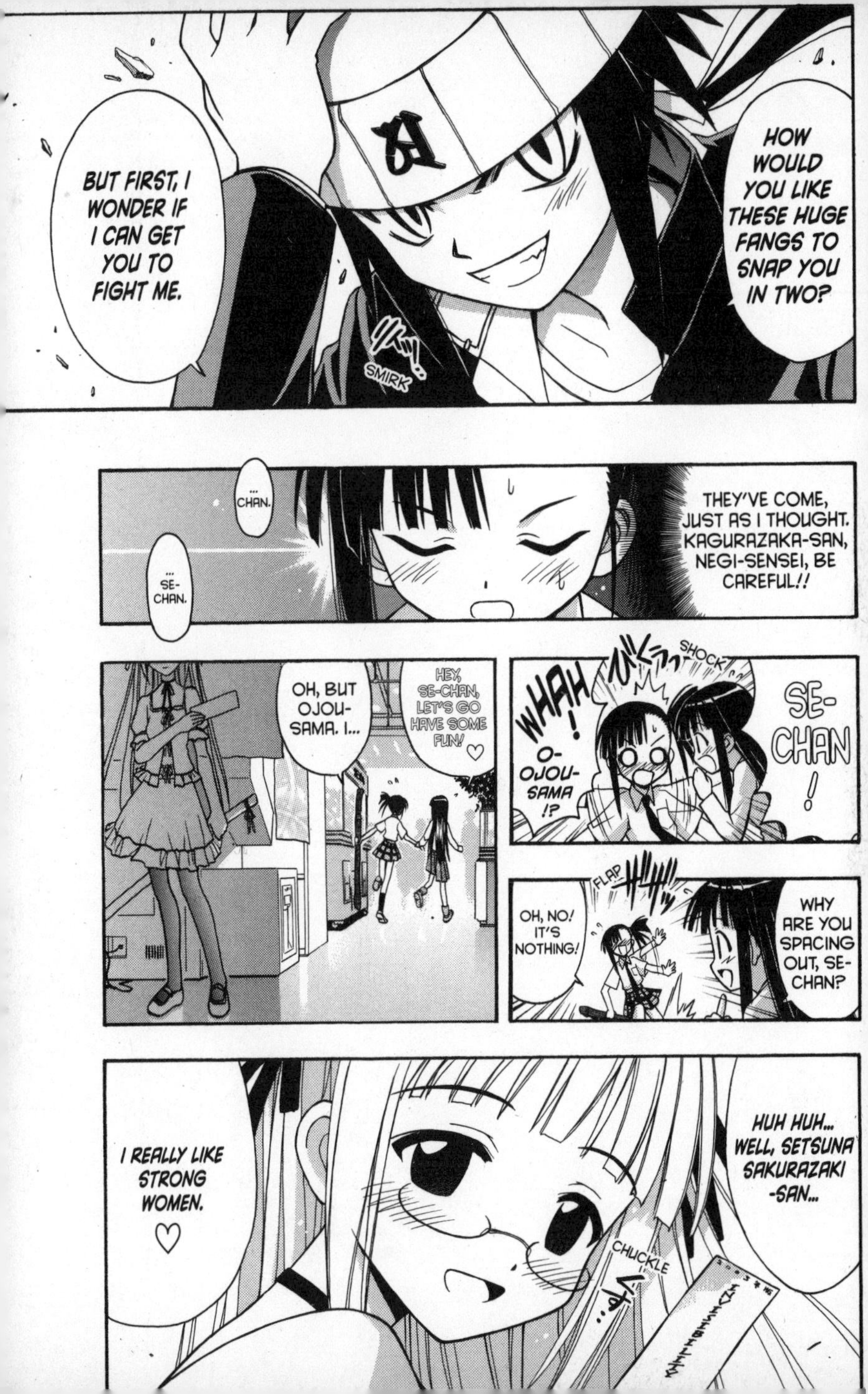
HOW WOULD YOU LIKE THESE HUGE FANGS TO SNAP YOU IN TWO?
BUT FIRST, I WONDER IF I CAN GET YOU TO FIGHT ME.
SMIRK
THEY'VE COME, JUST AS I THOUGHT. KAGURAZAKA-SAN, NEGI-SENSEI, BE CAREFUL!!
...CHAN.
...SE-CHAN.
SE-CHAN!
SHOCK
WHAH!
O-OJOU-SAMA!?
WHY ARE YOU SPACING OUT, SE-CHAN?
FLAP
OH, NO! IT'S NOTHING!
HEY, SE-CHAN, LET'S GO HAVE SOME FUN! ♡
OH, BUT OJOU-SAMA. I...
HUH HUH... WELL, SETSUNA SAKURAZAKI-SAN...
CHUCKLE
I REALLY LIKE STRONG WOMEN. ♡

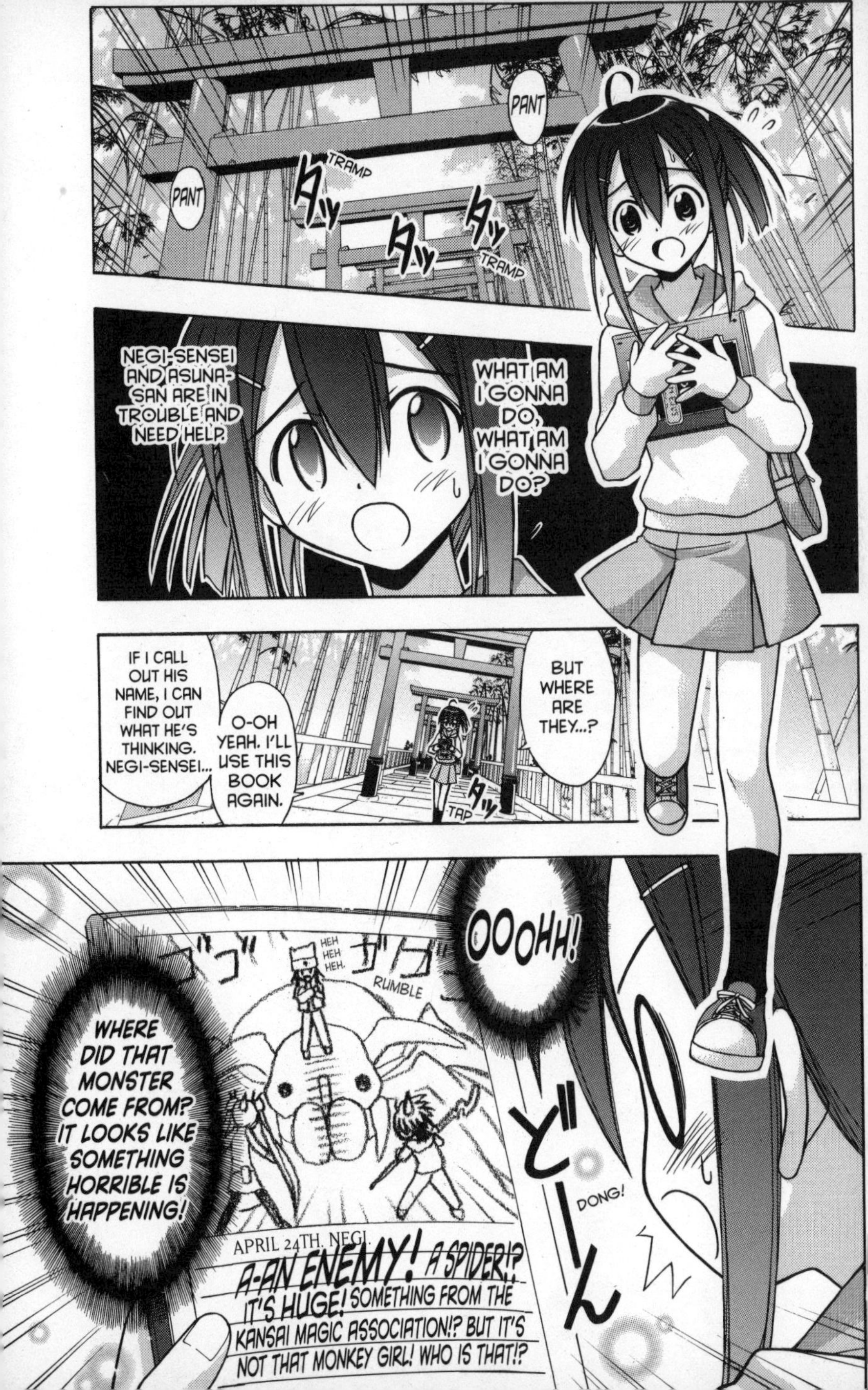

PANT
TRAMP
PANT
TRAMP
WHAT AM I GONNA DO, WHAT AM I GONNA DO?
NEGI-SENSEI AND ASUNA-SAN ARE IN TROUBLE AND NEED HELP.
BUT WHERE ARE THEY...?
O-OH YEAH. I'LL USE THIS BOOK AGAIN.
IF I CALL OUT HIS NAME, I CAN FIND OUT WHAT HE'S THINKING. NEGI-SENSEI...
TAP
OOOHH!
DONG!
RUMBLE
HEH HEH HEH.
WHERE DID THAT MONSTER COME FROM? IT LOOKS LIKE SOMETHING HORRIBLE IS HAPPENING!
APRIL 24TH. NEGI.
A-AN ENEMY! A SPIDER!? IT'S HUGE! SOMETHING FROM THE KANSAI MAGIC ASSOCIATION!? BUT IT'S NOT THAT MONKEY GIRL! WHO IS THAT!?

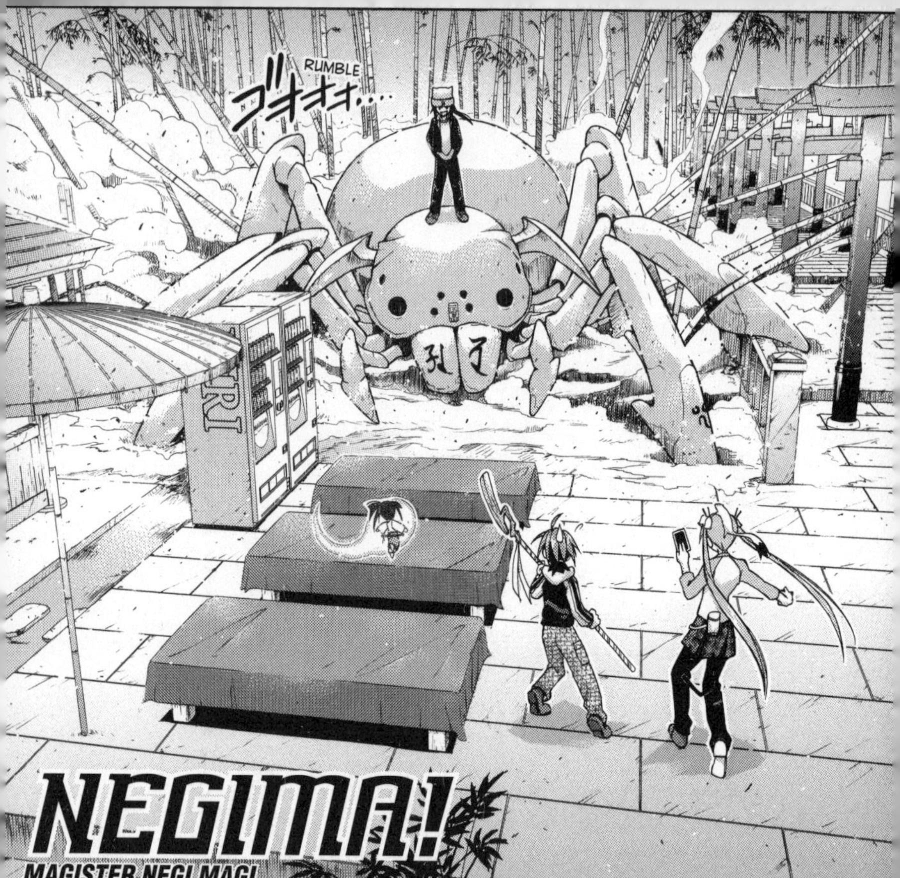
RUMBLE
ゴオオオ…
NEGIMA!
MAGISTER NEGI MAGI
FORTIETH PERIOD:
IN ORDER TO GET OFF THE ROAD WE'RE LOST ON
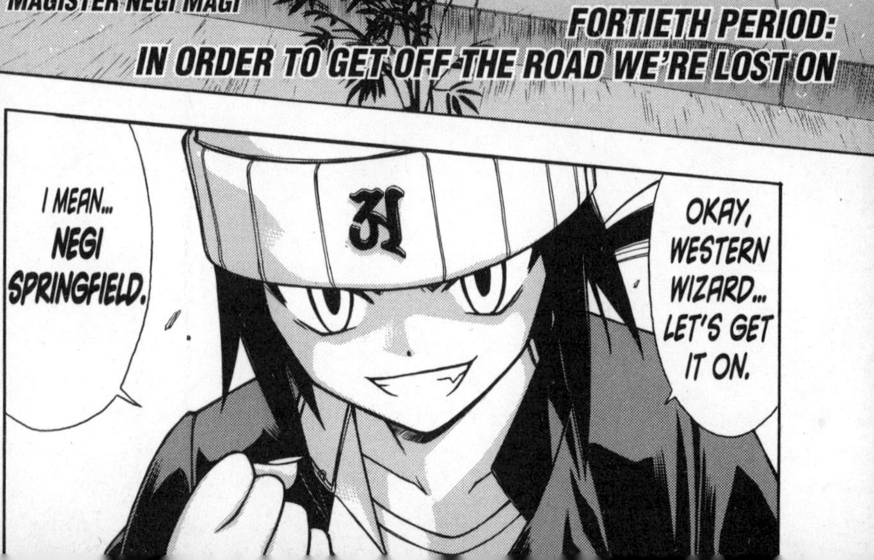
OKAY, WESTERN WIZARD... LET'S GET IT ON.
I MEAN... NEGI SPRINGFIELD.

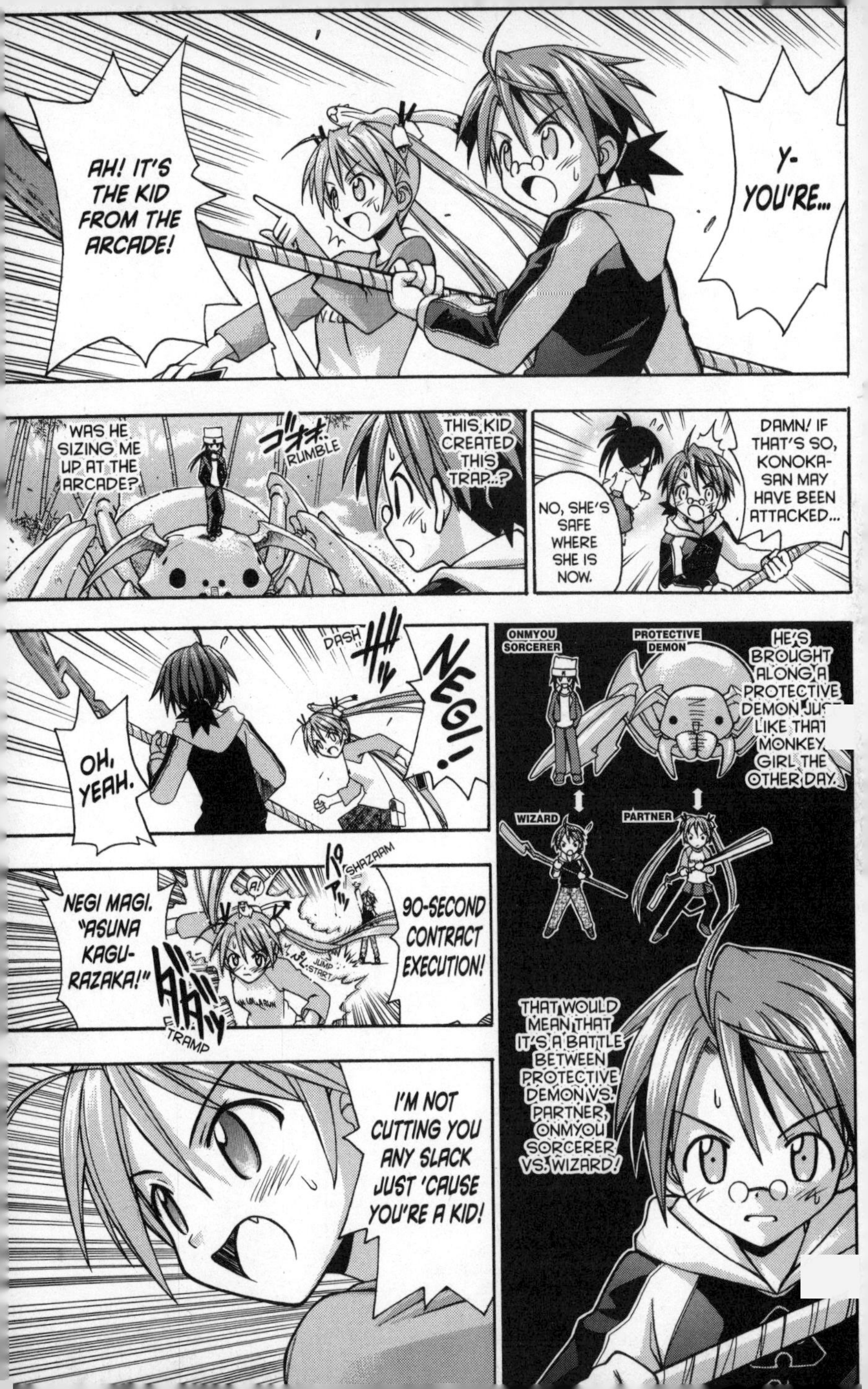

Y- YOU'RE...
AH! IT'S THE KID FROM THE ARCADE!
DAMN! IF THAT'S SO, KONOKA-SAN MAY HAVE BEEN ATTACKED...
NO, SHE'S SAFE WHERE SHE IS NOW.
THIS KID CREATED THIS TRAP...?
RUMBLE
WAS HE SIZING ME UP AT THE ARCADE?
ONMYOU SORCERER
PROTECTIVE DEMON
HE'S BROUGHT ALONG A PROTECTIVE DEMON JUST LIKE THAT MONKEY GIRL THE OTHER DAY.
WIZARD
PARTNER
THAT WOULD MEAN THAT IT'S A BATTLE BETWEEN PROTECTIVE DEMON VS. PARTNER, ONMYOU SORCERER VS. WIZARD!
NEGI!!
DASH
OH, YEAH.
SHAZAAM
90-SECOND CONTRACT EXECUTION!
JUMP START
NEGI MAGI. "ASUNA KAGURAZAKA!"
TRAMP
I'M NOT CUTTING YOU ANY SLACK JUST 'CAUSE YOU'RE A KID!

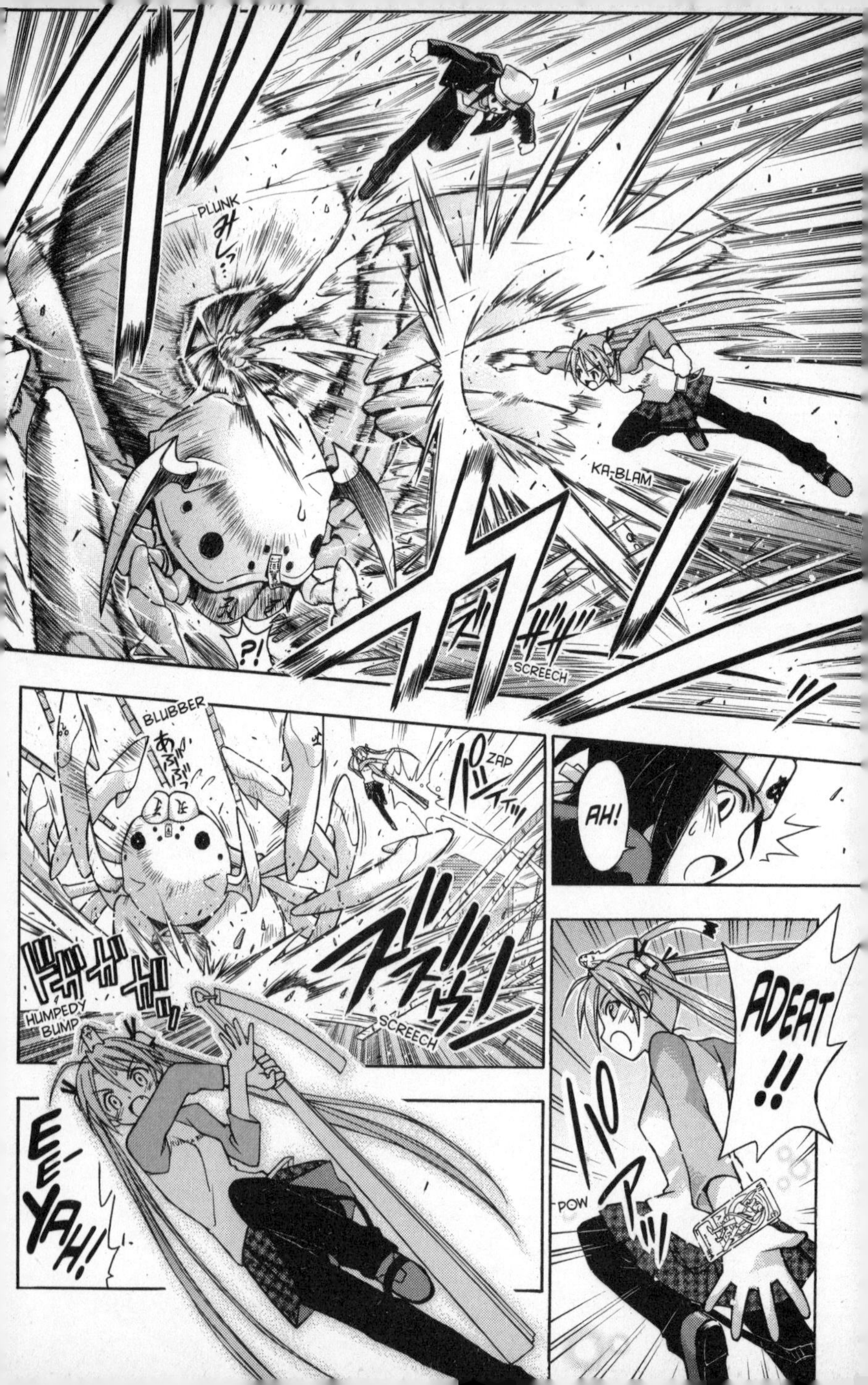

PLUNK
KA-BLAM
?!
SCREECH
AH!
ADEAT!!
POW
ZAP
BLUBBER
SCREECH
HUMPEDY BUMP
EEYAH!

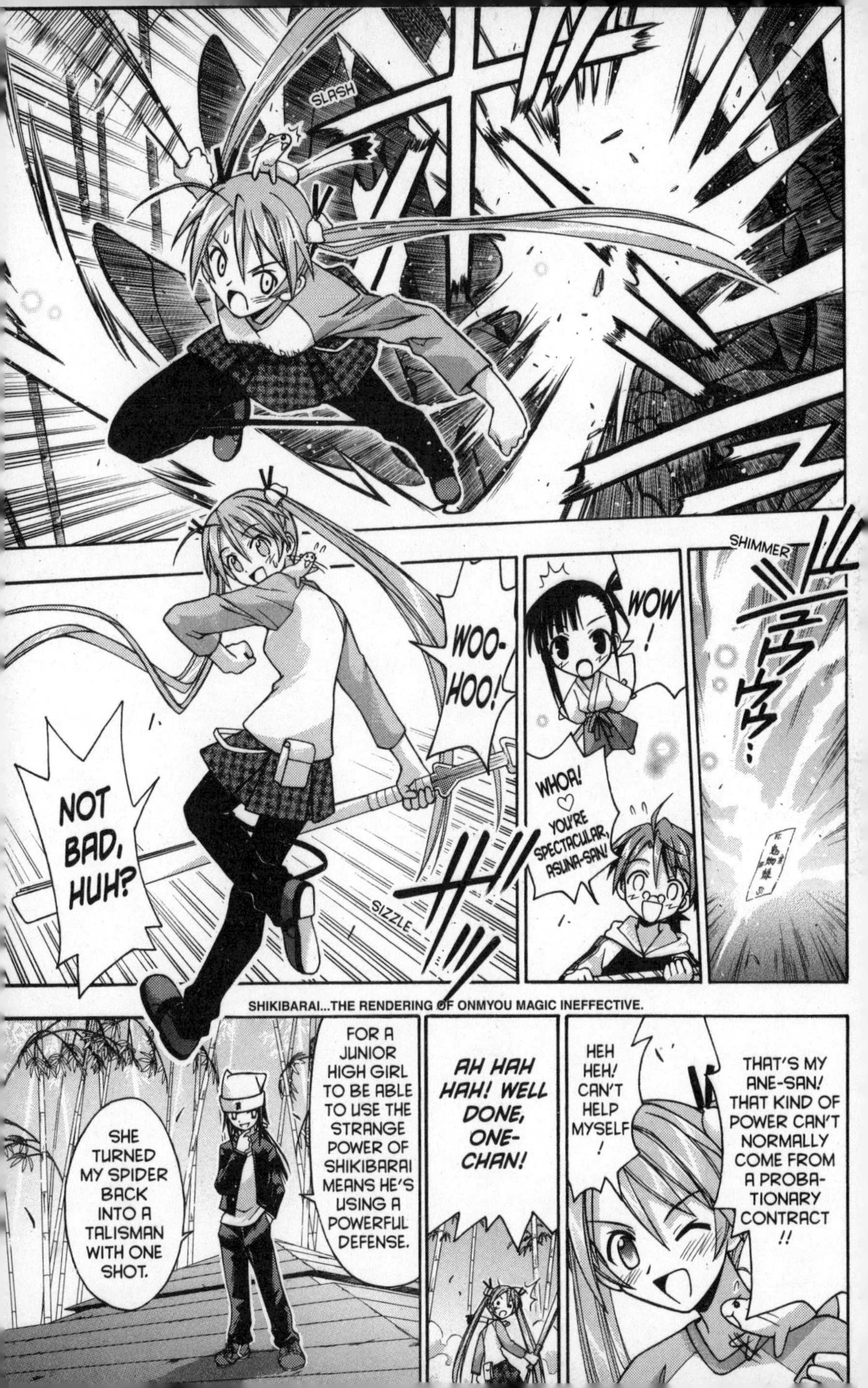
SLASH
SHIMMER
WOW!
WHOA! ♡ YOU'RE SPECTACULAR, ASUNA-SAN!
WOO-HOO!
SIZZLE
NOT BAD, HUH?
SHIKIBARAI...THE RENDERING OF ONMYOU MAGIC INEFFECTIVE.
THAT'S MY ANE-SAN! THAT KIND OF POWER CAN'T NORMALLY COME FROM A PROBATIONARY CONTRACT!!
HEH HEH! CAN'T HELP MYSELF!
AH HAH HAH! WELL DONE, ONE-CHAN!
FOR A JUNIOR HIGH GIRL TO BE ABLE TO USE THE STRANGE POWER OF SHIKIBARAI MEANS HE'S USING A POWERFUL DEFENSE.
SHE TURNED MY SPIDER BACK INTO A TALISMAN WITH ONE SHOT.

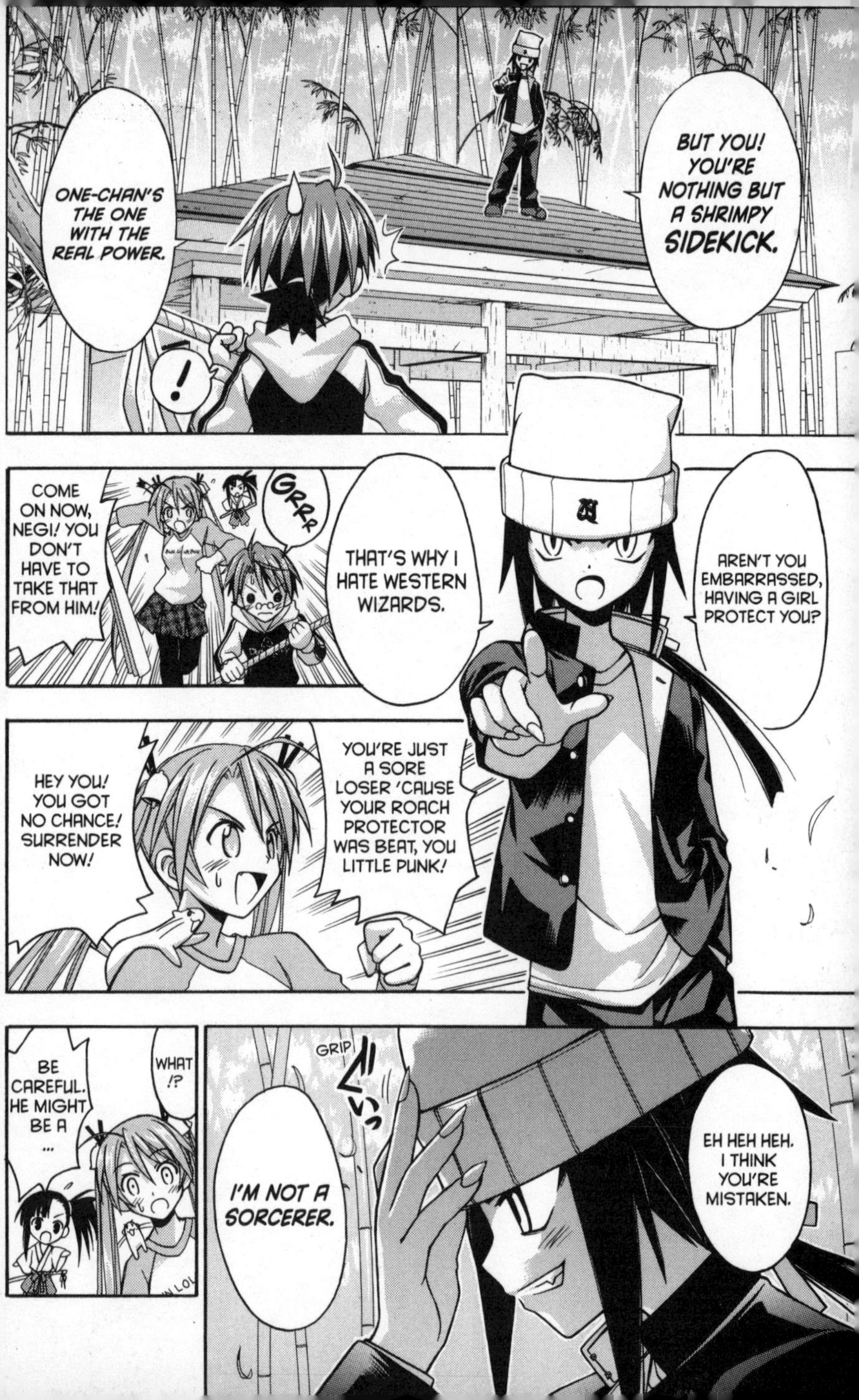
BUT YOU! YOU'RE NOTHING BUT A SHRIMPY SIDEKICK.
ONE-CHAN'S THE ONE WITH THE REAL POWER.
!
AREN'T YOU EMBARRASSED, HAVING A GIRL PROTECT YOU?
THAT'S WHY I HATE WESTERN WIZARDS.
GRRR
COME ON NOW, NEGI! YOU DON'T HAVE TO TAKE THAT FROM HIM!
YOU'RE JUST A SORE LOSER 'CAUSE YOUR ROACH PROTECTOR WAS BEAT, YOU LITTLE PUNK!
HEY YOU! YOU GOT NO CHANCE! SURRENDER NOW!
EH HEH HEH. I THINK YOU'RE MISTAKEN.
GRIP
I'M NOT A SORCERER.
WHAT !?
BE CAREFUL. HE MIGHT BE A ...

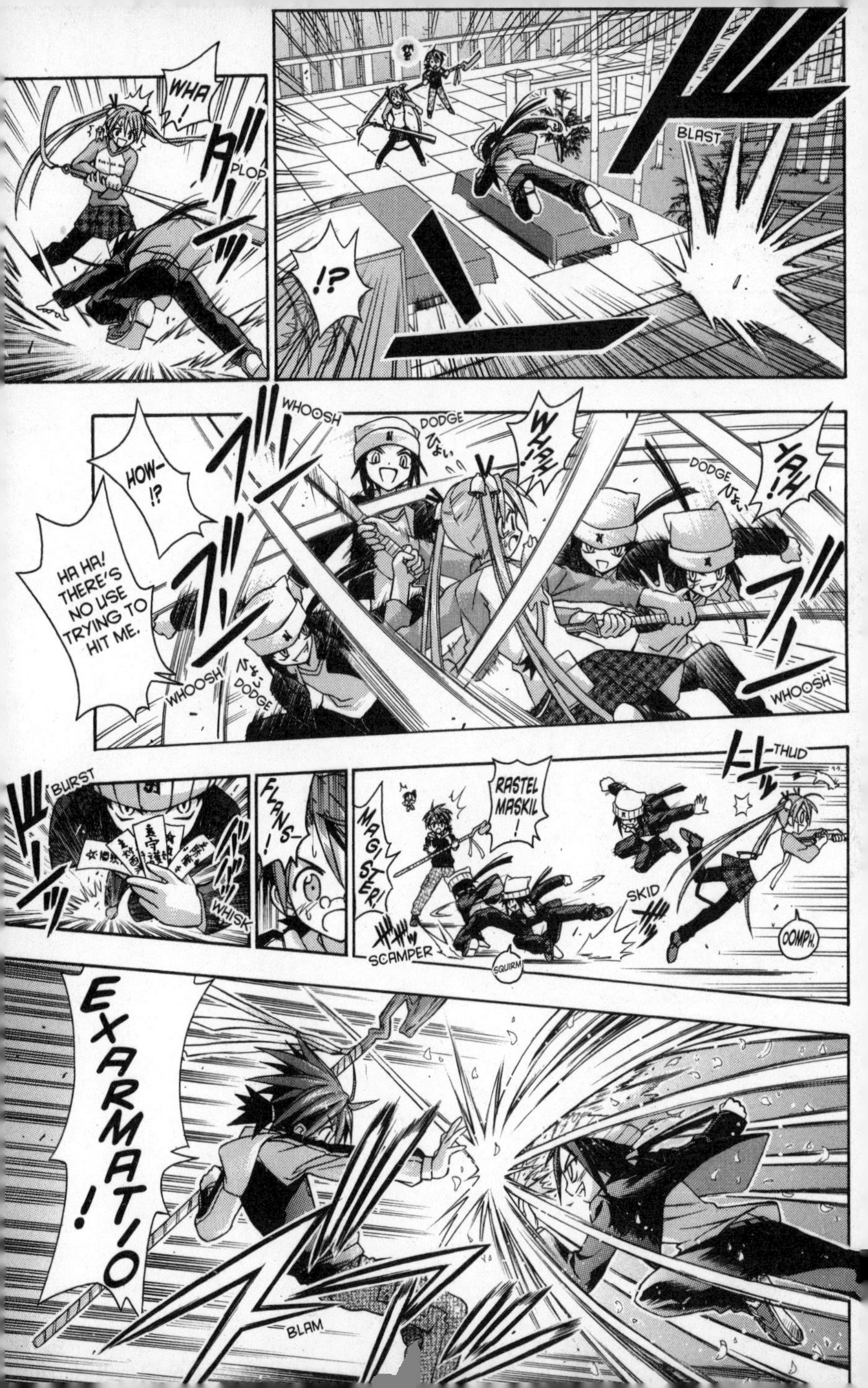
BLAST
!?
WHA!
PLOP
WHOOSH
YAH!
DODGE
WHAH!
DODGE
WHOOSH
HOW-!?
HA HA! THERE'S NO USE TRYING TO HIT ME.
WHOOSH
DODGE
THUD
OOMPH
SKID
RASTEL MASKIL!
MAGISTER!
SQUIRM
SCAMPER
FLANS-!
BURST
WHISK
EXARMATIO!
BLAM

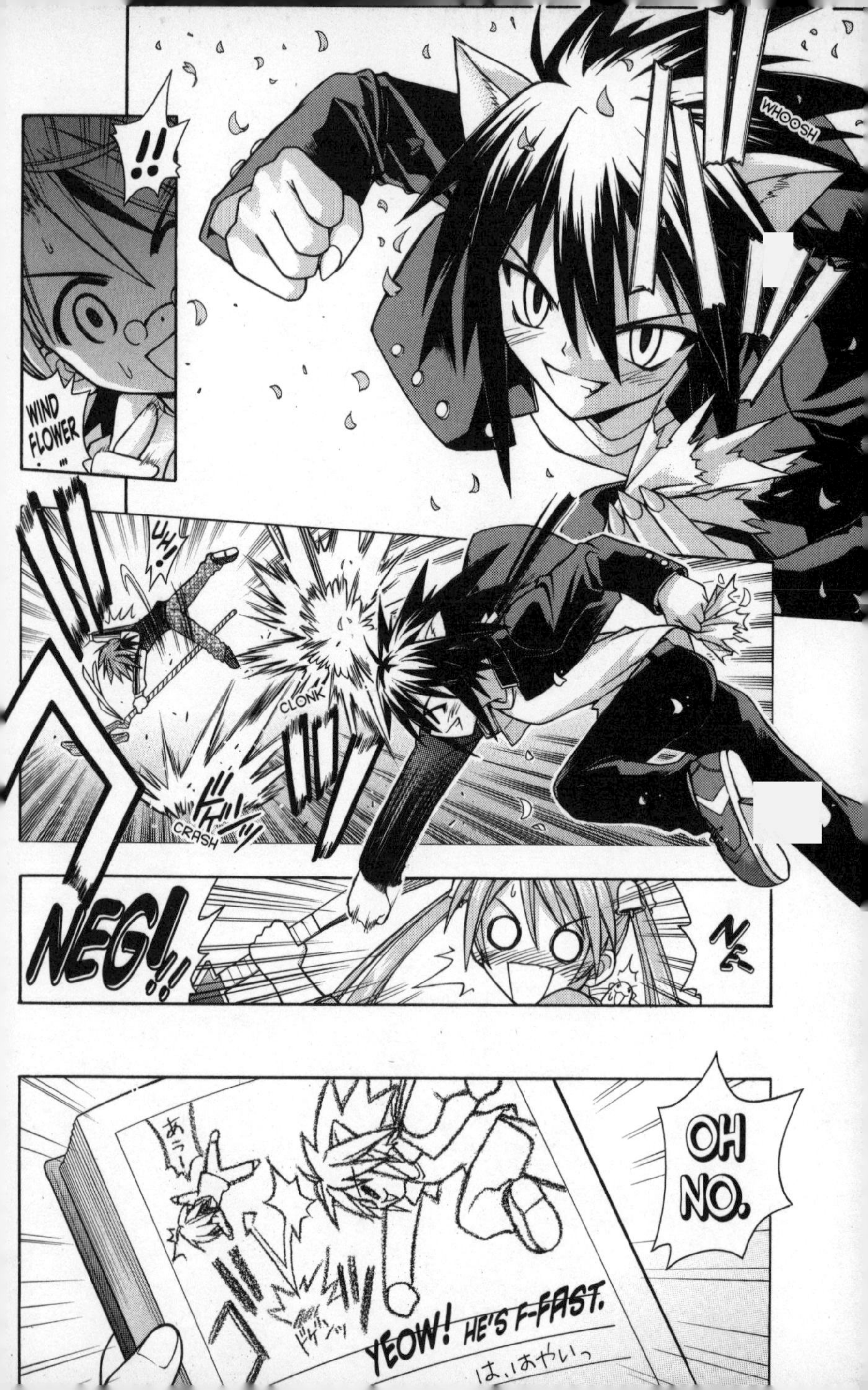
WHOOSH
!!
WIND FLOWER...
UH!
CLONK
CRASH
N-
NEG!!!
OH NO.
YEOW! HE'S F-FAST.

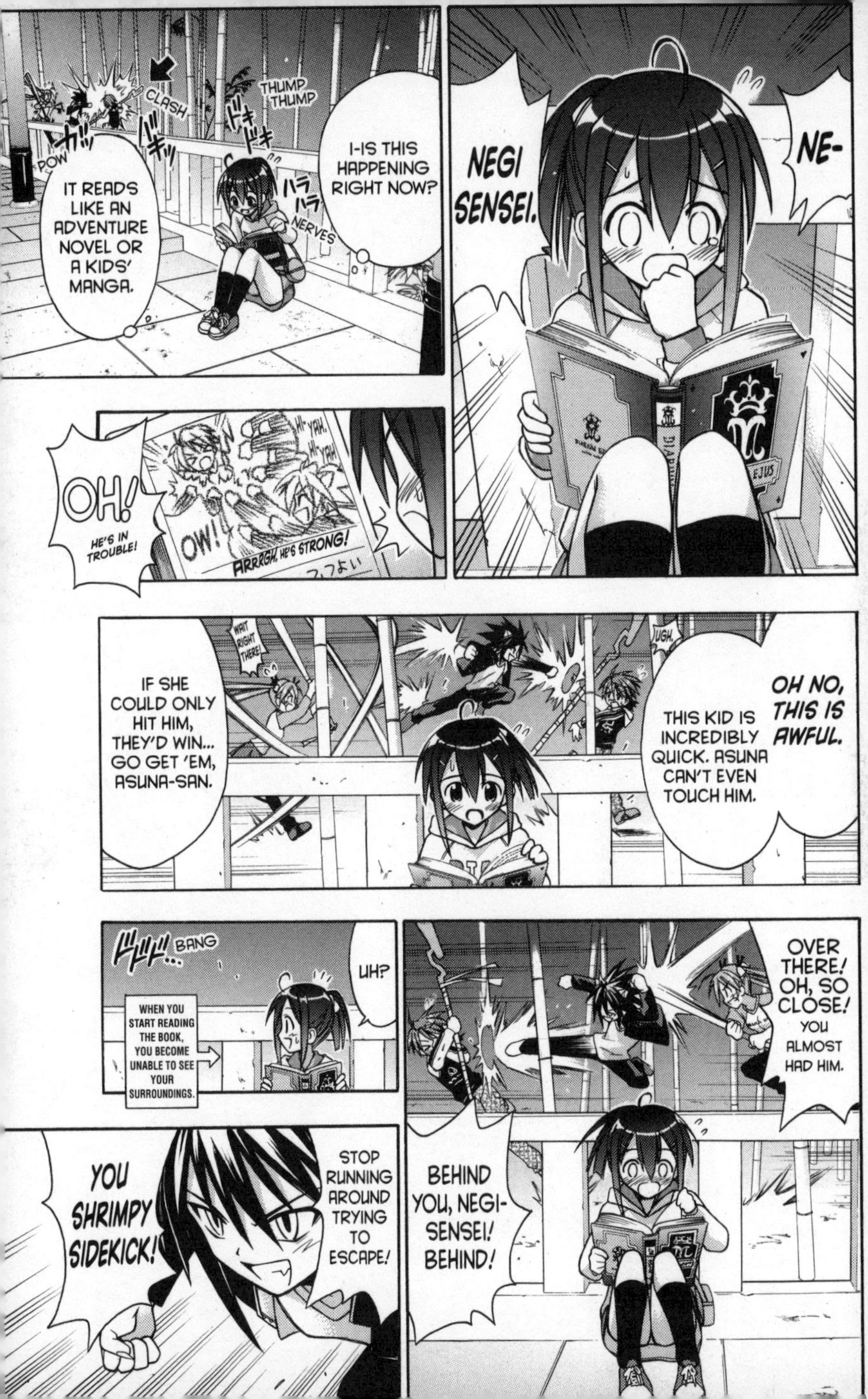
NE-
NEGI SENSEI.
THUMP THUMP
I-IS THIS HAPPENING RIGHT NOW?
CLASH
POW
NERVES
IT READS LIKE AN ADVENTURE NOVEL OR A KIDS' MANGA.
HI-YAH, HI-YAH
OW!
ARRRGH, HE'S STRONG!
OH!
HE'S IN TROUBLE!
OH NO, THIS IS AWFUL.
THIS KID IS INCREDIBLY QUICK. ASUNA CAN'T EVEN TOUCH HIM.
UGH,
WAIT RIGHT THERE!
IF SHE COULD ONLY HIT HIM, THEY'D WIN... GO GET 'EM, ASUNA-SAN.
OVER THERE! OH, SO CLOSE!
YOU ALMOST HAD HIM.
BEHIND YOU, NEGI-SENSEI! BEHIND!
UH?
BANG...
WHEN YOU START READING THE BOOK, YOU BECOME UNABLE TO SEE YOUR SURROUNDINGS.
STOP RUNNING AROUND TRYING TO ESCAPE!
YOU SHRIMPY SIDEKICK!

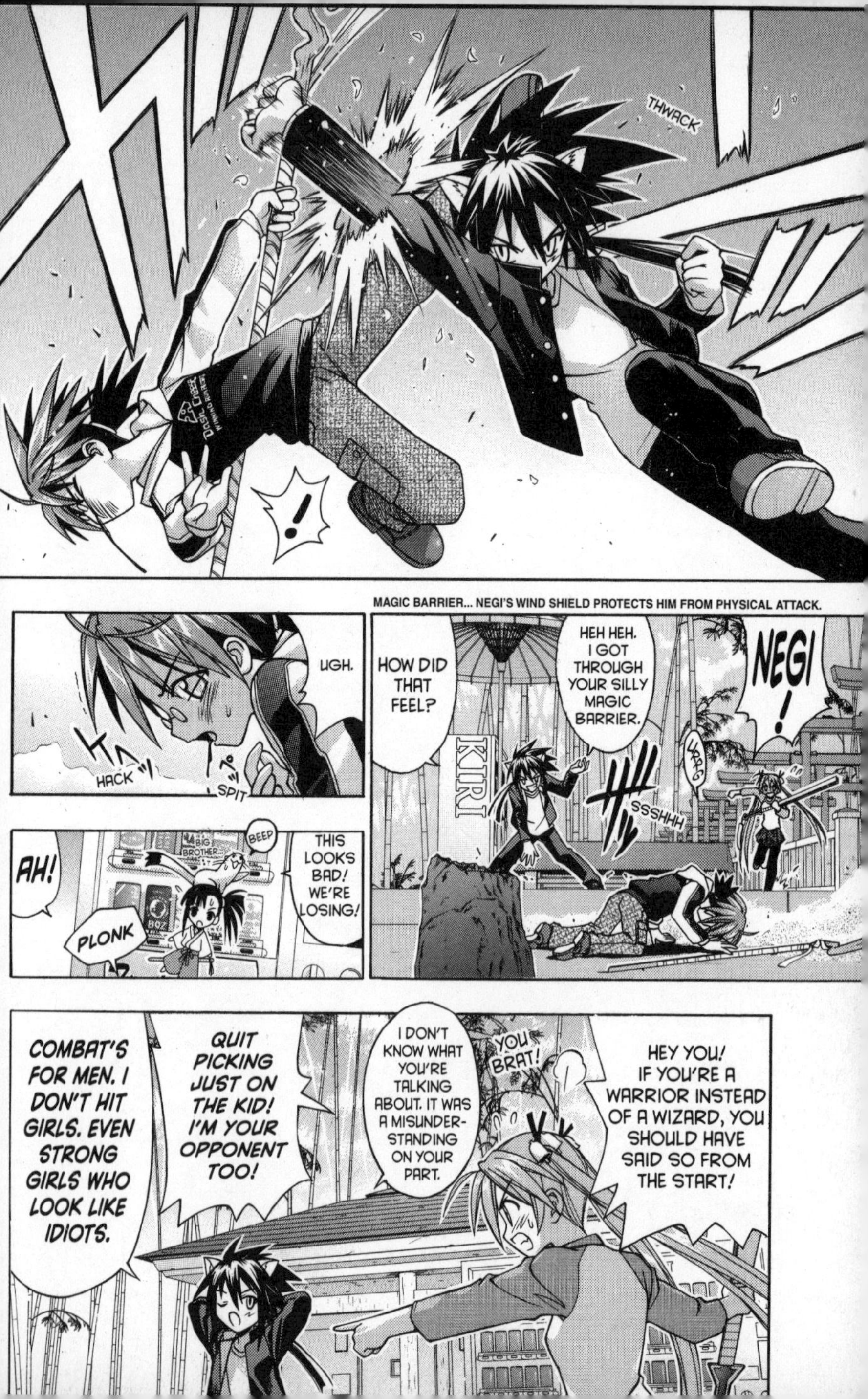
THWACK
!
MAGIC BARRIER... NEGI'S WIND SHIELD PROTECTS HIM FROM PHYSICAL ATTACK.
NEGI!
URRG
SSSHHH
HEH HEH. I GOT THROUGH YOUR SILLY MAGIC BARRIER.
HOW DID THAT FEEL?
KIRI
UGH.
SPIT
HACK
THIS LOOKS BAD! WE'RE LOSING!
BEEP
BIG BROTHER...
AH!
PLONK
HEY YOU! IF YOU'RE A WARRIOR INSTEAD OF A WIZARD, YOU SHOULD HAVE SAID SO FROM THE START!
YOU BRAT!
I DON'T KNOW WHAT YOU'RE TALKING ABOUT. IT WAS A MISUNDERSTANDING ON YOUR PART.
QUIT PICKING JUST ON THE KID! I'M YOUR OPPONENT TOO!
COMBAT'S FOR MEN. I DON'T HIT GIRLS. EVEN STRONG GIRLS WHO LOOK LIKE IDIOTS.

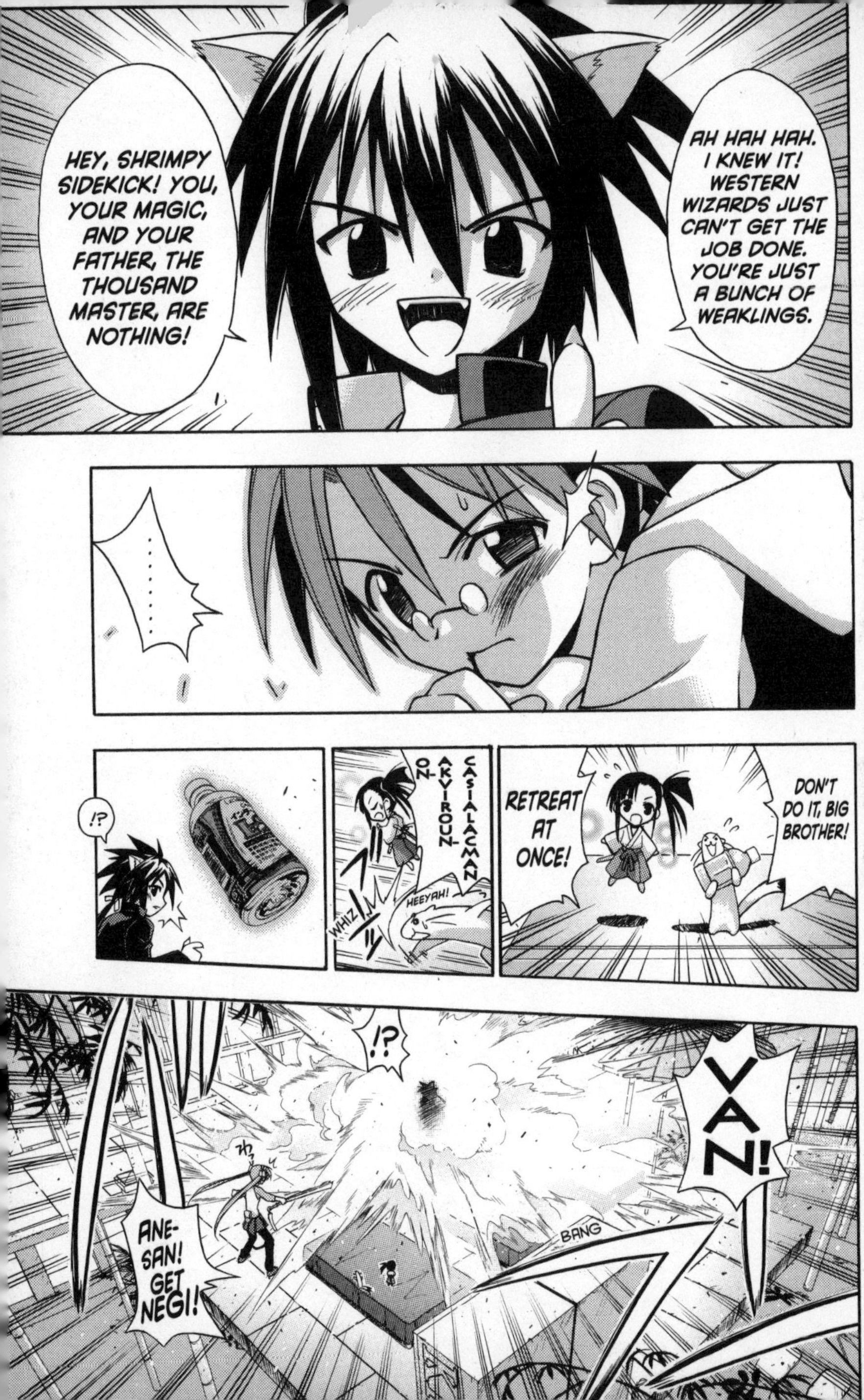
AH HAH HAH. I KNEW IT! WESTERN WIZARDS JUST CAN'T GET THE JOB DONE. YOU'RE JUST A BUNCH OF WEAKLINGS.
HEY, SHRIMPY SIDEKICK! YOU, YOUR MAGIC, AND YOUR FATHER, THE THOUSAND MASTER, ARE NOTHING!
......
DON'T DO IT, BIG BROTHER!
RETREAT AT ONCE!
ON- AKVIROUN- CASIALACMAN
HEEYAH!
WHIZ
!?
VAN!
!?
BANG
ANE-SAN! GET NEGI!

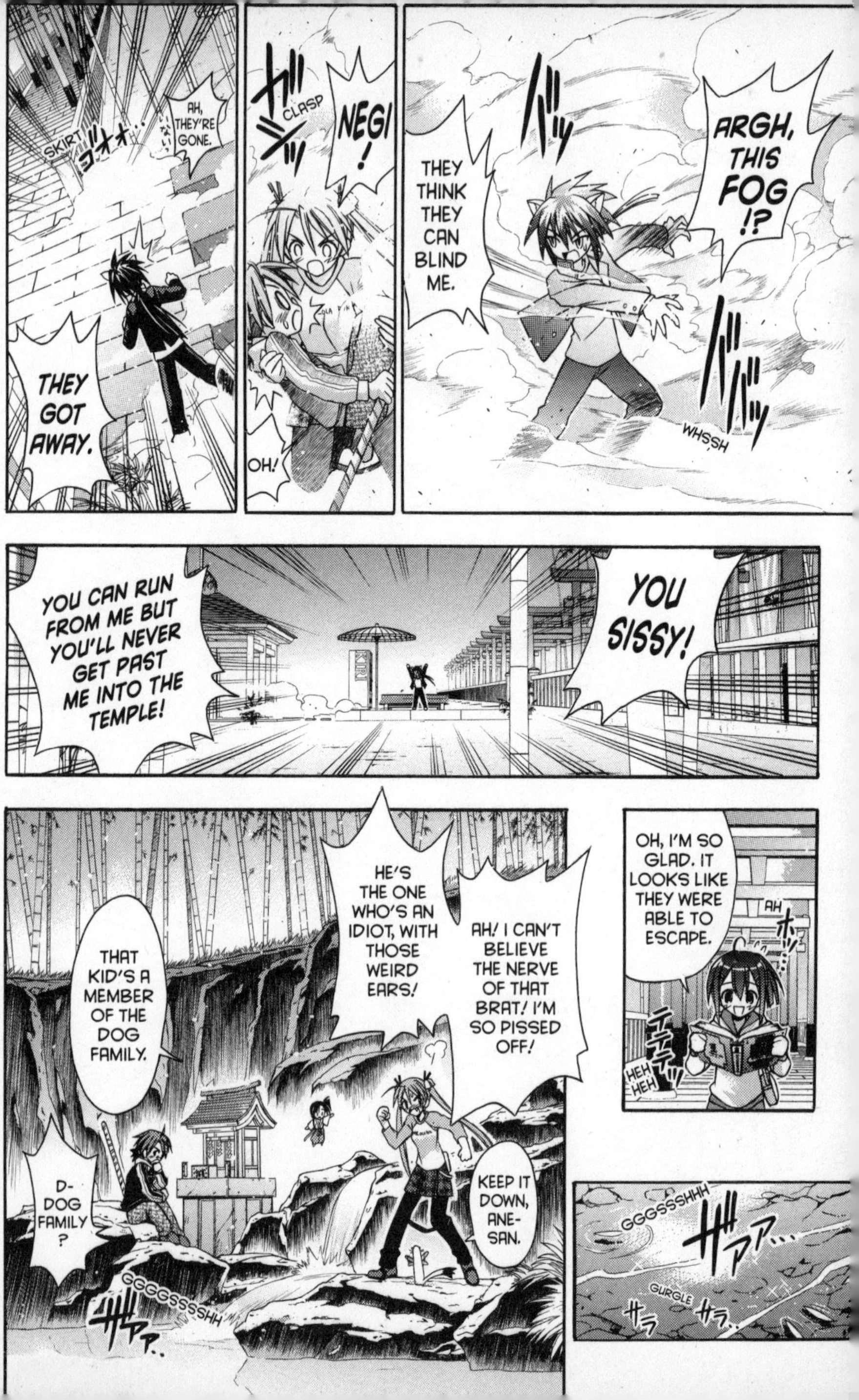
ARGH, THIS FOG !?
THEY THINK THEY CAN BLIND ME.
WHSSH
NEGI!
CLASP
OH!
AH, THEY'RE GONE.
SKIRT
THEY GOT AWAY.
YOU SISSY!
YOU CAN RUN FROM ME BUT YOU'LL NEVER GET PAST ME INTO THE TEMPLE!
OH, I'M SO GLAD. IT LOOKS LIKE THEY WERE ABLE TO ESCAPE.
AH
HEH HEH
GGGSSSHHH
GURGLE
AH! I CAN'T BELIEVE THE NERVE OF THAT BRAT! I'M SO PISSED OFF!
HE'S THE ONE WHO'S AN IDIOT, WITH THOSE WEIRD EARS!
THAT KID'S A MEMBER OF THE DOG FAMILY.
KEEP IT DOWN, ANE-SAN.
D-DOG FAMILY?
GGGGSSSSSHH

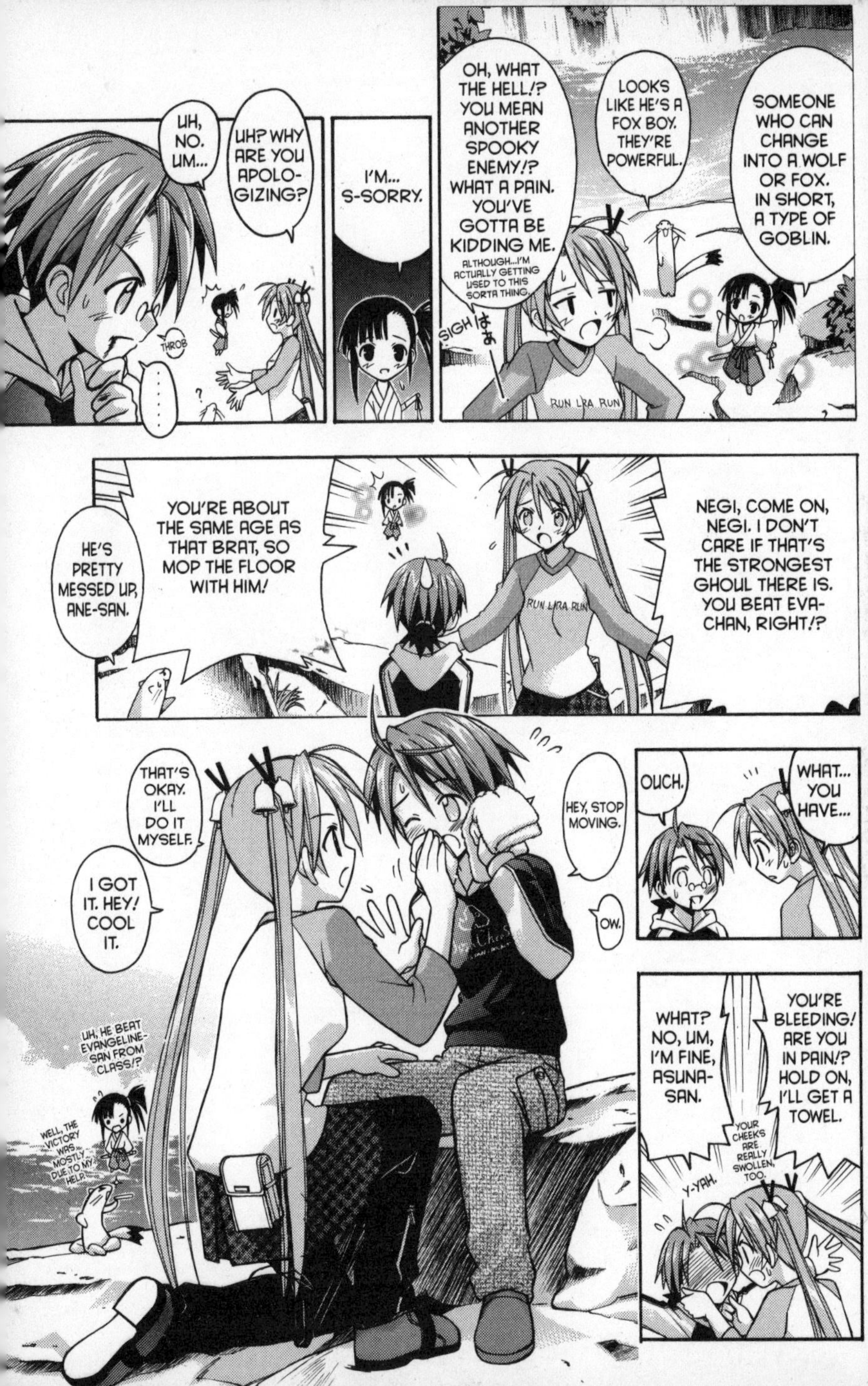
SOMEONE WHO CAN CHANGE INTO A WOLF OR FOX. IN SHORT, A TYPE OF GOBLIN.
LOOKS LIKE HE'S A FOX BOY. THEY'RE POWERFUL.
OH, WHAT THE HELL!? YOU MEAN ANOTHER SPOOKY ENEMY!? WHAT A PAIN. YOU'VE GOTTA BE KIDDING ME.
ALTHOUGH...I'M ACTUALLY GETTING USED TO THIS SORTA THING.
SIGH
はぁ
I'M... S-SORRY.
UH? WHY ARE YOU APOLOGIZING?
UH, NO. UM...
THROB
......
NEGI, COME ON, NEGI. I DON'T CARE IF THAT'S THE STRONGEST GHOUL THERE IS. YOU BEAT EVA-CHAN, RIGHT!?
YOU'RE ABOUT THE SAME AGE AS THAT BRAT, SO MOP THE FLOOR WITH HIM!
HE'S PRETTY MESSED UP, ANE-SAN.
WHAT... YOU HAVE...
OUCH.
YOU'RE BLEEDING! ARE YOU IN PAIN!? HOLD ON, I'LL GET A TOWEL.
WHAT? NO, UM, I'M FINE, ASUNA-SAN.
YOUR CHEEKS ARE REALLY SWOLLEN, TOO.
Y-YAH.
HEY, STOP MOVING.
OW.
THAT'S OKAY. I'LL DO IT MYSELF.
I GOT IT. HEY! COOL IT.
UH, HE BEAT EVANGELINE-SAN FROM CLASS!?
WELL, THE VICTORY WAS MOSTLY DUE TO MY HELP.

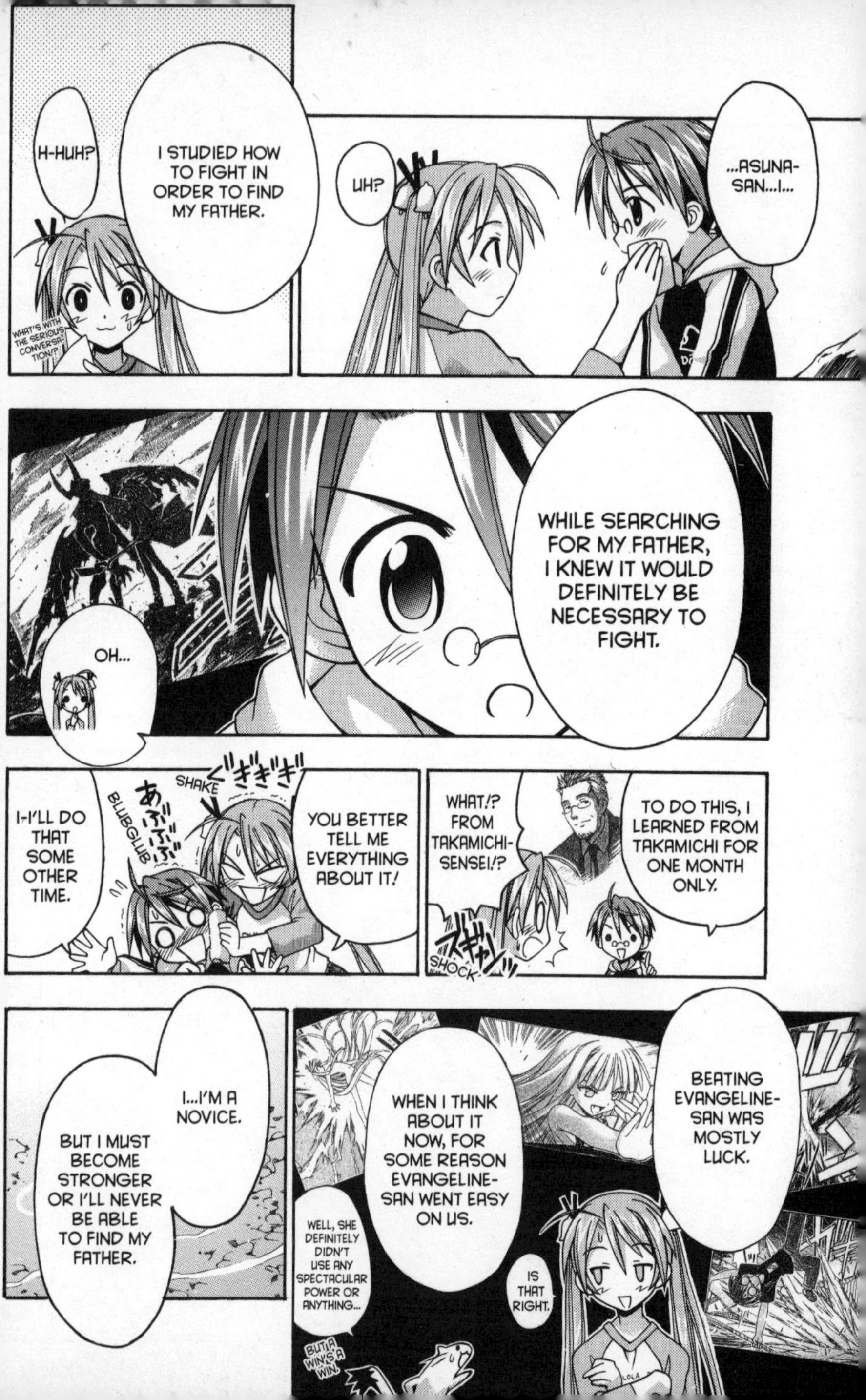
...ASUNA-SAN...I...
UH?
I STUDIED HOW TO FIGHT IN ORDER TO FIND MY FATHER.
H-HUH?
WHAT'S WITH THE SERIOUS CONVERSATION!?
WHILE SEARCHING FOR MY FATHER, I KNEW IT WOULD DEFINITELY BE NECESSARY TO FIGHT.
OH...
TO DO THIS, I LEARNED FROM TAKAMICHI FOR ONE MONTH ONLY.
WHAT!? FROM TAKAMICHI-SENSEI!?
SHOCK
SHAKE
YOU BETTER TELL ME EVERYTHING ABOUT IT!
BLUBGLUB
I-I'LL DO THAT SOME OTHER TIME.
BEATING EVANGELINE-SAN WAS MOSTLY LUCK.
WHEN I THINK ABOUT IT NOW, FOR SOME REASON EVANGELINE-SAN WENT EASY ON US.
IS THAT RIGHT.
WELL, SHE DEFINITELY DIDN'T USE ANY SPECTACULAR POWER OR ANYTHING...
BUT A WIN'S A WIN.
I...I'M A NOVICE.
BUT I MUST BECOME STRONGER OR I'LL NEVER BE ABLE TO FIND MY FATHER.

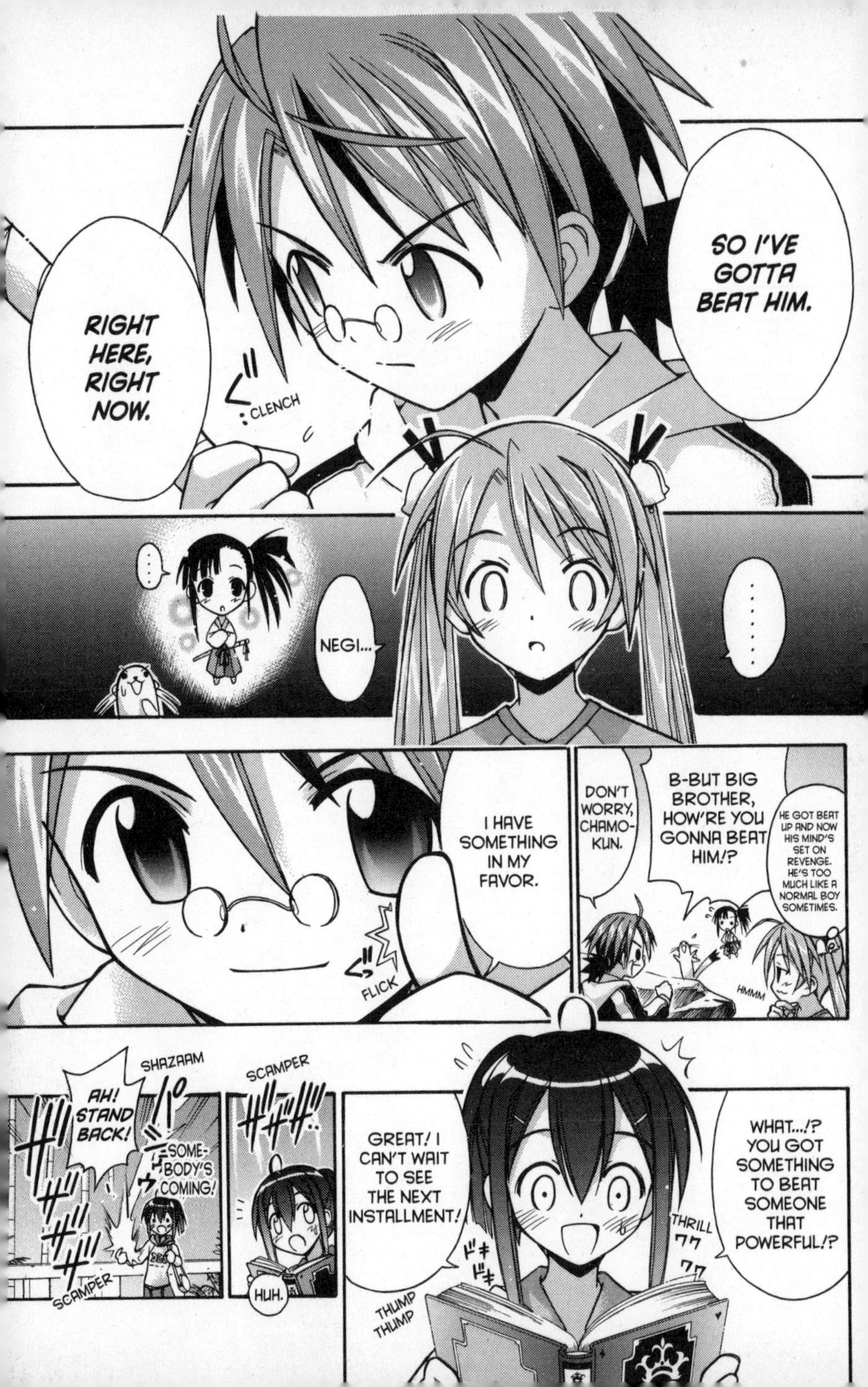
SO I'VE GOTTA BEAT HIM.
RIGHT HERE, RIGHT NOW.
CLENCH
......
NEGI...
...
B-BUT BIG BROTHER, HOW'RE YOU GONNA BEAT HIM!?
HE GOT BEAT UP AND NOW HIS MIND'S SET ON REVENGE. HE'S TOO MUCH LIKE A NORMAL BOY SOMETIMES.
DON'T WORRY, CHAMO-KUN.
HMMM
I HAVE SOMETHING IN MY FAVOR.
FLICK
WHAT...!? YOU GOT SOMETHING TO BEAT SOMEONE THAT POWERFUL!?
THRILL
GREAT! I CAN'T WAIT TO SEE THE NEXT INSTALLMENT!
THUMP THUMP
SCAMPER
HUH.
SHAZAAM
AH! STAND BACK!
SOMEBODY'S COMING!
SCAMPER

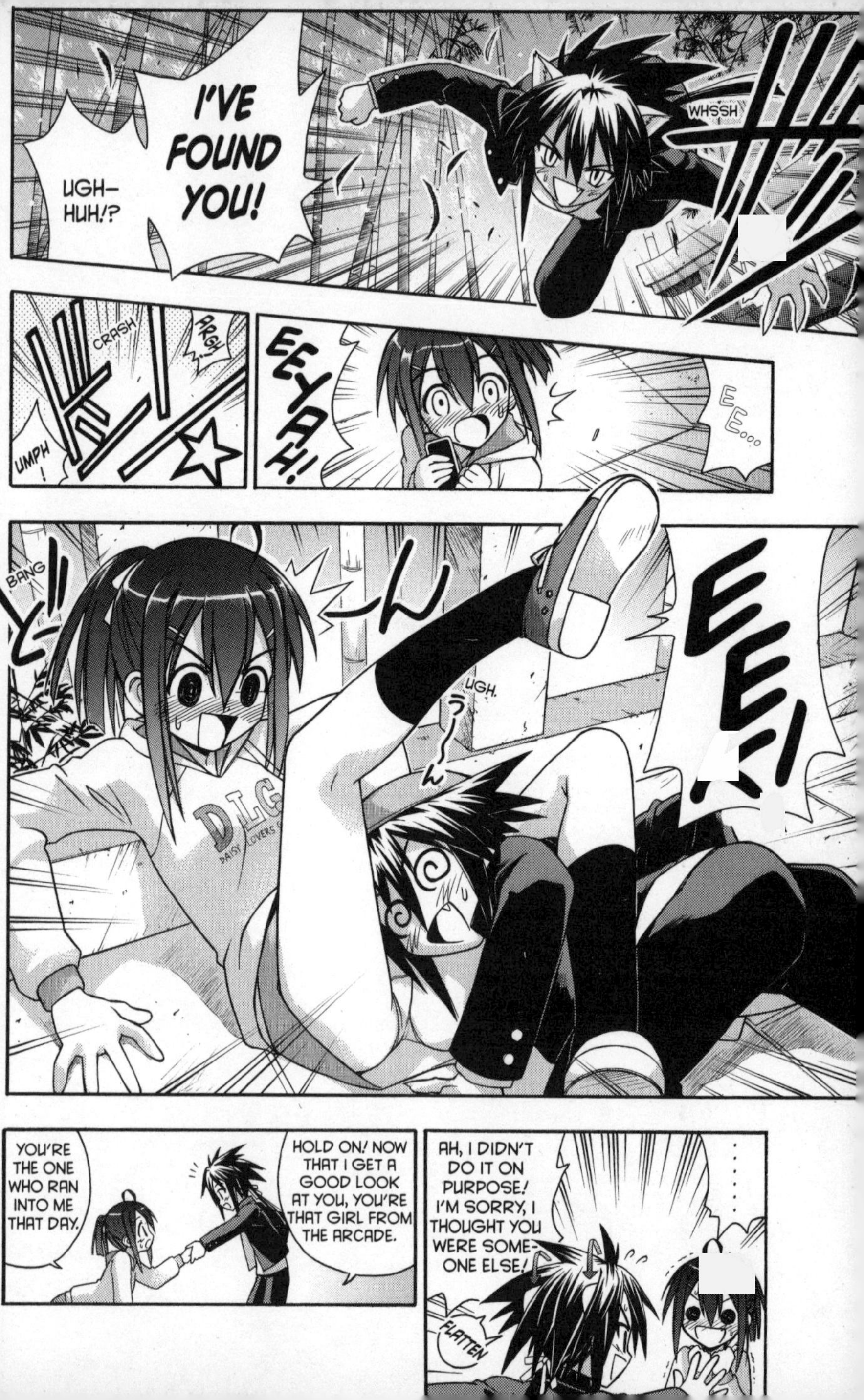
WHSSH
I'VE FOUND YOU!
UGH—HUH!?
EEYAH!
EE...
ARGH
CRASH
UMPH!
EEE!
UGH.
BANG
AH, I DIDN'T DO IT ON PURPOSE! I'M SORRY, I THOUGHT YOU WERE SOME-ONE ELSE!
......
FLATTEN
HOLD ON! NOW THAT I GET A GOOD LOOK AT YOU, YOU'RE THAT GIRL FROM THE ARCADE.
YOU'RE THE ONE WHO RAN INTO ME THAT DAY.

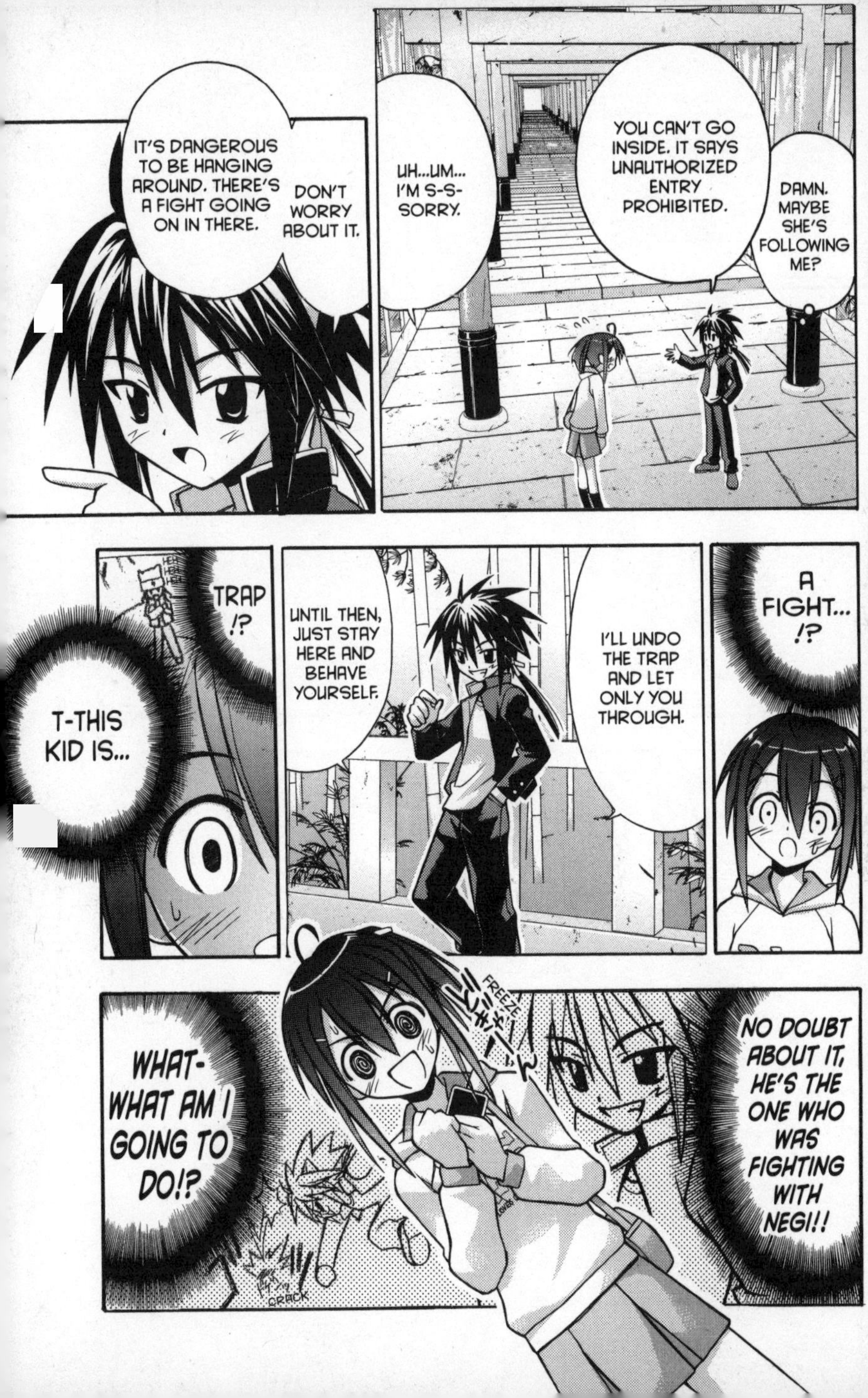
DAMN. MAYBE SHE'S FOLLOWING ME?
YOU CAN'T GO INSIDE. IT SAYS UNAUTHORIZED ENTRY PROHIBITED.
UH...UM... I'M S-S-SORRY.
DON'T WORRY ABOUT IT.
IT'S DANGEROUS TO BE HANGING AROUND. THERE'S A FIGHT GOING ON IN THERE.
A FIGHT...!?
I'LL UNDO THE TRAP AND LET ONLY YOU THROUGH.
UNTIL THEN, JUST STAY HERE AND BEHAVE YOURSELF.
TRAP!?
T-THIS KID IS...
NO DOUBT ABOUT IT, HE'S THE ONE WHO WAS FIGHTING WITH NEGI!!
FREEZE
WHAT-WHAT AM I GOING TO DO!?
CRACK

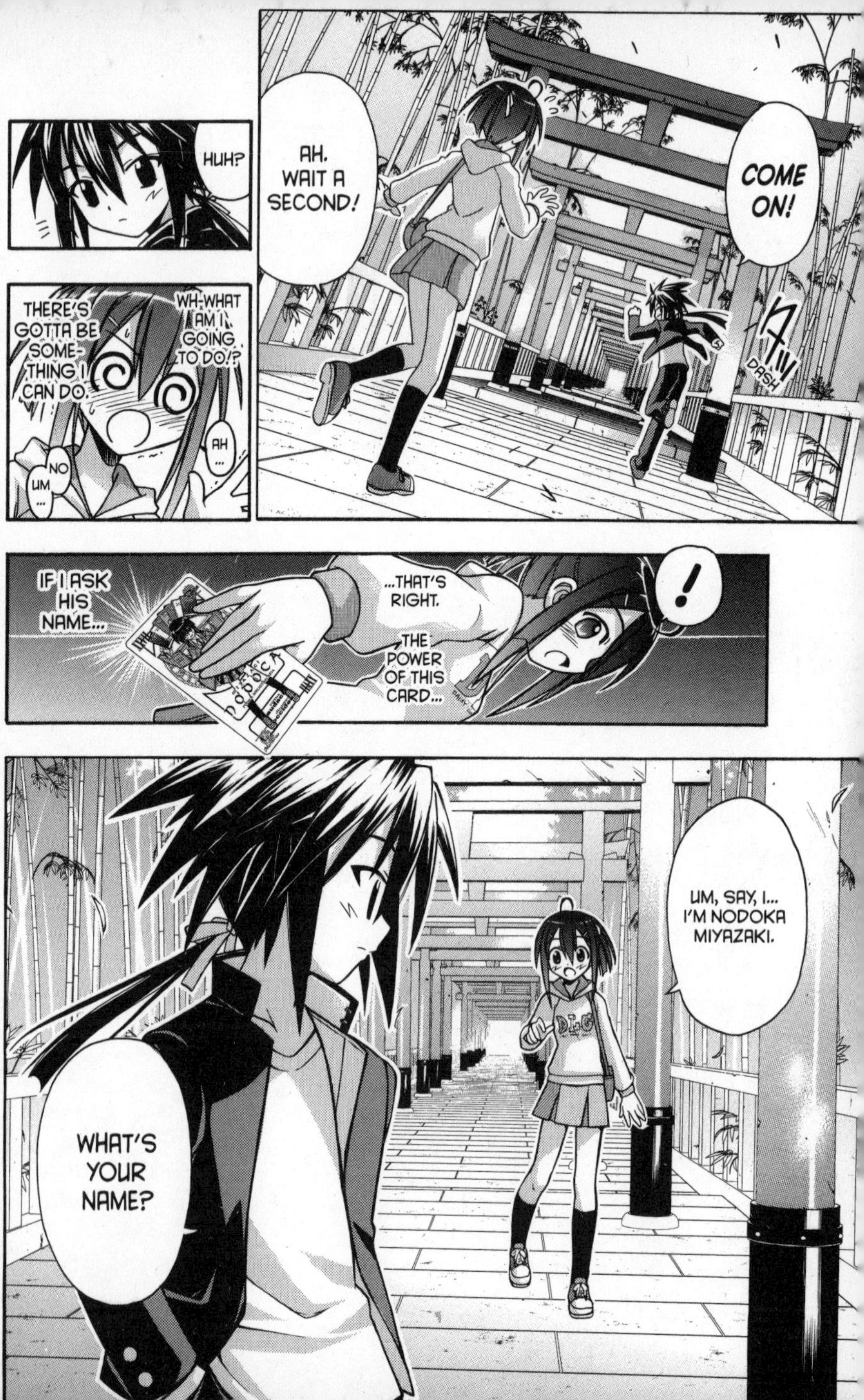
COME ON!
DASH
AH. WAIT A SECOND!
HUH?
WH-WHAT AM I GOING TO DO!?
THERE'S GOTTA BE SOMETHING I CAN DO.
AH...
NO
UM...
!
...THAT'S RIGHT.
THE POWER OF THIS CARD...
IF I ASK HIS NAME...
UM, SAY, I... I'M NODOKA MIYAZAKI.
WHAT'S YOUR NAME?

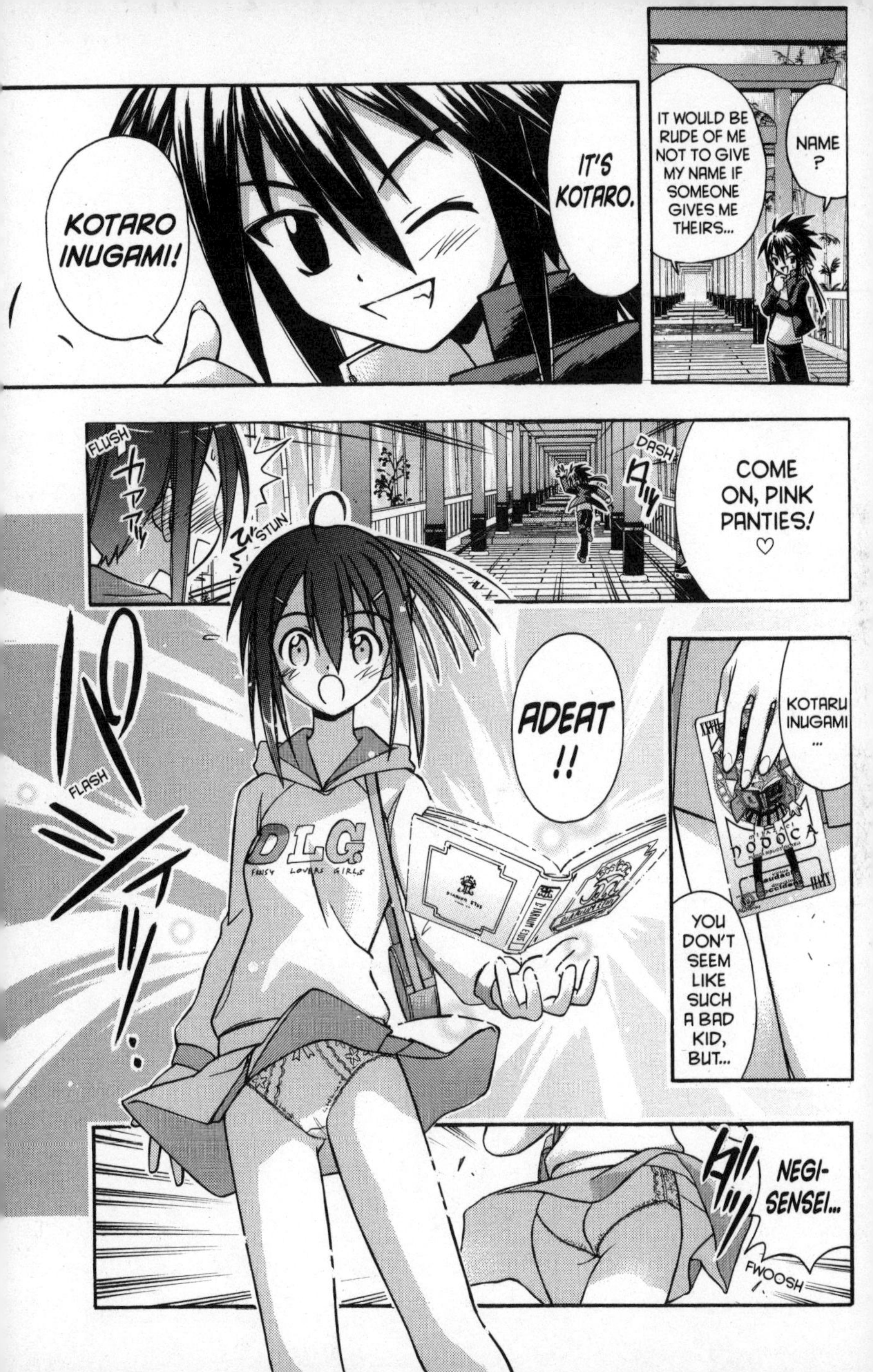
NAME ?
IT WOULD BE RUDE OF ME NOT TO GIVE MY NAME IF SOMEONE GIVES ME THEIRS...
IT'S KOTARO.
KOTARO INUGAMI!
COME ON, PINK PANTIES! ♡
DASH
FLUSH
STUN
KOTARU INUGAMI ...
YOU DON'T SEEM LIKE SUCH A BAD KID, BUT...
NEGI-SENSEI...
FWOOSH
ADEAT !!
FLASH

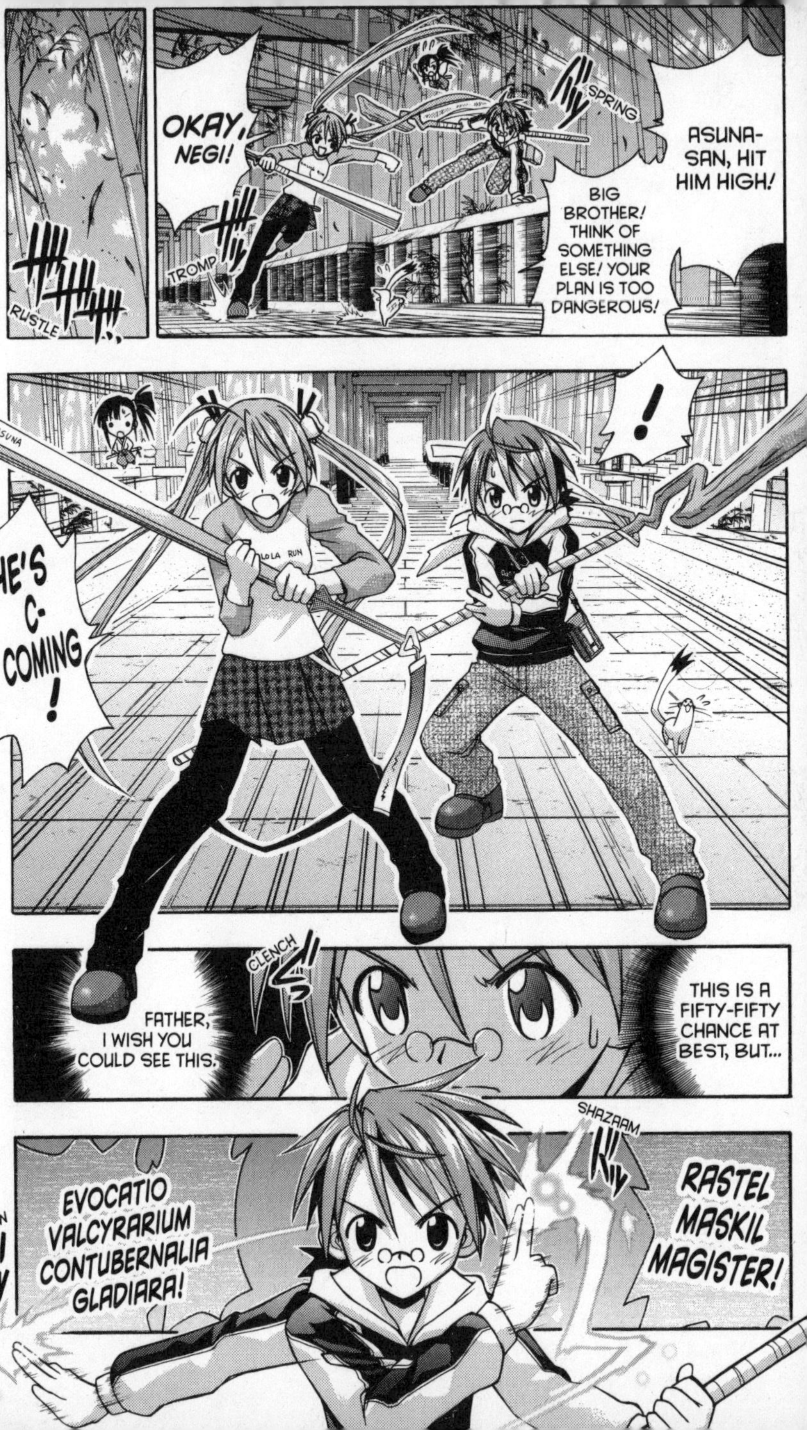
ASUNA-SAN, HIT HIM HIGH!
SPRING
BIG BROTHER! THINK OF SOMETHING ELSE! YOUR PLAN IS TOO DANGEROUS!
OKAY, NEGI!
TROMP
RUSTLE
!
MINISTRA MAGI ASUNA
LOLA RUN
HE'S C-COMING!
THIS IS A FIFTY-FIFTY CHANCE AT BEST, BUT...
CLENCH
FATHER, I WISH YOU COULD SEE THIS.
SHAZAAM
RASTEL MASKIL MAGISTER!
EVOCATIO VALCYRARIUM CONTUBERNALIA GLADIARA!
GLOW

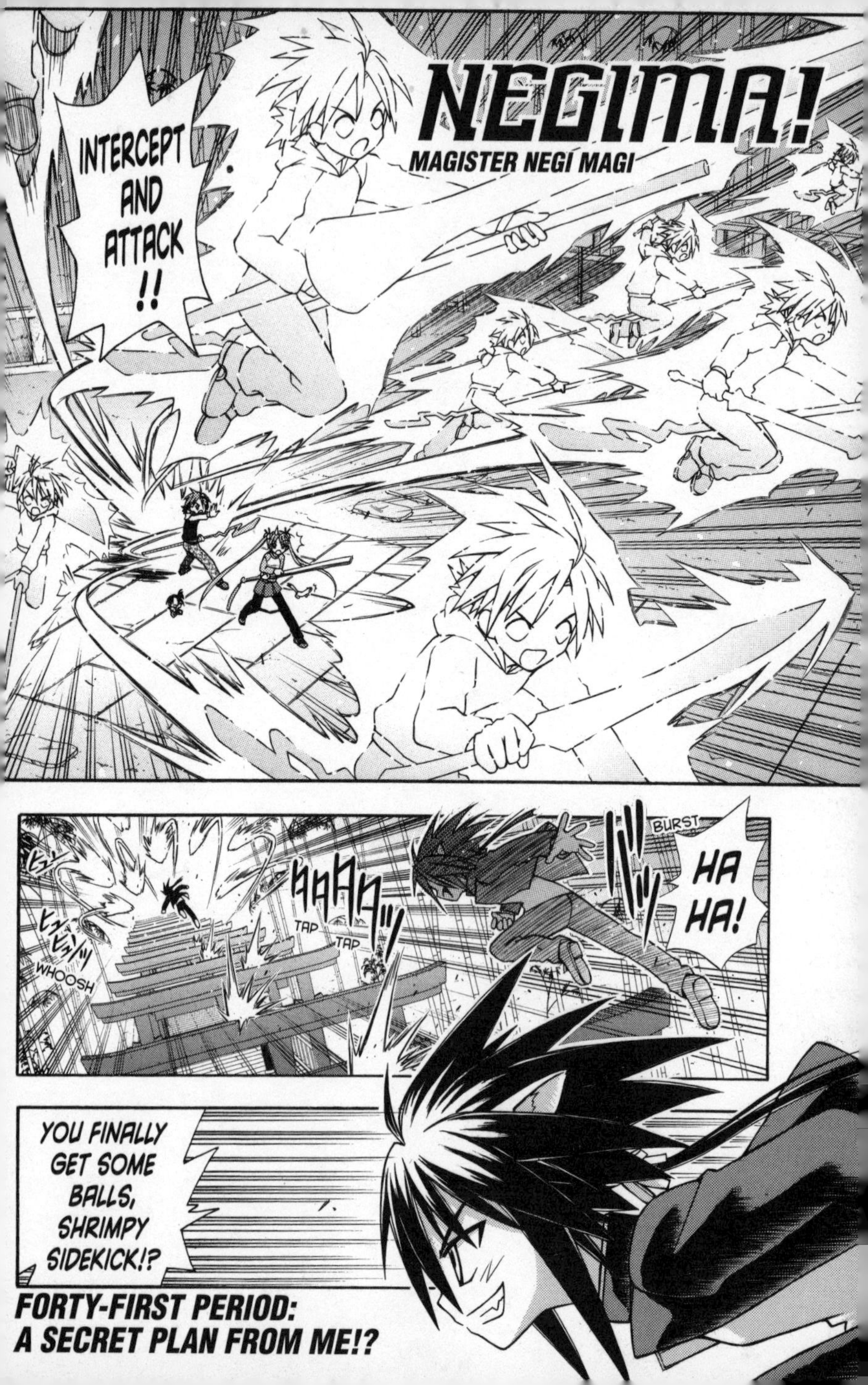
NEGIMA!
MAGISTER NEGI MAGI
INTERCEPT AND ATTACK!!
BURST
HA HA!
TAP TAP
WHOOSH
YOU FINALLY GET SOME BALLS, SHRIMPY SIDEKICK!?
FORTY-FIRST PERIOD: A SECRET PLAN FROM ME!?

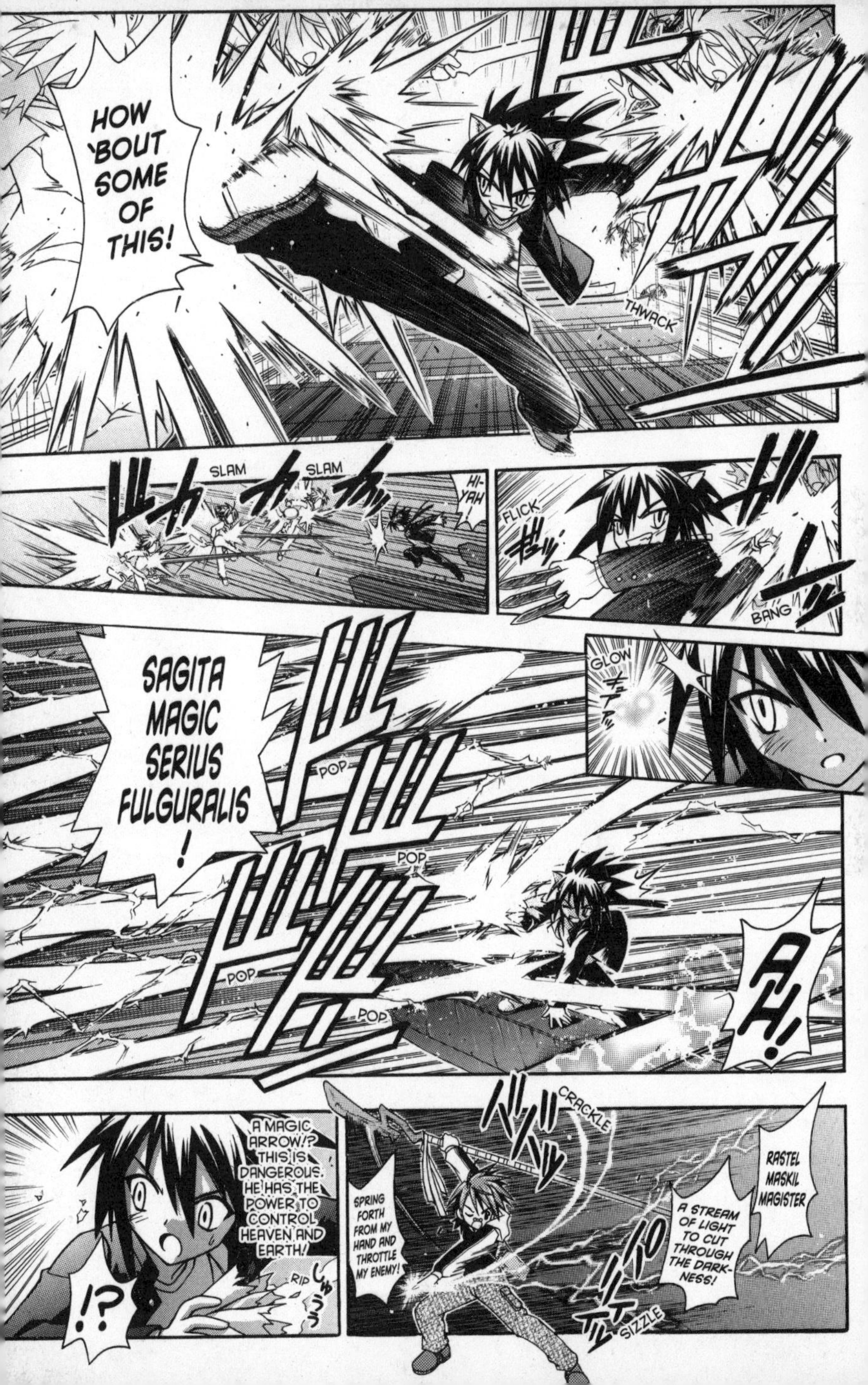
THWACK
HOW 'BOUT SOME OF THIS!
FLICK
BANG
HI-YAH!
SLAM
SLAM
GLOW
SAGITA MAGIC SERIUS FULGURALIS!
POP
POP
POP
POP
AH!
RASTEL MASKIL MAGISTER
A STREAM OF LIGHT TO CUT THROUGH THE DARKNESS!
CRACKLE
SPRING FORTH FROM MY HAND AND THROTTLE MY ENEMY!
SIZZLE
A MAGIC ARROW!? THIS IS DANGEROUS. HE HAS THE POWER TO CONTROL HEAVEN AND EARTH!
RIP
!?

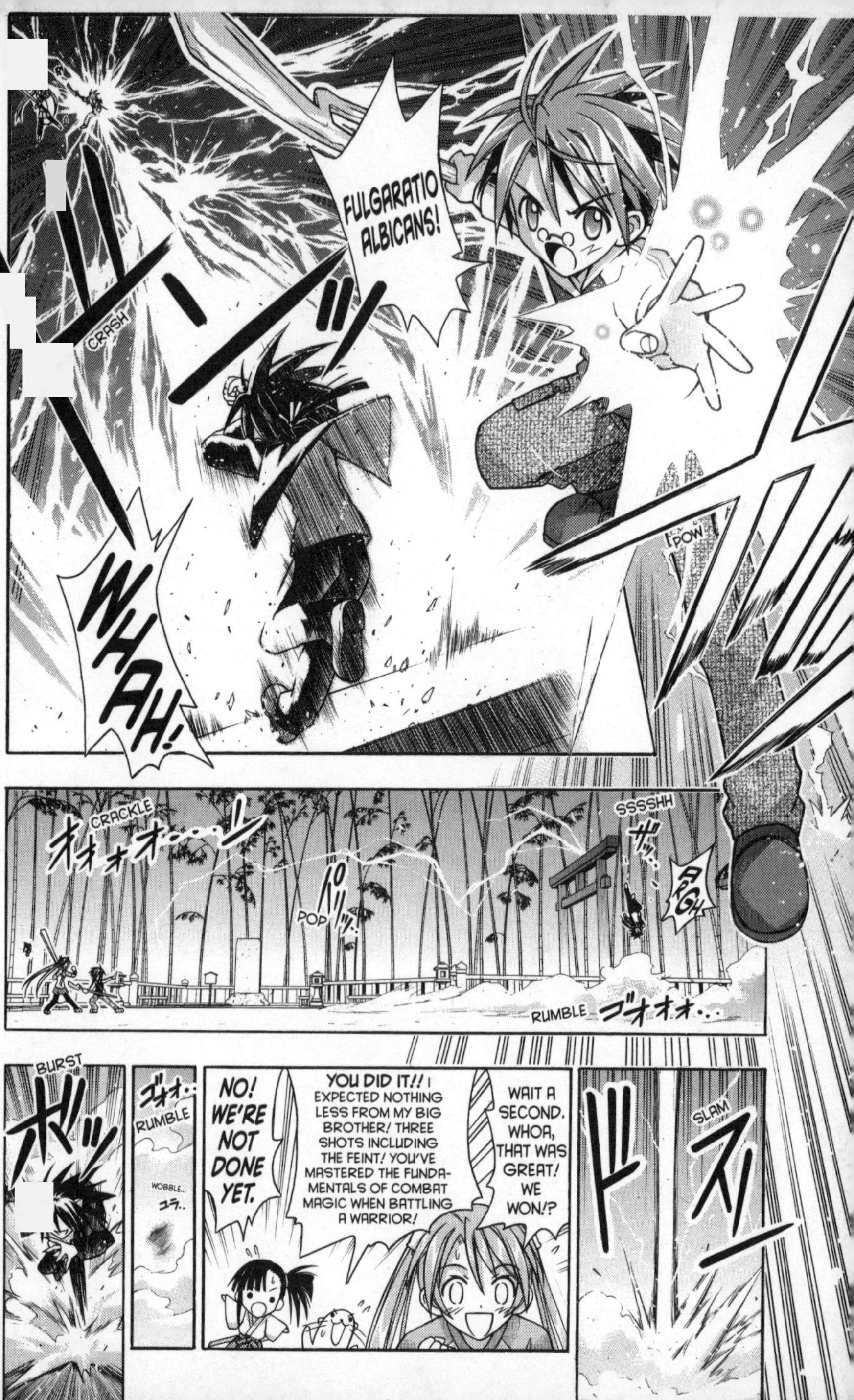
FULGARATIO ALBICANS!
CRASH
POW
WHAH!
SSSSHH
ARGH
CRACKLE
POP
RUMBLE
ゴオオオ…
SLAM
WAIT A SECOND. WHOA, THAT WAS GREAT! WE WON!?
YOU DID IT!! I EXPECTED NOTHING LESS FROM MY BIG BROTHER! THREE SHOTS INCLUDING THE FEINT! YOU'VE MASTERED THE FUNDAMENTALS OF COMBAT MAGIC WHEN BATTLING A WARRIOR!
NO! WE'RE NOT DONE YET.
ゴオ…
RUMBLE
WOBBLE…
ユラ..
BURST

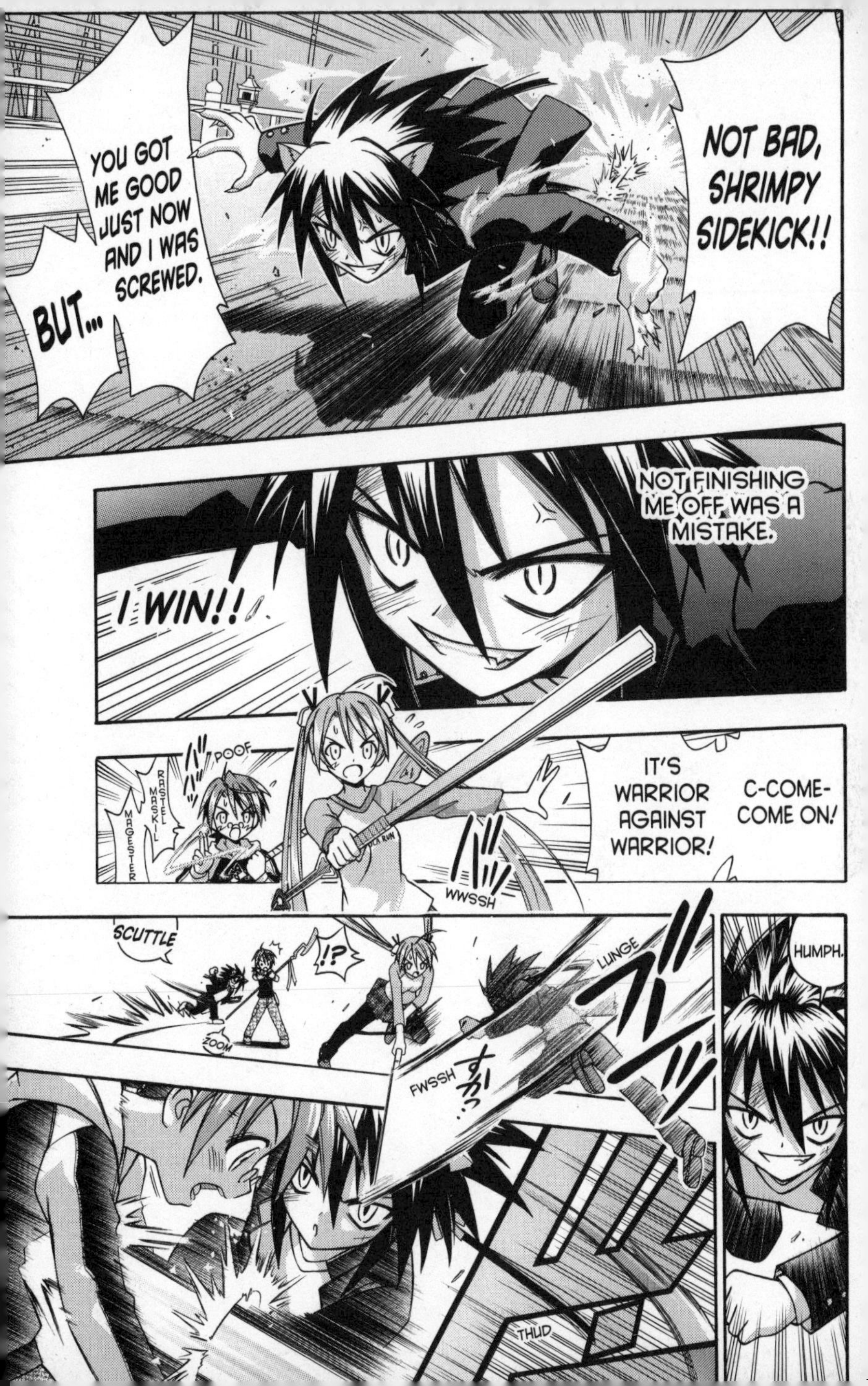
NOT BAD, SHRIMPY SIDEKICK!!
YOU GOT ME GOOD JUST NOW AND I WAS SCREWED.
BUT...
NOT FINISHING ME OFF WAS A MISTAKE.
I WIN!!
C-COME-COME ON!
IT'S WARRIOR AGAINST WARRIOR!
WWSSH
POOF
RASTEL MASKIL MAGESTER
HUMPH.
LUNGE
!?
SCUTTLE
ZOOM
FWSSH
すかっ
THUD

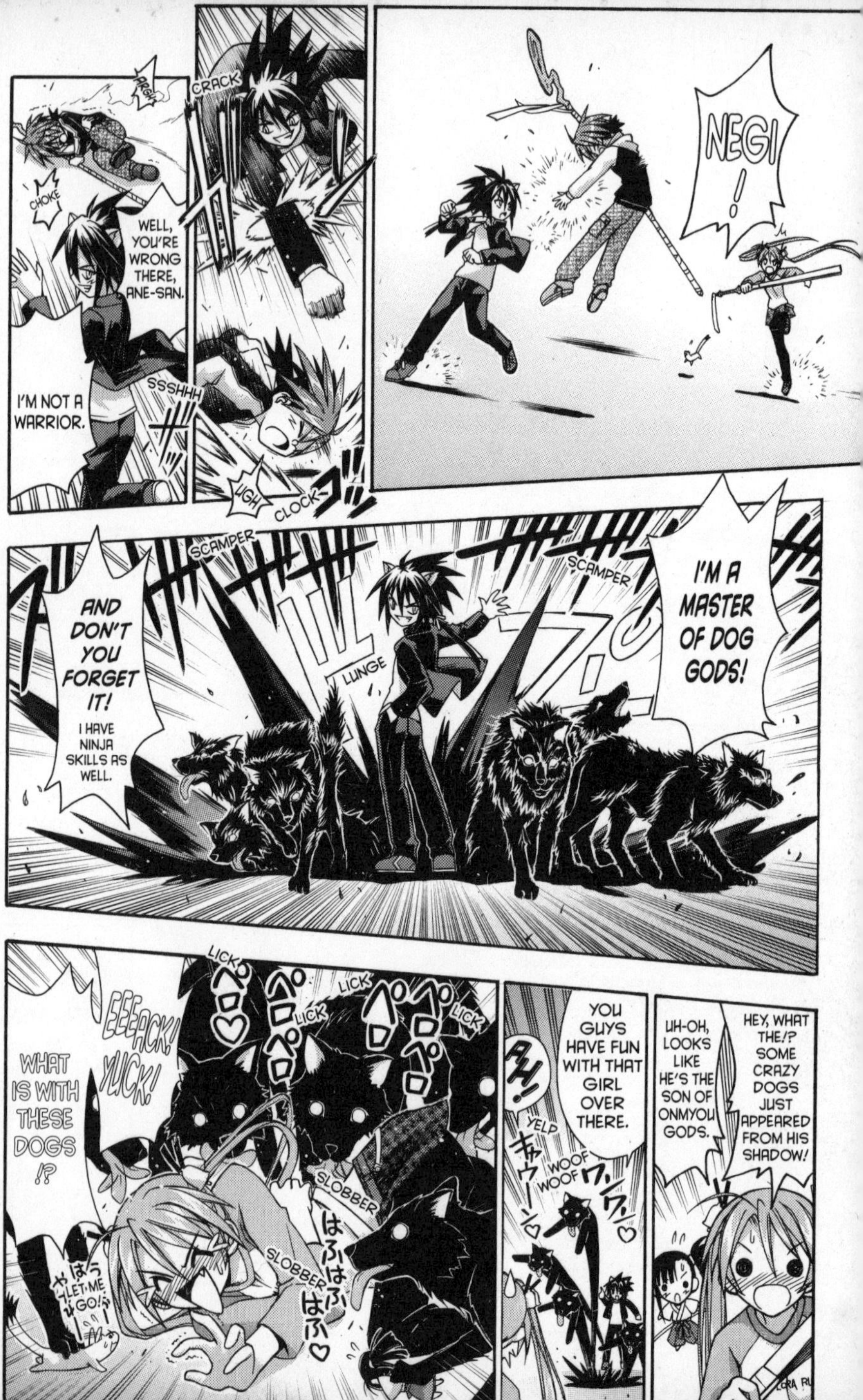
NEGI!
CRACK
SSSHHH
UGH
CLOCK
ARGH
CHOKE
WELL, YOU'RE WRONG THERE, ANE-SAN.
I'M NOT A WARRIOR.
I'M A MASTER OF DOG GODS!
SCAMPER
LUNGE
SCAMPER
AND DON'T YOU FORGET IT!
I HAVE NINJA SKILLS AS WELL.
HEY, WHAT THE!? SOME CRAZY DOGS JUST APPEARED FROM HIS SHADOW!
UH-OH, LOOKS LIKE HE'S THE SON OF ONMYOU GODS.
YOU GUYS HAVE FUN WITH THAT GIRL OVER THERE.
YELP
WOOF WOOF
LICK
LICK
LICK
LICK
EEEEACK! YUCK!
WHAT IS WITH THESE DOGS!?
SLOBBER
SLOBBER
LET ME GO!

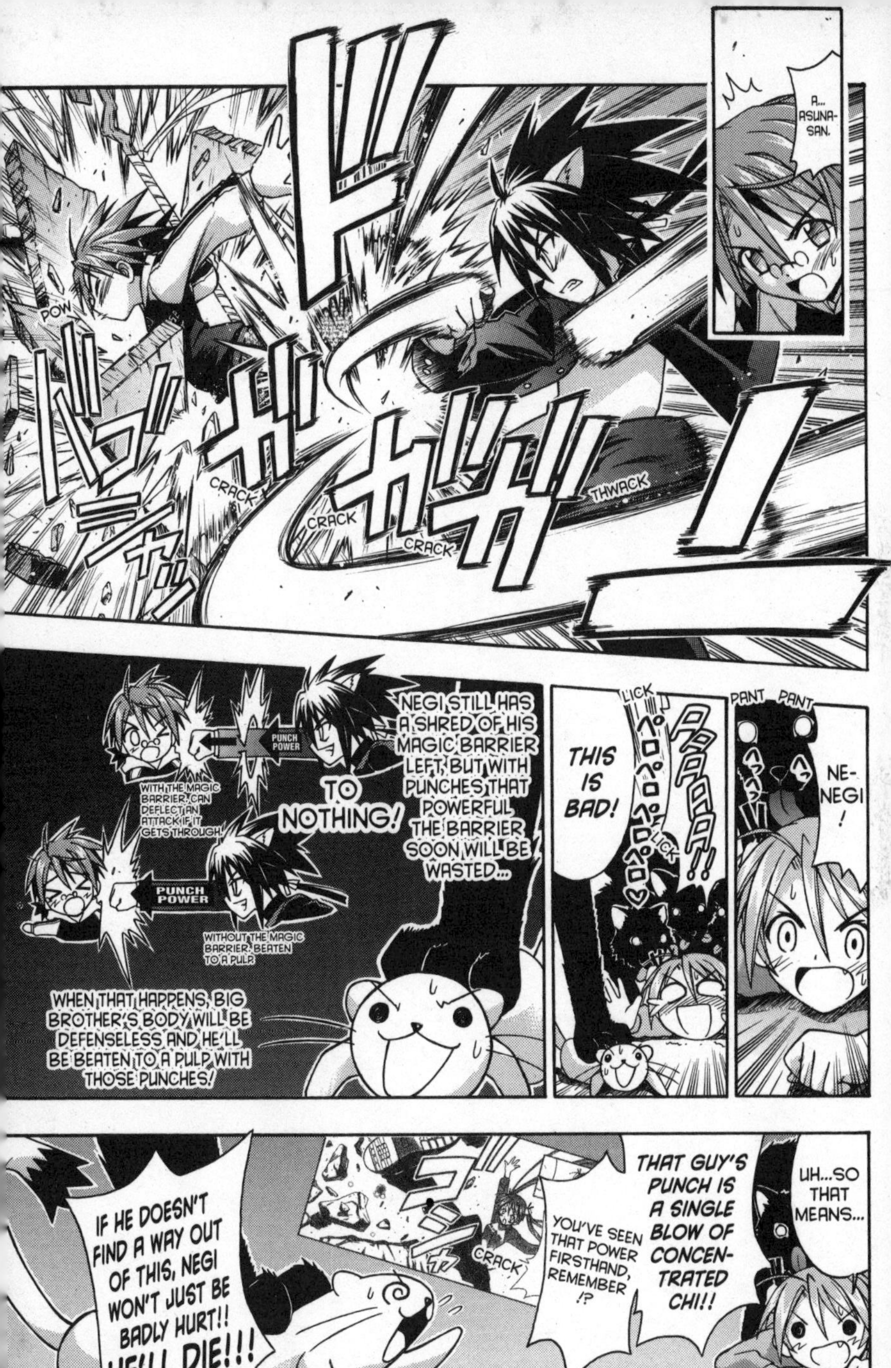
A... ASUNA-SAN.
POW
CRACK
CRACK
CRACK
THWACK
PANT PANT
NE-NEGI!
LICK
THIS IS BAD!
LICK
NEGI STILL HAS A SHRED OF HIS MAGIC BARRIER LEFT, BUT WITH PUNCHES THAT POWERFUL THE BARRIER SOON WILL BE WASTED...
PUNCH POWER
WITH THE MAGIC BARRIER, CAN DEFLECT AN ATTACK IF IT GETS THROUGH.
TO NOTHING!
PUNCH POWER
WITHOUT THE MAGIC BARRIER, BEATEN TO A PULP.
WHEN THAT HAPPENS, BIG BROTHER'S BODY WILL BE DEFENSELESS AND HE'LL BE BEATEN TO A PULP WITH THOSE PUNCHES!
UH...SO THAT MEANS...
THAT GUY'S PUNCH IS A SINGLE BLOW OF CONCEN-TRATED CHI!!
YOU'VE SEEN THAT POWER FIRSTHAND, REMEMBER!?
CRACK
IF HE DOESN'T FIND A WAY OUT OF THIS, NEGI WON'T JUST BE BADLY HURT!! HE'LL DIE!!!

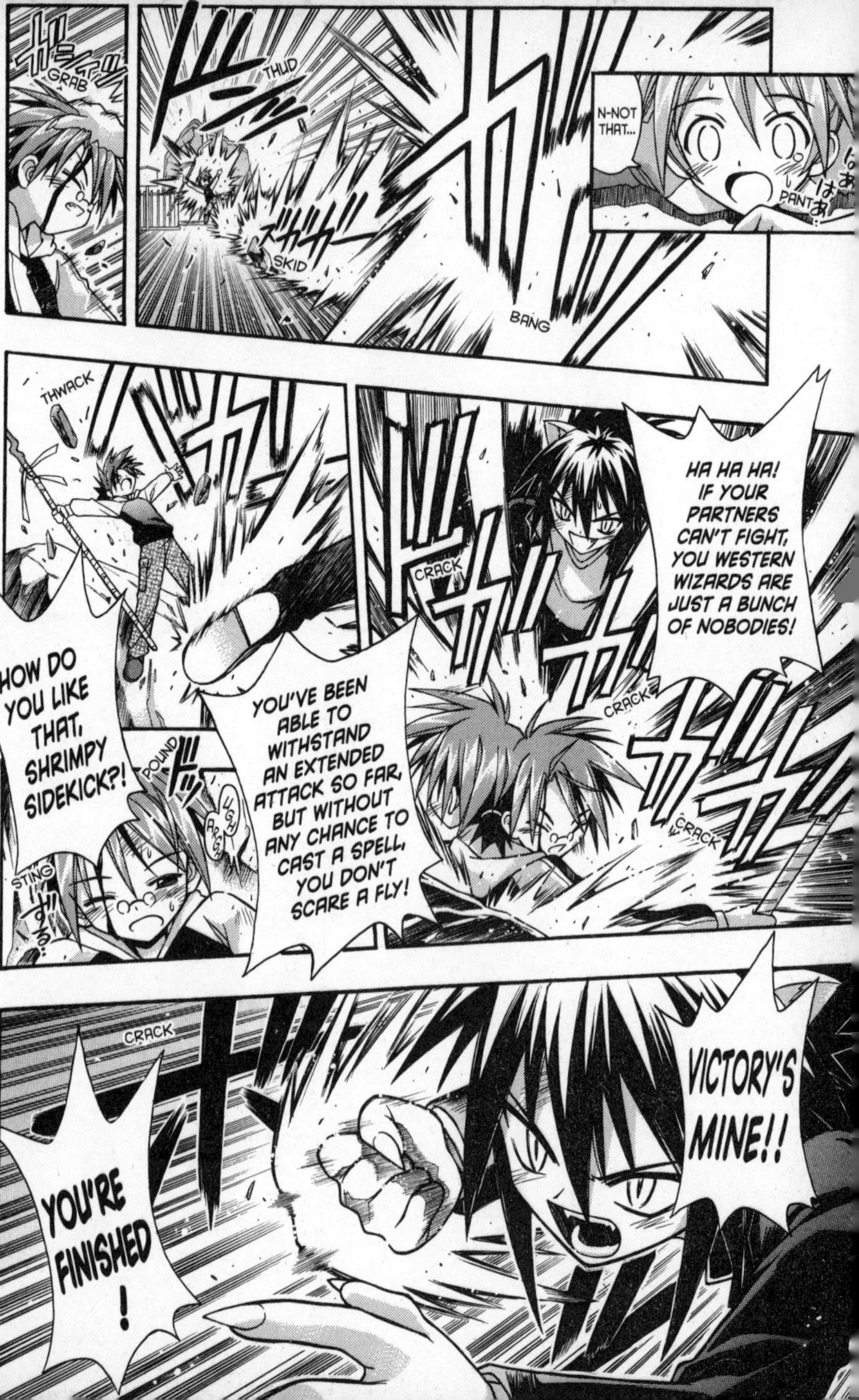
N-NOT THAT...
PANT
THUD
SKID
BANG
GRAB
HA HA HA! IF YOUR PARTNERS CAN'T FIGHT, YOU WESTERN WIZARDS ARE JUST A BUNCH OF NOBODIES!
CRACK
CRACK
CRACK
YOU'VE BEEN ABLE TO WITHSTAND AN EXTENDED ATTACK SO FAR, BUT WITHOUT ANY CHANCE TO CAST A SPELL, YOU DON'T SCARE A FLY!
THWACK
HOW DO YOU LIKE THAT, SHRIMPY SIDEKICK?!
POUND
UGH
ARGH
STING
CRACK
VICTORY'S MINE!!
YOU'RE FINISHED!

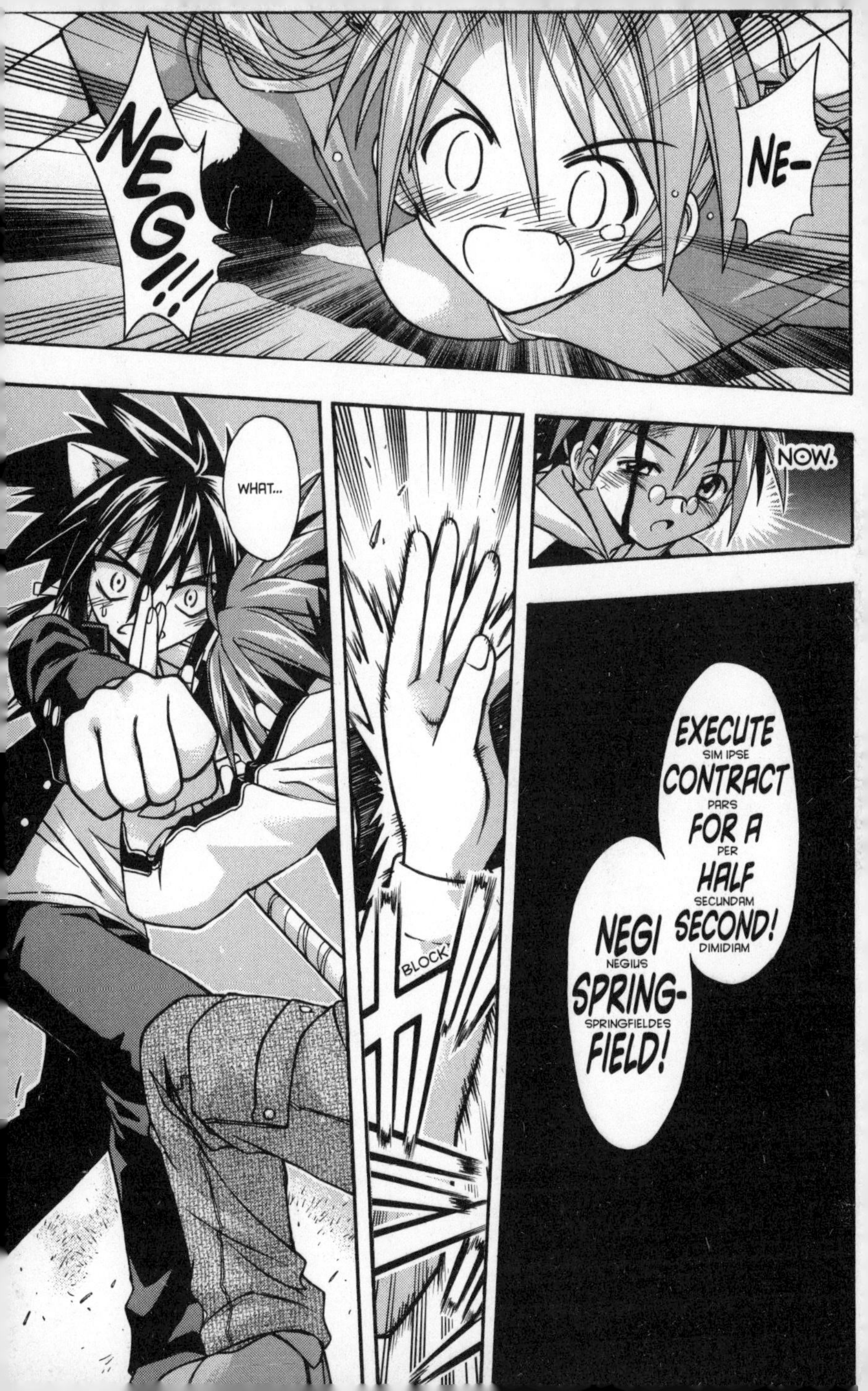
NE-
NEGI!!!
NOW.
EXECUTE SIM IPSE CONTRACT PARS FOR A PER HALF SECUNDAM SECOND! DIMIDIAM
NEGI NEGIUS SPRING- SPRINGFIELDES FIELD!
BLOCK
WHAT...

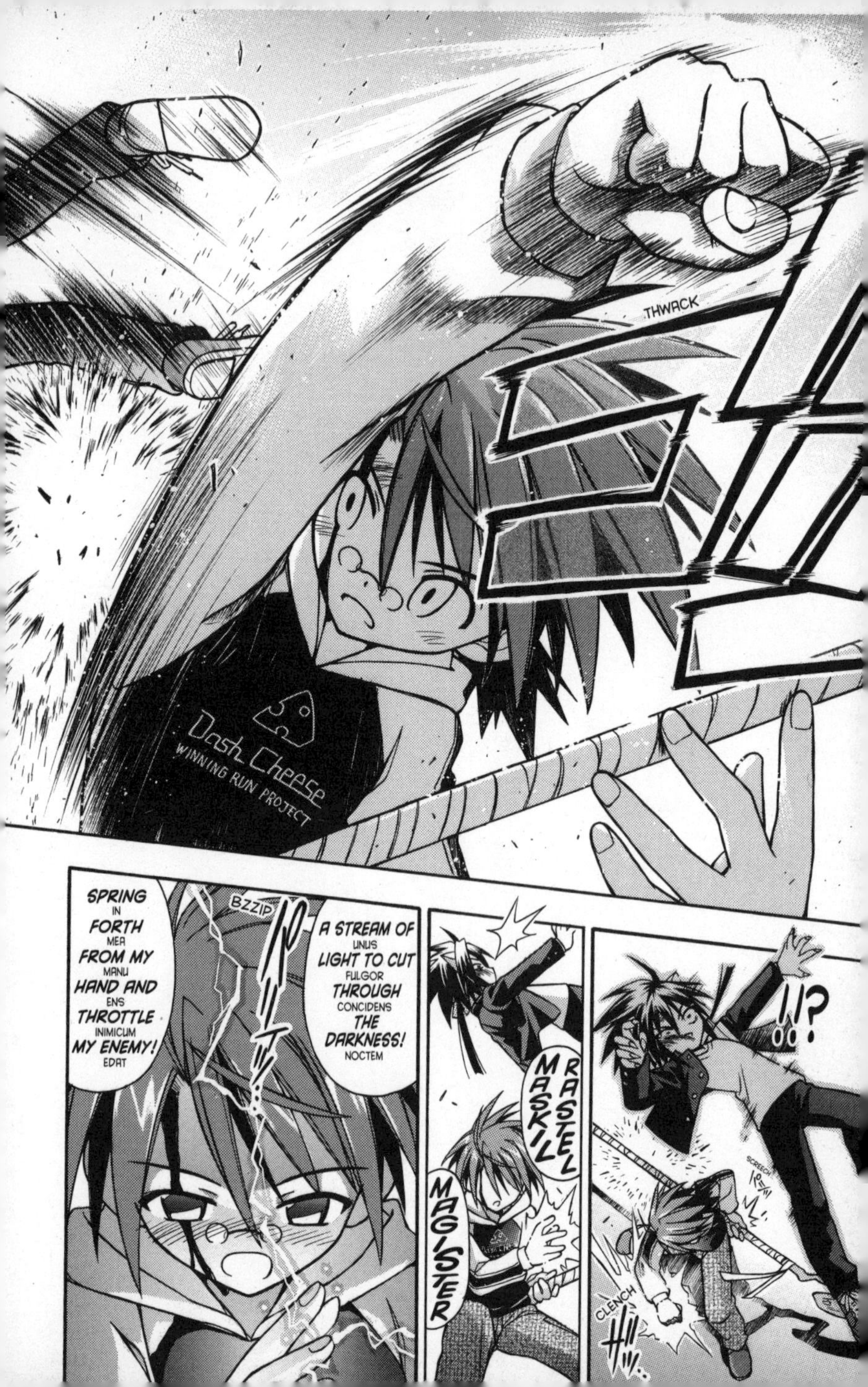
THWACK
!!?
SCREECH
CLENCH
RASTEL MASKIL MAGISTER
A STREAM OF UNUS LIGHT TO CUT FULGOR THROUGH CONCIDENS THE DARKNESS! NOCTEM
BZZIP
SPRING IN FORTH MEA FROM MY MANU HAND AND ENS THROTTLE INIMICUM MY ENEMY! EDAT

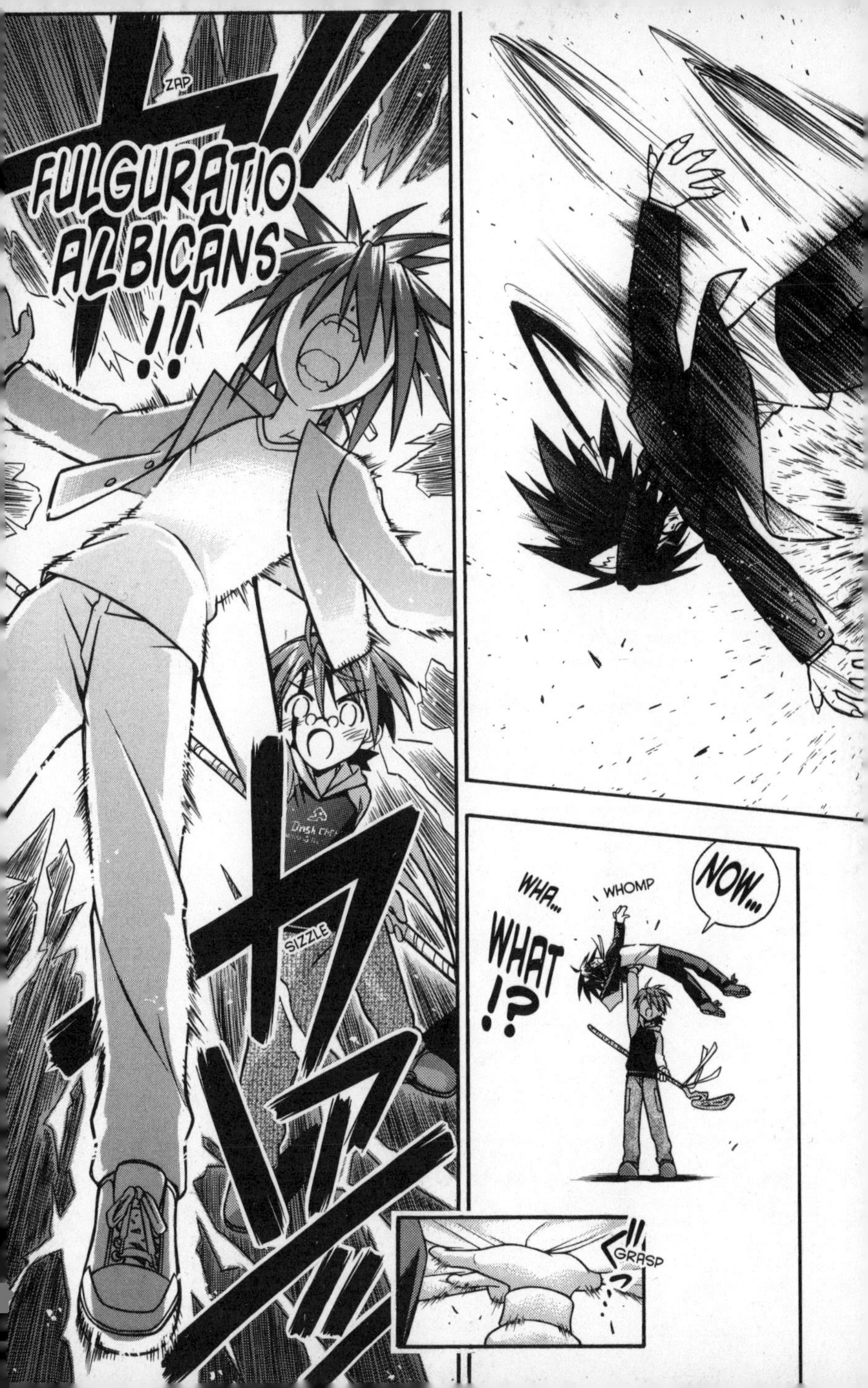
NOW...
WHOMP
WHA... WHAT!?
GRASP
ZAP
FULGURATIO ALBICANS!!
SIZZLE

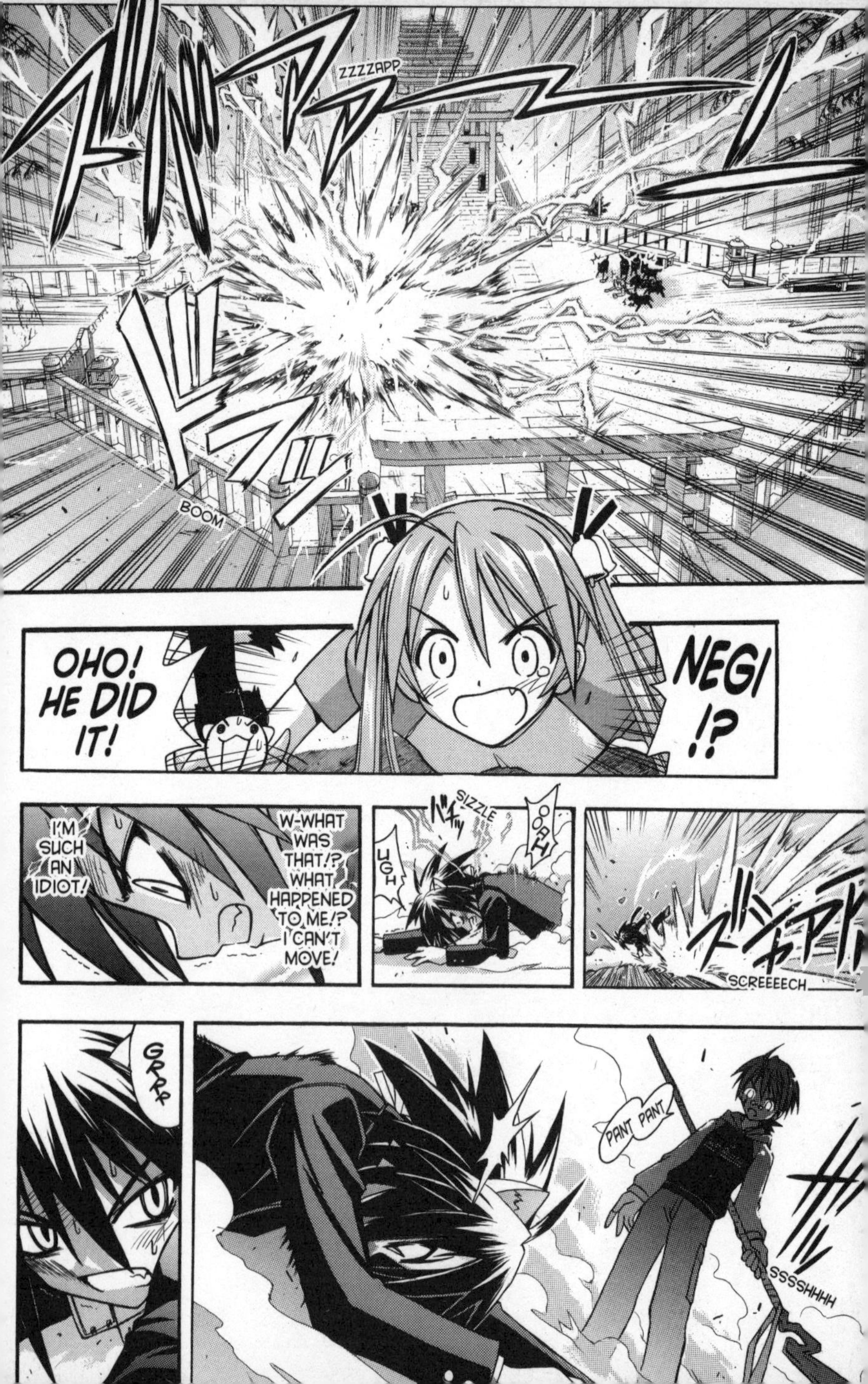
ZZZZAPP
BOOM
NEGI !?
OHO! HE DID IT!
SCREEEECH
SIZZLE
OORH
UGH
W-WHAT WAS THAT!? WHAT HAPPENED TO ME!? I CAN'T MOVE!
I'M SUCH AN IDIOT!
SSSSHHHH
PANT PANT
GRRR

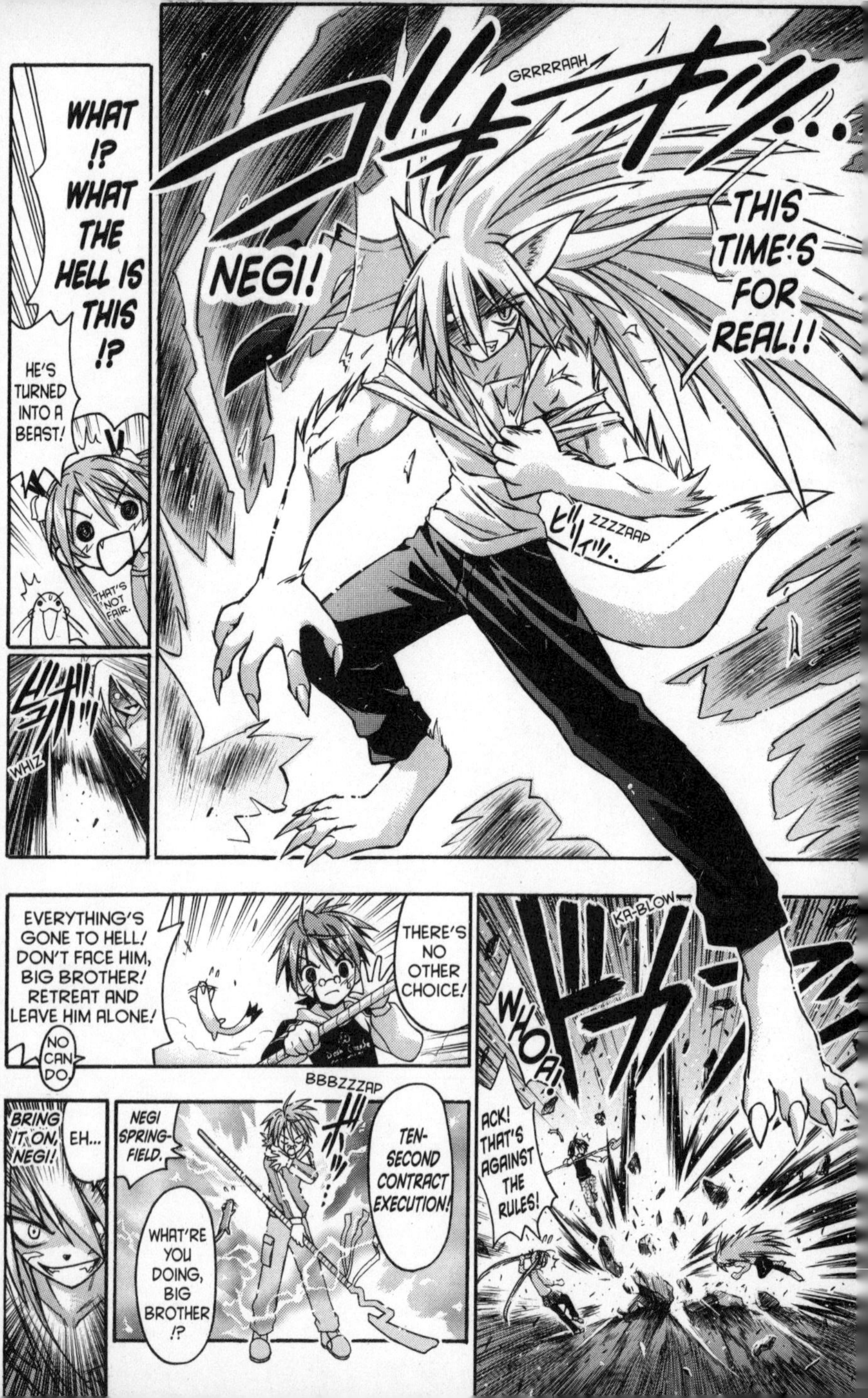
GRRRRAAH
THIS TIME'S FOR REAL!!
NEGI!
ZZZZAAP
WHAT!? WHAT THE HELL IS THIS!?
HE'S TURNED INTO A BEAST!
THAT'S NOT FAIR.
WHIZ
KA-BLOW
WHOA!
ACK! THAT'S AGAINST THE RULES!
THERE'S NO OTHER CHOICE!
EVERYTHING'S GONE TO HELL! DON'T FACE HIM, BIG BROTHER! RETREAT AND LEAVE HIM ALONE!
NO CAN DO.
BBBZZZAP
TEN-SECOND CONTRACT EXECUTION!
NEGI SPRING-FIELD.
WHAT'RE YOU DOING, BIG BROTHER!?
EH...
BRING IT ON, NEGI!

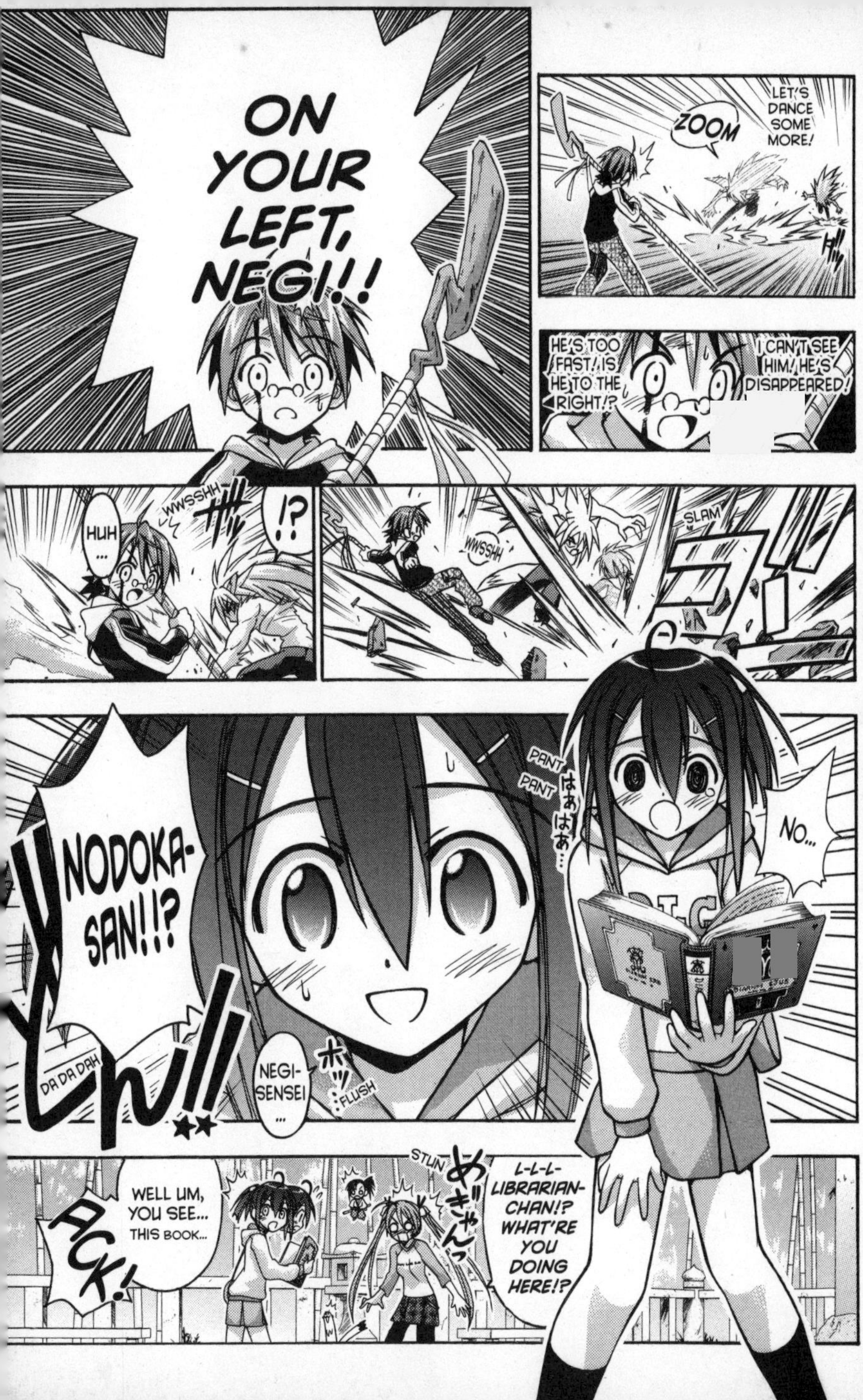
LET'S DANCE SOME MORE!
ZOOM
I CAN'T SEE HIM! HE'S DISAPPEARED!
HE'S TOO FAST! IS HE TO THE RIGHT!?
ON YOUR LEFT, NEGI!!
SLAM
WWSSHH
!?
WWSSHH
HUH...
NO...
PANT PANT
はあはあ…
NEGI-SENSEI...
FLUSH
NODOKA-SAN!!?
DA DA DAH
L-L-L-LIBRARIAN-CHAN!? WHAT'RE YOU DOING HERE!?
STUN
WELL UM, YOU SEE... THIS BOOK...
ACK!

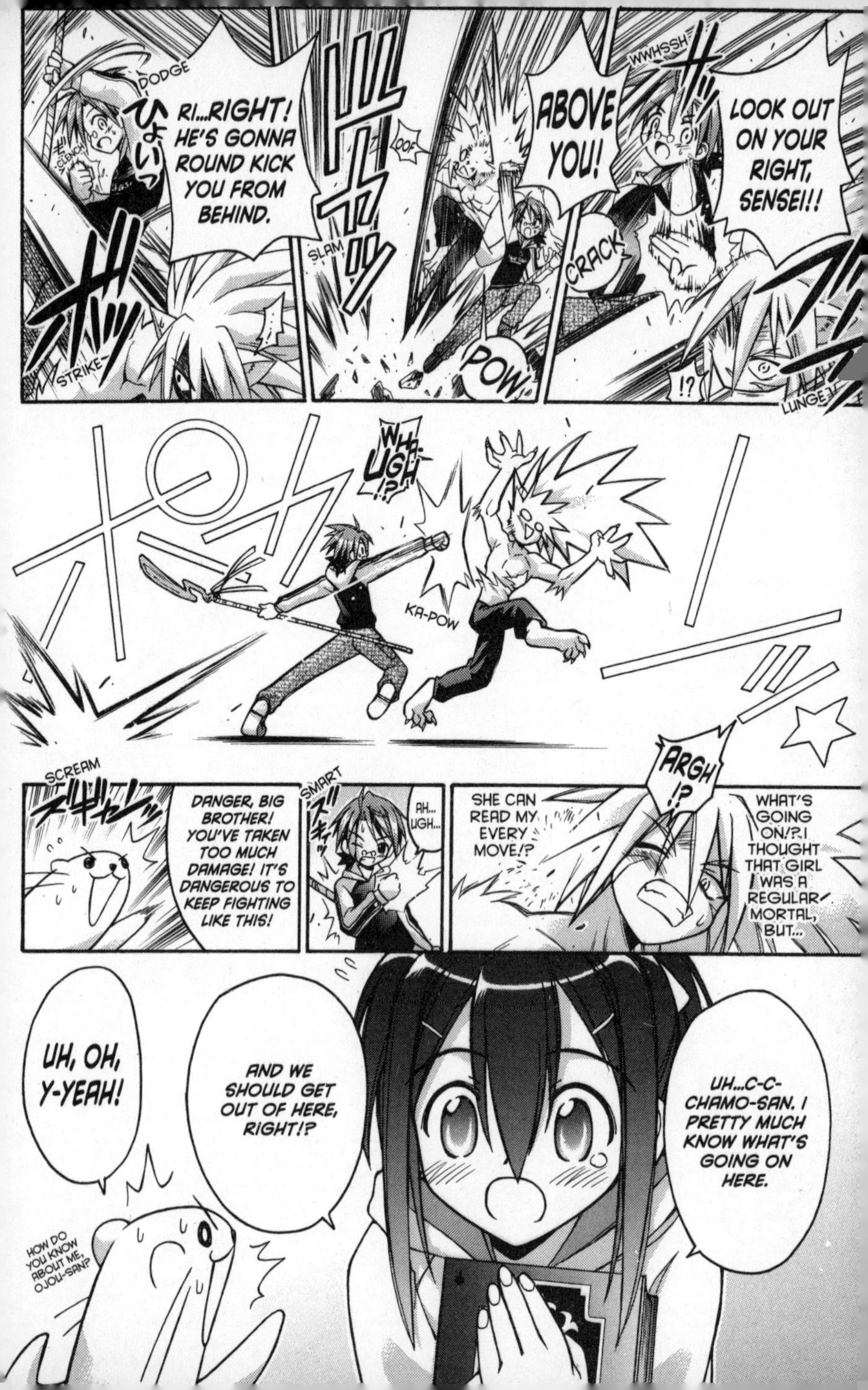
WWHSSH
LOOK OUT ON YOUR RIGHT, SENSEI!!
CRACK
!?
LUNGE
ABOVE YOU!
OOF
SLAM
POW
DODGE
ひょいっ
CLENCH
RI...RIGHT! HE'S GONNA ROUND KICK YOU FROM BEHIND.
STRIKE
WHA-UGH!?
KA-POW
WHAT'S GOING ON!? I THOUGHT THAT GIRL WAS A REGULAR MORTAL, BUT...
ARGH!?
SHE CAN READ MY EVERY MOVE!?
AH... UGH...
SMART
DANGER, BIG BROTHER! YOU'VE TAKEN TOO MUCH DAMAGE! IT'S DANGEROUS TO KEEP FIGHTING LIKE THIS!
SCREAM
UH...C-C-CHAMO-SAN. I PRETTY MUCH KNOW WHAT'S GOING ON HERE.
AND WE SHOULD GET OUT OF HERE, RIGHT!?
UH, OH, Y-YEAH!
HOW DO YOU KNOW ABOUT ME, OJOU-SAN?

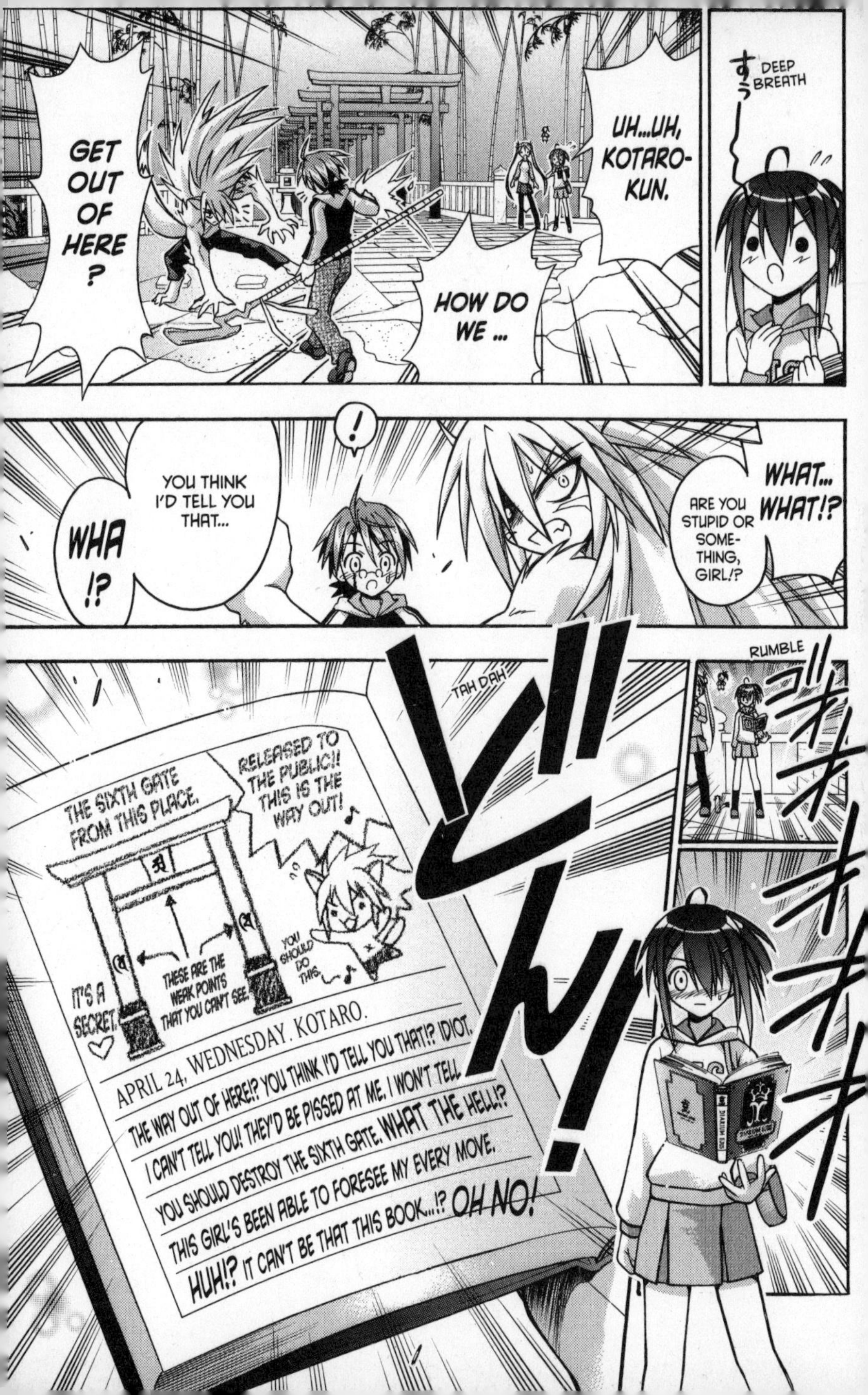

すぅ
DEEP BREATH
UH...UH, KOTARO-KUN.
HOW DO WE ...
GET OUT OF HERE ?
WHAT... WHAT!?
ARE YOU STUPID OR SOME-THING, GIRL!?
!
YOU THINK I'D TELL YOU THAT...
WHA !?
RUMBLE
TAH DAH
THE SIXTH GATE FROM THIS PLACE.
RELEASED TO THE PUBLIC!! THIS IS THE WAY OUT!
YOU SHOULD DO THIS.
THESE ARE THE WEAK POINTS THAT YOU CAN'T SEE.
IT'S A SECRET.
APRIL 24, WEDNESDAY. KOTARO.
THE WAY OUT OF HERE!? YOU THINK I'D TELL YOU THAT!? IDIOT.
I CAN'T TELL YOU! THEY'D BE PISSED AT ME. I WON'T TELL
YOU SHOULD DESTROY THE SIXTH GATE. WHAT THE HELL!?
THIS GIRL'S BEEN ABLE TO FORESEE MY EVERY MOVE.
HUH!? IT CAN'T BE THAT THIS BOOK...!? OH NO!

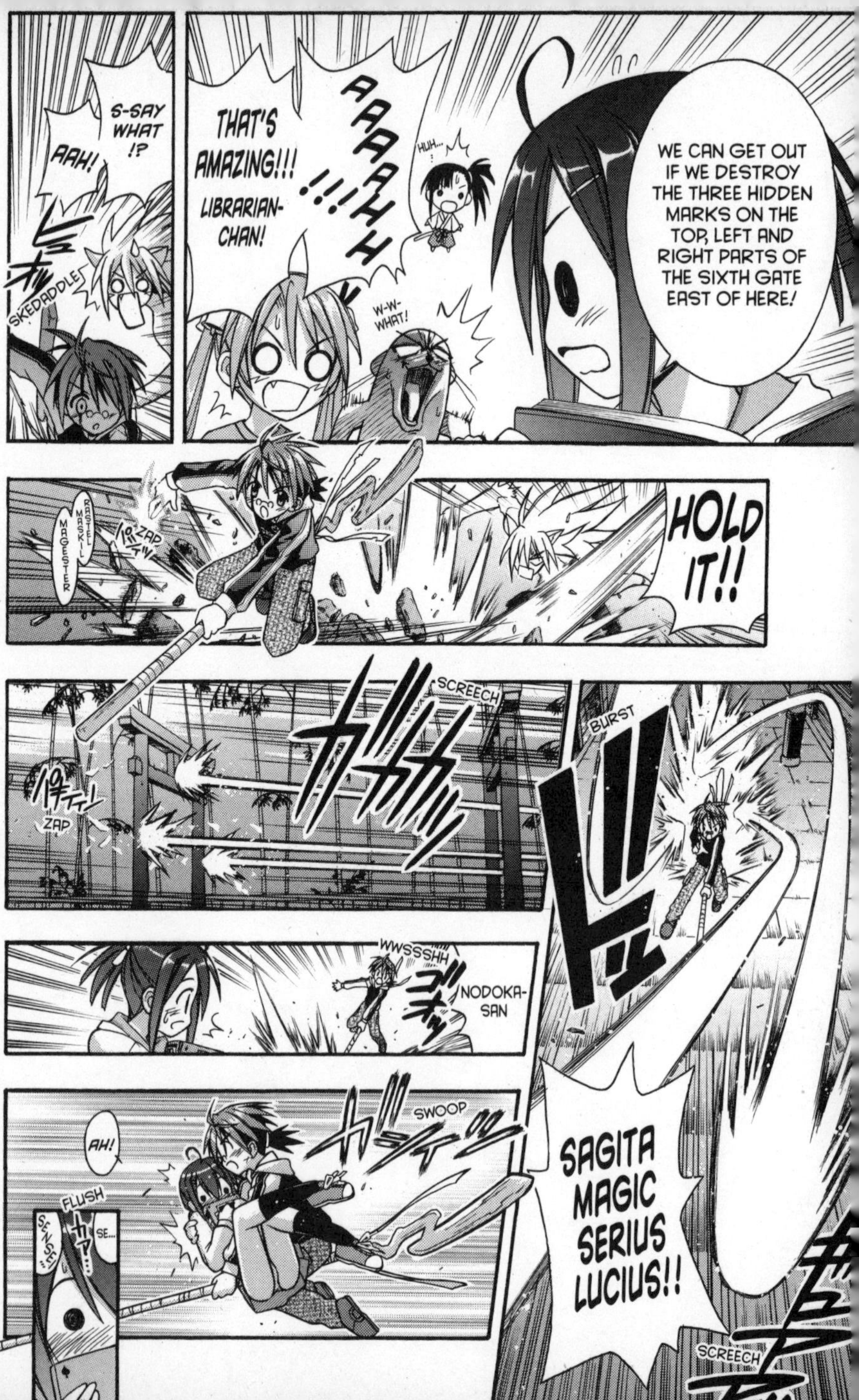

WE CAN GET OUT IF WE DESTROY THE THREE HIDDEN MARKS ON THE TOP, LEFT AND RIGHT PARTS OF THE SIXTH GATE EAST OF HERE!
AAAAAHHH!!!!
HUH...
THAT'S AMAZING!!! LIBRARIAN-CHAN!
W-W-WHAT!
S-SAY WHAT!?
AAH!
SKEDADDLE
HOLD IT!!
RASTEL MASKIL MAGESTER
ZAP
BURST
SAGITA MAGIC SERIUS LUCIUS!!
SCREECH
SCREECH
ZAP
NODOKA-SAN
WWSSSHH
SWOOP
AH!
FLUSH
SE...
SENSEI...

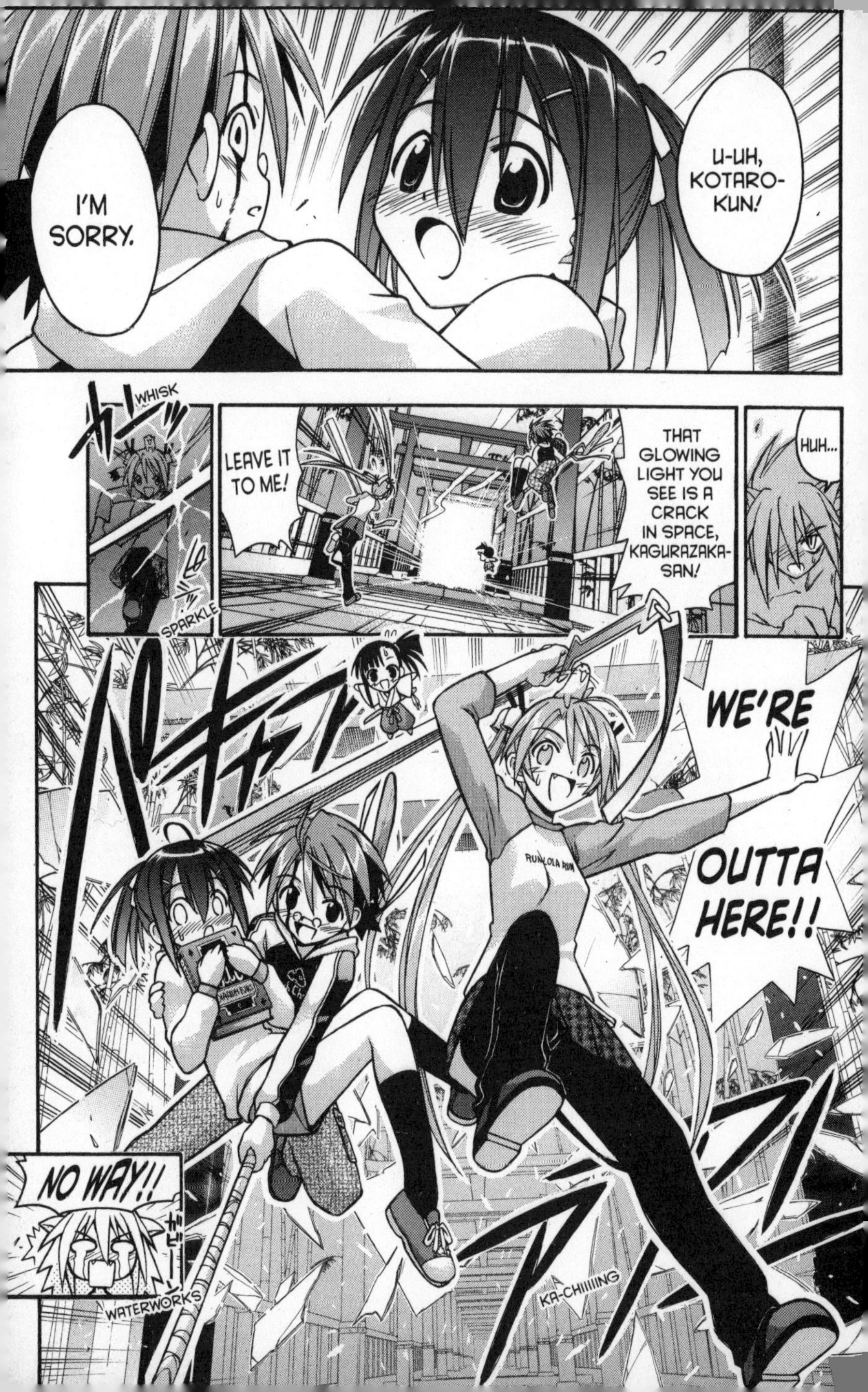
U-UH, KOTARO-KUN!
I'M SORRY.
HUH...
THAT GLOWING LIGHT YOU SEE IS A CRACK IN SPACE, KAGURAZAKA-SAN!
LEAVE IT TO ME!
WHISK
SPARKLE
WE'RE OUTTA HERE!!
RUN LOLA RUN
NO WAY!!
WATERWORKS
KA-CHIIIIING

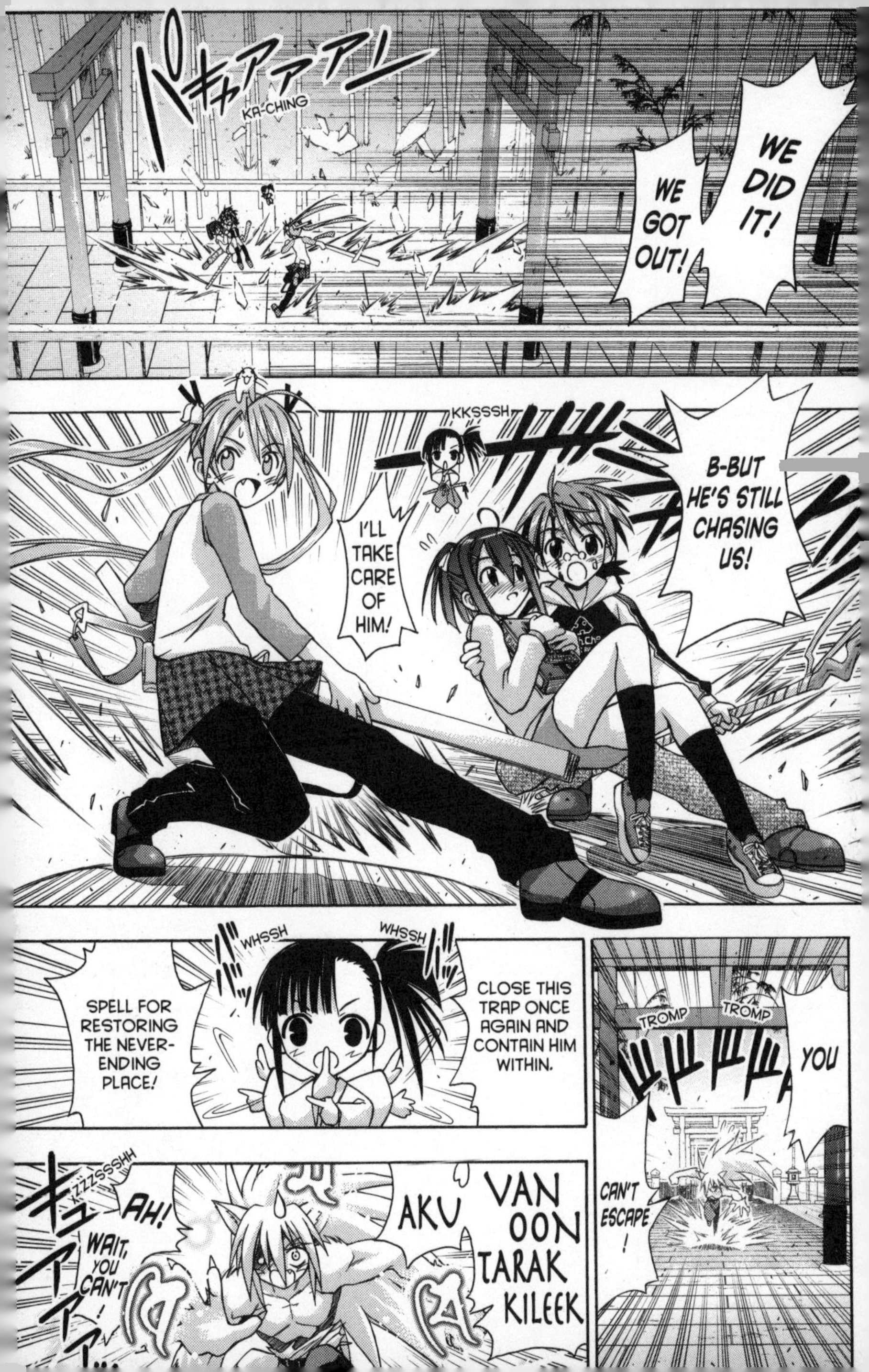

WE DID IT!
WE GOT OUT!
KA-CHING
B-BUT HE'S STILL CHASING US!
KKSSSH
I'LL TAKE CARE OF HIM!
TROMP
TROMP
YOU CAN'T ESCAPE!
WHSSH
WHSSH
CLOSE THIS TRAP ONCE AGAIN AND CONTAIN HIM WITHIN.
SPELL FOR RESTORING THE NEVER-ENDING PLACE!
VAN OON TARAK KILEEK
AKU
AH!
WAIT, YOU CAN'T!
ZZZSSSHH

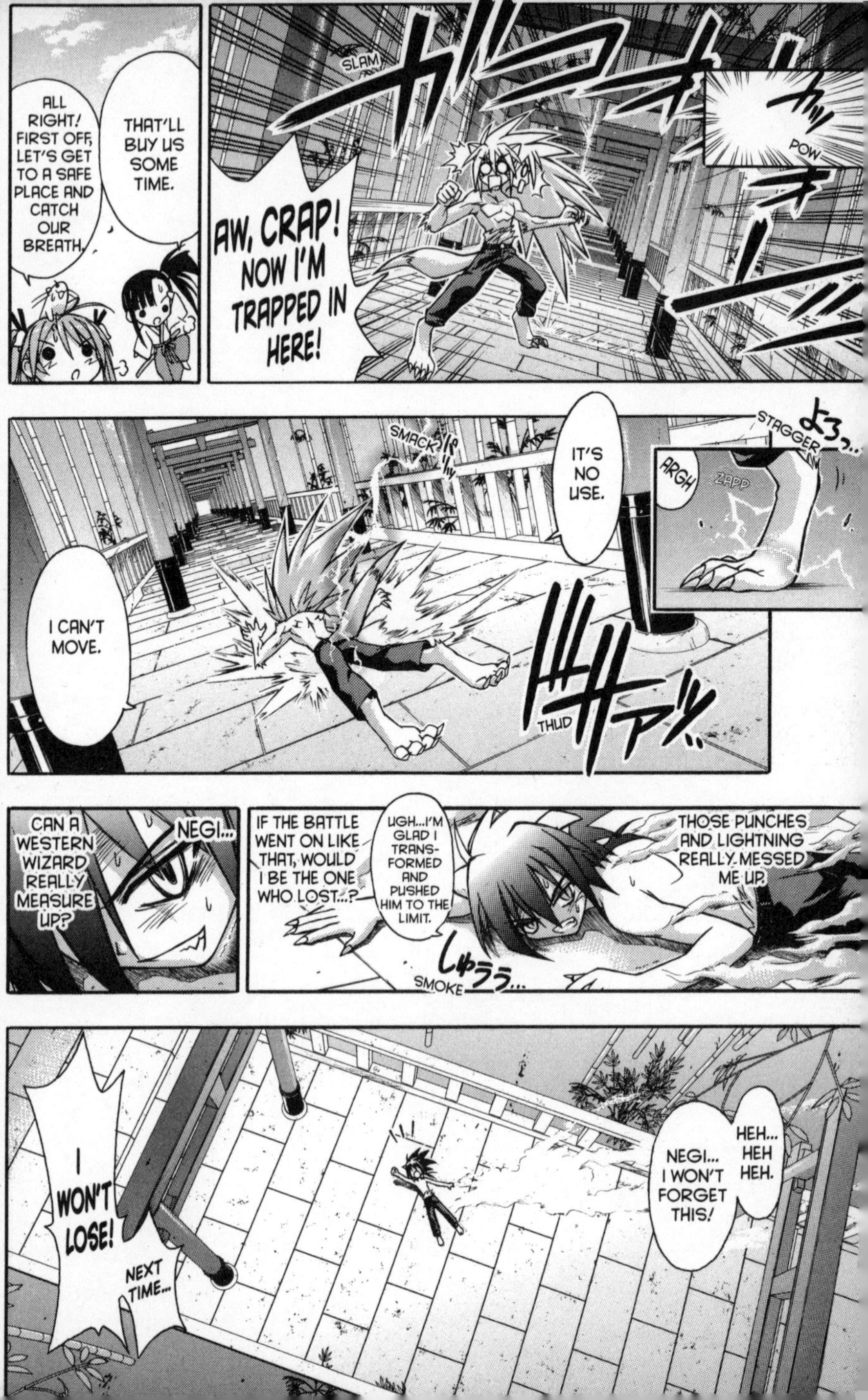
POW
SLAM
AW, CRAP! NOW I'M TRAPPED IN HERE!
THAT'LL BUY US SOME TIME.
ALL RIGHT! FIRST OFF, LET'S GET TO A SAFE PLACE AND CATCH OUR BREATH.
STAGGER
ARGH
ZAPP
SMACK
IT'S NO USE.
I CAN'T MOVE.
THUD
THOSE PUNCHES AND LIGHTNING REALLY MESSED ME UP.
UGH...I'M GLAD I TRANS-FORMED AND PUSHED HIM TO THE LIMIT.
IF THE BATTLE WENT ON LIKE THAT, WOULD I BE THE ONE WHO LOST...?
SMOKE
NEGI...
CAN A WESTERN WIZARD REALLY MEASURE UP?
HEH... HEH HEH.
NEGI... I WON'T FORGET THIS!
NEXT TIME...
I WON'T LOSE!

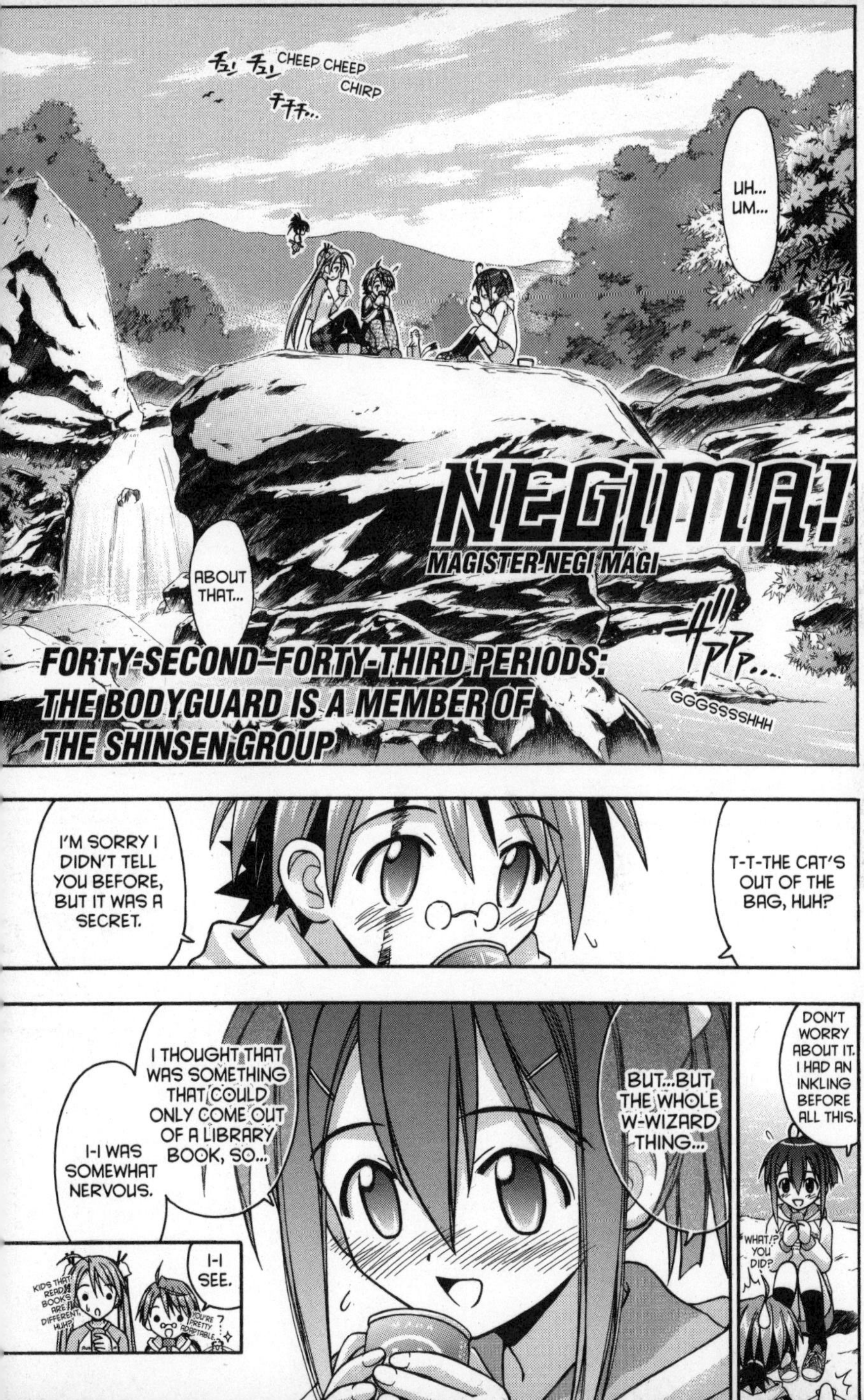
UH... UM...
チュン チュン CHEEP CHEEP
CHIRP
チチチ...
NEGIMA!
MAGISTER NEGI MAGI
ABOUT THAT...
FORTY-SECOND–FORTY-THIRD PERIODS: THE BODYGUARD IS A MEMBER OF THE SHINSEN GROUP
GGGSSSSHHH
T-T-THE CAT'S OUT OF THE BAG, HUH?
I'M SORRY I DIDN'T TELL YOU BEFORE, BUT IT WAS A SECRET.
DON'T WORRY ABOUT IT. I HAD AN INKLING BEFORE ALL THIS.
WHAT!? YOU DID?
BUT...BUT THE WHOLE W-WIZARD THING...
I THOUGHT THAT WAS SOMETHING THAT COULD ONLY COME OUT OF A LIBRARY BOOK, SO...
I-I WAS SOMEWHAT NERVOUS.
I-I SEE.
YOU'RE PRETTY ADAPTABLE...
KIDS THAT READ BOOKS ARE DIFFERENT, HUH?

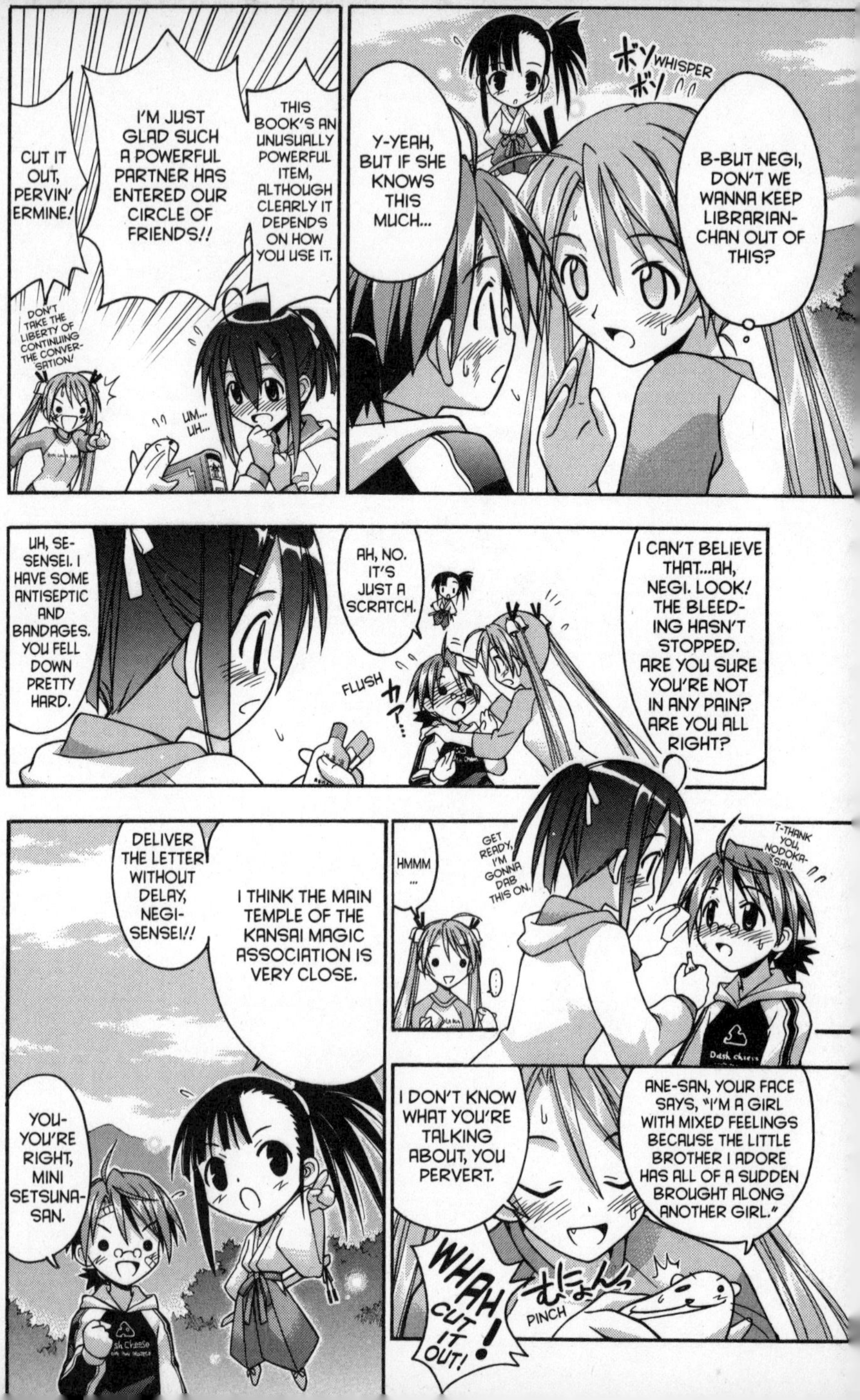
ボソ WHISPER ボソ
B-BUT NEGI, DON'T WE WANNA KEEP LIBRARIAN-CHAN OUT OF THIS?
Y-YEAH, BUT IF SHE KNOWS THIS MUCH...
THIS BOOK'S AN UNUSUALLY POWERFUL ITEM, ALTHOUGH CLEARLY IT DEPENDS ON HOW YOU USE IT.
I'M JUST GLAD SUCH A POWERFUL PARTNER HAS ENTERED OUR CIRCLE OF FRIENDS!!
CUT IT OUT, PERVIN' ERMINE!
DON'T TAKE THE LIBERTY OF CONTINUING THE CONVER-SATION!
UM... UH...
I CAN'T BELIEVE THAT...AH, NEGI. LOOK! THE BLEED-ING HASN'T STOPPED. ARE YOU SURE YOU'RE NOT IN ANY PAIN? ARE YOU ALL RIGHT?
AH, NO. IT'S JUST A SCRATCH.
FLUSH カァ...
UH, SE-SENSEI. I HAVE SOME ANTISEPTIC AND BANDAGES. YOU FELL DOWN PRETTY HARD.
T-THANK YOU, NODOKA-SAN.
GET READY, I'M GONNA DAB THIS ON.
HMMM ...
ANE-SAN, YOUR FACE SAYS, "I'M A GIRL WITH MIXED FEELINGS BECAUSE THE LITTLE BROTHER I ADORE HAS ALL OF A SUDDEN BROUGHT ALONG ANOTHER GIRL."
I DON'T KNOW WHAT YOU'RE TALKING ABOUT, YOU PERVERT.
むにょん PINCH
WHAH CUT IT OUT!
DELIVER THE LETTER WITHOUT DELAY, NEGI-SENSEI!!
I THINK THE MAIN TEMPLE OF THE KANSAI MAGIC ASSOCIATION IS VERY CLOSE.
YOU-YOU'RE RIGHT, MINI SETSUNA-SAN.

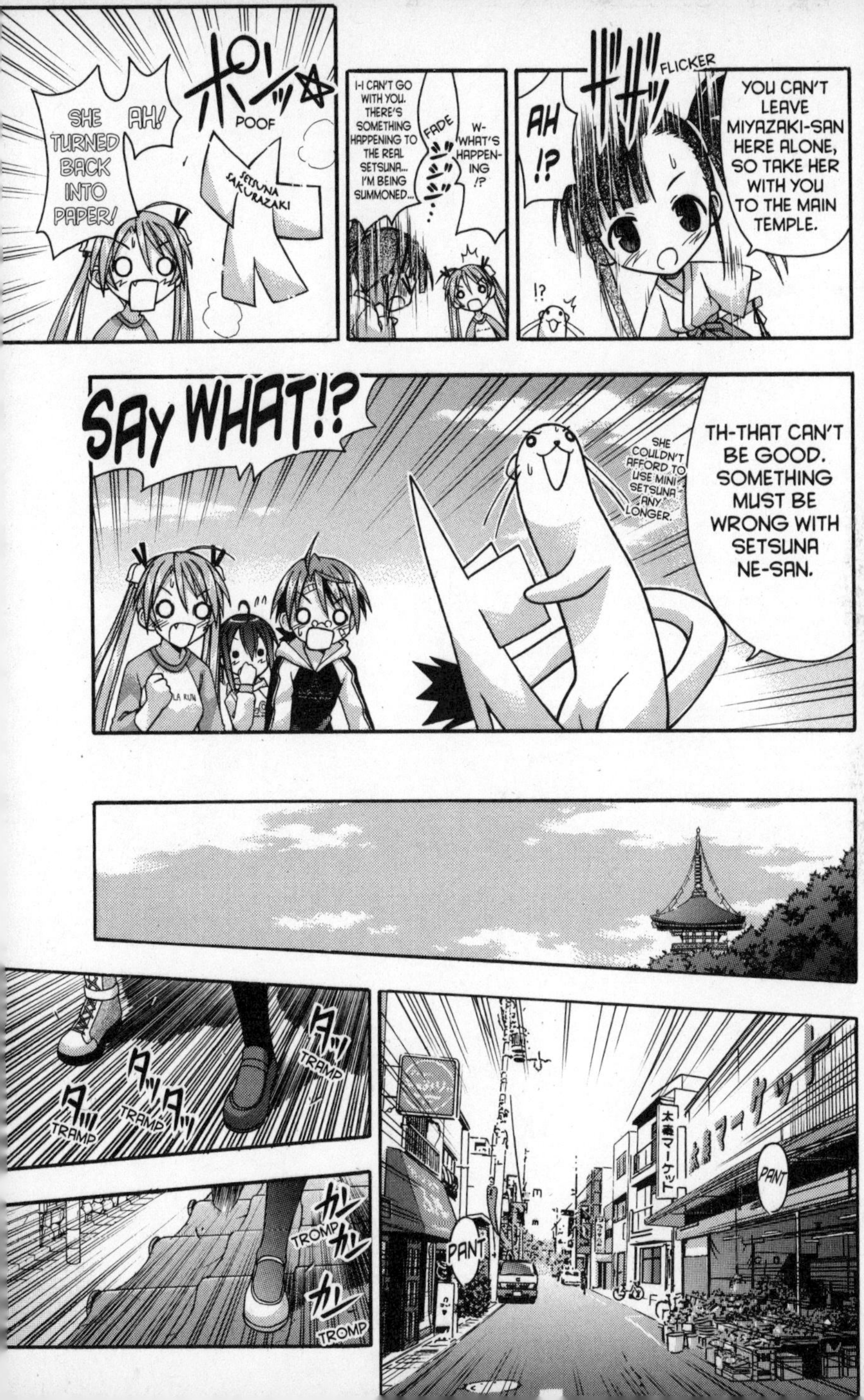
FLICKER
AH !?
YOU CAN'T LEAVE MIYAZAKI-SAN HERE ALONE, SO TAKE HER WITH YOU TO THE MAIN TEMPLE.
!?
W-WHAT'S HAPPENING !?
FADE
I-I CAN'T GO WITH YOU. THERE'S SOMETHING HAPPENING TO THE REAL SETSUNA... I'M BEING SUMMONED...
POOF
SETSUNA SAKURAZAKI
AH!
SHE TURNED BACK INTO PAPER!
TH-THAT CAN'T BE GOOD. SOMETHING MUST BE WRONG WITH SETSUNA NE-SAN.
SHE COULDN'T AFFORD TO USE MINI SETSUNA ANY LONGER.
SAY WHAT!?
PANT
PANT
TRAMP
TRAMP
TRAMP
TROMP
TROMP

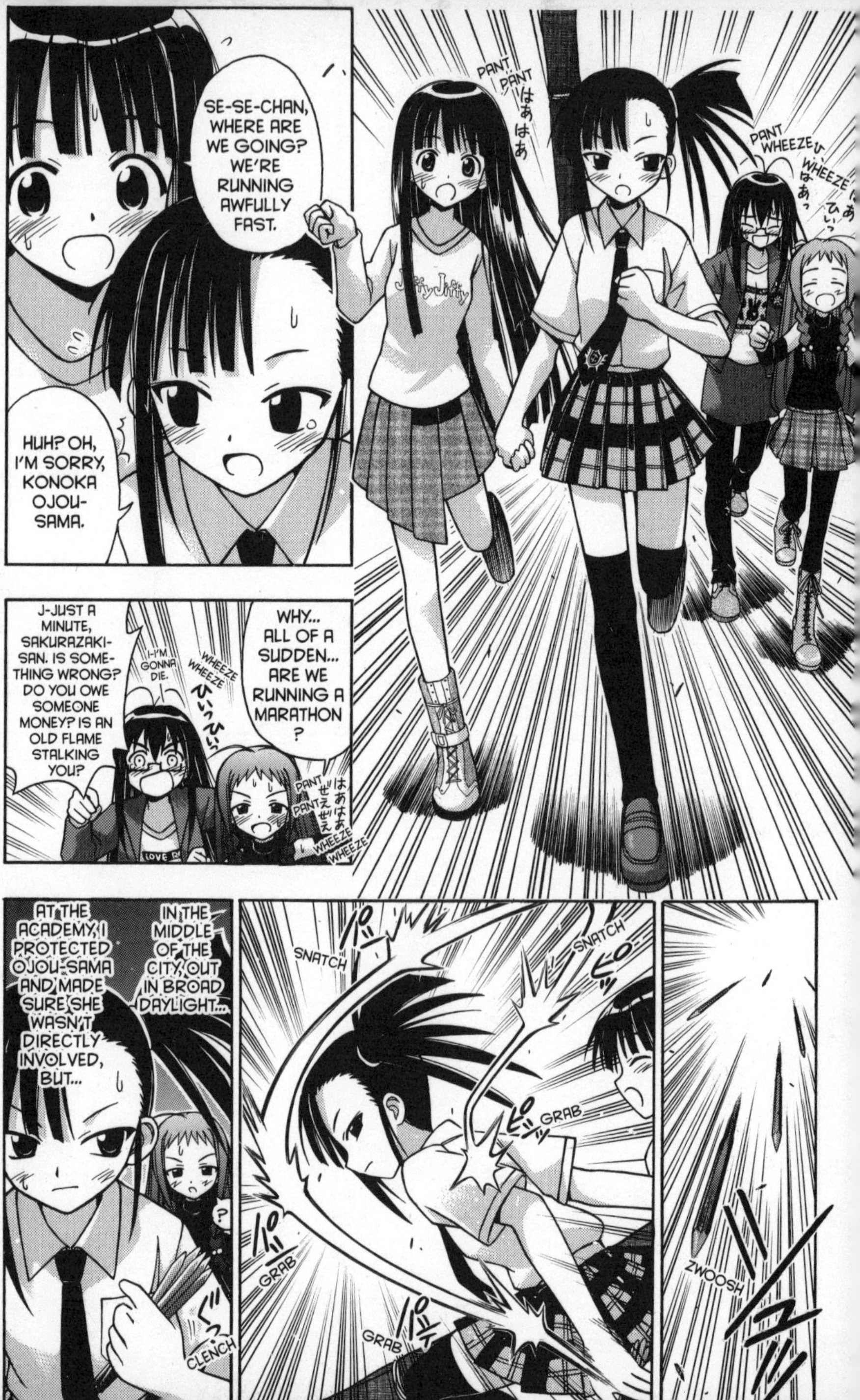
PANT PANT
はあはあ
PANT WHEEZE
ひぃ
WHEEZE
はあっ
ひぃっ
SE-SE-CHAN, WHERE ARE WE GOING? WE'RE RUNNING AWFULLY FAST.
HUH? OH, I'M SORRY, KONOKA OJOU-SAMA.
WHY... ALL OF A SUDDEN... ARE WE RUNNING A MARATHON?
WHEEZE WHEEZE
ひぃっひぃっ
I-I'M GONNA DIE.
J-JUST A MINUTE, SAKURAZAKI-SAN. IS SOMETHING WRONG? DO YOU OWE SOMEONE MONEY? IS AN OLD FLAME STALKING YOU?
PANT PANT
はあはあ
ぜえぜえ
WHEEZE WHEEZE
LOVE
ZWOOSH
SNATCH
SNATCH
GRAB
GRAB
GRAB
IN THE MIDDLE OF THE CITY, OUT IN BROAD DAYLIGHT...
AT THE ACADEMY, I PROTECTED OJOU-SAMA AND MADE SURE SHE WASN'T DIRECTLY INVOLVED, BUT...
?
CLENCH

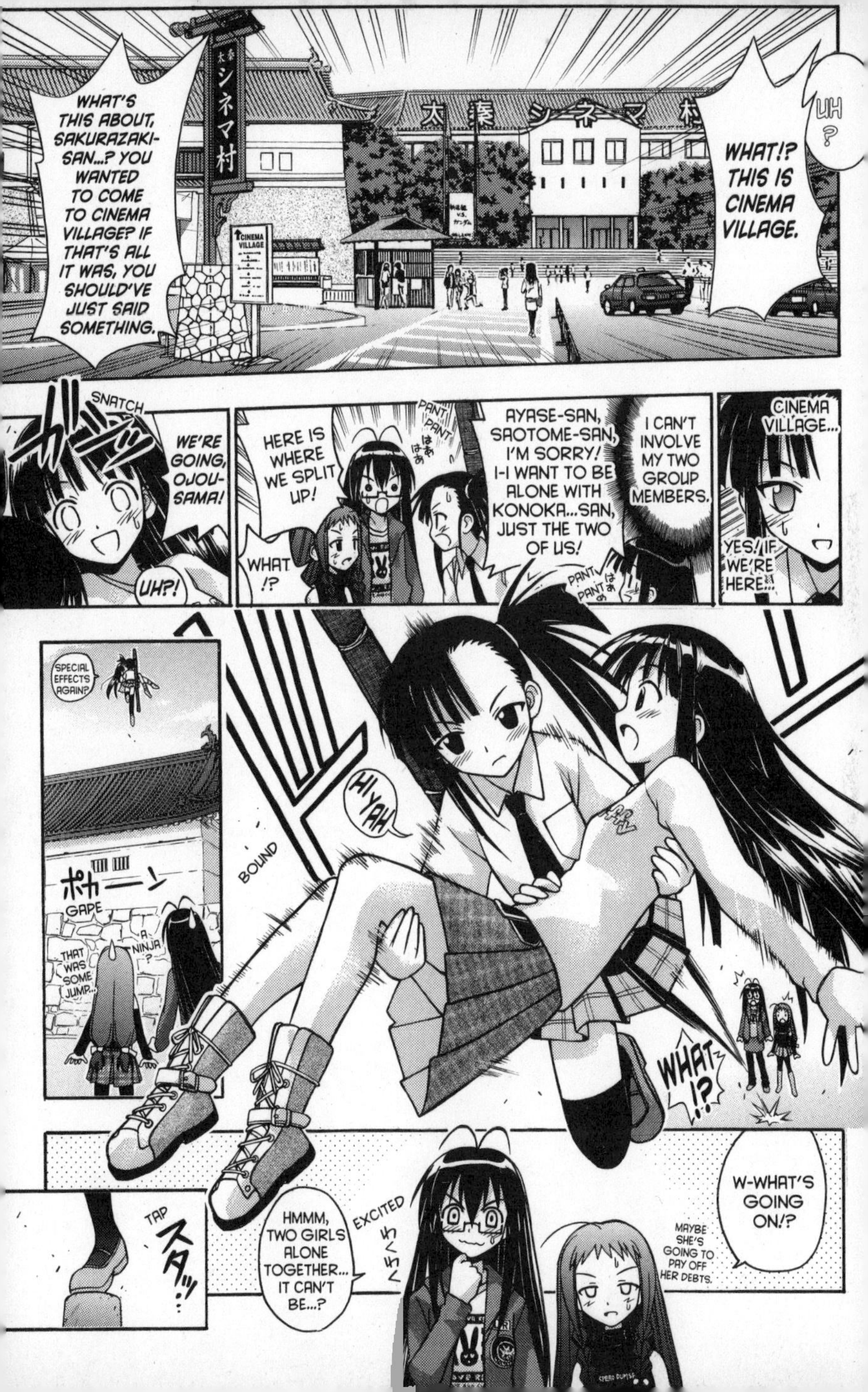

UH ?
WHAT!? THIS IS CINEMA VILLAGE.
WHAT'S THIS ABOUT, SAKURAZAKI-SAN...? YOU WANTED TO COME TO CINEMA VILLAGE? IF THAT'S ALL IT WAS, YOU SHOULD'VE JUST SAID SOMETHING.
太秦シネマ村
太秦 シネマ村
CINEMA VILLAGE
CINEMA VILLAGE...
YES! IF WE'RE HERE...
I CAN'T INVOLVE MY TWO GROUP MEMBERS.
AYASE-SAN, SAOTOME-SAN, I'M SORRY! I-I WANT TO BE ALONE WITH KONOKA...SAN, JUST THE TWO OF US!
PANT PANT はあ はあ
PANT PANT はあ はあ
HERE IS WHERE WE SPLIT UP!
WHAT !?
WE'RE GOING, OJOU-SAMA!
SNATCH
UH?!
HI-YAH
BOUND
WHAT !?
SPECIAL EFFECTS AGAIN?
ポカーン
GAPE
A NINJA ?
THAT WAS SOME JUMP...
W-WHAT'S GOING ON!?
MAYBE SHE'S GOING TO PAY OFF HER DEBTS.
HMMM, TWO GIRLS ALONE TOGETHER... IT CAN'T BE...?
EXCITED
わくわく
TAP
スタッ

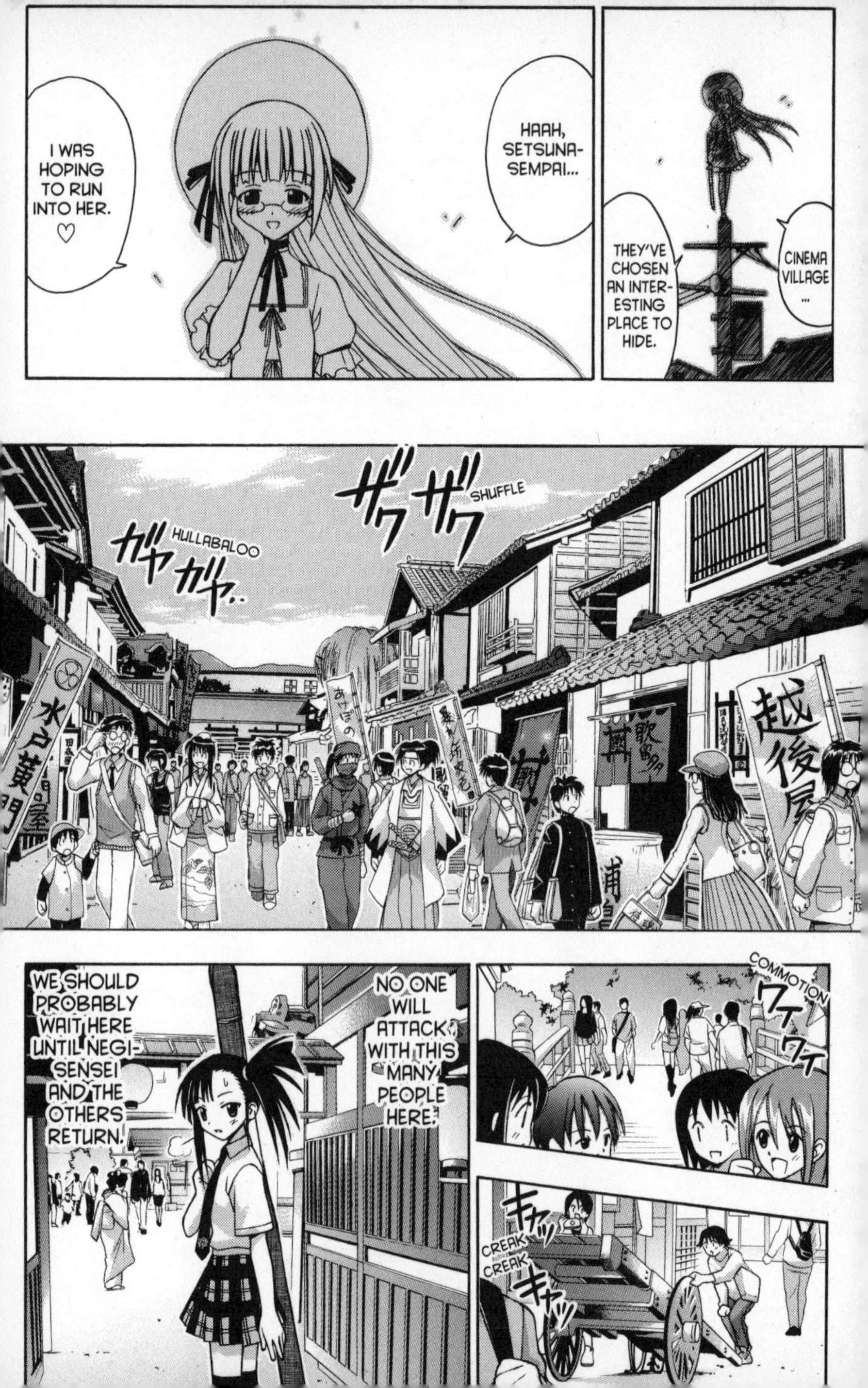
CINEMA VILLAGE ...
THEY'VE CHOSEN AN INTER-ESTING PLACE TO HIDE.
HAAH, SETSUNA-SEMPAI...
I WAS HOPING TO RUN INTO HER. ♡
ザワザワ
SHUFFLE
ガヤガヤ..
HULLABALOO
越後屋
ワイワイ
COMMOTION
キャッ
CREAK
CREAK
キャッ
NO ONE WILL ATTACK WITH THIS MANY PEOPLE HERE.
WE SHOULD PROBABLY WAIT HERE UNTIL NEGI-SENSEI AND THE OTHERS RETURN.

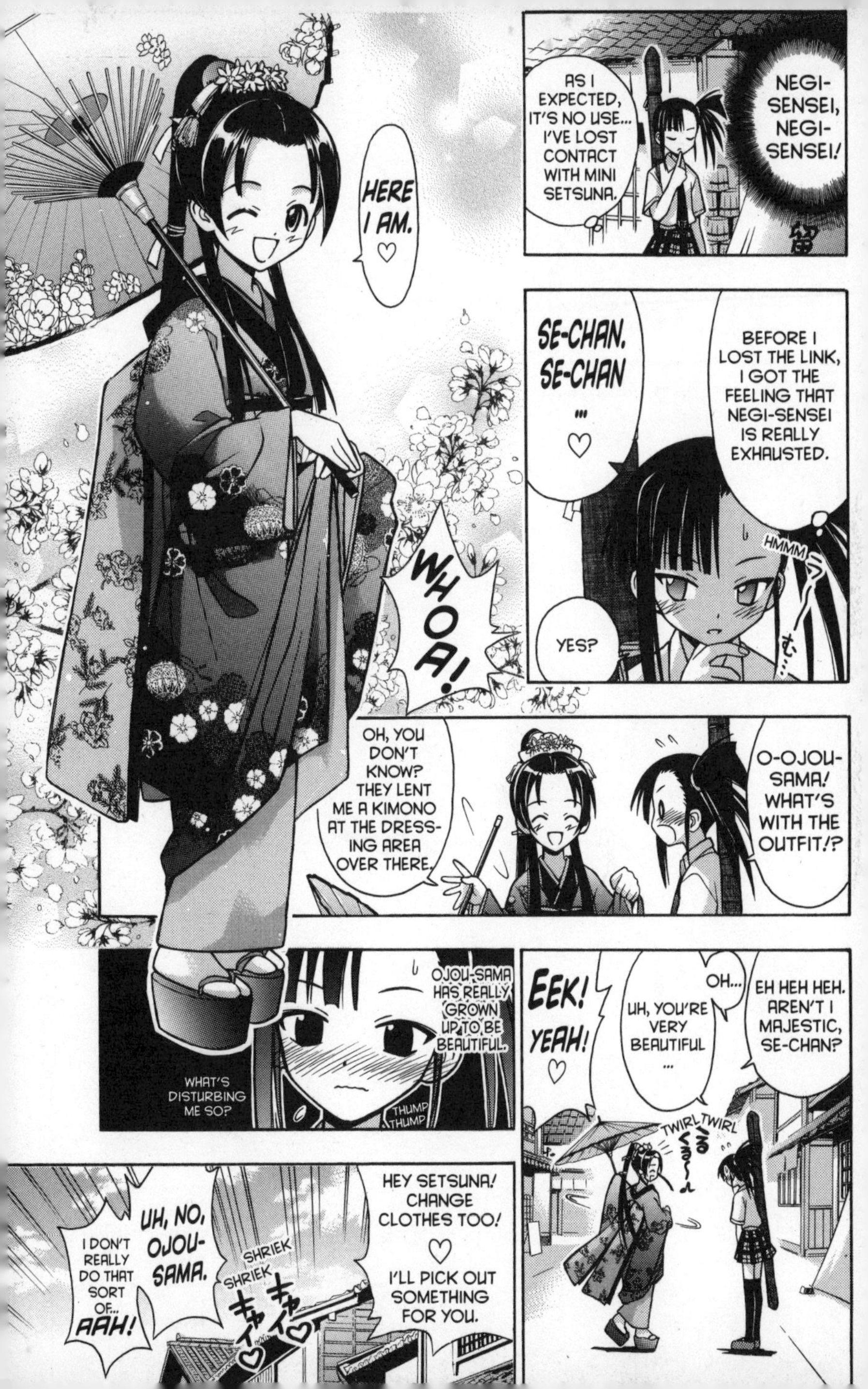
NEGI-SENSEI, NEGI-SENSEI!
AS I EXPECTED, IT'S NO USE... I'VE LOST CONTACT WITH MINI SETSUNA.
BEFORE I LOST THE LINK, I GOT THE FEELING THAT NEGI-SENSEI IS REALLY EXHAUSTED.
SE-CHAN. SE-CHAN ... ♡
HMMM
YES?
O-OJOU-SAMA! WHAT'S WITH THE OUTFIT!?
OH, YOU DON'T KNOW? THEY LENT ME A KIMONO AT THE DRESSING AREA OVER THERE.
HERE I AM. ♡
WHOA!
EH HEH HEH. AREN'T I MAJESTIC, SE-CHAN?
OH...
UH, YOU'RE VERY BEAUTIFUL ...
EEK! YEAH! ♡
TWIRL TWIRL
OJOU-SAMA HAS REALLY GROWN UP TO BE BEAUTIFUL.
WHAT'S DISTURBING ME SO?
THUMP THUMP
HEY SETSUNA! CHANGE CLOTHES TOO! ♡ I'LL PICK OUT SOMETHING FOR YOU.
SHRIEK SHRIEK
UH, NO, OJOU-SAMA.
I DON'T REALLY DO THAT SORT OF... AAH!

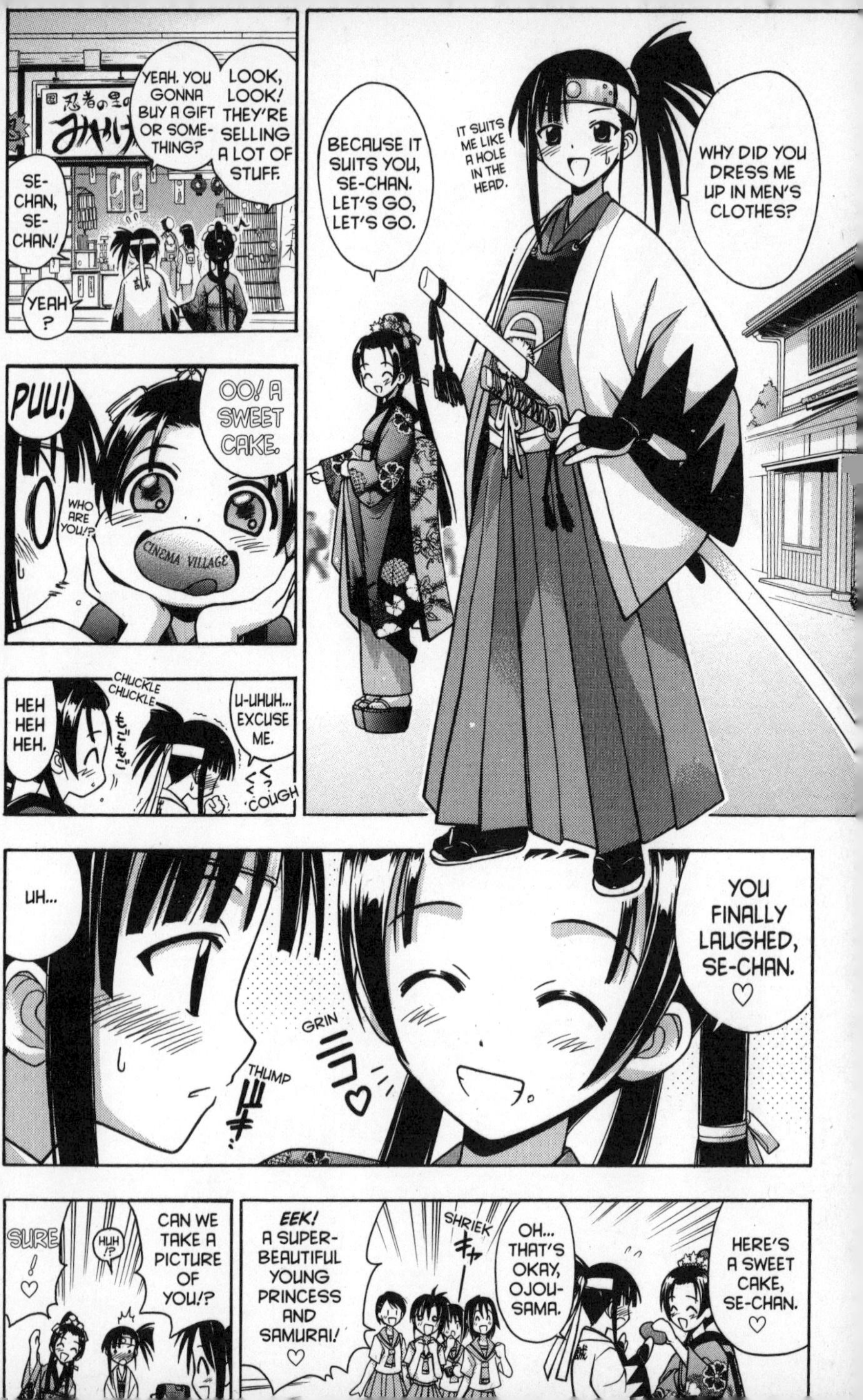

WHY DID YOU DRESS ME UP IN MEN'S CLOTHES?
IT SUITS ME LIKE A HOLE IN THE HEAD.
BECAUSE IT SUITS YOU, SE-CHAN. LET'S GO, LET'S GO.
LOOK, LOOK! THEY'RE SELLING A LOT OF STUFF.
YEAH. YOU GONNA BUY A GIFT OR SOME-THING?
忍者の里の
SE-CHAN, SE-CHAN!
YEAH?
OO! A SWEET CAKE.
PUU!
WHO ARE YOU!?
CINEMA VILLAGE
U-UHUH... EXCUSE ME.
COUGH
CHUCKLE CHUCKLE
HEH HEH HEH.
YOU FINALLY LAUGHED, SE-CHAN. ♡
GRIN
THUMP
UH...
HERE'S A SWEET CAKE, SE-CHAN. ♡
OH... THAT'S OKAY, OJOU-SAMA.
SHRIEK
EEK! A SUPER-BEAUTIFUL YOUNG PRINCESS AND SAMURAI! ♡
CAN WE TAKE A PICTURE OF YOU!?
HUH !?
SURE ! ♡

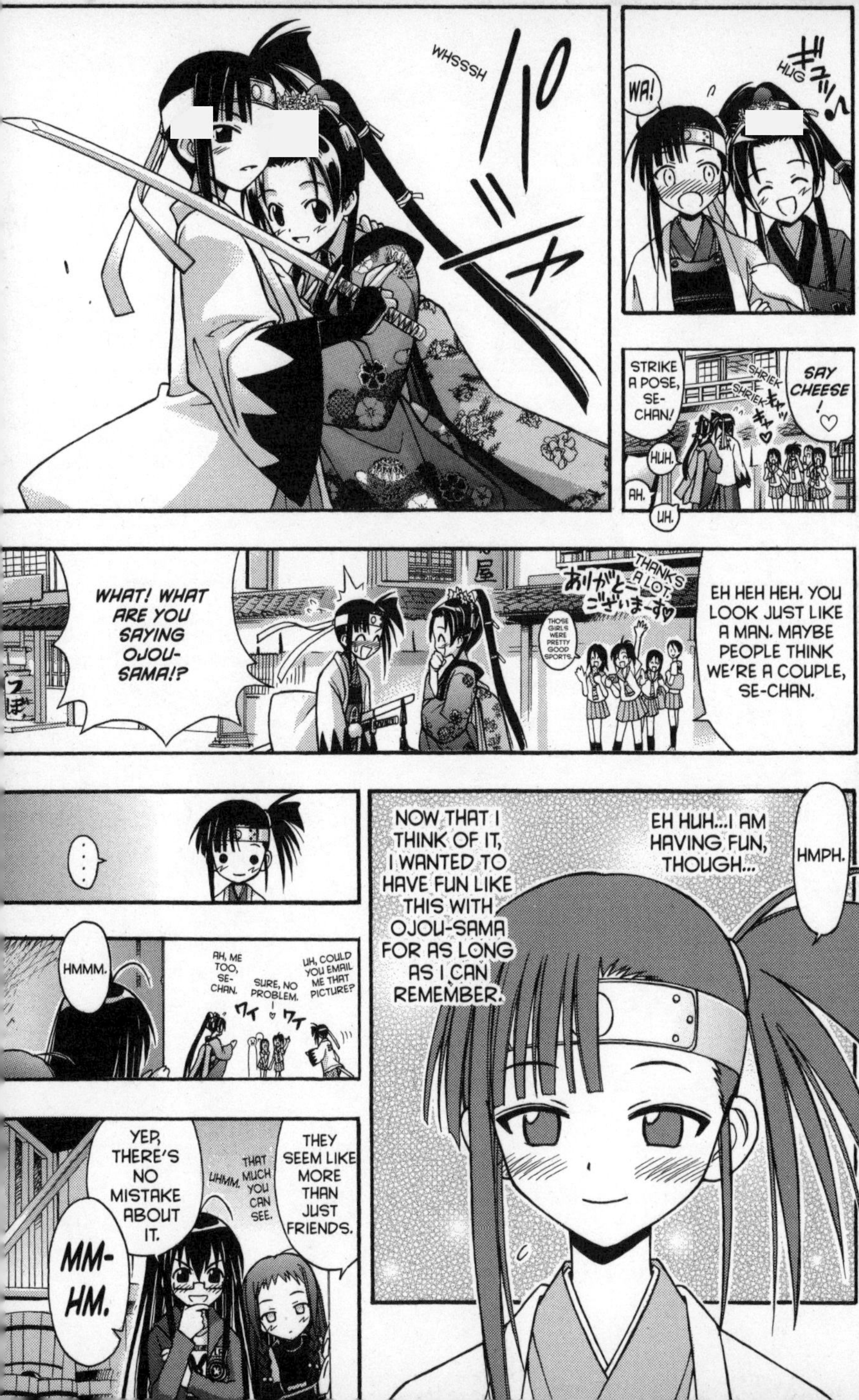

HUG
ギュッ♪
WA!
SAY CHEESE! ♡
SHRIEK SHRIEK
キャッ キャッ
STRIKE A POSE, SE-CHAN!
HUH.
AH.
UH.
WHSSSH
パッ
EH HEH HEH. YOU LOOK JUST LIKE A MAN. MAYBE PEOPLE THINK WE'RE A COUPLE, SE-CHAN.
THANKS A LOT.
ありがとーございまーす♡
THOSE GIRLS WERE PRETTY GOOD SPORTS.
WHAT! WHAT ARE YOU SAYING OJOU-SAMA!?
HMPH.
EH HUH...I AM HAVING FUN, THOUGH...
NOW THAT I THINK OF IT, I WANTED TO HAVE FUN LIKE THIS WITH OJOU-SAMA FOR AS LONG AS I CAN REMEMBER.
...
HMMM.
UH, COULD YOU EMAIL ME THAT PICTURE?
SURE, NO PROBLEM.
AH, ME TOO, SE-CHAN.
ワイ ワイ
THEY SEEM LIKE MORE THAN JUST FRIENDS.
THAT MUCH YOU CAN SEE.
UHMM.
YEP, THERE'S NO MISTAKE ABOUT IT.
MM-HM.

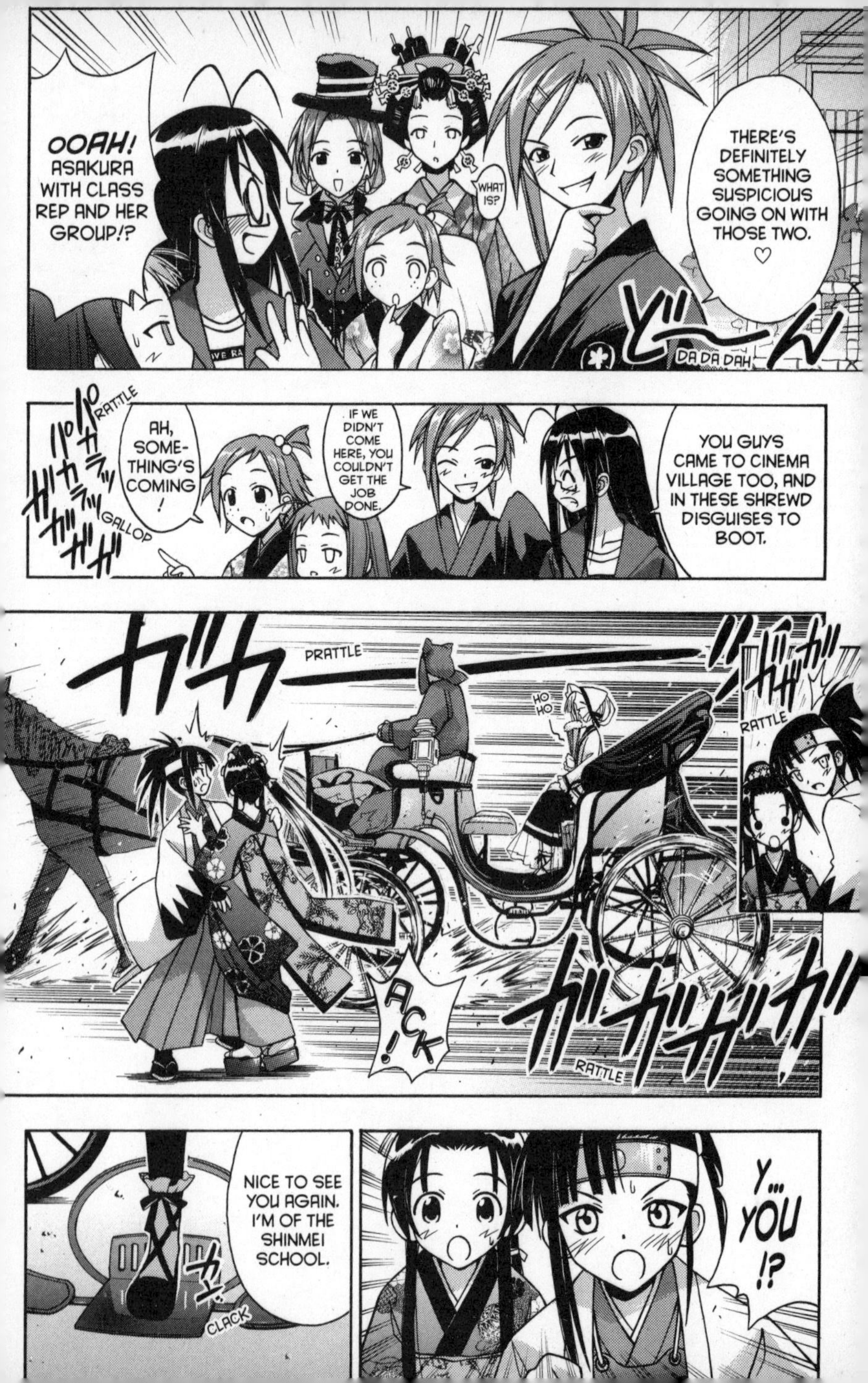

THERE'S DEFINITELY SOMETHING SUSPICIOUS GOING ON WITH THOSE TWO. ♡
DA DA DAH
WHAT IS?
OOAH! ASAKURA WITH CLASS REP AND HER GROUP!?
YOU GUYS CAME TO CINEMA VILLAGE TOO, AND IN THESE SHREWD DISGUISES TO BOOT.
IF WE DIDN'T COME HERE, YOU COULDN'T GET THE JOB DONE.
AH, SOMETHING'S COMING!
RATTLE
GALLOP
RATTLE
PRATTLE
HO HO
ACK!
RATTLE
Y... YOU!?
NICE TO SEE YOU AGAIN. I'M OF THE SHINMEI SCHOOL.
CLACK

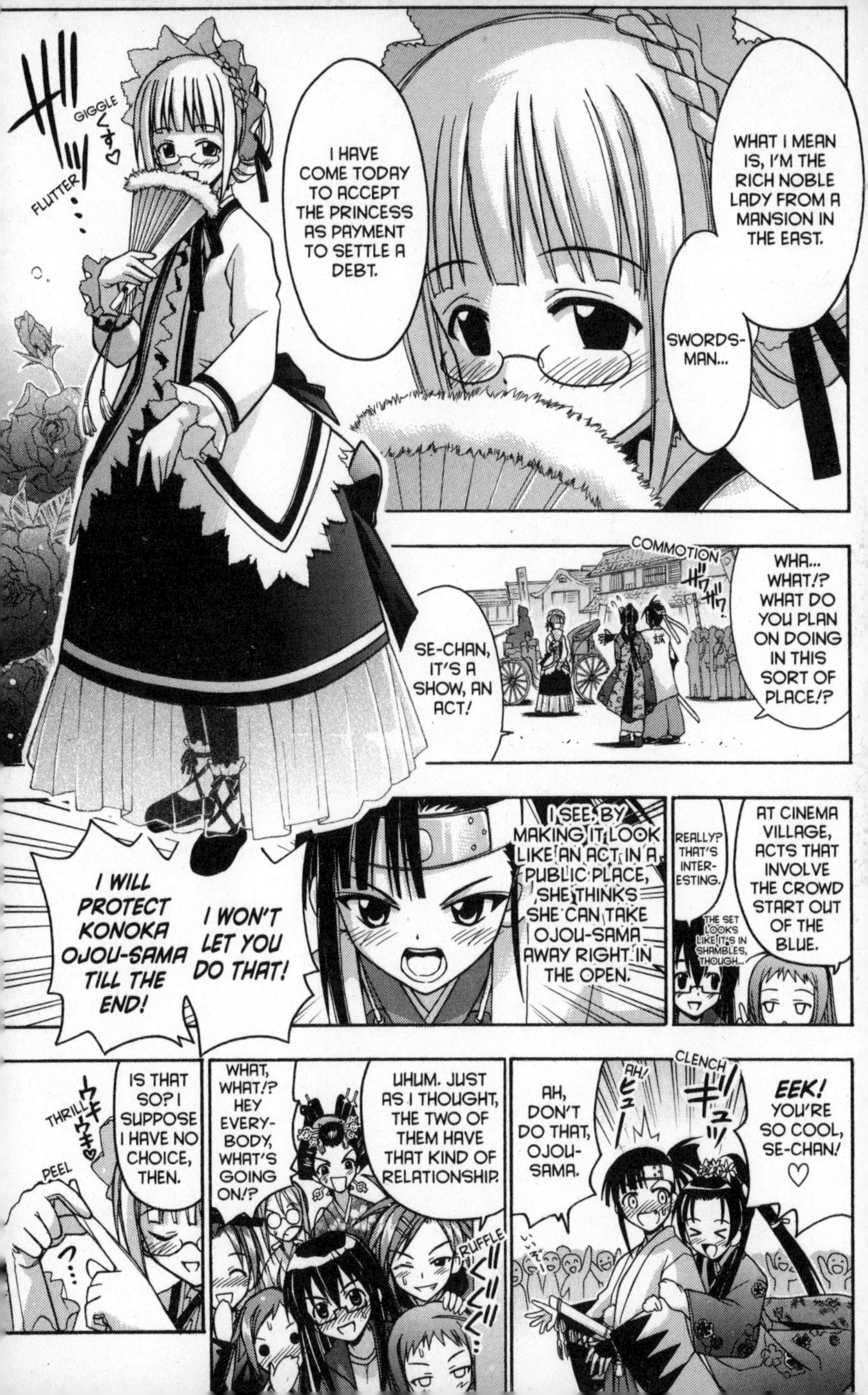
WHAT I MEAN IS, I'M THE RICH NOBLE LADY FROM A MANSION IN THE EAST.
SWORDS-MAN...
I HAVE COME TODAY TO ACCEPT THE PRINCESS AS PAYMENT TO SETTLE A DEBT.
COMMOTION
ザワ ザワ
WHA... WHAT!? WHAT DO YOU PLAN ON DOING IN THIS SORT OF PLACE!?
SE-CHAN, IT'S A SHOW, AN ACT!
GIGGLE
くす♡
FLUTTER
AT CINEMA VILLAGE, ACTS THAT INVOLVE THE CROWD START OUT OF THE BLUE.
REALLY? THAT'S INTER-ESTING.
THE SET LOOKS LIKE IT'S IN SHAMBLES, THOUGH...
I SEE. BY MAKING IT LOOK LIKE AN ACT IN A PUBLIC PLACE, SHE THINKS SHE CAN TAKE OJOU-SAMA AWAY RIGHT IN THE OPEN.
I WON'T LET YOU DO THAT!
I WILL PROTECT KONOKA OJOU-SAMA TILL THE END!
CLENCH
ギュッ
AH!
EEK! YOU'RE SO COOL, SE-CHAN! ♡
AH, DON'T DO THAT, OJOU-SAMA.
UHUM. JUST AS I THOUGHT, THE TWO OF THEM HAVE THAT KIND OF RELATIONSHIP.
WHAT, WHAT!? HEY EVERY-BODY, WHAT'S GOING ON!?
RUFFLE
IS THAT SO? I SUPPOSE I HAVE NO CHOICE, THEN.
THRILL
ウキウキ♡
PEEL
?...

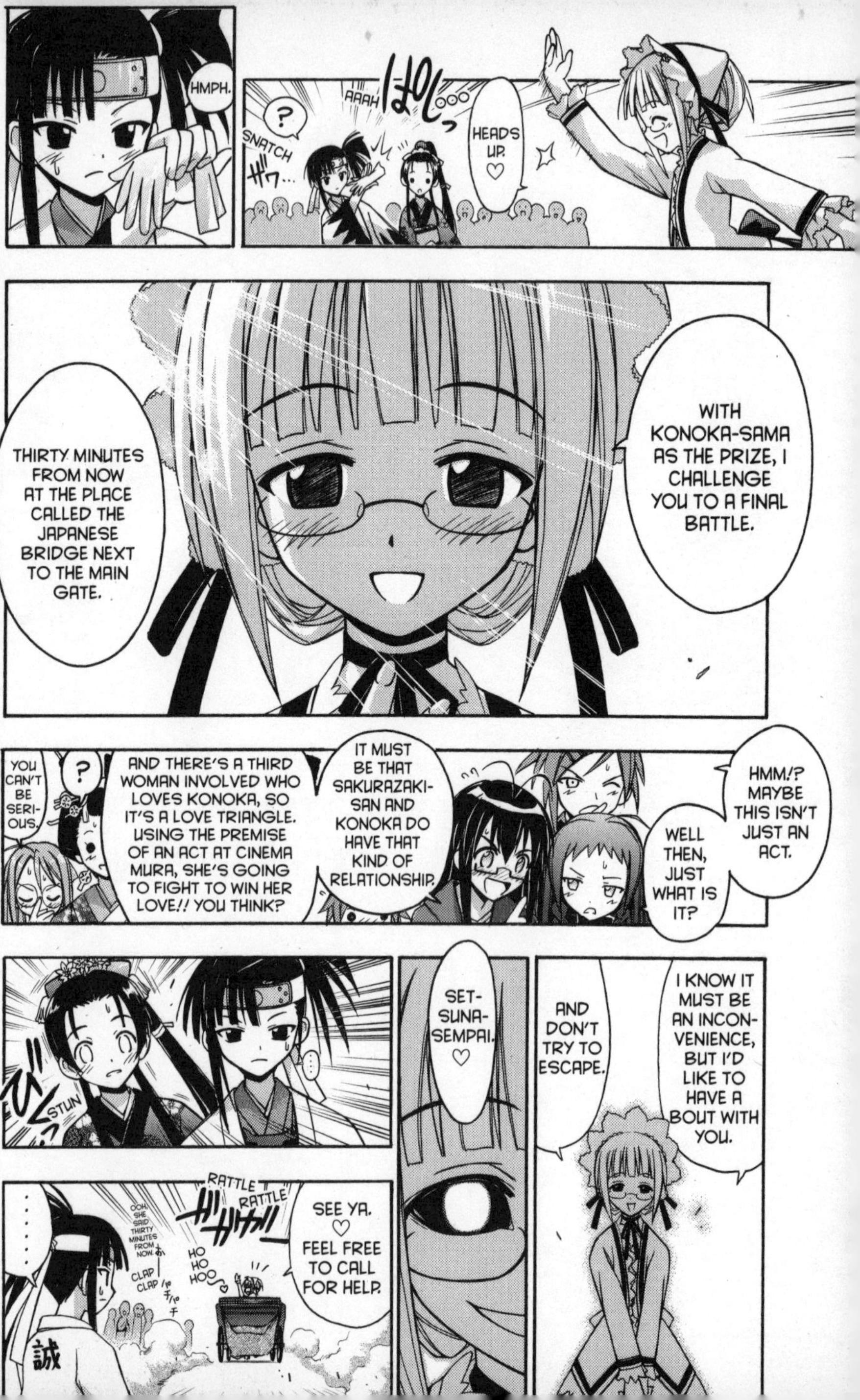
HEADS UP. ♡
AAAH
OOO
?
SNATCH
HMPH.
WITH KONOKA-SAMA AS THE PRIZE, I CHALLENGE YOU TO A FINAL BATTLE.
THIRTY MINUTES FROM NOW AT THE PLACE CALLED THE JAPANESE BRIDGE NEXT TO THE MAIN GATE.
HMM!? MAYBE THIS ISN'T JUST AN ACT.
WELL THEN, JUST WHAT IS IT?
IT MUST BE THAT SAKURAZAKI-SAN AND KONOKA DO HAVE THAT KIND OF RELATIONSHIP.
AND THERE'S A THIRD WOMAN INVOLVED WHO LOVES KONOKA, SO IT'S A LOVE TRIANGLE. USING THE PREMISE OF AN ACT AT CINEMA MURA, SHE'S GOING TO FIGHT TO WIN HER LOVE!! YOU THINK?
?
YOU CAN'T BE SERIOUS.
I KNOW IT MUST BE AN INCONVENIENCE, BUT I'D LIKE TO HAVE A BOUT WITH YOU.
AND DON'T TRY TO ESCAPE.
SETSUNA-SEMPAI. ♡
...
STUN
SEE YA. ♡ FEEL FREE TO CALL FOR HELP.
RATTLE RATTLE
HO HO HOO
OOH, SHE SAID THIRTY MINUTES FROM NOW.
CLAP CLAP
......
誠

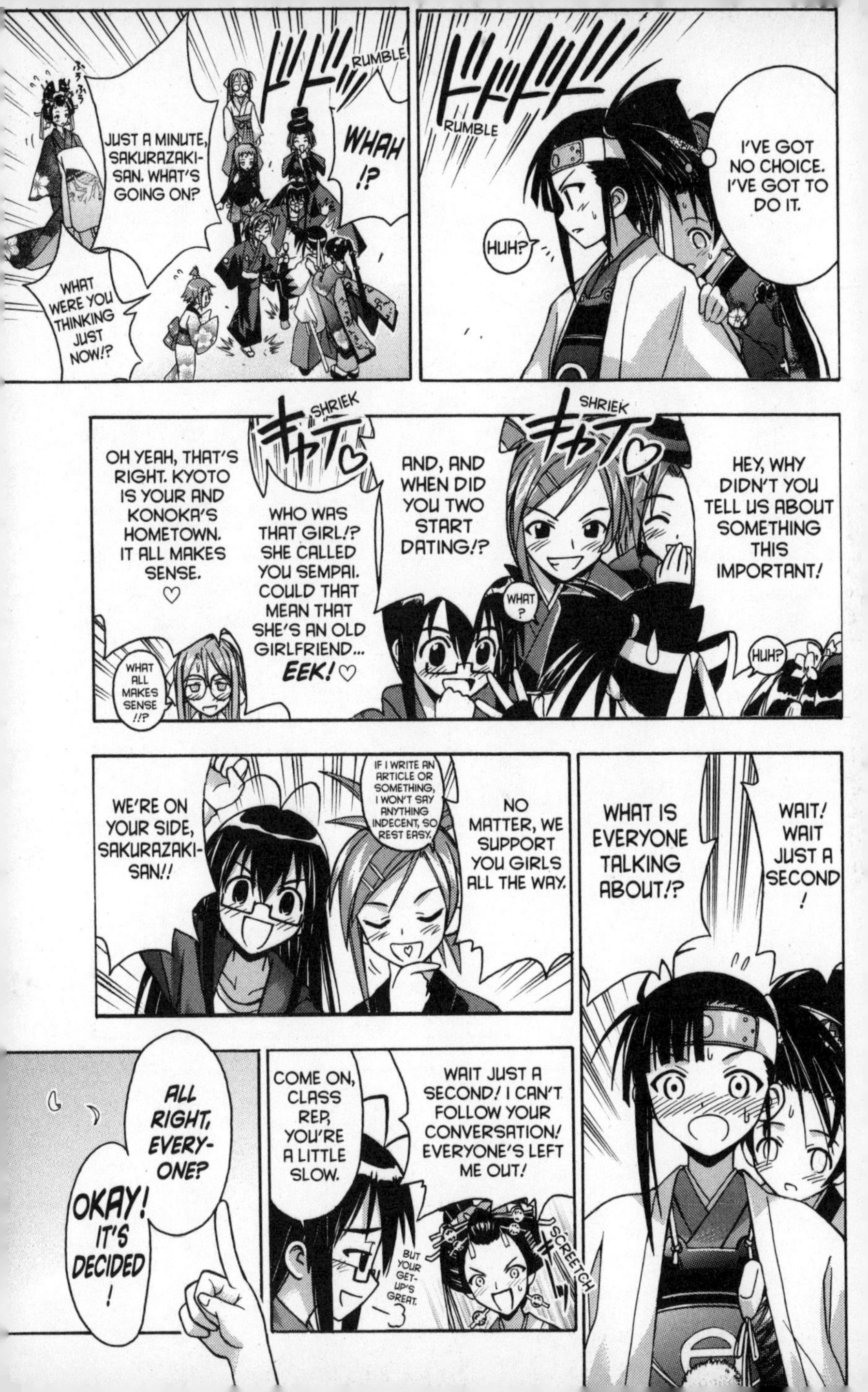
ドドドドド
RUMBLE
I'VE GOT NO CHOICE. I'VE GOT TO DO IT.
HUH?
ドドド
RUMBLE
WHAH!?
JUST A MINUTE, SAKURAZAKI-SAN. WHAT'S GOING ON?
WHAT WERE YOU THINKING JUST NOW!?
HEY, WHY DIDN'T YOU TELL US ABOUT SOMETHING THIS IMPORTANT!
HUH?
キャー
SHRIEK
AND, AND WHEN DID YOU TWO START DATING!?
WHAT?
キャー
SHRIEK
WHO WAS THAT GIRL!? SHE CALLED YOU SEMPAI. COULD THAT MEAN THAT SHE'S AN OLD GIRLFRIEND... EEK! ♡
OH YEAH, THAT'S RIGHT. KYOTO IS YOUR AND KONOKA'S HOMETOWN. IT ALL MAKES SENSE. ♡
WHAT ALL MAKES SENSE!!?
WAIT! WAIT JUST A SECOND!
WHAT IS EVERYONE TALKING ABOUT!?
NO MATTER, WE SUPPORT YOU GIRLS ALL THE WAY.
IF I WRITE AN ARTICLE OR SOMETHING, I WON'T SAY ANYTHING INDECENT, SO REST EASY.
WE'RE ON YOUR SIDE, SAKURAZAKI-SAN!!
WAIT JUST A SECOND! I CAN'T FOLLOW YOUR CONVERSATION! EVERYONE'S LEFT ME OUT!
SCREETCH
COME ON, CLASS REP, YOU'RE A LITTLE SLOW.
BUT YOUR GET-UP'S GREAT.
ALL RIGHT, EVERYONE?
OKAY! IT'S DECIDED!

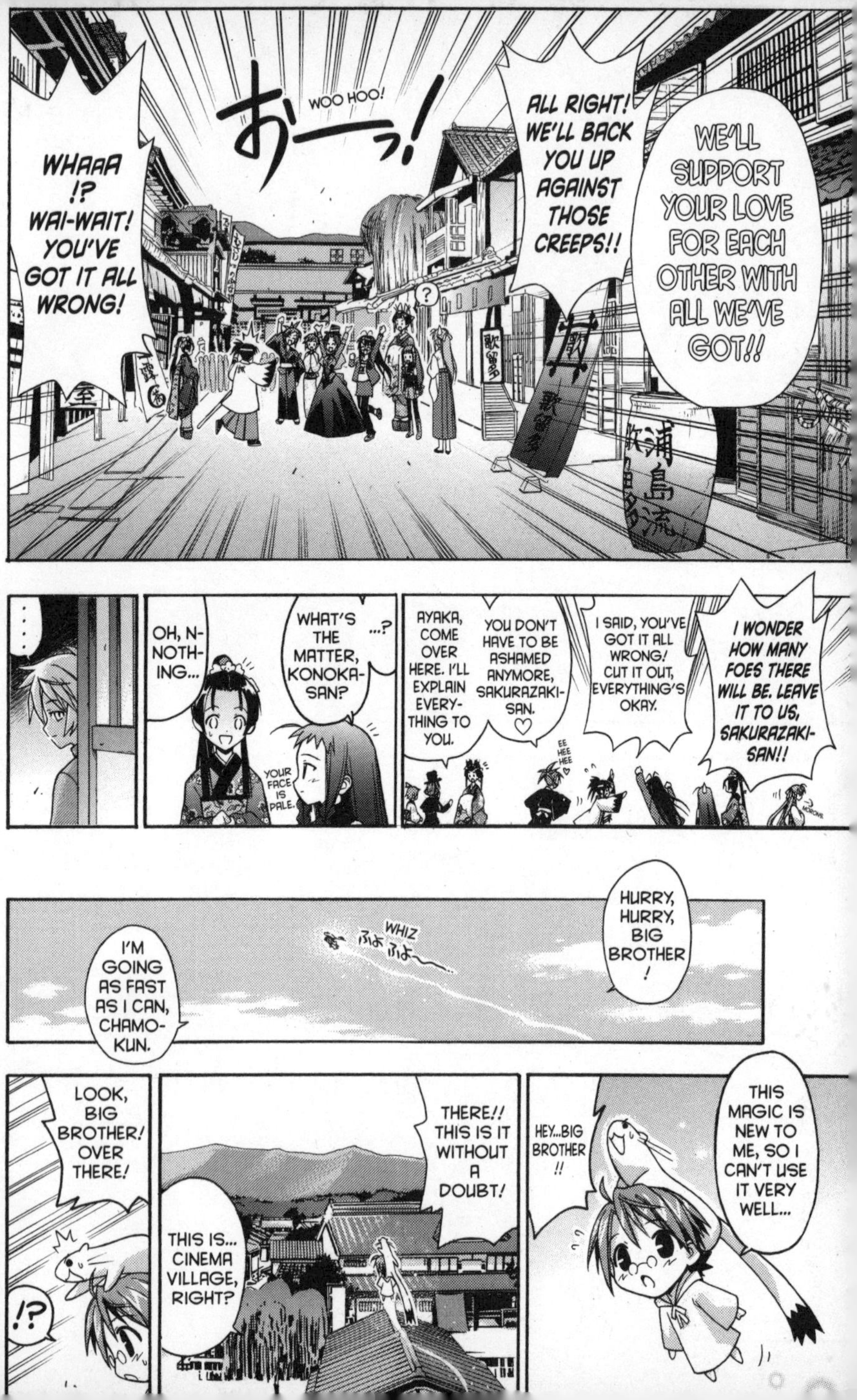
WE'LL SUPPORT YOUR LOVE FOR EACH OTHER WITH ALL WE'VE GOT!!
ALL RIGHT! WE'LL BACK YOU UP AGAINST THOSE CREEPS!!
WOO HOO!
WHAAA!? WAI-WAIT! YOU'VE GOT IT ALL WRONG!
I WONDER HOW MANY FOES THERE WILL BE. LEAVE IT TO US, SAKURAZAKI-SAN!!
I SAID, YOU'VE GOT IT ALL WRONG! CUT IT OUT, EVERYTHING'S OKAY.
YOU DON'T HAVE TO BE ASHAMED ANYMORE, SAKURAZAKI-SAN. ♡
EE HEE HEE
AYAKA, COME OVER HERE. I'LL EXPLAIN EVERYTHING TO YOU.
...?
WHAT'S THE MATTER, KONOKA-SAN?
OH, N-NOTHING...
YOUR FACE IS PALE.
...
HURRY, HURRY, BIG BROTHER!
WHIZ
I'M GOING AS FAST AS I CAN, CHAMO-KUN.
THIS MAGIC IS NEW TO ME, SO I CAN'T USE IT VERY WELL...
HEY...BIG BROTHER!!
THERE!! THIS IS IT WITHOUT A DOUBT!
THIS IS... CINEMA VILLAGE, RIGHT?
LOOK, BIG BROTHER! OVER THERE!
!?

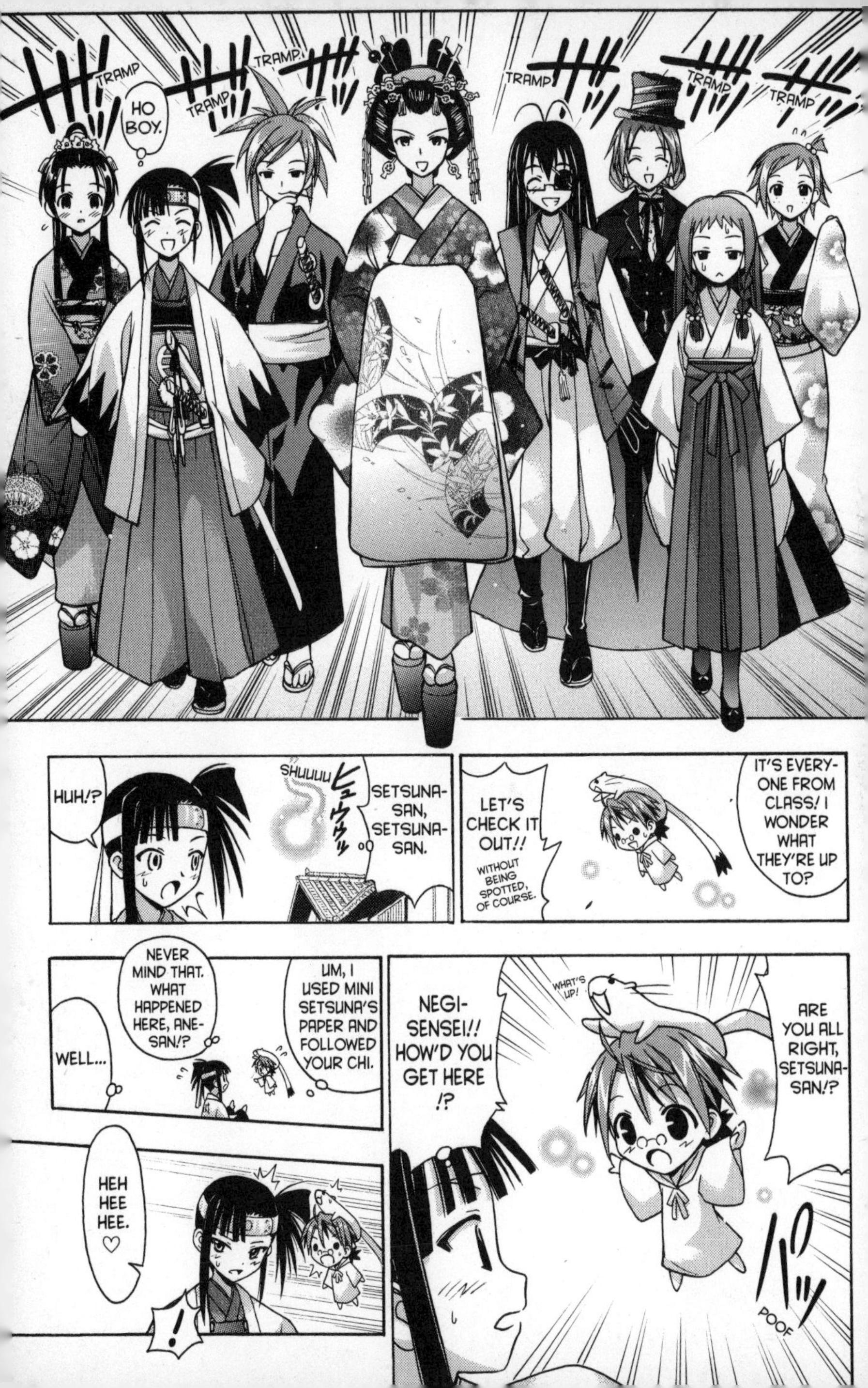
TRAMP
TRAMP
TRAMP
TRAMP
TRAMP.
TRAMP
HO BOY.
TRAMP
IT'S EVERY-ONE FROM CLASS! I WONDER WHAT THEY'RE UP TO?
LET'S CHECK IT OUT!!
WITHOUT BEING SPOTTED, OF COURSE.
SETSUNA-SAN, SETSUNA-SAN.
SHUUUU
HUH!?
ARE YOU ALL RIGHT, SETSUNA-SAN!?
WHAT'S UP!
NEGI-SENSEI!! HOW'D YOU GET HERE!?
POOF
UM, I USED MINI SETSUNA'S PAPER AND FOLLOWED YOUR CHI.
NEVER MIND THAT. WHAT HAPPENED HERE, ANE-SAN!?
WELL...
HEH HEE HEE. ♡
!

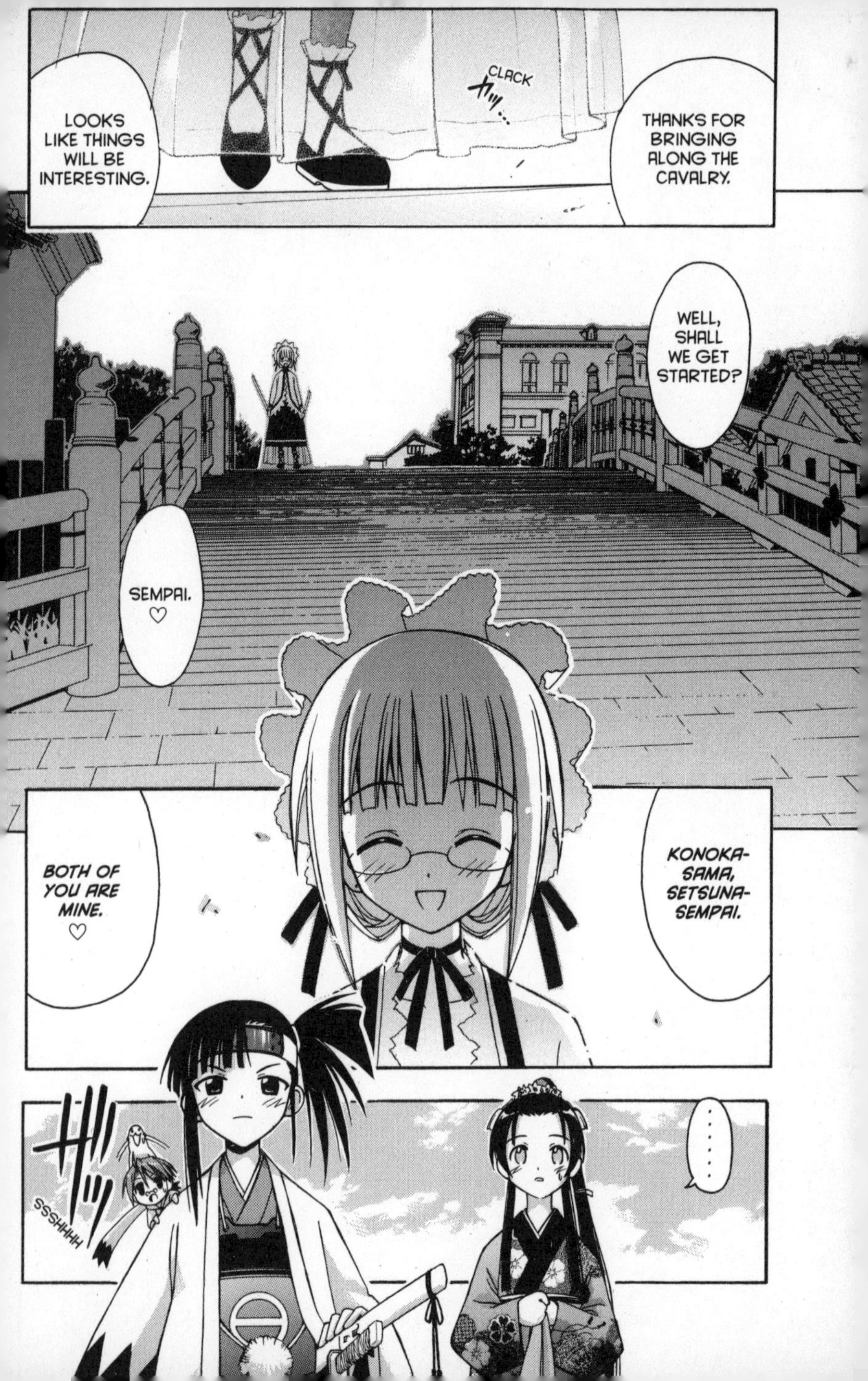
THANKS FOR BRINGING ALONG THE CAVALRY.
CLACK
LOOKS LIKE THINGS WILL BE INTERESTING.
WELL, SHALL WE GET STARTED?
SEMPAI. ♡
KONOKA-SAMA, SETSUNA-SEMPAI.
BOTH OF YOU ARE MINE. ♡
......
SSSHHHH

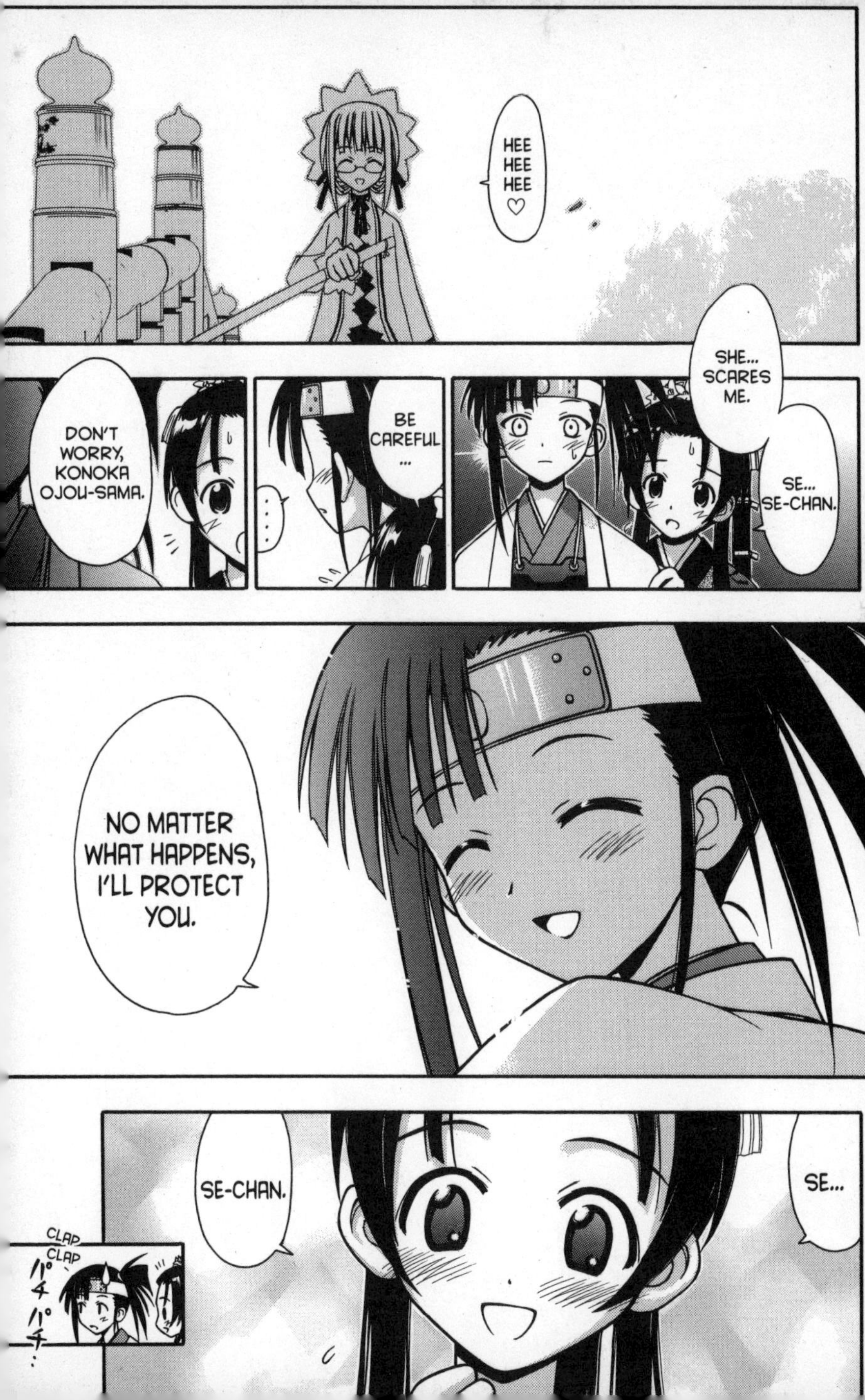
HEE HEE HEE ♡
SHE... SCARES ME.
SE... SE-CHAN.
BE CAREFUL ...
...
DON'T WORRY, KONOKA OJOU-SAMA.
NO MATTER WHAT HAPPENS, I'LL PROTECT YOU.
SE...
SE-CHAN.
CLAP CLAP
パチパチ…

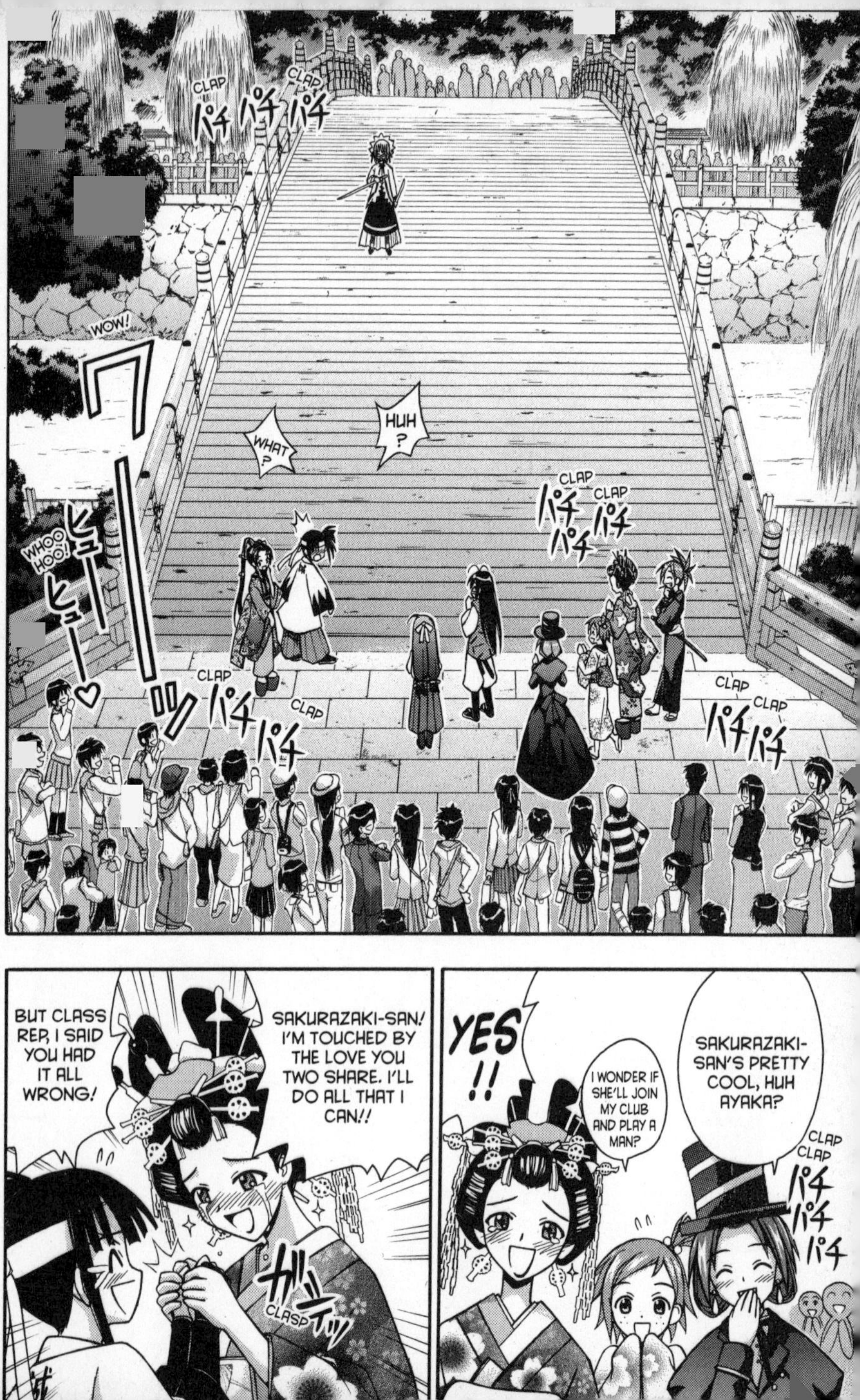
CLAP
パチ パチ パチ
CLAP
HUH?
WHAT?
CLAP CLAP
パチ パチ パチ
WOW!
「ワ――ッ」
WHOO HOO!
ヒューヒュー♥
CLAP CLAP
パチ パチ
CLAP
パチ パチ
CLAP
SAKURAZAKI-SAN'S PRETTY COOL, HUH AYAKA?
CLAP CLAP
パチ パチ パチ
YES!!
I WONDER IF SHE'LL JOIN MY CLUB AND PLAY A MAN?
SAKURAZAKI-SAN! I'M TOUCHED BY THE LOVE YOU TWO SHARE. I'LL DO ALL THAT I CAN!!
BUT CLASS REP, I SAID YOU HAD IT ALL WRONG!
CLASP
ガシッ

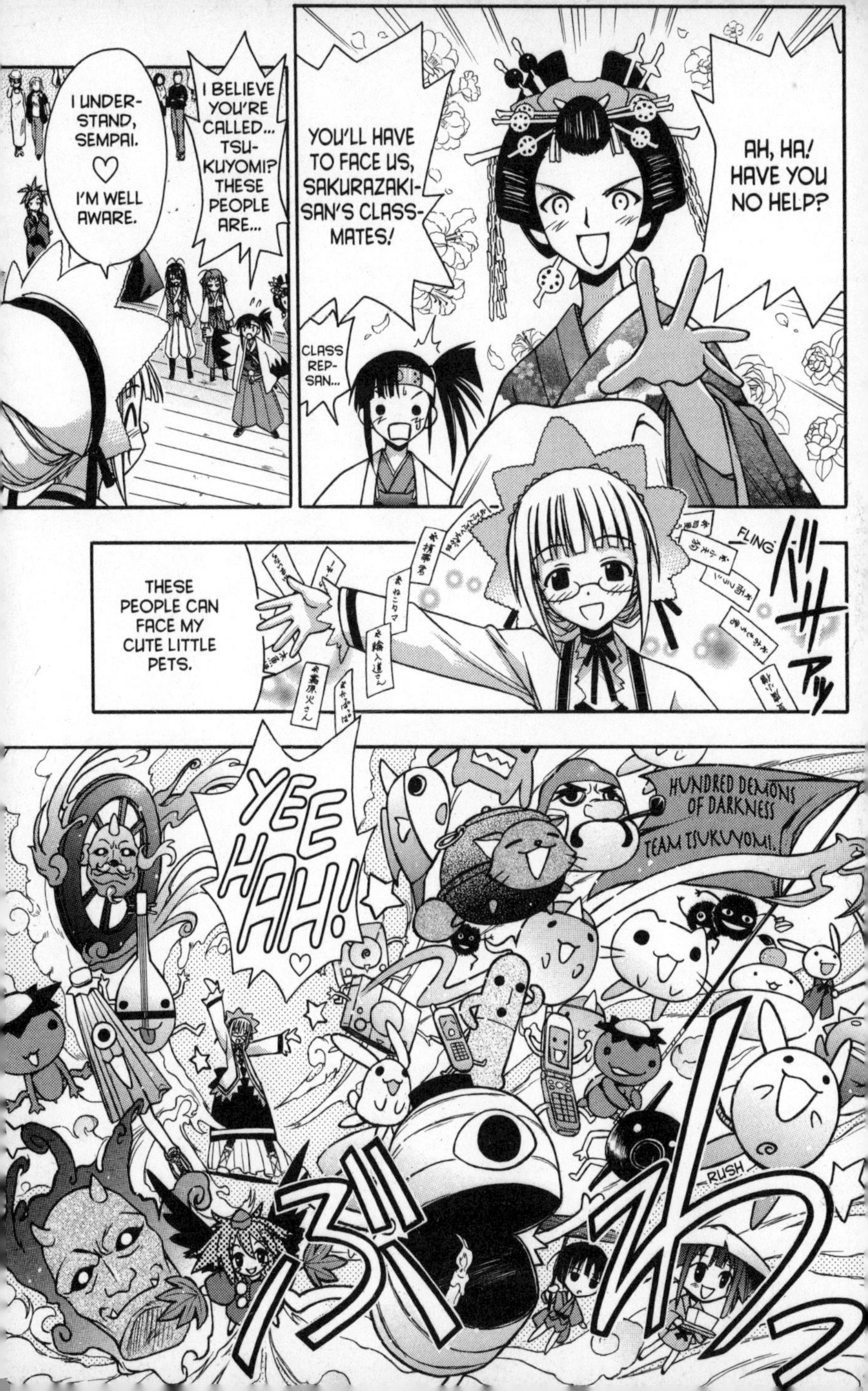
AH, HA! HAVE YOU NO HELP?
YOU'LL HAVE TO FACE US, SAKURAZAKI-SAN'S CLASS-MATES!
CLASS REP-SAN...
I BELIEVE YOU'RE CALLED... TSU-KUYOMI? THESE PEOPLE ARE...
I UNDER-STAND, SEMPAI. ♡ I'M WELL AWARE.
FLING
THESE PEOPLE CAN FACE MY CUTE LITTLE PETS.
YEE HAH! ♡
HUNDRED DEMONS OF DARKNESS
TEAM TSUKUYOMI.
RUSH

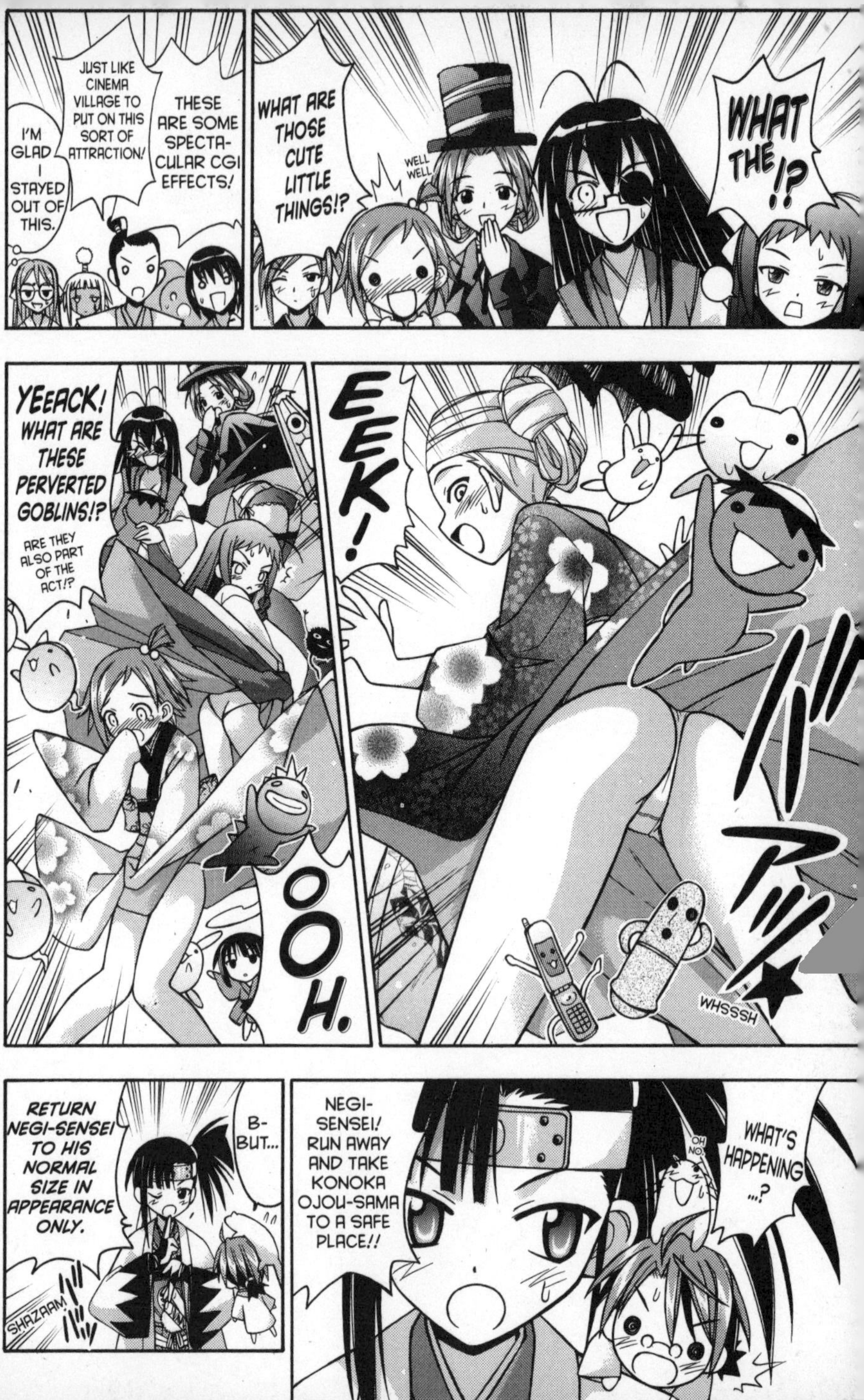
WHAT THE !?
WELL WELL
WHAT ARE THOSE CUTE LITTLE THINGS!?
THESE ARE SOME SPECTACULAR CGI EFFECTS!
JUST LIKE CINEMA VILLAGE TO PUT ON THIS SORT OF ATTRACTION!
I'M GLAD I STAYED OUT OF THIS.
EEK!
WHSSSH
OOOH.
YEEACK! WHAT ARE THESE PERVERTED GOBLINS!?
ARE THEY ALSO PART OF THE ACT!?
WHAT'S HAPPENING ...?
OH NO
NEGI-SENSEI! RUN AWAY AND TAKE KONOKA OJOU-SAMA TO A SAFE PLACE!!
B-BUT...
RETURN NEGI-SENSEI TO HIS NORMAL SIZE IN APPEARANCE ONLY.
SHAZAAM

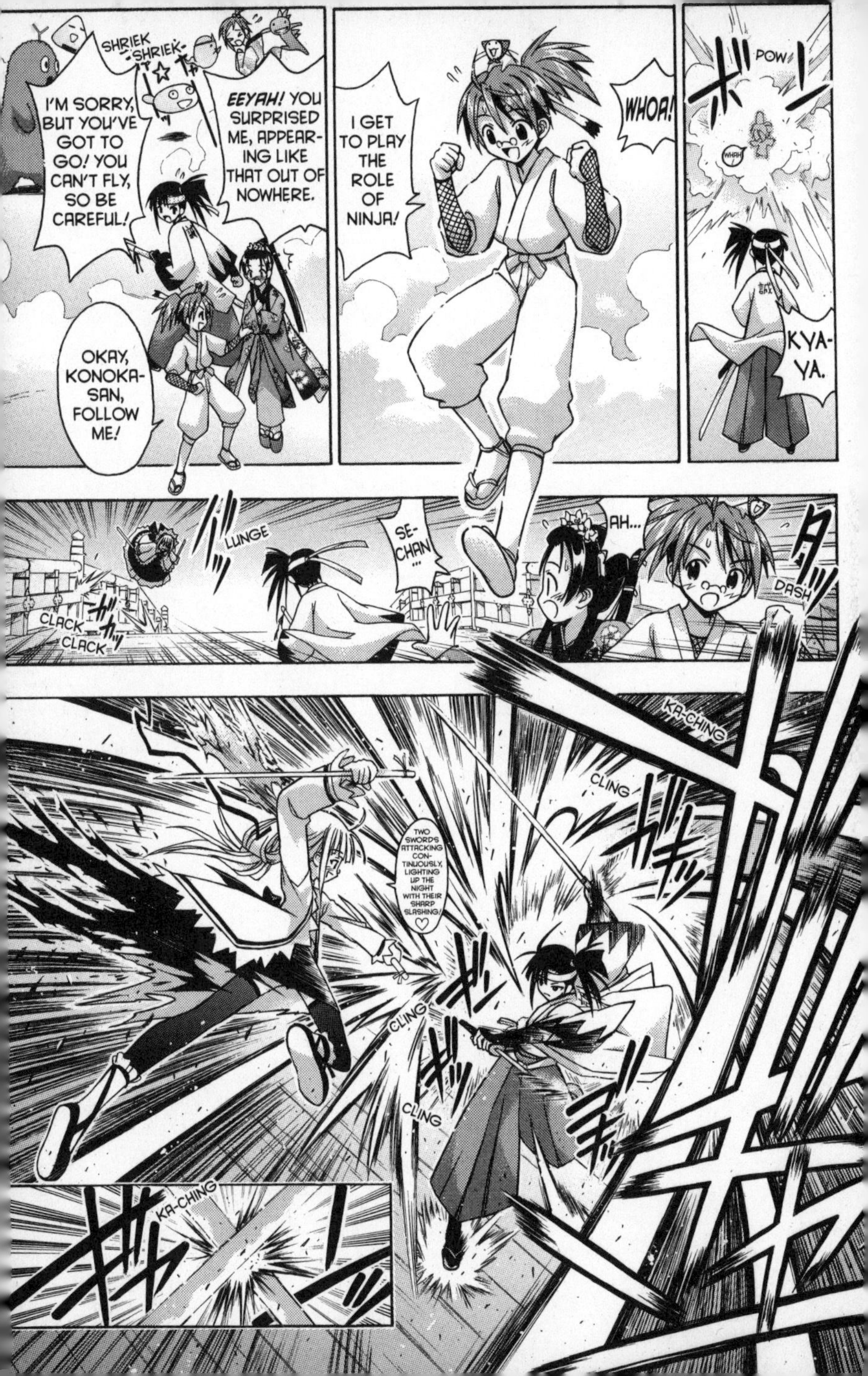
POW
WHAH
KYA-YA.
WHOA!
I GET TO PLAY THE ROLE OF NINJA!
SHRIEK SHRIEK
EEYAH! YOU SURPRISED ME, APPEARING LIKE THAT OUT OF NOWHERE.
I'M SORRY, BUT YOU'VE GOT TO GO! YOU CAN'T FLY, SO BE CAREFUL!
OKAY, KONOKA-SAN, FOLLOW ME!
DASH
AH...
SE-CHAN...
LUNGE
CLACK CLACK
KA-CHING
CLING
TWO SWORDS ATTACKING CONTINUOUSLY, LIGHTING UP THE NIGHT WITH THEIR SHARP SLASHING! ♡
CLING
CLING
KA-CHING

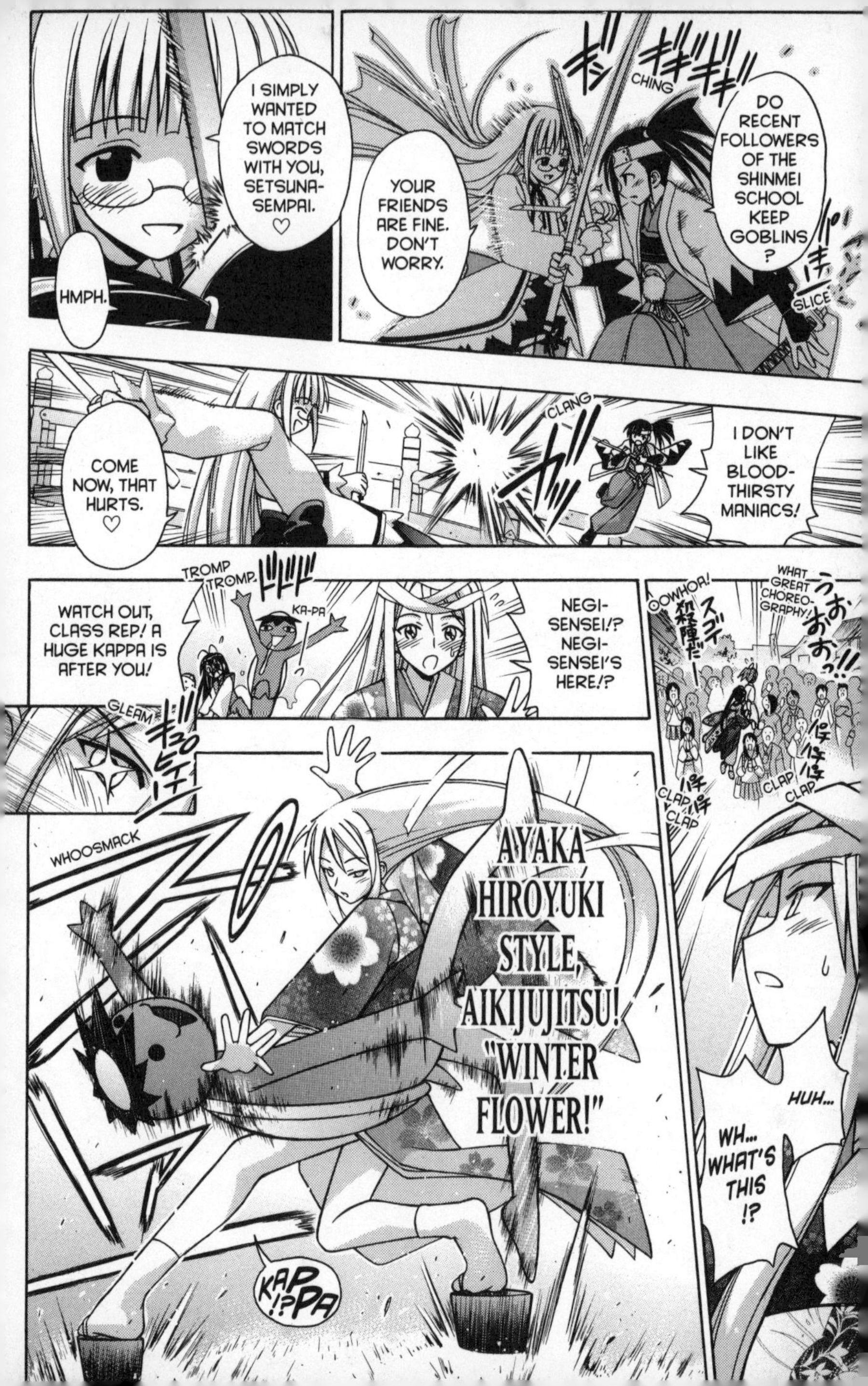
CHING
DO RECENT FOLLOWERS OF THE SHINMEI SCHOOL KEEP GOBLINS?
SLICE
YOUR FRIENDS ARE FINE. DON'T WORRY.
I SIMPLY WANTED TO MATCH SWORDS WITH YOU, SETSUNA-SEMPAI. ♡
HMPH.
CLANG
I DON'T LIKE BLOOD-THIRSTY MANIACS!
COME NOW, THAT HURTS. ♡
WHAT GREAT CHOREO-GRAPHY!
OOWHOA!
CLAP CLAP
CLAP CLAP
NEGI-SENSEI!? NEGI-SENSEI'S HERE!?
TROMP TROMP.
KA-PA
WATCH OUT, CLASS REP! A HUGE KAPPA IS AFTER YOU!
HUH...
WH... WHAT'S THIS!?
GLEAM
WHOOSMACK
AYAKA HIROYUKI STYLE, AIKIJUJITSU! "WINTER FLOWER!"
KAPPA!?

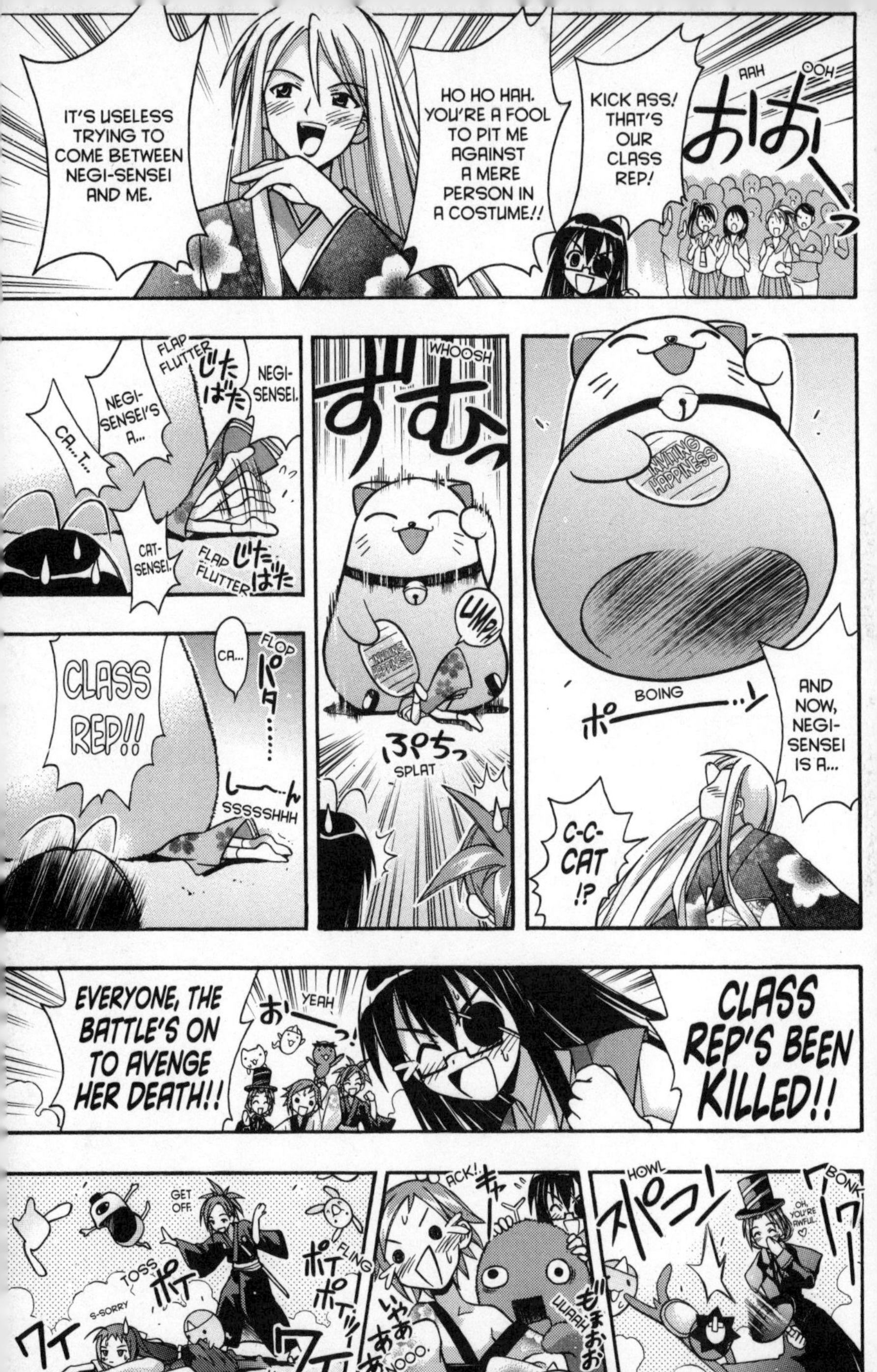
AAH
OOH
KICK ASS! THAT'S OUR CLASS REP!
HO HO HAH. YOU'RE A FOOL TO PIT ME AGAINST A MERE PERSON IN A COSTUME!!
IT'S USELESS TRYING TO COME BETWEEN NEGI-SENSEI AND ME.
BOING
ポー……ン
AND NOW, NEGI-SENSEI IS A...
C-C-CAT!?
INVITING HAPPINESS
WHOOSH
ずむっ
UMPH
INVITING HAPPINESS
ぷちっ
SPLAT
NEGI-SENSEI.
FLAP FLUTTER
じたばた
NEGI-SENSEI'S A...
CA...T...
CAT-SENSEI.
FLAP FLUTTER
じたばた
CA...
FLOP
パタ……
CLASS REP!!
しーん
SSSSSHHH
CLASS REP'S BEEN KILLED!!
YEAH
おーっ!
EVERYONE, THE BATTLE'S ON TO AVENGE HER DEATH!!
HOWL
スパコーン
BONK
OH, YOU'RE AWFUL. ♥
ワー
ACK!
キャー
UUAAH
いやあああ
NOOO.
GET OFF.
FLING
ポイポイッ
TOSS
ポイ
S-SORRY
ワイワイ
HUBBUB

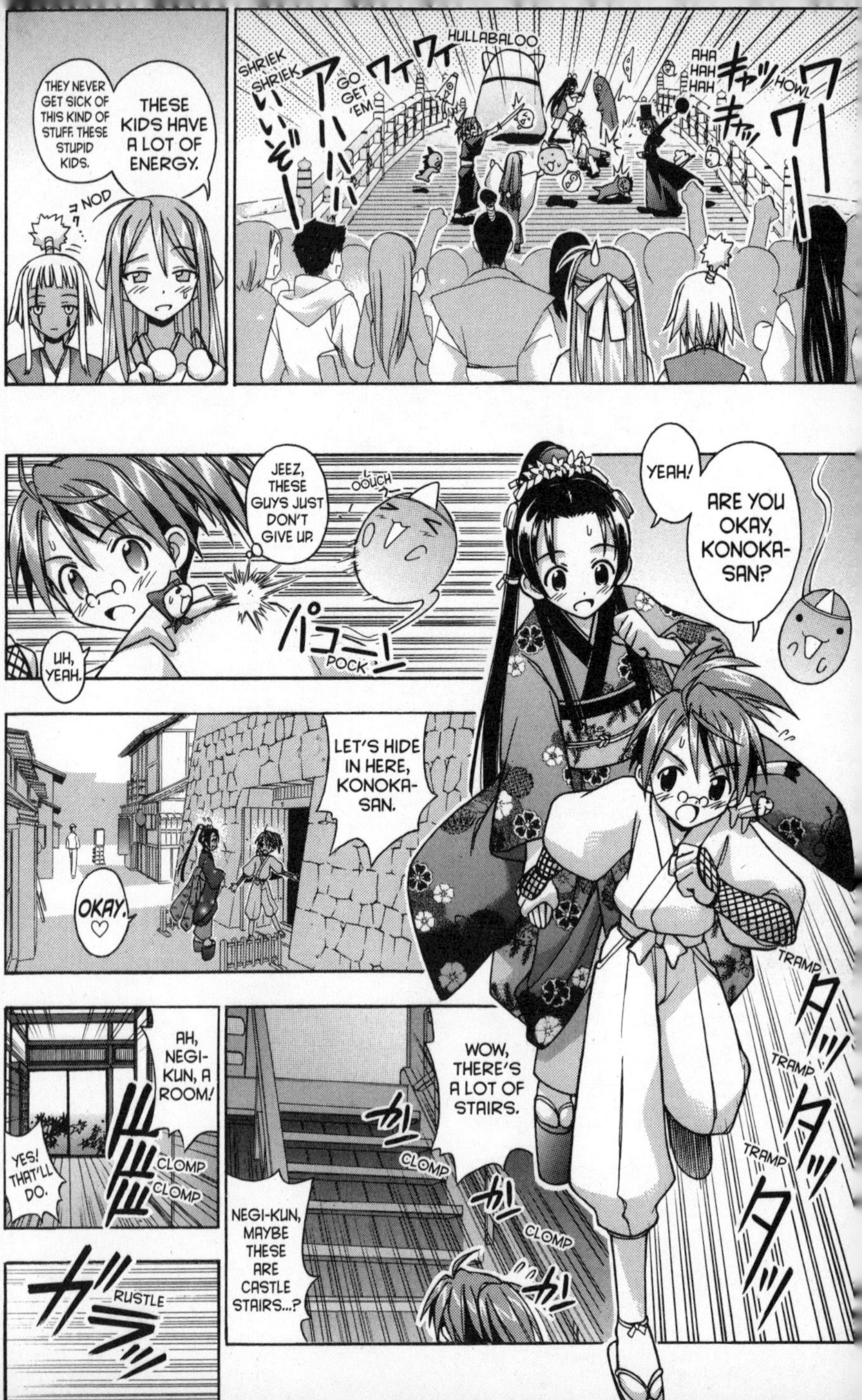

ワーワー
HOWL
キャッキャッ
AHA HAH HAH
HULLABALOO
ワイワイ
GO GET 'EM
アハハハハ
SHRIEK SHRIEK
いいぞー
THESE KIDS HAVE A LOT OF ENERGY.
THEY NEVER GET SICK OF THIS KIND OF STUFF. THESE STUPID KIDS.
コク
NOD
ARE YOU OKAY, KONOKA-SAN?
YEAH!
TRAMP
タッ
TRAMP
タッ
TRAMP
タッ
JEEZ, THESE GUYS JUST DON'T GIVE UP.
OOUCH
パコーン
POCK
UH, YEAH.
LET'S HIDE IN HERE, KONOKA-SAN.
OKAY. ♡
WOW, THERE'S A LOT OF STAIRS.
カッ
CLOMP
カッ
CLOMP
カッ
NEGI-KUN, MAYBE THESE ARE CASTLE STAIRS...?
AH, NEGI-KUN, A ROOM!
YES! THAT'LL DO.
CLOMP
CLOMP
ガラッ
RUSTLE

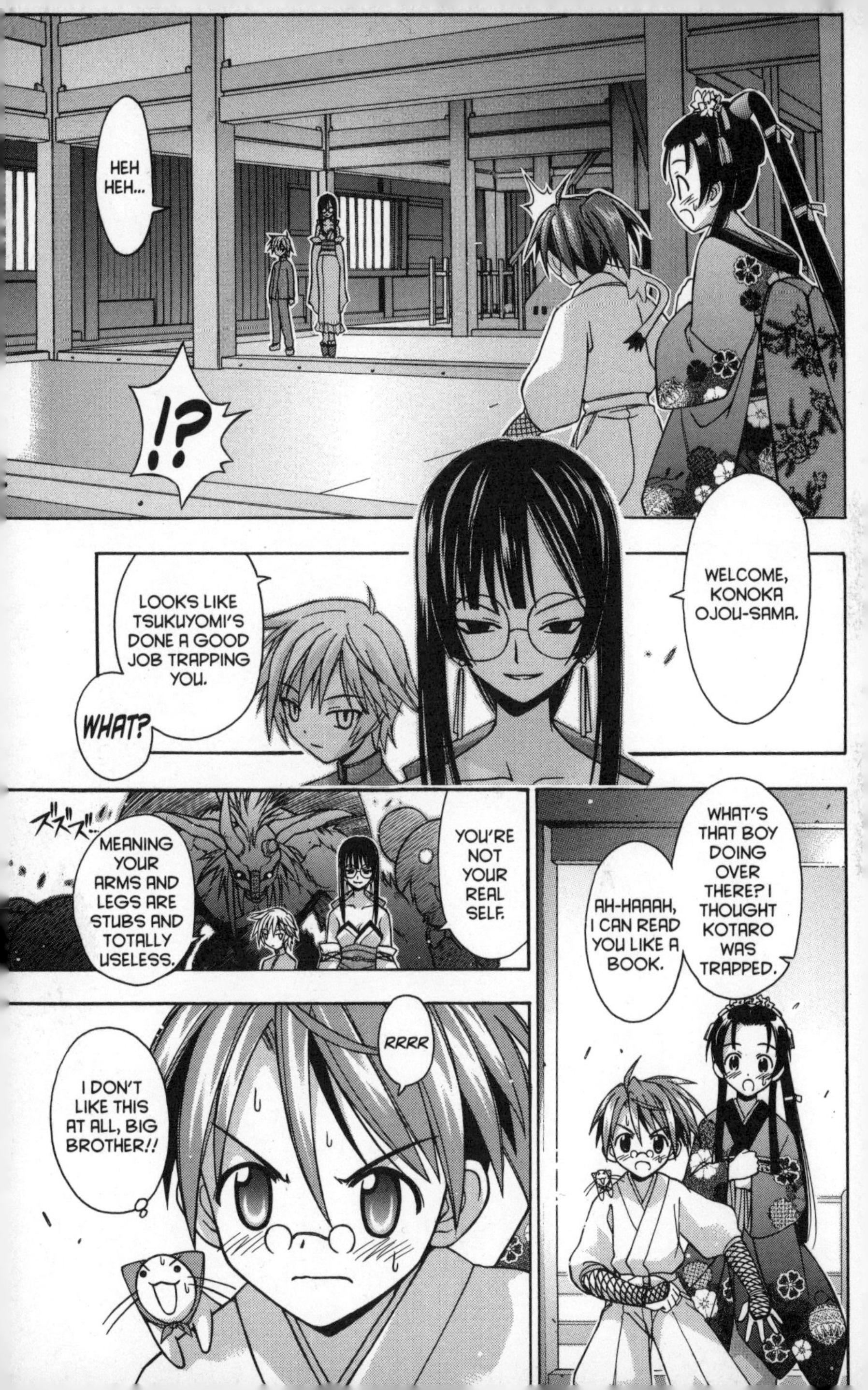
HEH HEH...
!?
WELCOME, KONOKA OJOU-SAMA.
LOOKS LIKE TSUKUYOMI'S DONE A GOOD JOB TRAPPING YOU.
WHAT?
WHAT'S THAT BOY DOING OVER THERE? I THOUGHT KOTARO WAS TRAPPED.
AH-HAAAH, I CAN READ YOU LIKE A BOOK.
YOU'RE NOT YOUR REAL SELF.
ズズズ...
MEANING YOUR ARMS AND LEGS ARE STUBS AND TOTALLY USELESS.
RRRR
I DON'T LIKE THIS AT ALL, BIG BROTHER!!

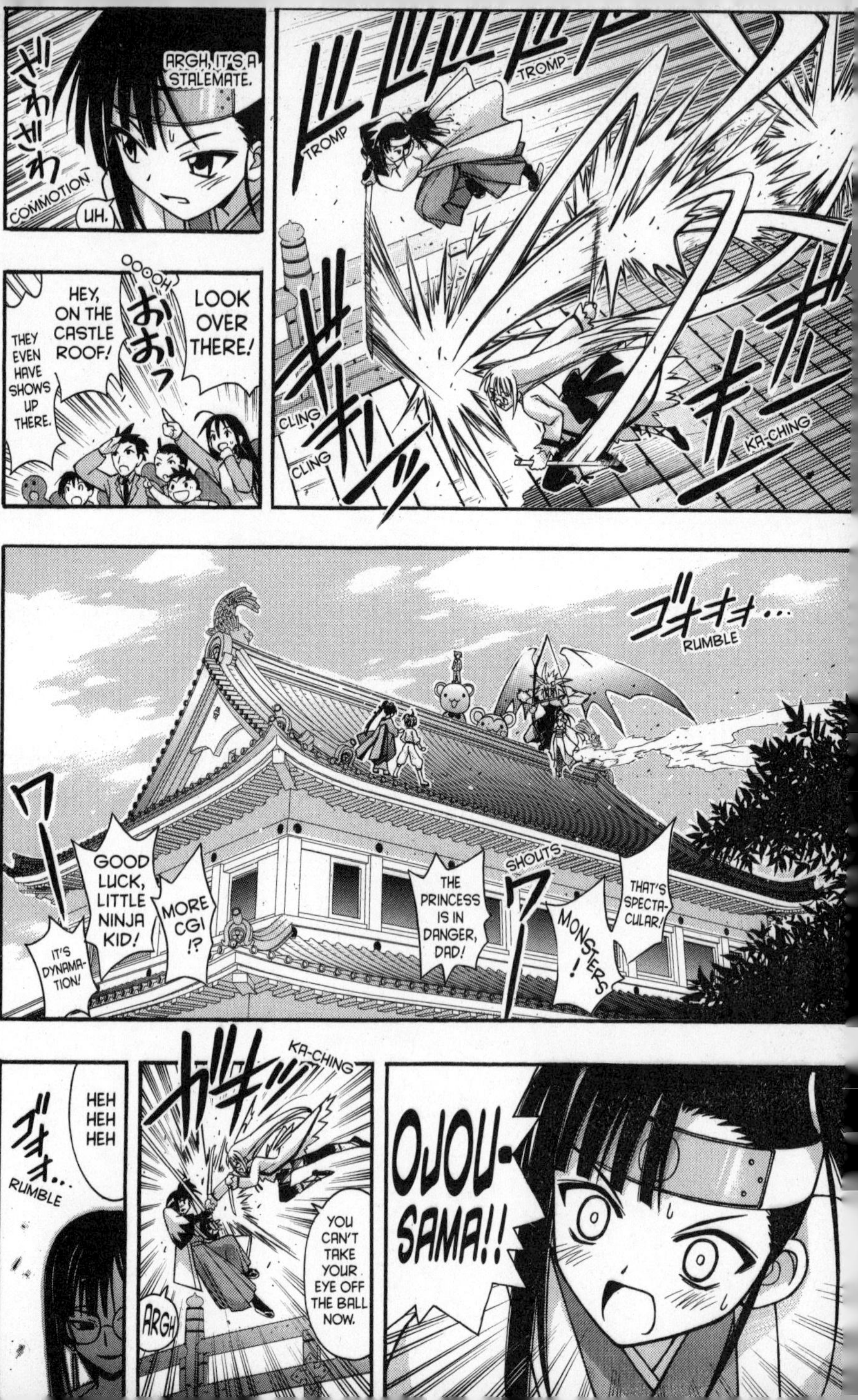
TROMP
TROMP
CLING
CLING
KA-CHING
ARGH, IT'S A STALEMATE.
ざわざわ
COMMOTION
UH.
LOOK OVER THERE!
おおっ
OOOOH
HEY, ON THE CASTLE ROOF!
THEY EVEN HAVE SHOWS UP THERE.
ゴオオオ…
RUMBLE
THAT'S SPECTACULAR!
MONSTERS!
SHOUTS
THE PRINCESS IS IN DANGER, DAD!
MORE CGI!?
GOOD LUCK, LITTLE NINJA KID!
IT'S DYNAMATION!
OJOU-SAMA!!
KA-CHING
YOU CAN'T TAKE YOUR EYE OFF THE BALL NOW.
ARGH
HEH HEH HEH
ゴオオ…
RUMBLE

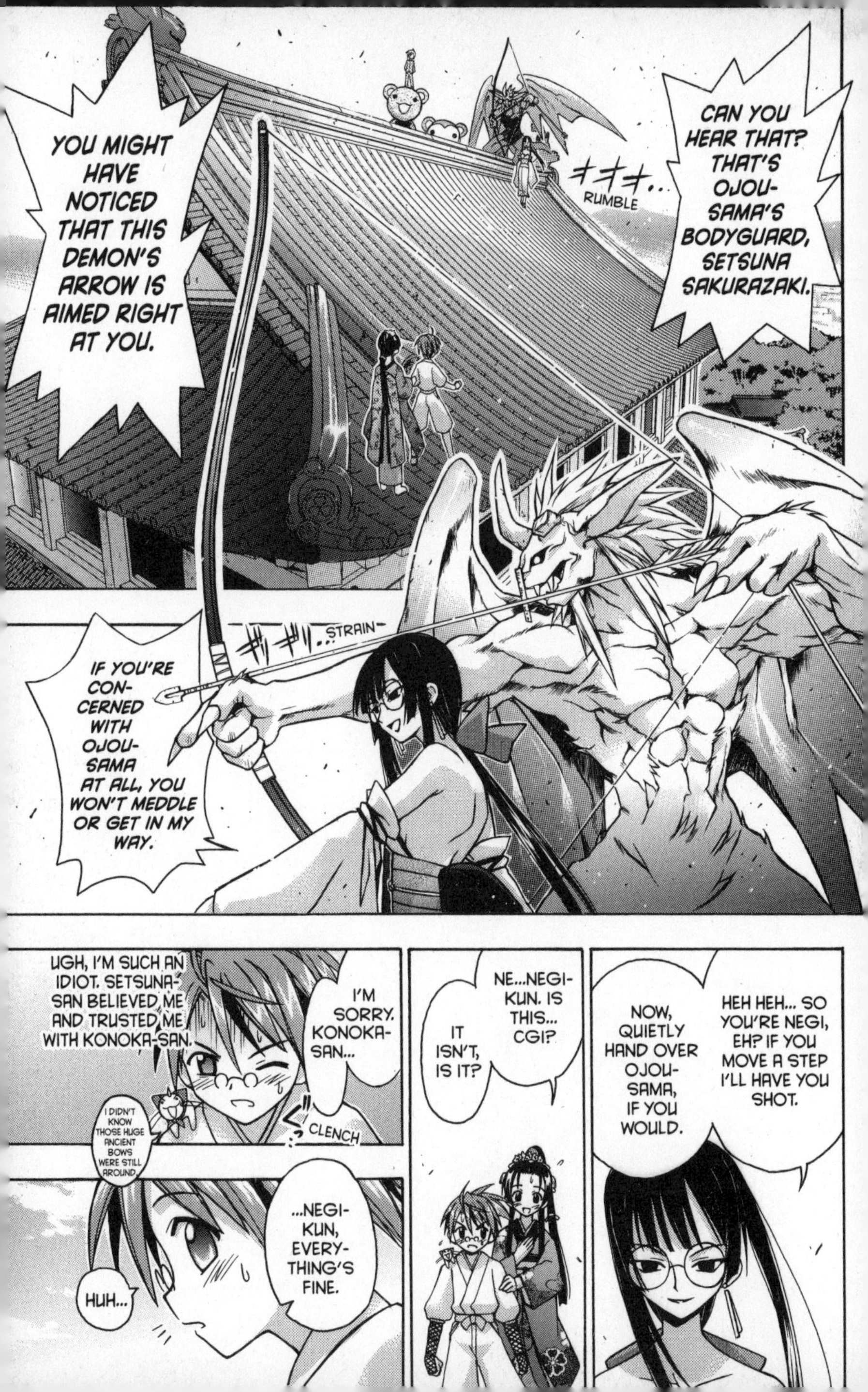
CAN YOU HEAR THAT? THAT'S OJOU-SAMA'S BODYGUARD, SETSUNA SAKURAZAKI.
RUMBLE
YOU MIGHT HAVE NOTICED THAT THIS DEMON'S ARROW IS AIMED RIGHT AT YOU.
STRAIN
IF YOU'RE CON-CERNED WITH OJOU-SAMA AT ALL, YOU WON'T MEDDLE OR GET IN MY WAY.
HEH HEH... SO YOU'RE NEGI, EH? IF YOU MOVE A STEP I'LL HAVE YOU SHOT.
NOW, QUIETLY HAND OVER OJOU-SAMA, IF YOU WOULD.
NE...NEGI-KUN. IS THIS... CGI?
IT ISN'T, IS IT?
I'M SORRY. KONOKA-SAN...
UGH, I'M SUCH AN IDIOT. SETSUNA-SAN BELIEVED ME AND TRUSTED ME WITH KONOKA-SAN.
CLENCH
I DIDN'T KNOW THOSE HUGE ANCIENT BOWS WERE STILL AROUND.
...NEGI-KUN, EVERY-THING'S FINE.
HUH...

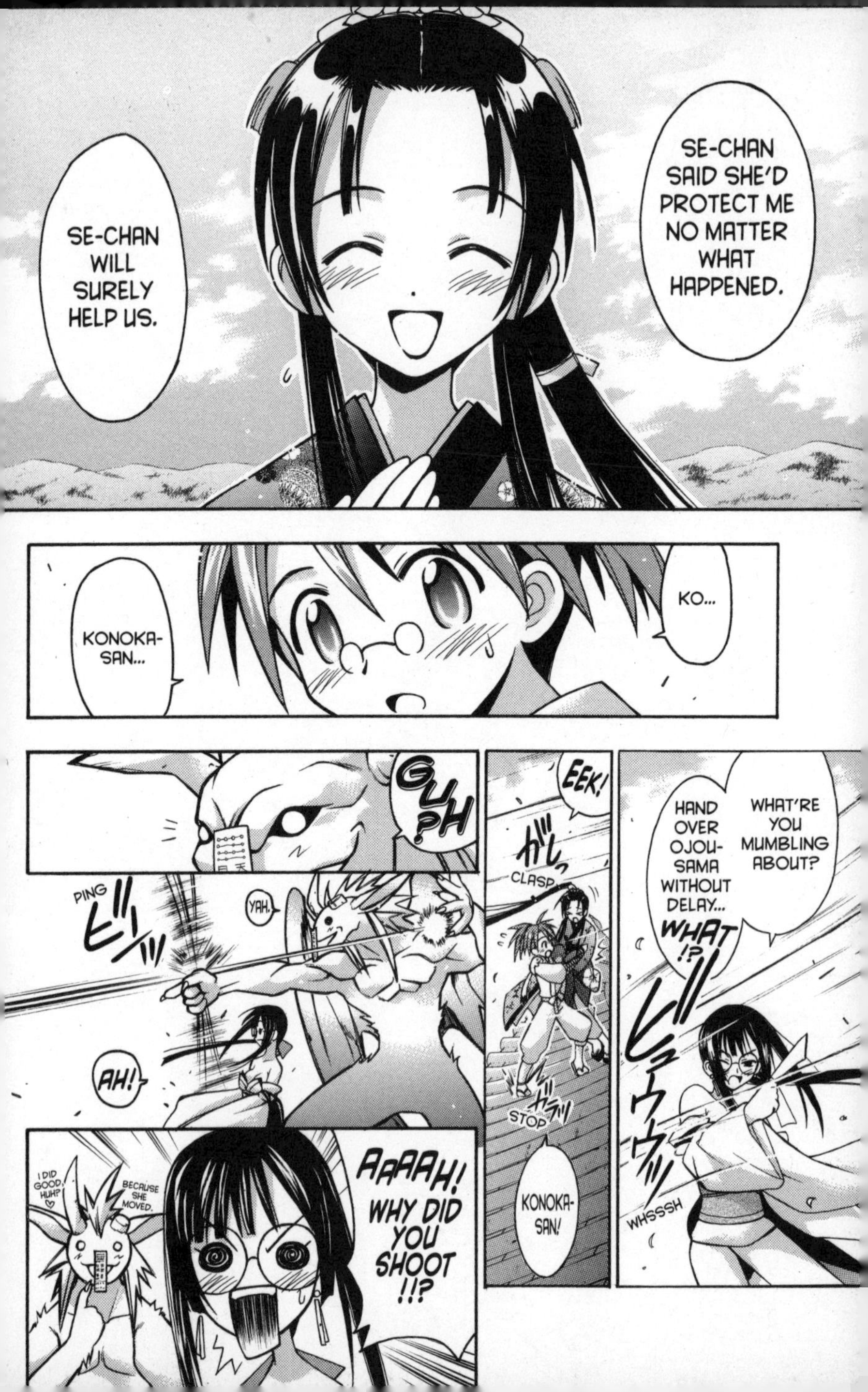
SE-CHAN SAID SHE'D PROTECT ME NO MATTER WHAT HAPPENED.
SE-CHAN WILL SURELY HELP US.
KO...
KONOKA-SAN...
WHAT'RE YOU MUMBLING ABOUT?
HAND OVER OJOU-SAMA WITHOUT DELAY...
WHAT !?
WHSSSH
EEK!
CLASP
STOP
KONOKA-SAN!
GUH?H
YAH.
PING
AH!
AAAAH! WHY DID YOU SHOOT !!?
BECAUSE SHE MOVED.
I DID GOOD, HUH? ♡

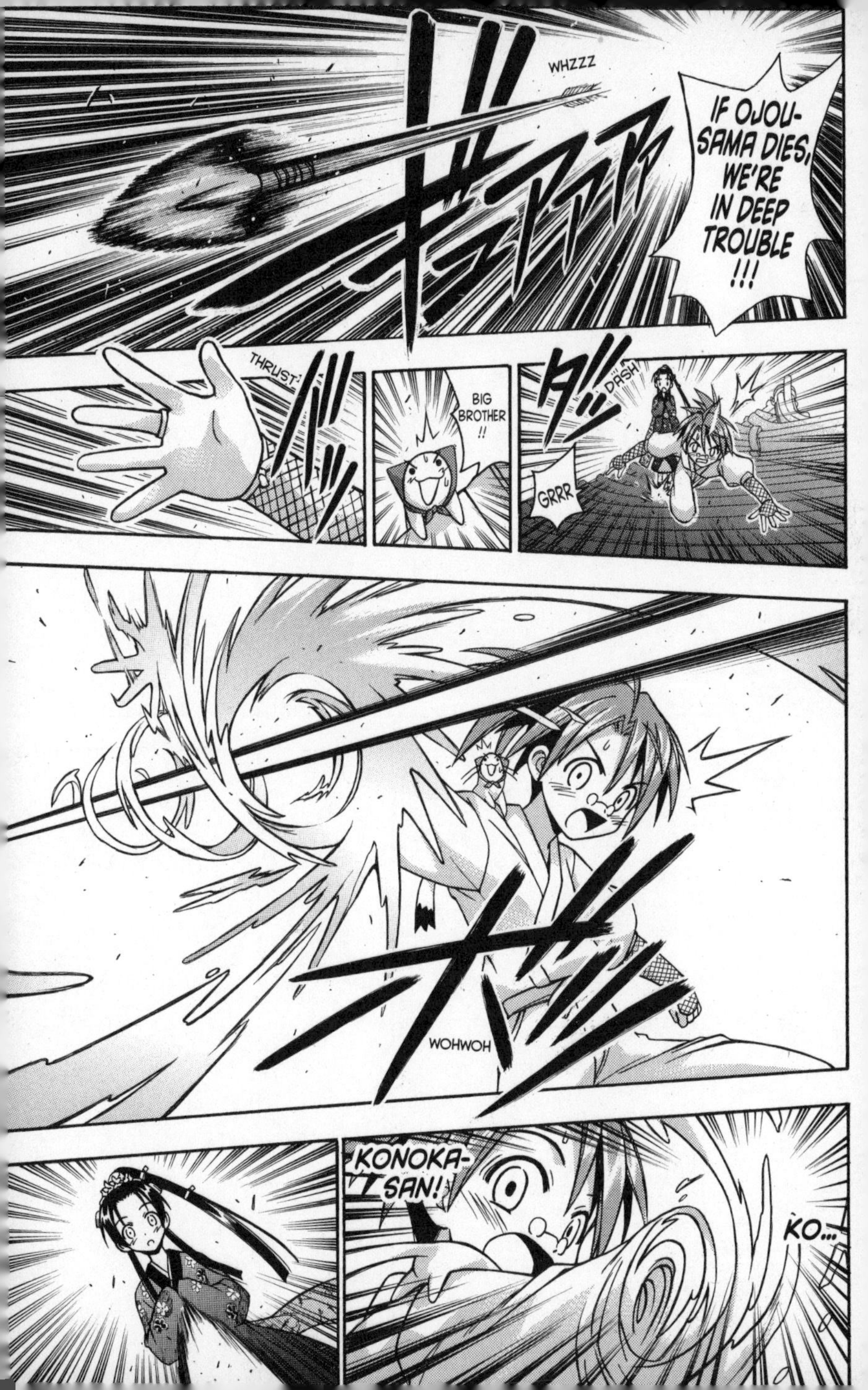
IF OJOU-SAMA DIES, WE'RE IN DEEP TROUBLE !!!
WHZZZ
DASH
GRRR
BIG BROTHER !!
THRUST
WOHWOH
KO...
KONOKA-SAN!

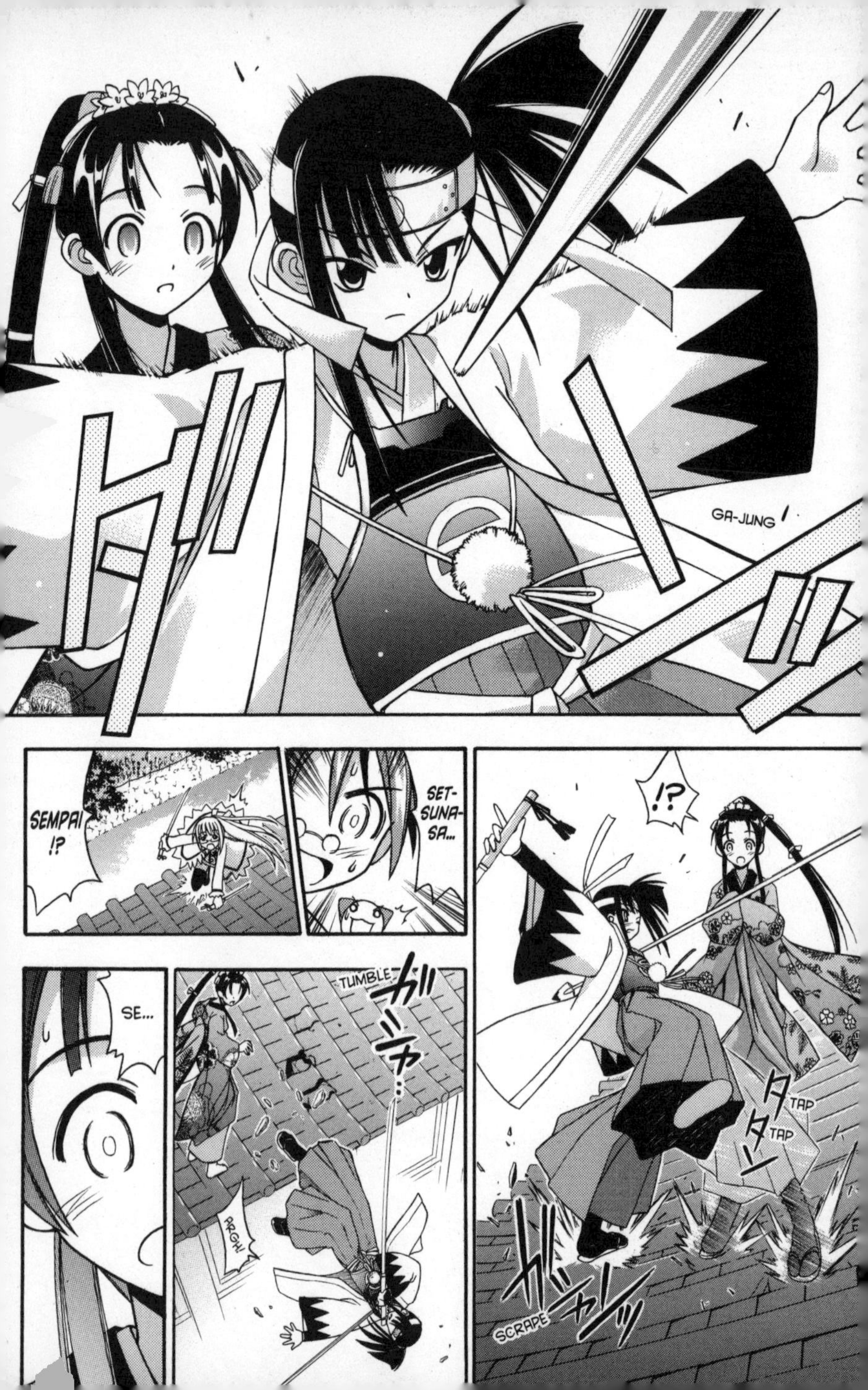
GA-JUNG!
!?
TAP
TAP
SCRAPE
SET-SUNA-SA...
SEMPAI !?
TUMBLE
ARGH!
SE...

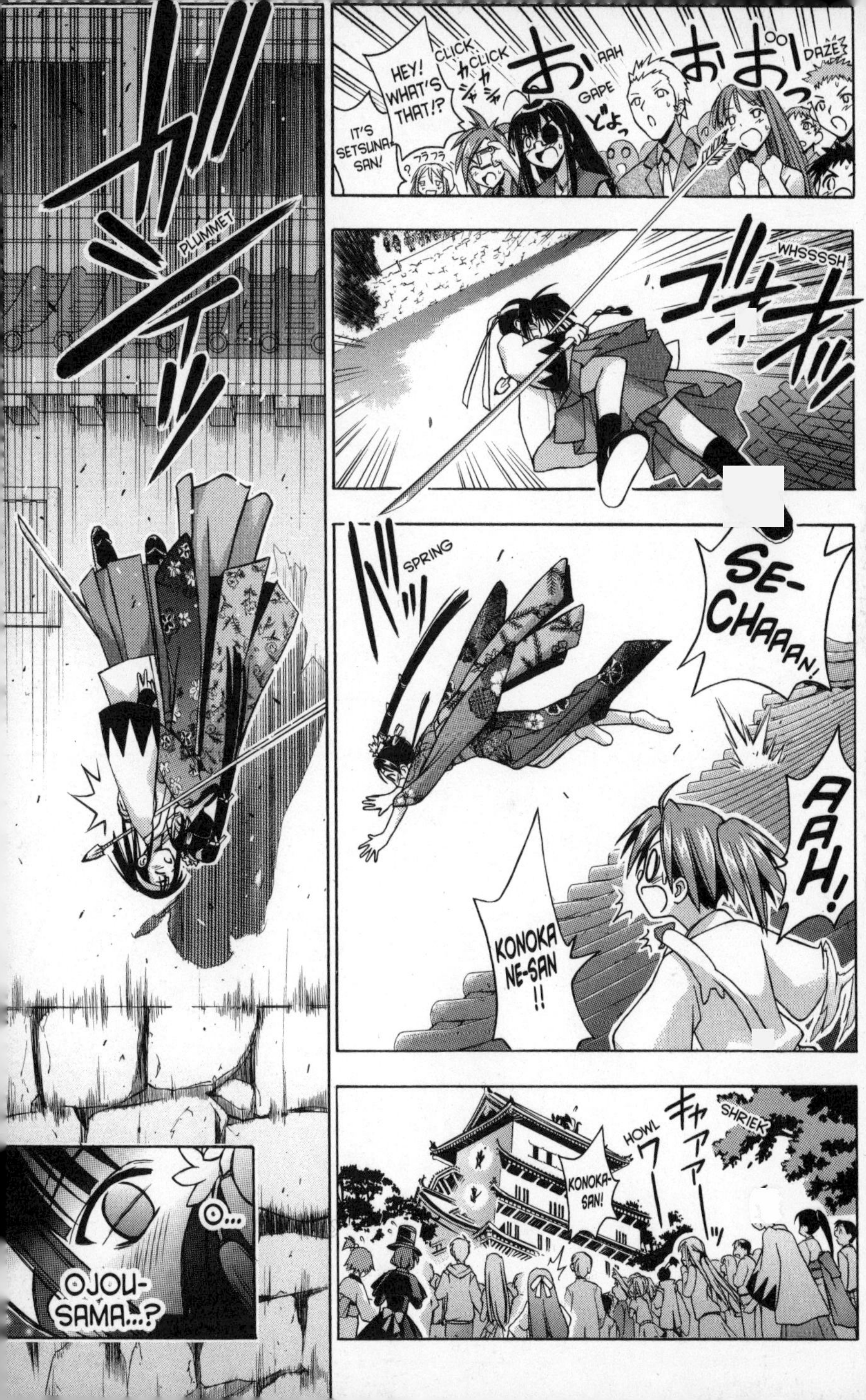

DAZE
おおっ
GAPE
どよっ
お AAH
CLICK CLICK
カシャ カシャ
HEY! WHAT'S THAT!?
IT'S SETSUNA-SAN!
WHSSSSH
ゴオオッ
SE-CHAAAAN!
SPRING
AAAH!
KONOKA NE-SAN!!
SHRIEK
キャアアーッ
HOWL
ワー
KONOKA-SAN!
PLUMMET
O...
OJOU-SAMA...?

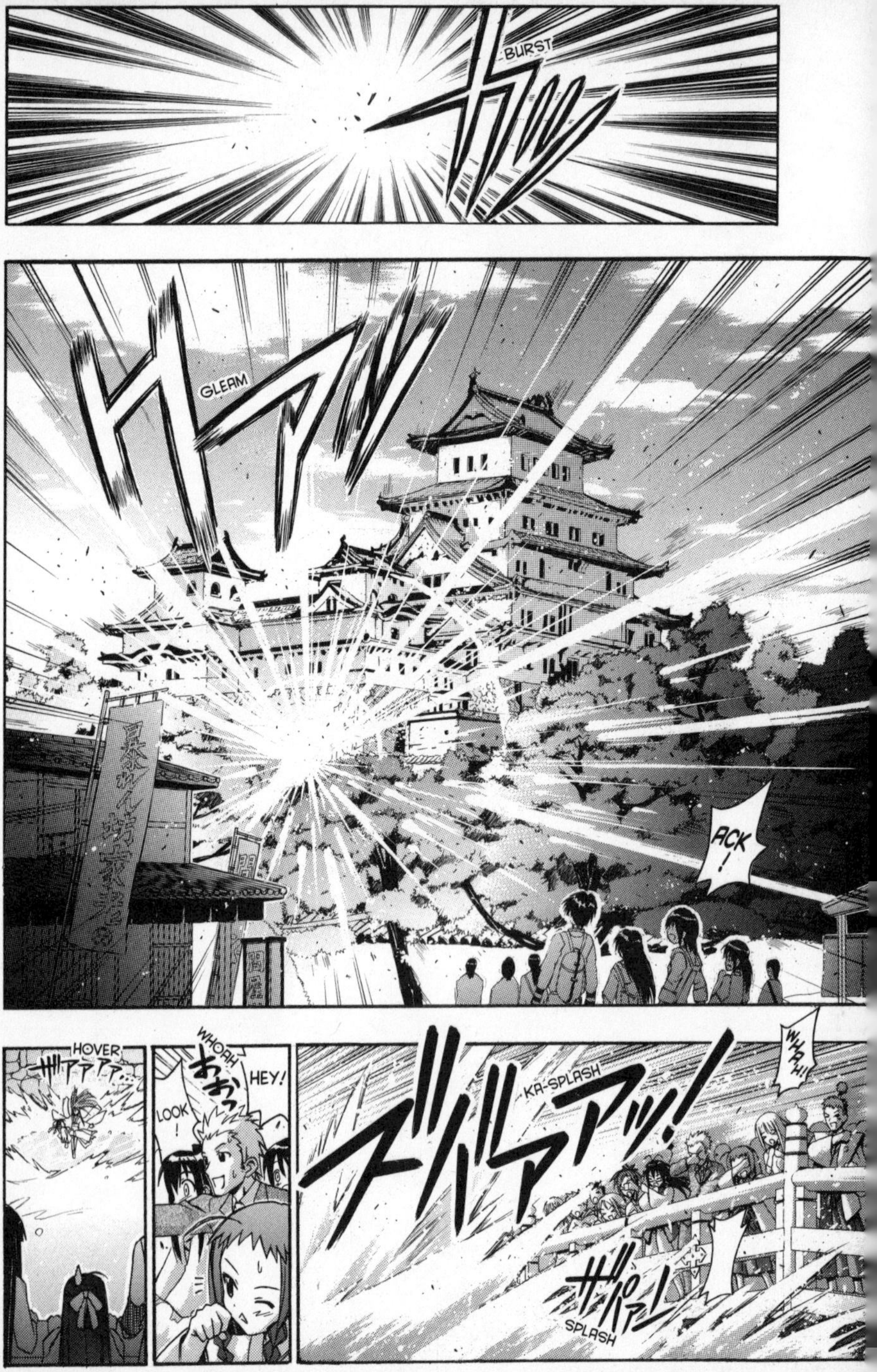
BURST
GLEAM
ACK!
WHOAH!!
KA-SPLASH
SPLASH
WHOAH
HEY!
LOOK!
HOVER

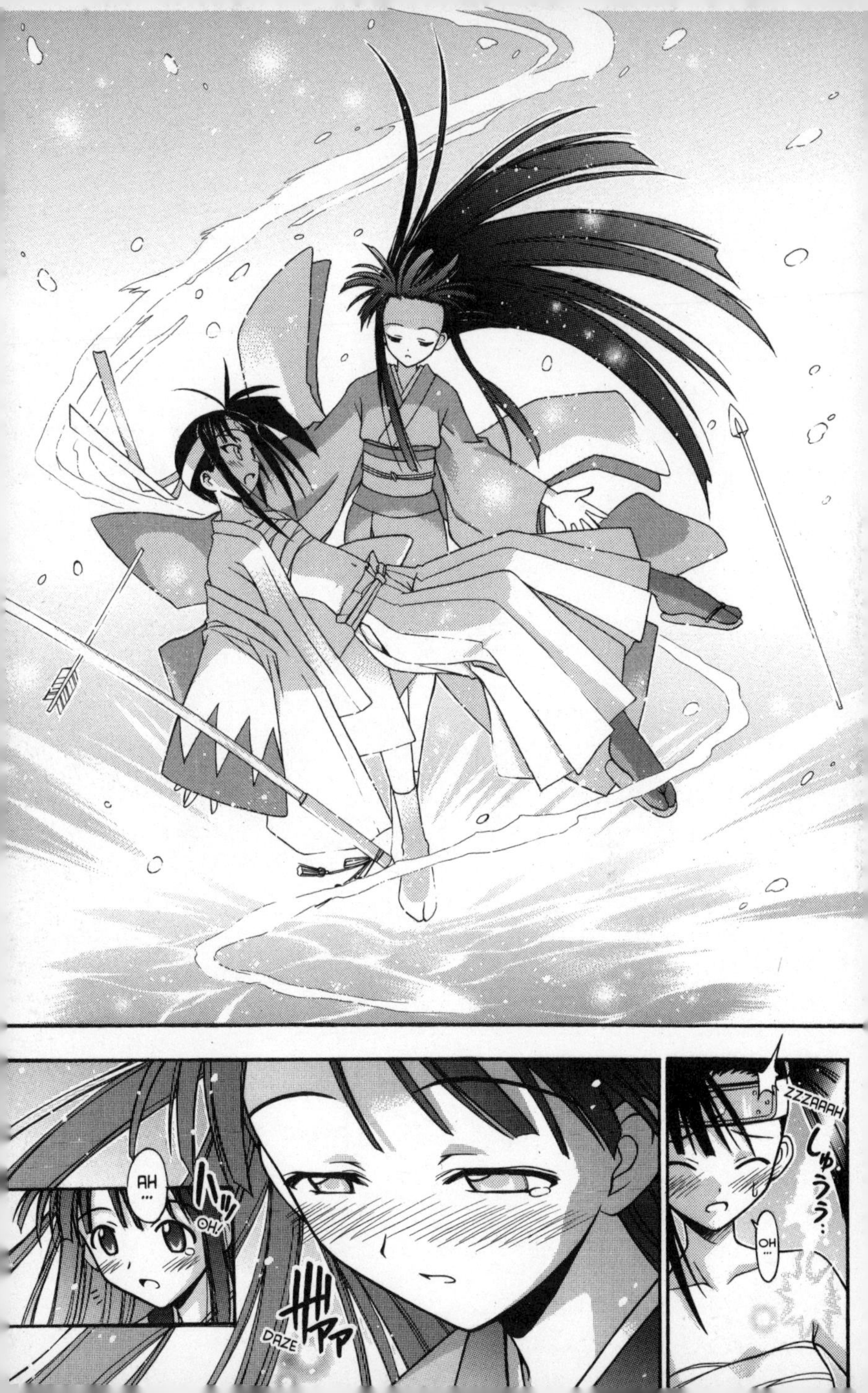
ZZZAAAAH
しゅううう…
OH ...
DAZE
ハッ
OH!
AH ...

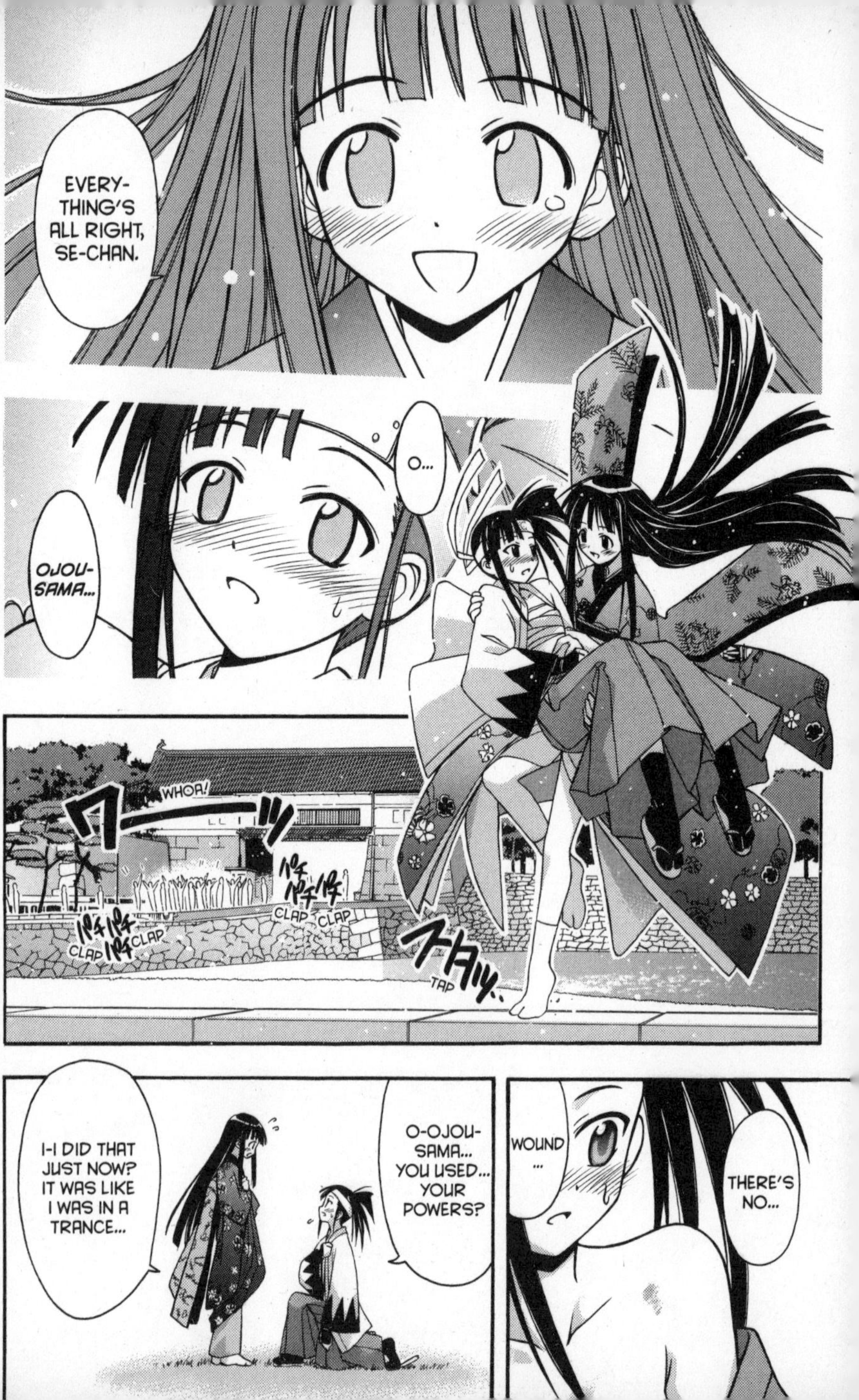
EVERY-THING'S ALL RIGHT, SE-CHAN.
O...
OJOU-SAMA...
TAP
CLAP CLAP
CLAP CLAP
WHOA!
THERE'S NO...
WOUND ...
O-OJOU-SAMA... YOU USED... YOUR POWERS?
I-I DID THAT JUST NOW? IT WAS LIKE I WAS IN A TRANCE...

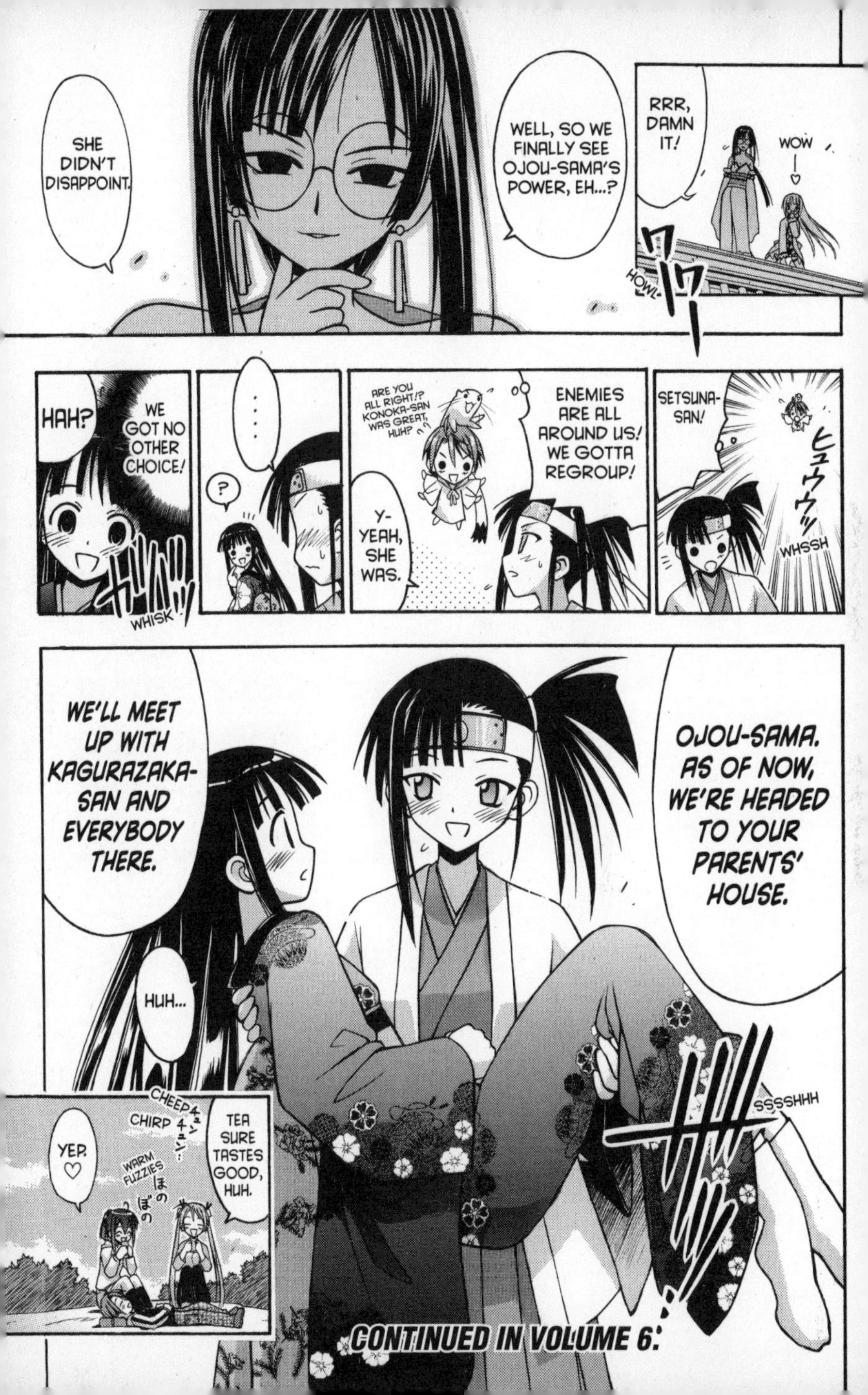
RRR, DAMN IT!
WOW
♡
HOWL
WELL, SO WE FINALLY SEE OJOU-SAMA'S POWER, EH...?
SHE DIDN'T DISAPPOINT.
SETSUNA-SAN!
WHSSH
ENEMIES ARE ALL AROUND US! WE GOTTA REGROUP!
ARE YOU ALL RIGHT!? KONOKA-SAN WAS GREAT, HUH?
Y-YEAH, SHE WAS.
....
?
WE GOT NO OTHER CHOICE!
HAH?
WHISK
OJOU-SAMA. AS OF NOW, WE'RE HEADED TO YOUR PARENTS' HOUSE.
WE'LL MEET UP WITH KAGURAZAKA-SAN AND EVERYBODY THERE.
HUH...
SSSSHHH
TEA SURE TASTES GOOD, HUH.
CHEEP チュン
CHIRP チュン
WARM FUZZIES ほのぼの
YEP. ♡
CONTINUED IN VOLUME 6.

- STAFF -

Ken Akamatsu
Takashi Takemoto
Kenichi Nakamura
Masaki Ohyama
Keiichi Yamashita
Chigusa Amagasaki
Takaaki Miyahara

Thanks To

Ran Ayanaga

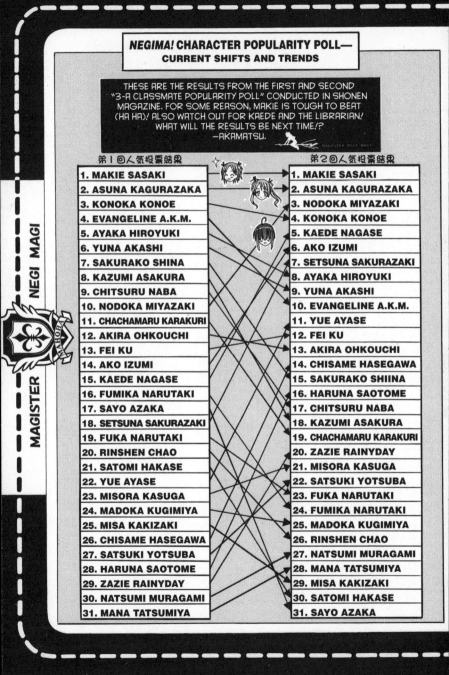

NEGIMA! CHARACTER POPULARITY POLL—
CURRENT SHIFTS AND TRENDS

THESE ARE THE RESULTS FROM THE FIRST AND SECOND
"3-A CLASSMATE POPULARITY POLL" CONDUCTED IN SHONEN
MAGAZINE. FOR SOME REASON, MAKIE IS TOUGH TO BEAT
(HA HA)! ALSO WATCH OUT FOR KAEDE AND THE LIBRARIAN!
WHAT WILL THE RESULTS BE NEXT TIME!?
—AKAMATSU.

第1回人気投票結果

1. MAKIE SASAKI
2. ASUNA KAGURAZAKA
3. KONOKA KONOE
4. EVANGELINE A.K.M.
5. AYAKA HIROYUKI
6. YUNA AKASHI
7. SAKURAKO SHINA
8. KAZUMI ASAKURA
9. CHITSURU NABA
10. NODOKA MIYAZAKI
11. CHACHAMARU KARAKURI
12. AKIRA OHKOUCHI
13. FEI KU
14. AKO IZUMI
15. KAEDE NAGASE
16. FUMIKA NARUTAKI
17. SAYO AZAKA
18. SETSUNA SAKURAZAKI
19. FUKA NARUTAKI
20. RINSHEN CHAO
21. SATOMI HAKASE
22. YUE AYASE
23. MISORA KASUGA
24. MADOKA KUGIMIYA
25. MISA KAKIZAKI
26. CHISAME HASEGAWA
27. SATSUKI YOTSUBA
28. HARUNA SAOTOME
29. ZAZIE RAINYDAY
30. NATSUMI MURAGAMI
31. MANA TATSUMIYA

第2回人気投票結果

1. MAKIE SASAKI
2. ASUNA KAGURAZAKA
3. NODOKA MIYAZAKI
4. KONOKA KONOE
5. KAEDE NAGASE
6. AKO IZUMI
7. SETSUNA SAKURAZAKI
8. AYAKA HIROYUKI
9. YUNA AKASHI
10. EVANGELINE A.K.M.
11. YUE AYASE
12. FEI KU
13. AKIRA OHKOUCHI
14. CHISAME HASEGAWA
15. SAKURAKO SHIINA
16. HARUNA SAOTOME
17. CHITSURU NABA
18. KAZUMI ASAKURA
19. CHACHAMARU KARAKURI
20. ZAZIE RAINYDAY
21. MISORA KASUGA
22. SATSUKI YOTSUBA
23. FUKA NARUTAKI
24. FUMIKA NARUTAKI
25. MADOKA KUGIMIYA
26. RINSHEN CHAO
27. NATSUMI MURAGAMI
28. MANA TATSUMIYA
29. MISA KAKIZAKI
30. SATOMI HAKASE
31. SAYO AZAKA

MAGISTER NEGI MAGI

MAHORA

COMPILATION OF MATERIAL FOR THE BEGINNING OF *NEGIMA!*

THE ORIGINAL CHARACTER SKETCHES

[YUE AYASE]

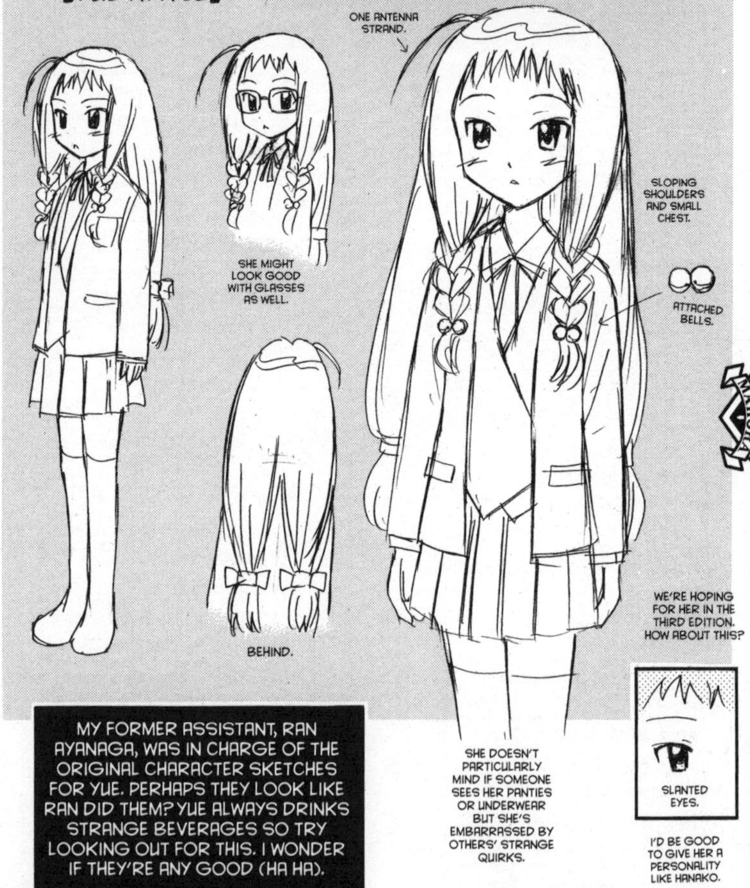
ONE ANTENNA STRAND.
SHE MIGHT LOOK GOOD WITH GLASSES AS WELL.
SLOPING SHOULDERS AND SMALL CHEST.
ATTACHED BELLS.
BEHIND.
WE'RE HOPING FOR HER IN THE THIRD EDITION. HOW ABOUT THIS?
SLANTED EYES.
SHE DOESN'T PARTICULARLY MIND IF SOMEONE SEES HER PANTIES OR UNDERWEAR BUT SHE'S EMBARRASSED BY OTHERS' STRANGE QUIRKS.
I'D BE GOOD TO GIVE HER A PERSONALITY LIKE HANAKO.
NAME: SUZUCHAN.

MY FORMER ASSISTANT, RAN AYANAGA, WAS IN CHARGE OF THE ORIGINAL CHARACTER SKETCHES FOR YUE. PERHAPS THEY LOOK LIKE RAN DID THEM? YUE ALWAYS DRINKS STRANGE BEVERAGES SO TRY LOOKING OUT FOR THIS. I WONDER IF THEY'RE ANY GOOD (HA HA).

MAGISTER NEGI MAGI

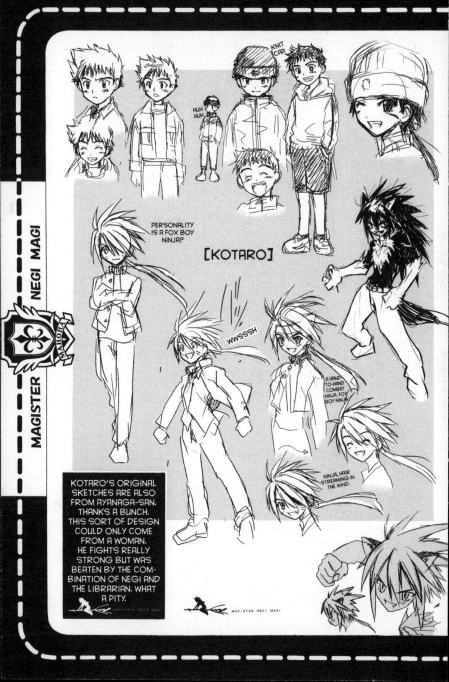

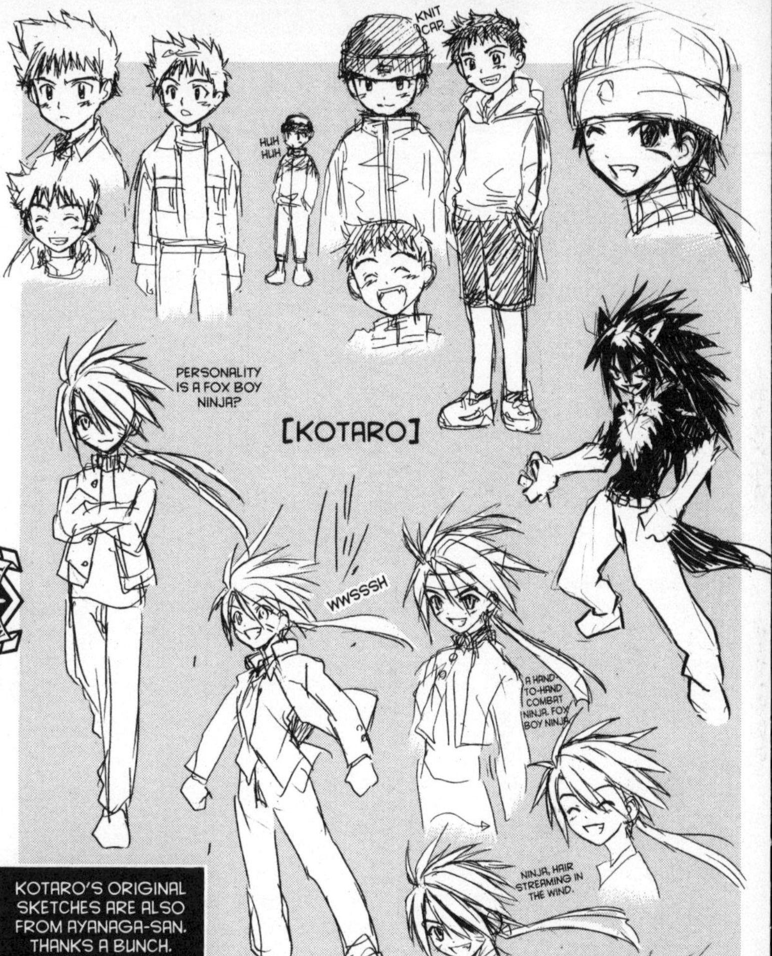
KNIT CAP
HUH HUH
PERSONALITY IS A FOX BOY NINJA?
[KOTARO]
WWSSSH
A HAND TO-HAND COMBAT NINJA, FOX BOY NINJA
NINJA, HAIR STREAMING IN THE WIND.
MAGISTER NEGI MAGI

KOTARO'S ORIGINAL SKETCHES ARE ALSO FROM AYANAGA-SAN. THANKS A BUNCH. THIS SORT OF DESIGN COULD ONLY COME FROM A WOMAN. HE FIGHTS REALLY STRONG BUT WAS BEATEN BY THE COMBINATION OF NEGI AND THE LIBRARIAN. WHAT A PITY.

MAGISTER NEGI MAGI

NEGIMA!

DICTIONARY OF VARIOUS TERMS OF BLACK MAGIC

"The island nation of Japan is a prosperous country with a mystical language so there is great joy."
— From the Manyoushu (an ancient collection of Japanese songs), Volume 13.

38th Period

Adeat/Abeat. A spell used by wizards' partners to summon the specially tailored weapons that have been given to them. *Adeat* means "Come!" and *abeat* means "Go away!" Because Asuna, who doesn't study magic, can use it, it doesn't appear that it's necessary to understand the meaning of the spell.

Diarium Ejus. The specially tailored weapon given to Negi's partner, Nodoka Miyazaki, according to the contract's power. *Diarium* derives from the English word *diary,* and means "everyday assignments," and from that gained the meaning of "a record of every day" or "journal." *Ejus* is the genitive case of the Latin pronoun *id* meaning "that thing" or "that person." This book gives one the ability to read a person's outward feelings, as well as what Freud called the subconscious, or the "id."

The Sanskrit character on Kotaro's cap. This character represents all Buddhas, with Tahagata, the Supreme Buddha of Sino-Japanese Esoteric Buddhism, at the top of the list. Tahagata's literal meaning is "the ultimate truth of nonexistence" or "the unobtainable." Esoteric Buddhism's take on the universe, which Tahagata revered and respected, incorporated many beliefs and magic arts from the people that practiced Shugendo, a kind of Japanese shamanism that encorporates Shinto and Buddhist concepts.

39th Period

Om. A word that's attached at the beginning of a mantra. The literal meaning is "the ultimate truth of nonexistence." Shingon is Sanskrit for "mantra" and can be translated as "spell." Originally they were magic spells used by the Brahman class in India, and those spells were recorded in the Veda (an ancient Indian religious text). In 1816, the

German Franz Bopp discovered that the grammatical structure of Greek and Latin closely resembled that of the European and Sanskrit classics, and he established the modern subject of comparative literature. In the same way, the structure of the spells of eastern magic and that of the western magic of Negi and company are distant relatives of each other.

Kagabikonoyashiro. A shrine with a thousand gates, like the Fushimi Grand Shrine. It's the main temple of the Kansai Magic Association not far from Arashiyama and Sagano, but details are unknown. *Kagabikonoyashiro* is, in the first volume of the Kojiki (a three-volume history of ancient Japan), a fire god also known as Obuto. When he was born, he burned his mother, Nami Iya, killing her. Because she also gave birth to the six gods corresponding to metal, earth, water, and wood in the process of dying, the *Kagabikonoyashiro* became connected to the five flows of the life force, also known as the five elements (wood, fire, earth, metal, and water) as the first important gods.

Ja/A/Ii/Da. The Sanskrit characters cut into the legs of the spider demon. *Ja* means "battle enemy," *Ii* means "disaster," and *Da* means "Hold a grudge." It's most likely a kind of magic for controlling Onmyou Gods.

Deflexio. (Wind Shield) Makes appear a magic shield that parries a physical attack. Wizards unleash a magic barrier in order to protect themselves from physical damage. In contrast to the extremely powerful barrier that's unleashed for an instant—the "Wind Flower! Wall of Wind" used in the 34th Period—this magic is comparatively weak but is constant. Negi's specialty is wind magic, so he broke out the "Wind Shield."

Om ak vi ra un kya sha rak man. This mantra is called the eight-character spell, and can be recited in various ways. It's called the eight-character spell even though it has nine characters because the first *Om* at the beginning of the mantra is a decorative attachment.

Van. A Sanskrit character that represents Tahagata of the Vajradhatu Mandala (the mandala is the Buddhist visual schema of the enlightened mind). But the character of *van* also represents water in the "earth, water, fire, wind, sky, knowledge" of the *Pillars of the Worship of Shugen* which states, "the character of *van* is water, everything and everyone in the universe obeys water." In order to unleash the fog from the drink bought at the vending machine, the character of *van* was recited.

41st Period

Contra Pugnent. ("Intercept and Attack") The call Negi used to summon the spirits. *Contra* means "confront" and *pugnent* means "fight."

Unus fulgor concidens noctem, in mea manu ens inimicum edat. FULGURATIO ALBICANS.(A stream of light to cut through the darkness! Spring forth from my hand and throttle my enemy! White Lightning!) Magic that wounds or kills the enemy with an intense electric shock that springs from the user's palm. It doesn't have the power to completely destroy things, but it's a full-on battle spell with an extremely high offensive effectiveness with regards to people and animals.

Sim ipse pars per secundam dimidiam Negius Springfieldes. (Execute Contract For A Half Second! Negi Springfield!) A spell that turns back on themselves the magic powers received by the wizard according to the contract; in this case, on Negi himself. Normally, with *sis mea pars* ("thou art a part of me") two people's names are recited, but here it becomes a phrase with the strange meaning *sim ipse pars* ("I myself become a part"). Perhaps because it's an experimental technique, it takes a heavy toll on Negi's body.

A Vi Ci. The Sanskrit characters carved into the thousand gates. They mean "endless hell" and they establish the boundaries for the "never-ending place spell."

42nd Period

Van Oon Tarak Kileek Aku. An Onmyoudou spell known widely by the name of *Seman* and used in a variety of ways. Originally, they were the Sanskrit characters for esoteric Buddhism's Five Buddhas of the Vajradhatu and were not related to common Onmyoudou. However, in Volume 4 of the *Five Pages of the Earth God (Chijingoyou)* it says, "the present four Buddhas will increase to five Buddhas, changing to consist of the earth god of the five elements." In this way, the five Buddhas were arranged to correspond to the five elements. The five elements were the five life forces—wood, fire, earth, metal, and water—and the study of the flow of those life forces was the important task of the common Onmyou wizards. From the beginning, before the division of Shintoism and Buddhism in 1868 (the first year of the Meiji Era), Shintoism and Buddhism were jointly practiced everywhere. Before modern times, the Japanese openly incorporated a variety of religions and magic into their lives without concern. This single Onmyoudou spell that comes from the Sanskrit characters of Esoteric Buddhism gives us a glimpse of the history of those Japanese people.

43rd Period

Kya-ya. A word that means the "bodily actions" in the Bodily Actions, Speech, Thought of esoteric Buddhism. In short, it means the body and is a spell used, using the talisman arts, in order to give Negi the temporary, doll-like figure that he used.

References:
Iwanami Dictionary of Buddhism; "Examination of Shinto in the Middle Ages," *Compendium of Japanese Thought 19*, Iwanami Publishing; "Compendium of Shinto Articles," Volume 17, Shugendou (Shinto Compendium Editorial Foundation Society)

PARTNER CARDS EXPLAINED

Charta Ministralis

—PARTNER CARD—

VIII
Charta Ministralis
Rubor
tonus
CAGURAZACA
ASUNA
BELLATRIX SAUCIATA
virtus
audacia
directio
oriens
astralitas
Mars

Mysterious Roman numbers. There are various mysterious interpretations of numbers, especially numbers 1-13 where there are particular peculiarities in the prime numbers. For example, in contrast to the number 1, which means a unified complete whole, the number 2 means the fluctuation in activity brought on by the power of Onmyou. Lucky number 7 is a powerful number, being that it's the largest prime number in the decimal system. 13, which is not found in the duodecimal system, represents death in this world and rebirth in the next. It's very interesting that when you analyze the prime factor of the numbers written on Asuna and Nodoka's cards, you can see that they have the same logarithmic number of 3.

The contract's magic base. A simple thing made up of the 12 zodiac signs and a six pointed star. Pactio is a simple magic that even the ermine fairies can use, so the magic base is small.

Partner's title. The partner's ability and personality are frankly stated.

virtus—VIRTUES

The virtue section of the partner's card mentions the seven virtues,

Knowledge *(sapientia)*
Bravery *(audacia)*
Temperance *(temterantia)*
Justice *(justitia)*
Faith *(fides)*
Hope *(spes)*
Love *(caritas)*

These are known as the seven European original virtues. The first four are found in Plato's Nation-State (427E, especially 441E-444A) and the next three are often written into marriage vows and found in Paulos' Corinthians I (13:13). Virtue is defined here as the virtue talked of in modern times. It means the advantages and usefulness of people and things and in the study of western classics, and it's often translated as "excellence." However, the principal meaning is the broad idea of "bravery" or "courageousness." The theme of "bravery is the real magic" is expounded here.

astralitas—ASTROLOGY

The various partners have astrological attributes, in short, an astrological sign that corresponds to their birth.

Moon *(Luna)*
Sun *(Sol)*
Mars *(Mars)*
Venus *(Venus)*
Mercury *(Mercurius)*
Jupiter *(Jupiter)*
Saturn *(Saturnus)*
Uranus *(Uranus)*
Neptune *(Neptunus)*
Pluto *(Pluto)*
Comet *(cometes)*
Falling Star *(fax)*
Fixed Star *(caelus sideralis)*
Black Hole *(nigrum foramen)*

The astrology relating to the seven astral bodies of the Moon, Sun, Mars, Venus, Mercury, Jupiter, and Saturn was established by the Sumerians and were inherited by the Sem peoples of Assyria and Babylonia. Later, through Alexander the Great's expeditions to the east, middle-eastern astronomy flowed through Greece and into Europe.

tonus—COLORS

In most modern natural sciences, color is nothing more than a uniform electromagnetic wave within a wavelength but, in premodern cultures, color had important symbolism.

For example, in the Revelation of John (2:18), the son of God had eyes that were red like fire and, as you can see with the mother goddess, Cybele, of Asia Minor, black symbolizes the darkness that contrasts with light, death contrasting with life, and also symbolizes rebirth from that death.

The colors that are at the top of the partner card are known to be:

Red *(rubor)*
Blue *(caerula)*
Green *(virude)*
Yellow *(flavum)*
Purple *(cyaneum)*
Violet *(viola)*
Orange *(luteum)*
Rose *(roseum)*
White *(album)*
Black *(nigror)*
Gold *(aurum)*
Silver *(argentums)*
Crimson *(prisma)*

The respective colors reflect the symbolism of the partner's birth, development, and destiny. The gold, silver, and crimson cards are extremely rare and as their equally rare magic weapons are high in value, they are often traded on the black market.

directio—DIRECTION

In astrology, back in the era of Ptolemy, it was known that the earth was a sphere. Therefore, the five directions on the top of the partner card—

East *(oriens)*
West *(occidens)*
South *(auster)*
North *(septentrio)*
Center *(centrum)*

—don't merely mean directions on a plane. For example, there was the widely held belief that paradise lies in a westerly direction, and in the north was the North Star, which symbolized the center of space. The east is the direction the sun rises and had the temporal meaning of the coming of a new day.

12 YELLOW tonus

AI-YAH.

FEI KU
STOIC KUNGFU CHINA.

SPECIAL SKILL:
PONKEN KASHI-FU KICK!
astralita LIKES: IT'S TOO BAD THERE'S
NO ONE STRONGER THAN ME!

☆ HO-CHA.

12

THE PROBATIONARY
CONTRACT SYSTEM IS
DIFFERENT FROM THAT OF
THE REAL CONTRACT AND
BECAUSE ITS CHECK SYSTEM
IS EXTREMELY LENIENT, CARDS
STILL APPEAR EVEN WITH
A KISS ON THE CHEEK OR
KISSING AN ALTER EGO. BUT
WHAT APPEARS IS A BOTCHED
CARD. AS YOU CAN SEE, THESE
ARE SOME CARDS THAT WERE
MISTAKES (HA HA). DURING
THE MAKING OF THIS, NINE
CARDS WERE CREATED. YOU
CAN'T REALLY SEE THEM TOO
WELL SO WE PRINTED THEM
HERE. THEY'RE PRETTY CUTE...
SORT OF!

MAGISTER NEGI MAGI

13 WHITE tonus

HAH

KONOE KONOKA
EASYGOING WIZARD.

SPECIAL SKILL:
HAMMERTHRUST.
astralitas LIKES: CAKE, THE SWEET KIND

☆ CONK.

13

8 RED tonus

GRRR

ASUNA KAGURAZAKA
JUNIOR HIGH SCHOOL GIRL WITH THE FLYING KICK!

SPECIAL SKILL:
ASUNA PUNCH. ASUNA KICK.
astralitas LIKES: MOVIES THAT HAVE
DANDY OLD MEN

☆ KEEYAH.

8

NEGI MA!

MAHORA

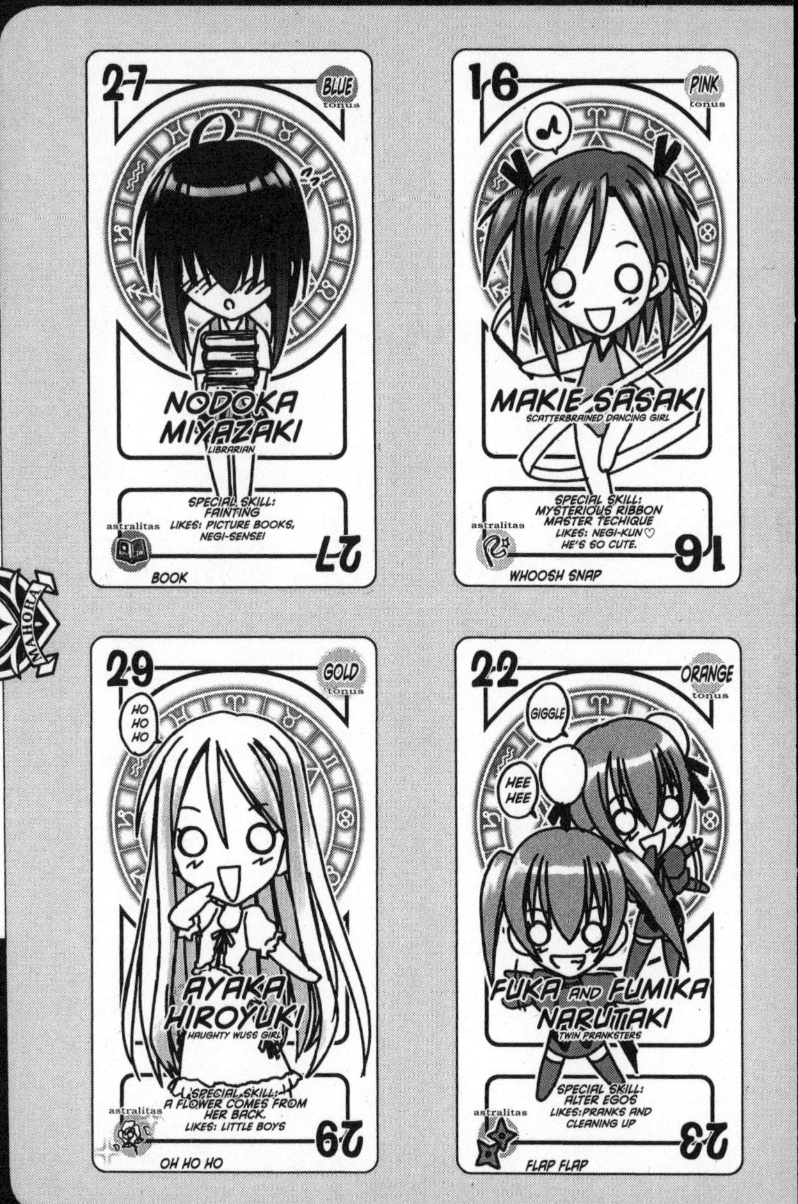

16
PINK
tonus
MAKIE SASAKI
SCATTERBRAINED DANCING GIRL
astralitas
SPECIAL SKILL: MYSTERIOUS RIBBON MASTER TECHIQUE
LIKES: NEGI-KUN♡ HE'S SO CUTE.
16
WHOOSH SNAP
27
BLUE
tonus
NODOKA MIYAZAKI
LIBRARIAN
astralitas
SPECIAL SKILL: FAINTING
LIKES: PICTURE BOOKS, NEGI-SENSEI
27
BOOK
22
ORANGE
tonus
GIGGLE
HEE HEE
FUKA AND FUMIKA NARUTAKI
TWIN PRANKSTERS
astralitas
SPECIAL SKILL: ALTER EGOS
LIKES: PRANKS AND CLEANING UP
23
FLAP FLAP
29
GOLD
tonus
HO HO HO
AYAKA HIROYUKI
HAUGHTY WUSS GIRL
astralitas
SPECIAL SKILL: A FLOWER COMES FROM HER BACK.
LIKES: LITTLE BOYS
29
OH HO HO

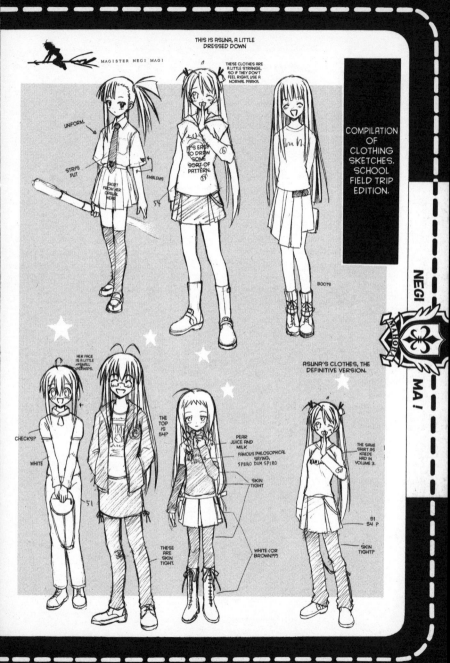

THIS IS ASUNA, A LITTLE
DRESSED DOWN

MAGISTER NEGI MAGI

THESE CLOTHES ARE
A LITTLE STRANGE,
SO IF THEY DON'T
FEEL RIGHT, USE A
NORMAL PARKA.

UNIFORM.

STRAY'S
PLIT

EMBLEMS

IT'S EASY
TO DRAW
SOME
SORT OF
PATTERN.

SKIRT
FROM HER
CASUAL
HERE

54

COMPILATION
OF
CLOTHING
SKETCHES.
SCHOOL
FIELD TRIP
EDITION.

BOOTS

HER FACE
IS A LITTLE
SMALL,
PERHAPS.

ASUNA'S CLOTHES, THE
DEFINITIVE VERSION.

CHECKS?

WHITE

THE
TOP
IS
5HP

51

THESE
ARE
SKIN
TIGHT.

PEAR
JUICE AND
MILK

FAMOUS PHILOSOPHICAL
SAYING,
SPERO DUM SPIRO

SKIN
TIGHT

WHITE (OR
BROWN??)

THE SAME
SHIRT AS
KAEDE
HAD IN
VOLUME 3.

51
54 P

SKIN
TIGHT?

NEGI
MA!

NEGIMA! LETTER CORNER ☆

THESE ARE SOME RECENT LETTERS. WE FOCUSED OUR ATTENTION ON THE PORTRAIT ILLUSTRATIONS AND COMPILED THEM FOR YOU! —MAX ASHI.

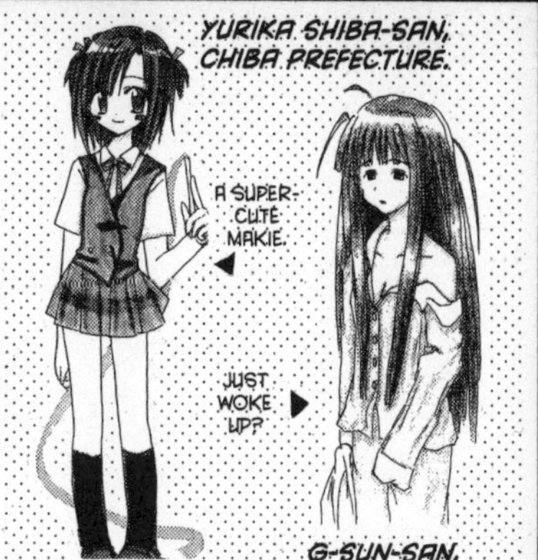
A SUPER-CUTE MAKIE.
JUST WOKE UP?

YURIKA SHIBA-SAN, CHIBA PREFECTURE.

G-SUN-SAN, TOKYO CITY.

A MAKIE WHO'S EYELASHES ARE SPOT ON (DIFFICULT TO DRAW?)

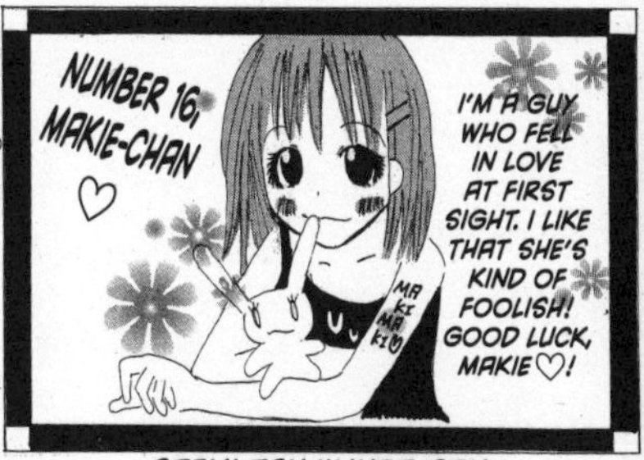
NUMBER 16, MAKIE-CHAN ♡
I'M A GUY WHO FELL IN LOVE AT FIRST SIGHT. I LIKE THAT SHE'S KIND OF FOOLISH! GOOD LUCK, MAKIE♡!
MA KI MA KI♡

SAEMI TSUJIMURA-SAN, KANAGAWA PREFECTURE.

AN UNOBTRUSIVE CHACHAMARU.

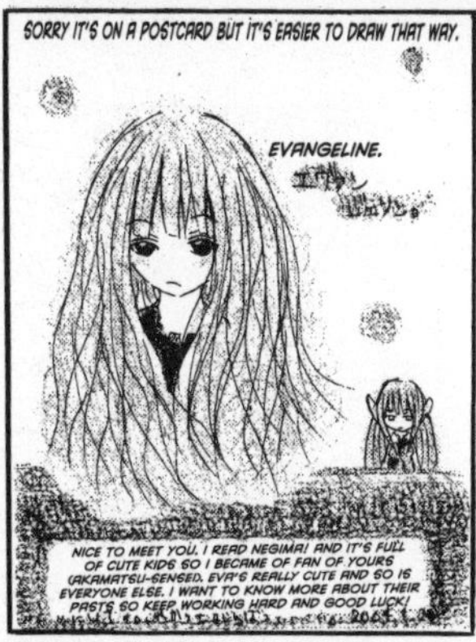
SORRY IT'S ON A POSTCARD BUT IT'S EASIER TO DRAW THAT WAY.
EVANGELINE.
NICE TO MEET YOU. I READ NEGIMA! AND IT'S FULL OF CUTE KIDS SO I BECAME OF FAN OF YOURS (AKAMATSU-SENSEI). EVA'S REALLY CUTE AND SO IS EVERYONE ELSE. I WANT TO KNOW MORE ABOUT THEIR PASTS SO KEEP WORKING HARD AND GOOD LUCK!

AYAKA INAMI-SAN, TOKYO CITY.

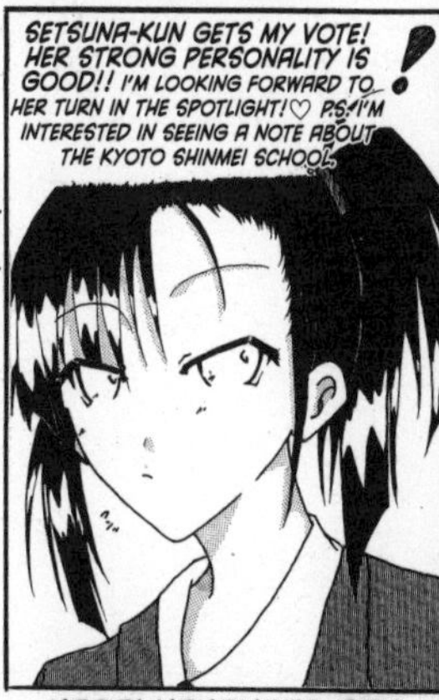
SETSUNA-KUN GETS MY VOTE! HER STRONG PERSONALITY IS GOOD!! I'M LOOKING FORWARD TO HER TURN IN THE SPOTLIGHT!♡ P.S. I'M INTERESTED IN SEEING A NOTE ABOUT THE KYOTO SHINMEI SCHOOL.

KAORI NAKAMOTO-SAN, WAKAYAMA PREFECTURE.

AN ENERGETIC NEGI.

A COOL SETSUNA. ☆

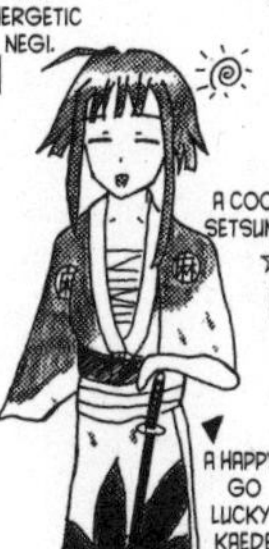

A HAPPY-GO LUCKY-KAEDE (HA HA).

NORI-SAN, OKAYAMA PREFECTURE.

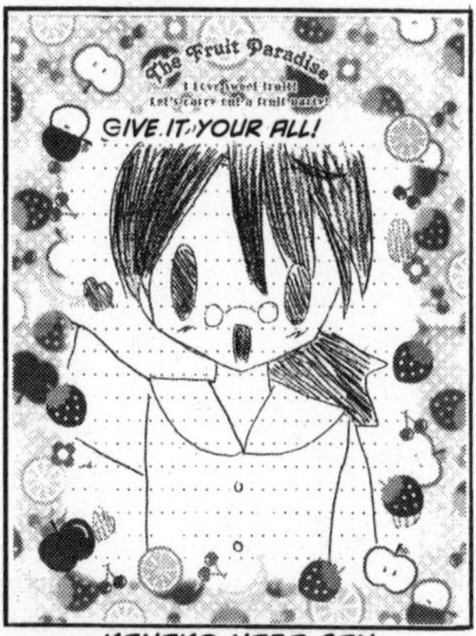
The Fruit Paradise
GIVE IT YOUR ALL!

KANAKO HABA-SAN, SAITAMA PREFECTURE.

Translation Notes

Japanese is a tricky language for most westerners, and translation is often more art than science. For your edification and reading pleasure, here are notes on some of the places where we could have gone in a different direction in our translation of the work, or where a Japanese cultural reference is used.

Seiza, page 10

In Japanese, the word *seiza* is made up of the characters for *correct* and *sit* and refers to the position used in the tea ceremony and in Zen meditation. It involves folding the lower legs under your thighs, and if you're not used to it, it can be very uncomfortable if maintained for prolonged periods.

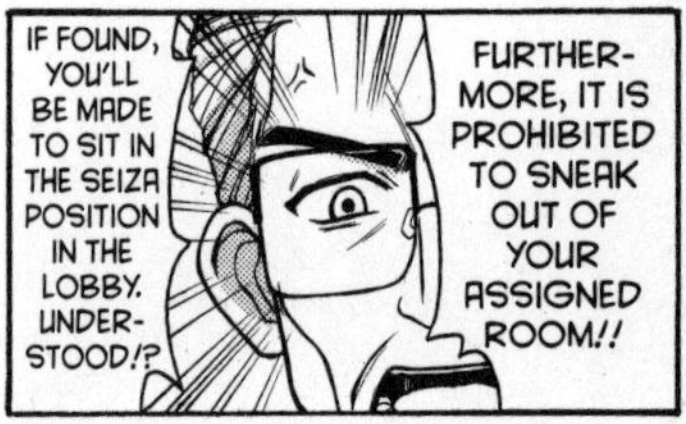
FURTHERMORE, IT IS PROHIBITED TO SNEAK OUT OF YOUR ASSIGNED ROOM!!
IF FOUND, YOU'LL BE MADE TO SIT IN THE SEIZA POSITION IN THE LOBBY. UNDERSTOOD!?

Katakana, page 20

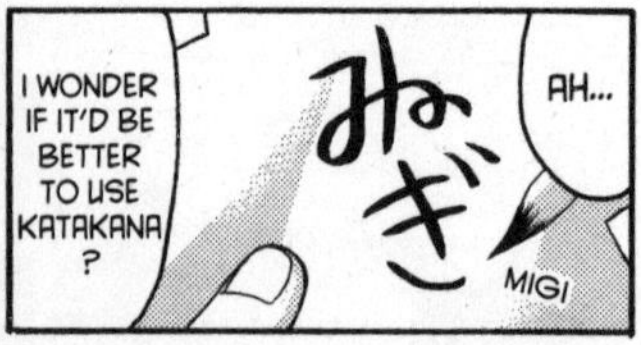
AH...
みぎ
MIGI
I WONDER IF IT'D BE BETTER TO USE KATAKANA?

Katakana is one of three Japanese systems (alphabets, really) for spelling words (the other two are hiragana and kanji). Katakana is usually used for writing western names or words of non-Japanese origin.

Kouga, page 33

Kouga is a county in Shiga Prefecture, and presumably Fuka and Fumika's home.

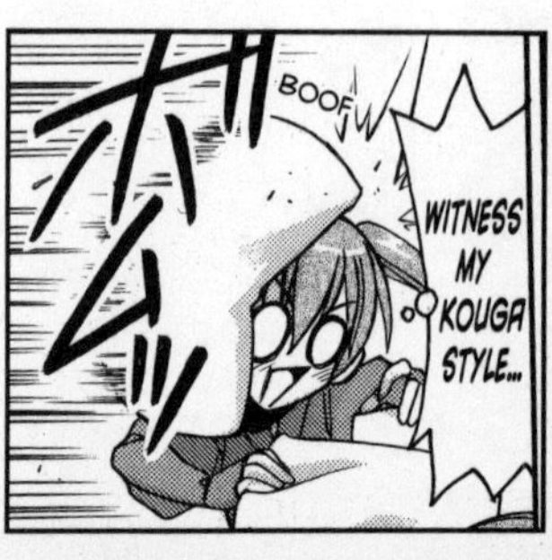
BOOF
WITNESS MY KOUGA STYLE...

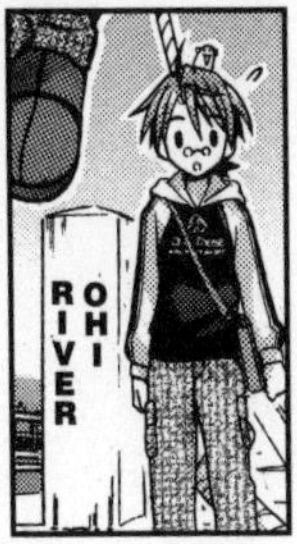
OHI RIVER

Ohi River, page 72

The Ohi River runs through Kyoto. With its source at the southern Japan Alps, it is most famous for the Ohi River Railroad, which used old steam locomotives and is still running today.

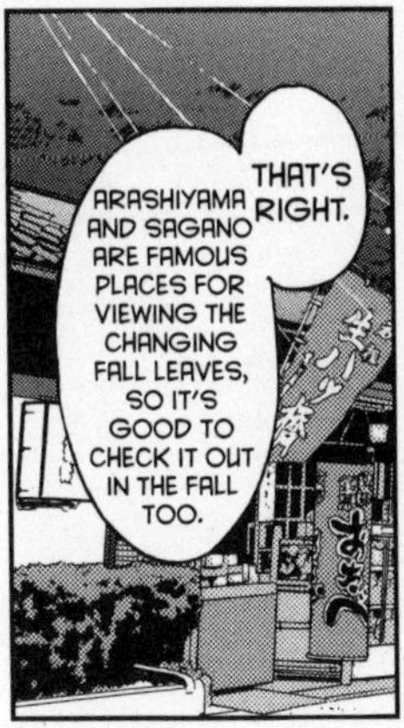
THAT'S RIGHT.
ARASHIYAMA AND SAGANO ARE FAMOUS PLACES FOR VIEWING THE CHANGING FALL LEAVES, SO IT'S GOOD TO CHECK IT OUT IN THE FALL TOO.

Arashiyama and Sagano, page 74

This is the area in the vicinity of Saga in Ukyo Ward in Kyoto.

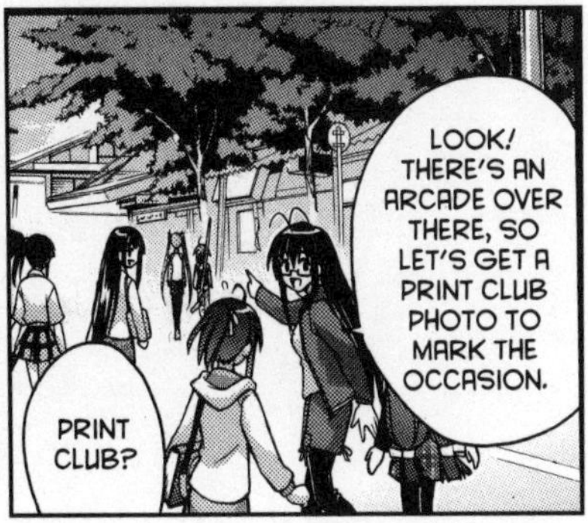
LOOK! THERE'S AN ARCADE OVER THERE, SO LET'S GET A PRINT CLUB PHOTO TO MARK THE OCCASION.
PRINT CLUB?

Print Club, page 75

Print Club (or *purikurabu*) refers to machines in arcades that take your picture and turn them into little stickers that you can customize. They are very popular in Japan.

Om, page 83

The sound used by followers of Buddhism in certain types of meditation.

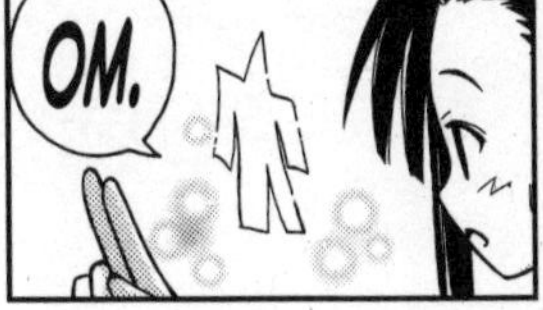
OM.

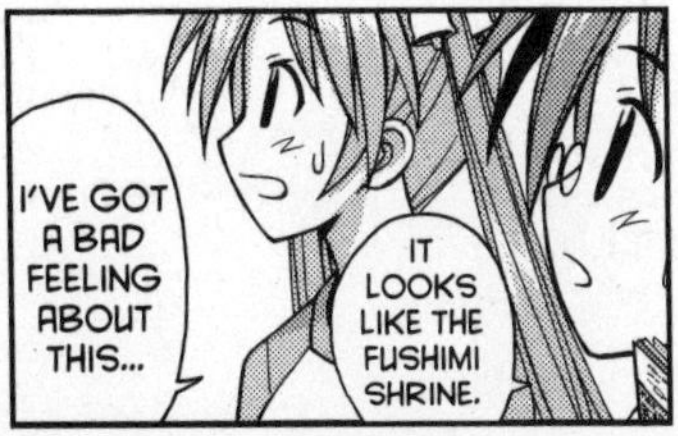
IT LOOKS LIKE THE FUSHIMI SHRINE.
I'VE GOT A BAD FEELING ABOUT THIS...

Fushimi, page 86

Fushimi is a ward in southern Kyoto known for its pure water and, by extension, its delicious sake. Several famous breweries large and small are located here, including Gekkeikan.

O-Shiruko, page 94

A beverage made from sweet azuki beans (also called *anko*), water, and sugar.

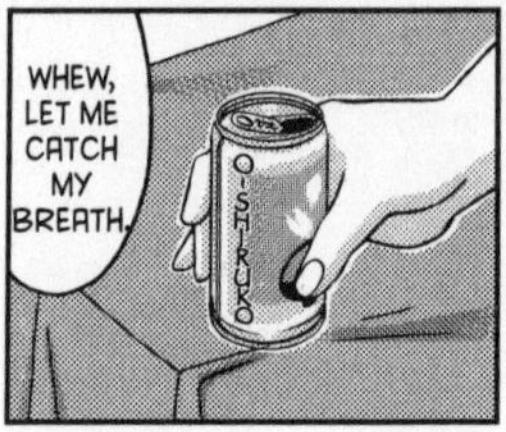
WHEW, LET ME CATCH MY BREATH.
O-SHIRUKO

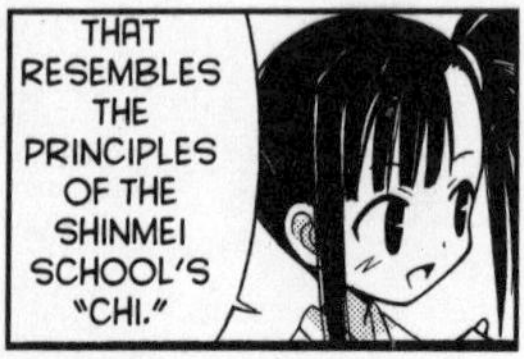
THAT RESEMBLES THE PRINCIPLES OF THE SHINMEI SCHOOL'S "CHI."

Chi, page 96

Chi is the power that martial artists and others believe you can harness from inside yourself through training and meditation.

Inugami, page 121

The name *Inugami* is written in Japanese using the characters for "dog" and "upper" or "above."

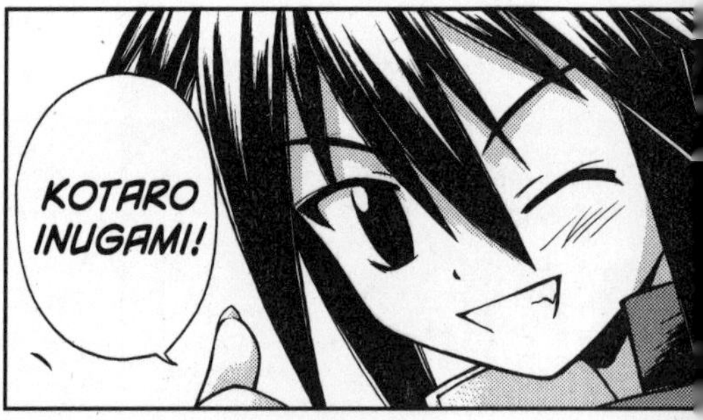
KOTARO INUGAMI!

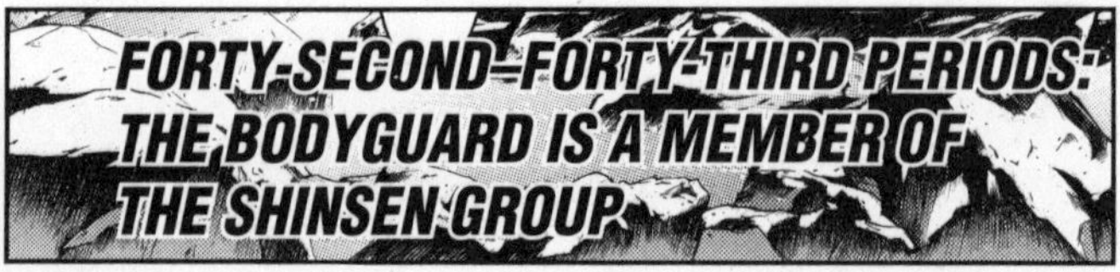
FORTY-SECOND–FORTY-THIRD PERIODS:
THE BODYGUARD IS A MEMBER OF THE SHINSEN GROUP

Shinsen, page 145

The Shinsen Group (*Shinsengumi*) was a group of twenty to fifty ronin (masterless samurai) formed at the end of the Edo Era to protect and control Kyoto. They revered the Emperor and sought the overthrow of the Shogunate.

Cinema Village, page 149

There is an amusement park in Kyoto called Eiga Mura (literally, Movie Village), which is a reproduction of Edo-era Japan, featuring reproductions of samurai movie sets, and also actors who recreate the era for tourists.

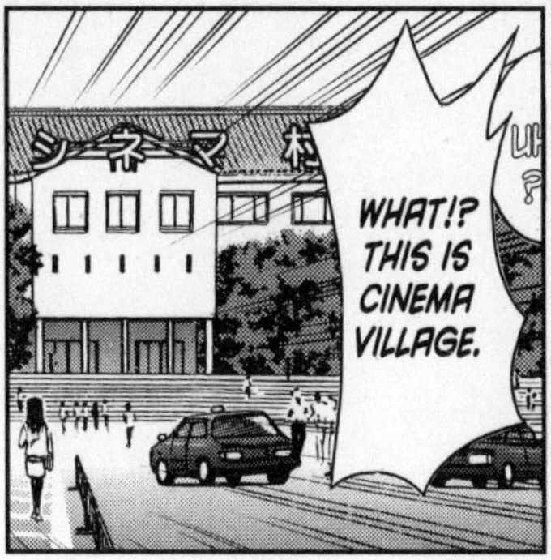
WHAT!? THIS IS CINEMA VILLAGE.

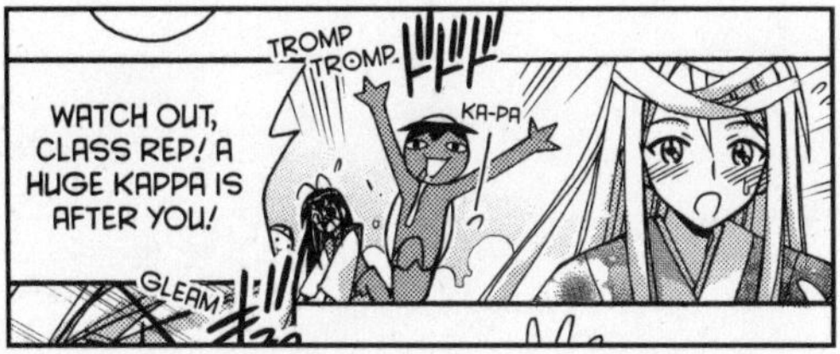
TROMP TROMP
KA-PA
WATCH OUT, CLASS REP! A HUGE KAPPA IS AFTER YOU!
GLEAM

Kappa, page 166

A *kappa* is a creature from Japanese mythology. It is an amphibian, sort of a cross between a turtle and a human, that drags people under water and sucks their blood.

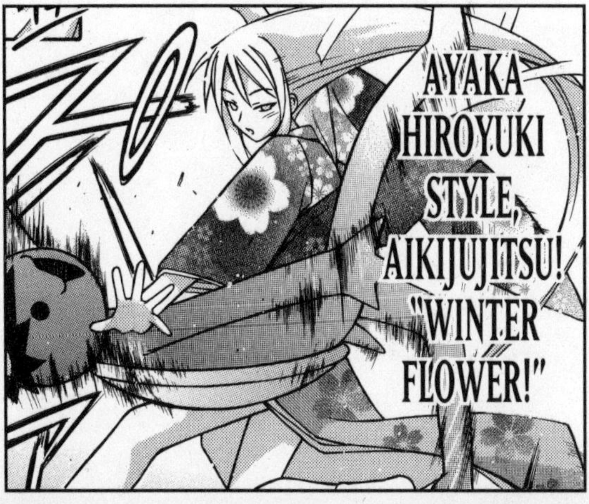
AYAKA HIROYUKI STYLE, AIKIJUJITSU! "WINTER FLOWER!"

AikiJujitsu, page 166

AikiJujitsu is a traditional Japanese martial art. Modern martial arts such as aikido, judo and hapkido can trace their roots to *Aikijujitsu*.

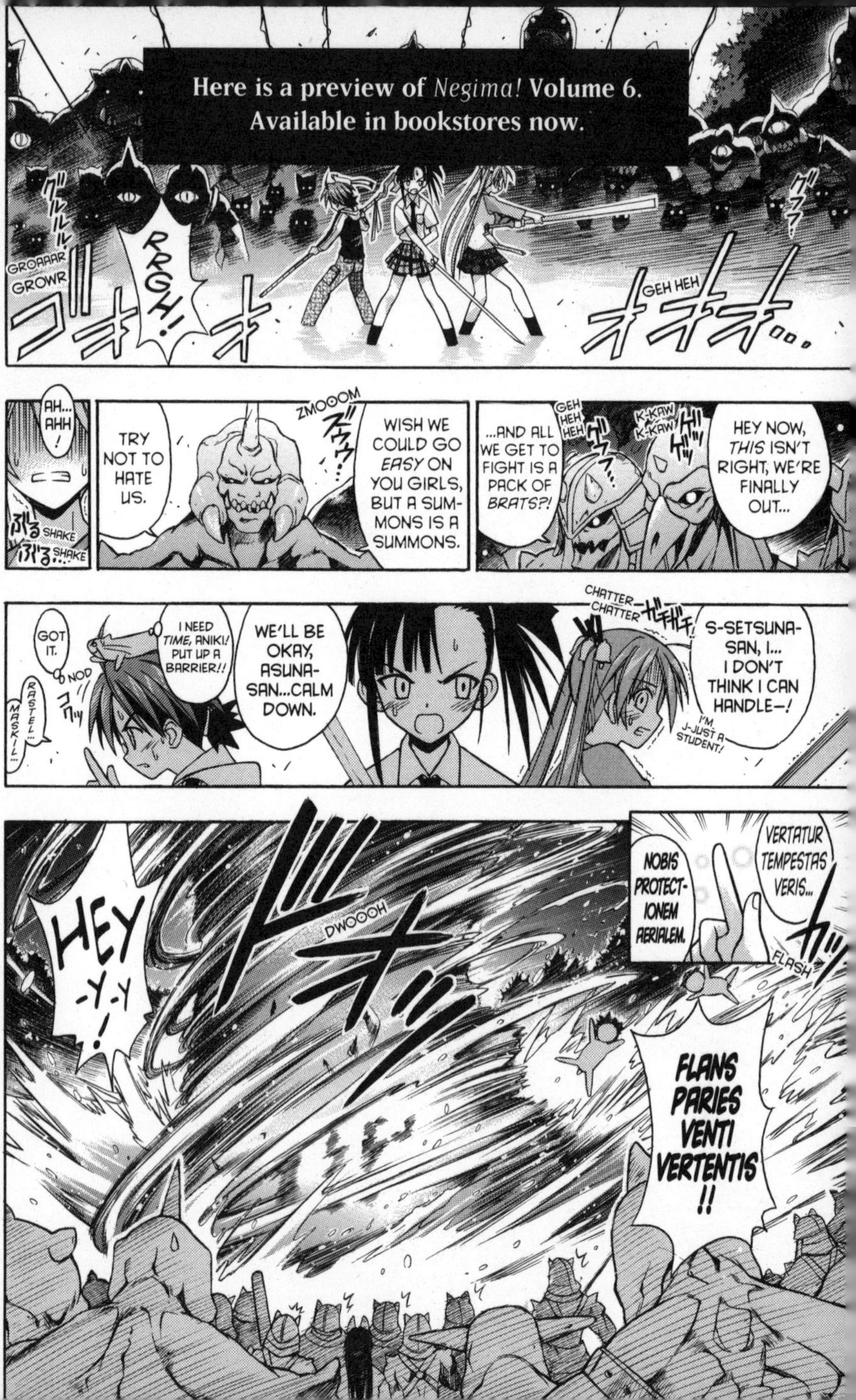
Here is a preview of *Negima!* Volume 6.
Available in bookstores now.
GEH HEH
RRGH!!
GROAAAR
GROWR
HEY NOW, *THIS* ISN'T RIGHT, WE'RE FINALLY OUT...
K-KAW K-KAW
GEH HEH HEH
...AND ALL WE GET TO FIGHT IS A PACK OF *BRATS?!*
ZMOOOM
WISH WE COULD GO *EASY* ON YOU GIRLS, BUT A SUMMONS IS A SUMMONS.
TRY NOT TO HATE US.
AH... AHH!
SHAKE
SHAKE...
CHATTER CHATTER
S-SETSUNA-SAN, I... I DON'T THINK I CAN HANDLE–!
I'M J-JUST A STUDENT!
WE'LL BE OKAY, ASUNA-SAN...CALM DOWN.
I NEED *TIME,* ANIKI! PUT UP A BARRIER!!
GOT IT.
NOD
RASTEL... MASKIL...
VERTATUR TEMPESTAS VERIS...
NOBIS PROTECT-IONEM AERIALEM.
FLASH
FLANS PARIES VENTI VERTENTIS!!
DWOOOH
HEY-Y-Y!

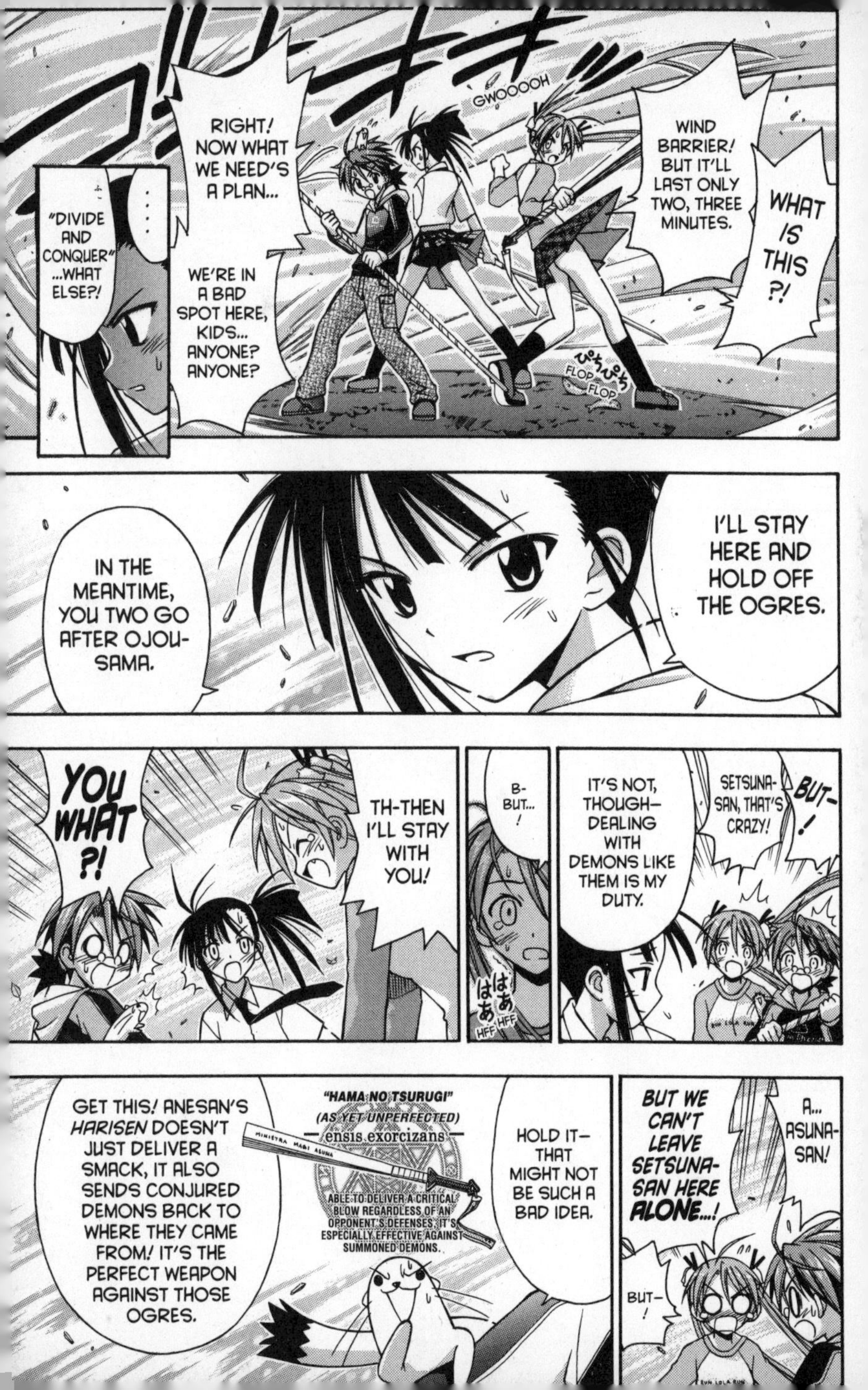

WHAT IS THIS?!
WIND BARRIER! BUT IT'LL LAST ONLY TWO, THREE MINUTES.
GWOOOOH
RIGHT! NOW WHAT WE NEED'S A PLAN...
WE'RE IN A BAD SPOT HERE, KIDS... ANYONE? ANYONE?
ぴちぴち FLOP FLOP
....
"DIVIDE AND CONQUER" ...WHAT ELSE?!
I'LL STAY HERE AND HOLD OFF THE OGRES.
IN THE MEANTIME, YOU TWO GO AFTER OJOU-SAMA.
BUT-!
SETSUNA-SAN, THAT'S CRAZY!
IT'S NOT, THOUGH— DEALING WITH DEMONS LIKE THEM IS MY DUTY.
B-BUT...!
はあはあ HFF HFF
TH-THEN I'LL STAY WITH YOU!
YOU WHAT?!
A... ASUNA-SAN!
BUT WE CAN'T LEAVE SETSUNA-SAN HERE ALONE...!
BUT—!
HOLD IT— THAT MIGHT NOT BE SUCH A BAD IDEA.
"HAMA NO TSURUGI"
(AS YET UNPERFECTED)
ensis exorcizans
MINISTRA MAGI ASUNA
ABLE TO DELIVER A CRITICAL BLOW REGARDLESS OF AN OPPONENT'S DEFENSES, IT'S ESPECIALLY EFFECTIVE AGAINST SUMMONED DEMONS.
GET THIS! ANESAN'S HARISEN DOESN'T JUST DELIVER A SMACK, IT ALSO SENDS CONJURED DEMONS BACK TO WHERE THEY CAME FROM! IT'S THE PERFECT WEAPON AGAINST THOSE OGRES.

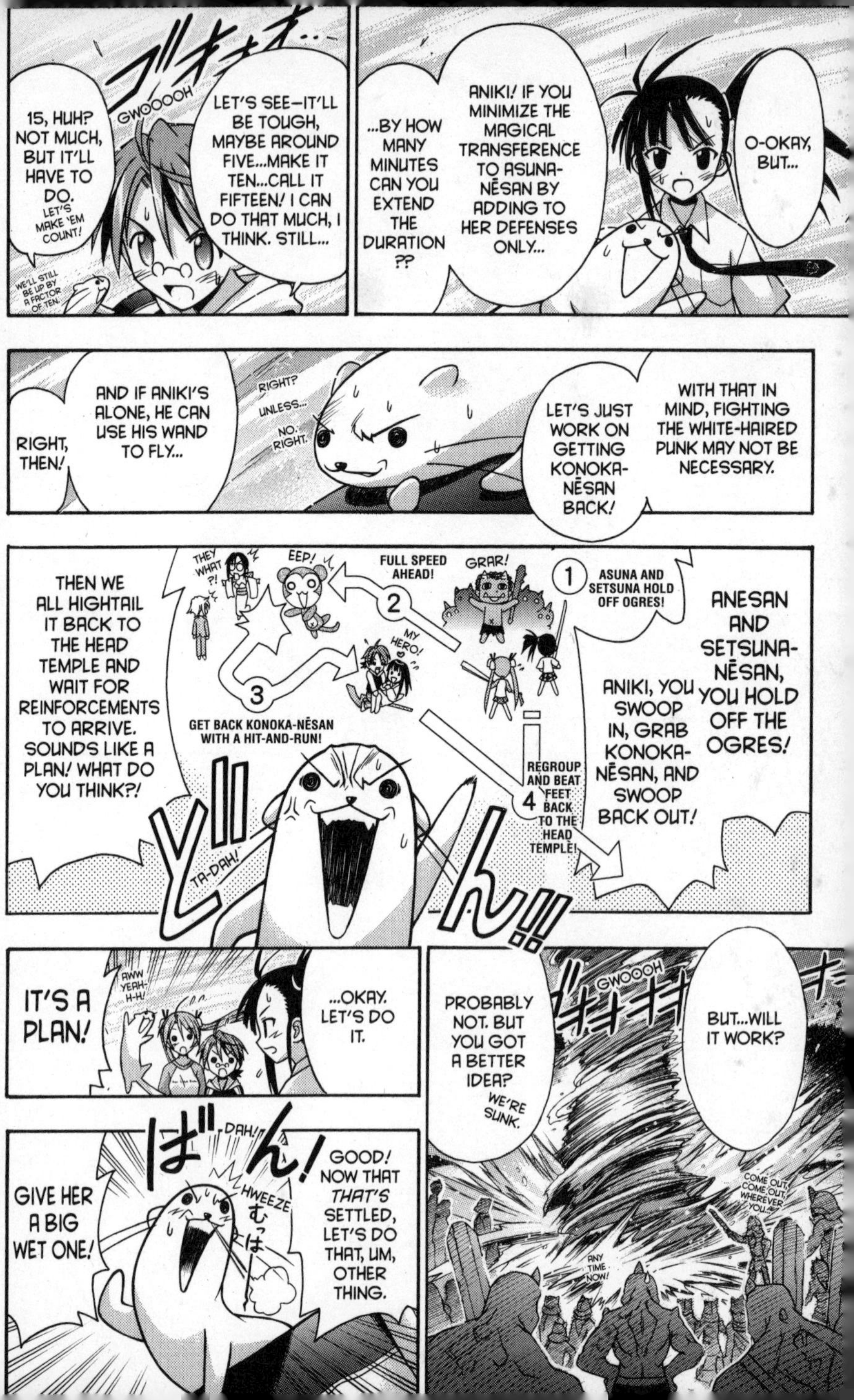
O-OKAY, BUT...
ANIKI! IF YOU MINIMIZE THE MAGICAL TRANSFERENCE TO ASUNA-NĒSAN BY ADDING TO HER DEFENSES ONLY...
...BY HOW MANY MINUTES CAN YOU EXTEND THE DURATION ??
GWOOOOH
LET'S SEE—IT'LL BE TOUGH, MAYBE AROUND FIVE...MAKE IT TEN...CALL IT FIFTEEN! I CAN DO THAT MUCH, I THINK. STILL...
15, HUH? NOT MUCH, BUT IT'LL HAVE TO DO.
LET'S MAKE 'EM COUNT!
WE'LL STILL BE UP BY A FACTOR OF TEN.
WITH THAT IN MIND, FIGHTING THE WHITE-HAIRED PUNK MAY NOT BE NECESSARY.
LET'S JUST WORK ON GETTING KONOKA-NĒSAN BACK!
RIGHT?
UNLESS...
NO. RIGHT.
AND IF ANIKI'S ALONE, HE CAN USE HIS WAND TO FLY...
RIGHT, THEN!
ANESAN AND SETSUNA-NĒSAN, YOU HOLD OFF THE OGRES!
ANIKI, YOU SWOOP IN, GRAB KONOKA-NĒSAN, AND SWOOP BACK OUT!
1 ASUNA AND SETSUNA HOLD OFF OGRES!
GRAR!
2 FULL SPEED AHEAD!
EEP!
THEY WHAT ?!
3 GET BACK KONOKA-NĒSAN WITH A HIT-AND-RUN!
MY HERO!
4 REGROUP AND BEAT FEET BACK TO THE HEAD TEMPLE!
THEN WE ALL HIGHTAIL IT BACK TO THE HEAD TEMPLE AND WAIT FOR REINFORCEMENTS TO ARRIVE. SOUNDS LIKE A PLAN! WHAT DO YOU THINK?!
TA-DAH!
BUT...WILL IT WORK?
GWOOOH
PROBABLY NOT. BUT YOU GOT A BETTER IDEA?
WE'RE SUNK.
COME OUT, COME OUT, WHEREVER YOU...
ANY TIME NOW!
...OKAY. LET'S DO IT.
AWW YEAH-H-H!
IT'S A PLAN!
GOOD! NOW THAT THAT'S SETTLED, LET'S DO THAT, UM, OTHER THING.
DAH!
HWEEZE
GIVE HER A BIG WET ONE!

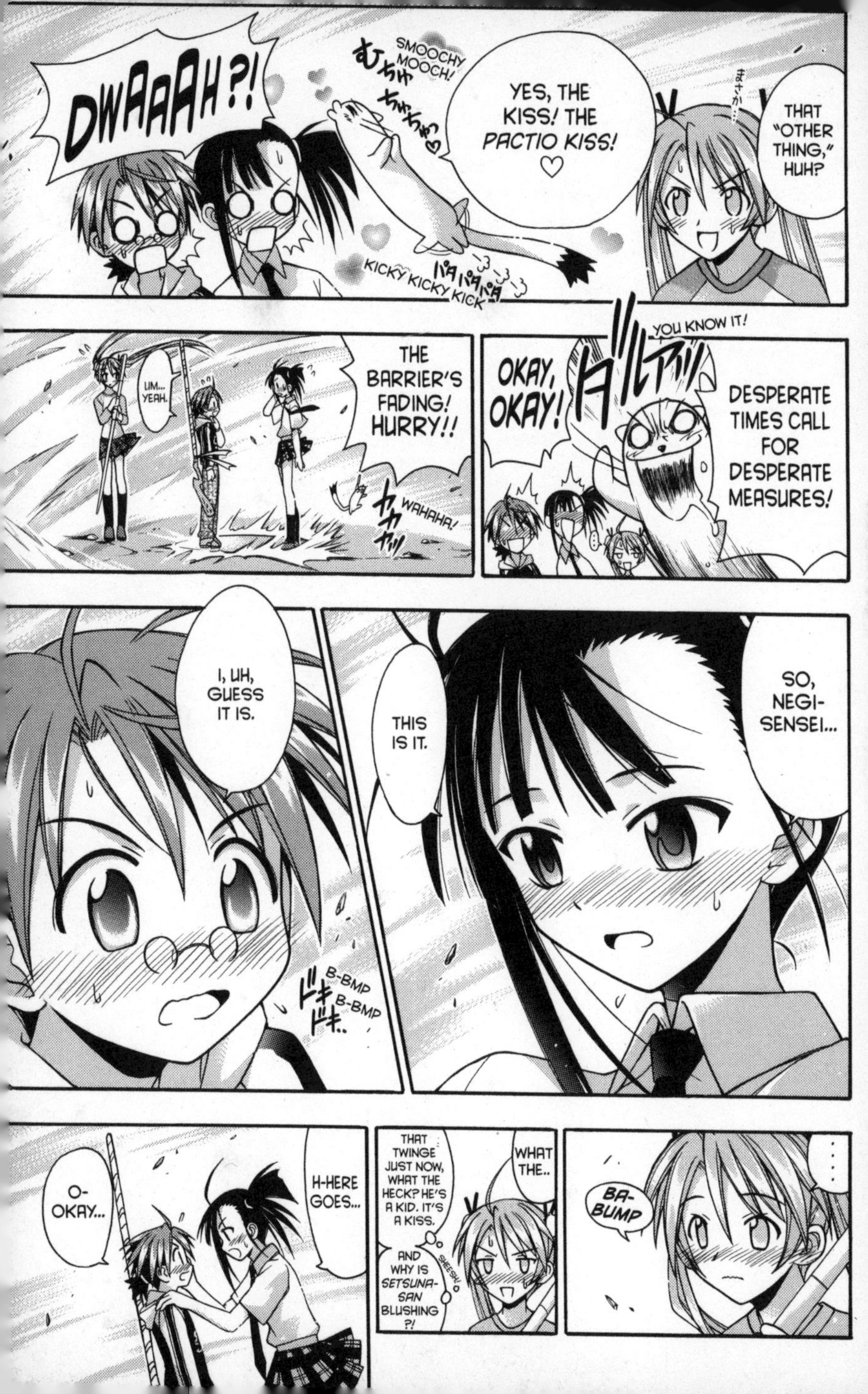
まさか…
THAT "OTHER THING," HUH?
YES, THE KISS! THE PACTIO KISS! ♡
SMOOCHY MOOCH!
KICKY KICKY KICK
DWAAAH?!
DESPERATE TIMES CALL FOR DESPERATE MEASURES!
YOU KNOW IT!
OKAY, OKAY!
THE BARRIER'S FADING! HURRY!!
UM... YEAH.
WAHAHA!
SO, NEGI-SENSEI...
THIS IS IT.
I, UH, GUESS IT IS.
B-BMP B-BMP
· · · ·
BA-BUMP
WHAT THE..
THAT TWINGE JUST NOW, WHAT THE HECK? HE'S A KID. IT'S A KISS.
AND WHY IS SETSUNA-SAN BLUSHING?!
SHEESH!
H-HERE GOES...
O-OKAY...

About the Creator

Negima! is only Ken Akamatsu's third manga, although he started working in the field in 1994 with *AI Ga Tomaranai*. Like all of Akamatsu's work to date, it was published in Kodansha's *Shonen Magazine*. *AI Ga Tomaranai* ran for five years before concluding in 1999. In 1998, however, Akamatsu began the work that would make him one of the most popular manga artists in Japan *Love Hina*. *Love Hina* ran for four years, and before its conclusion in 2002, it would cause Akamatsu to be granted the prestigious Manga of the Year award from Kodansha, as well as going on to become one of the best selling manga in the United Kingdom.

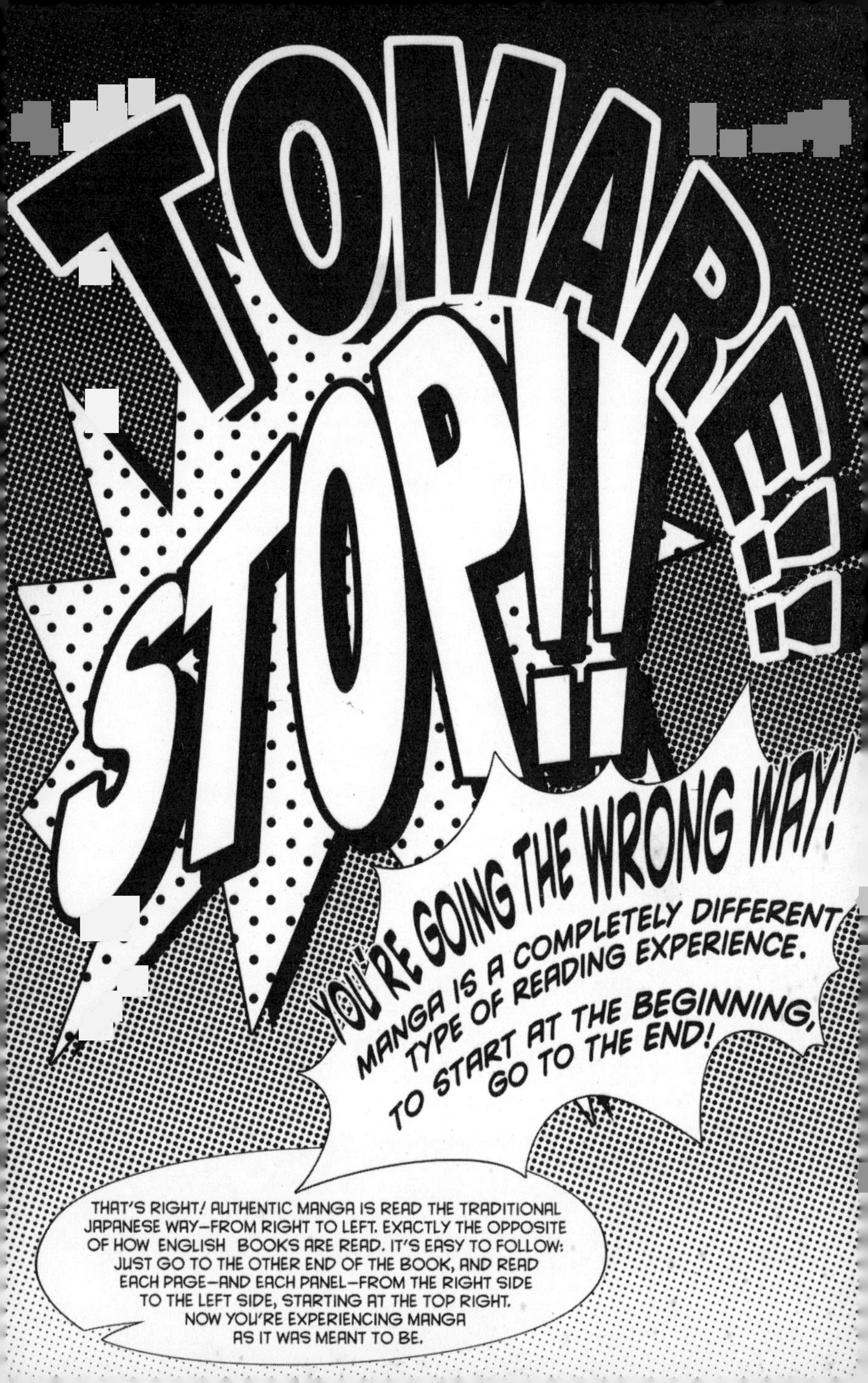
TOMARE!!
STOP!!
YOU'RE GOING THE WRONG WAY!
MANGA IS A COMPLETELY DIFFERENT TYPE OF READING EXPERIENCE.
TO START AT THE BEGINNING, GO TO THE END!
THAT'S RIGHT! AUTHENTIC MANGA IS READ THE TRADITIONAL JAPANESE WAY—FROM RIGHT TO LEFT. EXACTLY THE OPPOSITE OF HOW ENGLISH BOOKS ARE READ. IT'S EASY TO FOLLOW: JUST GO TO THE OTHER END OF THE BOOK, AND READ EACH PAGE—AND EACH PANEL—FROM THE RIGHT SIDE TO THE LEFT SIDE, STARTING AT THE TOP RIGHT. NOW YOU'RE EXPERIENCING MANGA AS IT WAS MEANT TO BE.